D1244416

standard catalog of ®
GTO
1961-2004

Jerry Heasley photo

John Gunnell

©2003 by Krause Publications
All rights reserved.

No portion of this publication may be reproduced or transmitted in any form or by any means, electronic or mechanical, including photocopy, recording, or any information storage and retrieval system, without permission in writing from the publisher, except by a reviewer who may quote brief passages in a critical article or review to be printed in a magazine or newspaper, or electronically transmitted on radio or television.

Published by

krause publications
An F&W Publications Company

700 East State Street • Iola, WI 54990-0001
715-445-2214 • 888-457-2873
www.krause.com

Please call or write for our free catalog of publications. Our toll-free number to place an order or obtain a free catalog is (800) 258-0929.

Library of Congress Catalog Number: 2003108894
ISBN: 0-87349-689-2

Edited by Brian Earnest
Designed by Jamie Griffin
Front cover photography by Jerry Heasley (bottom)
and Daniel B. Lyons
Back cover photography by Daniel B. Lyons

Daniel B. Lyons photo

3

About this Book

This book was compiled from a variety of reliable sources. The historical and technical facts come from different forms of documentation including factory sales literature, product information manuals, used car books, repair manuals, industry trade journals and collector car publications. In some cases, factory or aftermarket information may have original errors that have slipped past the attention of automotive historians. In other cases, introductory facts or specifications may have been changed during a model year, after early editions of literature were printed.

Some of the VIN information breakdowns may contain codes for *all* General Motors vehicles because the factory-issued VIN cards do not always provide information specific to Tempests, LeMans, GTOs, Grand Ams and Can Ams. Therefore, we may, for example, show vehicle restraint systems not used on Pontiac products. Having too much information will not prevent you from interpreting the codes on your particular vehicle.

The data on options and accessories for many 1970s and 1980s models was supplied by Jim Mattison of Pontiac Historic Services in Sterling Heights, Michigan. PHS is an invaluable resource for Pontiac collectors and can tell you exactly what your car came equipped with from the factory. Prices for the options offered in these years were not given in the sheets that PHS supplied. However, we did include many option prices presented in our previous *Standard Catalog of Pontiac 1926-2002*.

Once this book is on the market, it is our hope that marque experts will read it and let us know of any ways in which we can make this standard catalog even better. We are always committed to improving future editions of our books so that hobbyists will have the latest automotive information at their fingertips.

The Tempest...The LeMans...and The GTO

In order to be a GTO, you gotta first be a LeMans. In order to be a LeMans, you gotta first be a Tempest. That's how it was back in 1964, and thanks to the painstaking research and the uncompromising desire for perfection, my good friend John Gunnell has assembled a magnificent study of this great slice of American automotive history.

I'm going to tell you about three great men, without whom there never would have been a Tempest or a LeMans or certainly not a GTO. Perhaps, there might not even be a Pontiac in existence today, were it not for the dedication and the creative determination of these three men: Semon E. "Bunkie" Knudsen, Elliot M. "Pete" Estes, and John Zachary DeLorean.

There have been the Henry Fords, the David Dunbar Buicks, the Ransom E. Olds, and the Walter Chryslers of our industry, all of who have had their contributions enshrined in history in the form of an automobile bearing their name. There is no Knudsen, or no Estes, and no longer a DeLorean, but there should be, and they should all be Pontiacs.

There would be no Bonneville, no Grand Prix, no GTO, no Firebird, no Trans Am, no LeMans, Tempest, Catalina, not even a Wide-Track were it not for these men and their determined leadership.

From the very beginning in 1961 when Pontiac introduced its new intermediate Tempest, it was Knudsen as the division general manager who insisted that this new Pontiac be an exciting and totally different car. With the help of engineering teams headed by Estes and DeLorean, the new trans-axle Tempest was born.

In 1962, the upgraded LeMans was added to the line, and with the advent of the 1964 model, again thanks to the dedication of new Chief Engineer DeLorean and a couple of his most trusted assistants, Bill Collins and Russ Gee, the history-making GTO "hit the streets." Perhaps the most famous GM "A-body" ever built; this new Pontiac brought to the world a popularly priced mass-produced version of every hot rodder's dream — a big engine in a little car.

As Pontiac reintroduces a new millennium version of this great nameplate, now more than ever it's time to get to know its real history.

—Jim Wangers

(Editor's note: Jim Wangers is one of the great movers and shakers in U.S. automotive history – a true luminary who left a distinctive mark on the industry. He has worked in various capacities at Kaiser-Frazer, Chevrolet, and Chrysler, but is probably best remembered for his groundbreaking work as an advertising man for Pontiac beginning in 1958. He became a muscle-car pioneer whose enthusiasm and foresight helped launch a bold new category of high-performance, all-American automobile. One of his greatest achievements was helping define and promote the GTO – a car considered by many to be the original, and ultimate, muscle car.)

Contents

Introduction

Tempest, LeMans, GTO: Multi-Personality Syndrome

The Pontiac Tempest, LeMans, GTO story is one affected by "multiple-personality syndrome." These cars do not fit neatly into the GM midsize category, as does the Chevelle. The first Tempest was a compact car. The midsize permeation was first called the Tempest and later became known as the LeMans. Even the GTO, which was midsized for nearly 90 percent of its life, wound up with a different personality; the last edition in 1974 was based on the Ventura, a "senior compact" model. Then, we have the early Grand Ams and the one-year-only Can Am, which were not called a LeMans, but actually were.

Of the group, the GTO is the more interesting and more collectible car (unless, of course, you own one of the other models). The GTO is credited with starting the muscle-car era and did, if you take the term "muscle car" in its purest sense. Undoubtedly, cars like the Chrysler 300, the Plymouth Fury, the Dodge D-500, the Pontiac Bonneville, the Olds J-2, and even the Chevy Super Sport pointed in the same direction, but the GTO stuffed the big-car V-8 drive train into a small body just like a real hot rodder would. No one in Detroit had done that before.

The "Great One" was a reflection of the creative genius of Mr. John Z. DeLorean, who sired this street racer with the same defiance of authority figures that later proved his undoing. He stuck it to The General's politically correct "bean counters" and came out smelling like a rose, then capitalized on his brashness for the next 10 years. And the funny thing is that DeLorean's flawed genius hasn't ever been forgotten, as evidenced by the fact that the GTO is due back again soon.

The Tempest, for its part, was another of DeLorean's triumphs and perhaps even more revealing of his eccentricity. Unfortunately, he didn't have it quite right for the public's taste, although he was damn close. I have always seen the early Tempest as part of a Pontiac continuum that starts with a show car design called the 1954 Bonneville Special and ends with the production-line Fiero. You could not bring out a two-seat American sports car in 1960, so I believe that DeLorean tried to disguise one as a sedan.

Innovations like the use of a half-a-V-8 engine, a rope drive shaft, and a rear-mounted transaxle were all part of an attempt to make an exciting little car. We know Pontiac built standard '57 models with some of these features, but by 1960 the two-seat T-Bird had passed from the scene and the Corvette was just clinging to life. So Pontiac wisely launched the Tempest as a sedan and a wagon and carved out some strong sales numbers at first. But neither the Tempest sedan nor Safari were the essence of the car — that role was played by the Monte Carlo, a show-car version that pretended to be a two-seater. A two-seat "Super-Duty" coupe called the GT was also on the drawing board.

Unfortunately, the sales allure of the little Tempest wore off quickly, but that was because the recession of the late-'50s was over. Back then it took Detroit longer to get new cars out and by the time the small ones arrived, big ones were back in demand. The Tempest got bigger in '63 and a lot more conventional in '64. And of course, by that time the LeMans model (introduced in mid-1961) was playing to the demand for sportiness that carved a market for Ford's Mustang.

The Tempest-LeMans models of the late '60s are interesting because they once again reflected DeLorean's eccentric thinking — at least under their hoods where an overhead-cam six-cylinder engine resided. It's almost as if the success of the GTO concept gave John Z. carte blanche to try more of his ideas out on the American public.

While it did not achieve the notoriety of the GTO, the Tempest Lemans of this era helped make Pontiac America's best-selling brand and keep it there for more than a decade. Just look at how many body styles were offered and how many sedans and Safari station wagons were sold and you can tell how the Tempest helped to fill Pontiac's coffers. It was image cars like the GTO and the LeMans and Sprint coupes and the convertibles that were seen in most of the advertising, but it was the grocery-getter models that people really plunked down their hard-earned dollars for.

DeLorean's Pontiac, with the help of ad man Jim Wangers, was a selling machine in the '60s and when sales started dipping the innovators got going again. Take the '68 GTO with its hidden headlamps, hidden wipers, Ram Air engines, and Endura nose as an example of a "Tempest" that picked up the slack in midstream. As PMD walked away with "Car of the Year" honors time and again, it kept the public coming back to Pontiac showrooms. It took the U.S. government and the entire insurance industry, acting like Alan Greenspan at the height of the tech-stock boom, to bring Pontiac down from its third-rung perch.

It can be debated whether the last two or three GTOs were lesser cars than those that came before them, but there's no doubt that the image changed. Pontiac made this clear in 1972, when the GTO goodies reverted to option status, as they had been in 1964-1965. Rather than emasculating the car, like some manufacturers were forced to do to their performance models, Pontiac chose to retire the GTO name.

By this time, the Tempest tag had also disappeared in favor of LeMans for the whole group. To try to keep pace with the leisure suit set, Pontiac gussied things up with a Luxury LeMans that tried to be a big car on a short wheelbase. A number of performance options remained buried in the extras list and some were hotter than the competition, but the competition wasn't much.

DeLorean was gone, of course, and Pontiac was lost in the disco decade. The Grand Am came along in 1973 and was themed as an import fighter because the four-door sedan was made available with bucket seats. A few people wound up with an unusually nice-looking Pontiac, but the "Euro" push was over in three short years. Few, if any, BMW and Mercedes buyers switched to Grand Ams. 1977 brought a show-car-inspired Americanized version dubbed the Can Am. It was a bright-looking car, and rare, but it sold for only one year.

In the last four years of its existence, the A-body LeMans became a trimmer machine with a family-car flavor and enough customers to push Pontiac sales to new-record levels. The down-sized LeMans Group and its Gen II Grand Am spin-off contributed to the totals along with the hot-selling Firebird of the late '70s. It was not to last, however. Political and economic unrest sent production skidding in 1980 when the Lemans Group and Grand Am went from 137,000 to 84,000 in 12 months. The last A-body LeMans was built in 1981.

The LeMans name returned in 1988 on a badge-engineered Korean car that survived until 1991. Some felt this econobox ought to be included in this catalog, but our answer was, "We're not going there!" We did, of course, leave room for the new GTO that's coming from Australia and promises to kick like a kangaroo when it hits the street of America.

Alex Gabbard photo

With a rope drive shaft, rear transaxle, independent rear suspension, and other technical advancements, the '61 Tempest was a first-year hit.

A radical new compact car named the Tempest was introduced as Pontiac's entry in the growing small-car marketplace. In appearance the Tempest was pure Pontiac with twin grilles, sculptured body panels, a V-contour hood and body-side windsplits. It was technically innovative and featured an integral body and frame, a flexible "rope" drive shaft, torque-tube drive, an independent rear suspension, a rear-mounted transaxle, and a four-cylinder base power plant created by cutting a 389-cid V-8 in half. As *Ward's 1961 Automotive Yearbook* stated, "Three sparkling nuggets of engineering ingenuity, incorporated into a one-half bank engine, lent new luster during 1960, to Pontiac's shining achievements in the automotive realm. The Tempest Four, reaping honors from many quarters as 'the car of the year,' embodied probably the most revolutionary design the industry saw in 1960."

It was the first car built in the United States to combine a transaxle (rear-end transmission) and front-mounted engine. The "Indianapolis Four," as Pontiac dubbed the engine, was actually a chopped-off standard-size V-8 with only slight modifications. It displaced a healthy 194.5 cid and, with a one-barrel carburetor and 8.6:1 compression ratio, pumped out 130 hp at 4100 rpm. Optional four-barrel carburetors and pistons could hike compression to 10.25:1 and increase horsepower to 155 at 4800 rpm. A floor-flattening flexible drive shaft 5/8 of an inch thick linked the engine with the transaxle. An optional Buick-built aluminum V-8 was offered for

the Tempest, but it was the four-cylinder engine that characterized it as a unique engineering exercise. In appearance, the Tempest Four was all Pontiac, with twin-grille styling and other design characteristics of its proud parent.

I.D. NUMBERS

VIN on left front door post. First symbol tells series: 21=Tempest. Second and third symbols tell year: 61=1961. Fourth symbol tells assembly plant: P=Pontiac, Michigan, and S=South Gate, California. Fifth through last symbols are the sequential numbers starting at 1001 for each assembly plant. Body/style number plate under hood tells manufacturer, Fisher style number, assembly plant, trim code, paint code, accessory codes. Style number consists of 61 (for 1961) prefix and four symbols that appear in second column of charts below. First two symbols indicate series, second two symbols indicate body type. VIN appears on front of engine at right-hand cylinder bank along with an alphanumerical engine production code. Engine production codes included: (195-cid/110-hp four) DA/DS, (195-cid/120-hp four) OSY, (195-cid/155-hp four) XS/YS/XA, (195-cid/140-hp four) OA, (215-cid/155-hp aluminum V-8) YA.

COLORS

Paint color codes for 1961 were: A=Regent Black, C=Shelltone Ivory, D=Richmond Gray, E=Bristol Blue,

From Maine to California, the happiest season of the year is ushered in with the selection of the family Christmas tree . . . joining in the holiday fun are Pontiac's stunning new Safari Wagon and Tempest 4-Door Sedan.

NEW CAR FOR FESTIVITY

A dazzling new General Motors car keeps family excitement at Christmas morning peak the whole year around! Why, even a trip to the corner store is a festive occasion . . . and you're sure to find more places to go and wonderful things to do, just because it's so much more fun getting there.

GM adds an extra measure of pleasure to motoring—and you'll find many reasons why. One is the handsome coachwork by Fisher Body. You'll like the looks, the lines, and the colors. You'll appreciate the wonderfully wide interiors that offer leg room, shoulder room, and wiggly-kid-room. On the road you will be impressed with the traditional General Motors reliability, which means confident and comfortable traveling. And you'll mentally tip your hat to GM engineers when you thrill to the performance of these '61's—GM's finest by far.

Don't forget! There's sure to be a new car for *your* family in the GM line . . . just look at all the models, sizes, colors, engines, transmissions and power options! It pays to do your Christmas shopping early—it pays more to start your Christmas shopping at your GM dealer's showroom.

For the car of your choice, GO GM GENERAL MOTORS

Chevrolet • Pontiac • Oldsmobile • Buick • Cadillac • All with Body by Fisher

Pontiac was able to stir up some excitement in 1961 with its Tempest line, claiming "even a trip to the corner store is a festive occasion" in one of its new cars.

In addition to the sedan and hardtop models, Pontiac also brought out a station wagon as part of its Tempest line in 1961. More than 23,000 wagons and Custom wagons were produced for the initial model year.

F=Richelieu Blue, H=Tradewind Blue, J=Jadestone Green, K=Seacrest Green, L=Coronado Red, M=Bamboo Cream, N=Cherrywood Bronze, P=Ranier Turquoise, R=Fernando Beige, S=Dawnfire Mist and T=Mayan Gold. Interior trim codes for 1961 were: 271/298=Gray vinyl, 262=Blue cloth and vinyl, 272=Blue vinyl, 263=Green cloth and vinyl, 273=Green Vinyl, 264=Fawn cloth and vinyl, 274=Fawn vinyl, 265=Maroon cloth and vinyl, and 275=Maroon vinyl.

TEMPEST — (FOUR-CYL) — SERIES 21

Features of the first Tempest included independent front-wheel compression-strut suspension, an inclined 45-degree short-stroke four-cylinder engine, solid one-piece unit-body and frame construction, a heavily-ribbed flat floor pan, a reduced-size transmission tunnel, a floor-mounted stick shift (automatic transmission optional), a curved torque-tube-type flexible triple-alloy-steel drive shaft, a rear-mounted transmission, independent swing-axle rear suspension and standard 15-in.-diameter wheels. Standard equipment included electric wipers, turn signals, dual sun visors and five tubeless black sidewall tires. A four-door sedan and Safari station wagon were first to appear. The sedan and station wagon models were joined by a pair of two-door hardtops (or sport coupes) later in the year. One of these was a deluxe model with bucket seats that was named the Le Mans.

Model Number	Body/Style Number	Body Type & Seating	Factory Price	Shipping Weight	Production Total
TEMPEST — (FOUR-CYL) — SERIES 21					
21	19	4d Sedan-6P	$2,702	2,800 lbs.	22,557
21	27	2d Hardtop-6P	$2,113	2,785 lbs.	7,432
21	35	4d Sta Wagon-6P	$2,438	2,980 lbs.	7,404
TEMPEST — (FOUR-CYL) — SERIES 21 (WITH CUSTOM TRIM PACKAGE)					
21	19	4d Sedan-6P	$2,884	2,800 lbs.	40,082
21	27	2d Le Mans HT-6P	$2,297	2,795 lbs.	7,455
21	35	4d Sta Wagon-6P	$2,611	2,980 lbs.	15,853

NOTE 1: 98,779 Tempest with four-cylinder engines were built.
NOTE 2: 26,737 Tempest fours had synchromesh and 72,042 had Hydra-Matic.
NOTE 3: 2,004 Tempests were built with optional (Buick) aluminum V-8s.
NOTE 4: Three Tempest V-8s had synchromesh and 2,001 had Hydra-Matic.

Paul Zazerine collection

One of the first Tempest sedans to roll off the assembly line in Pontiac, Michigan.

ENGINES

TEMPEST "INDY FOUR" BASE 194-CID FOUR-CYL (WITH SYNCHROMESH): Inline. Overhead valves. Cast-iron block. Displacement: 194.5 cid. Bore and stroke: 4.06 x 3.75 in. Compression ratio: 8.6:1. Brake hp: 110 at 3800 rpm. Torque: 110 lbs.-ft. at 3800 rpm. Five main bearings. Hydraulic valve lifters. Carburetor: Rochester one-barrel. Available with standard manual transmission and standard 3.55:1 rear axle. A 3.31:1 rear axle was optional with manual transmission on all models except station wagons and a 3.73:1 rear axle was optional on all models with manual transmission. Also available with automatic transmission and a 3.08:1 rear axle in sedans or a 3.55:1 rear axle in station wagons (3.55:1 rear axle was optional in sedans with automatic transmission and a 3.73:1 rear axle was optional in station wagons with automatic).

TEMPEST "INDY FOUR" BASE 194-CID FOUR-CYL (PREMIUM FUEL ENGINE WITH MANUAL TRANSMISSION): Inline. Overhead valves. Cast-iron block. Displacement: 194.5 cid. Bore and stroke: 4.06 x 3.75 in. Compression ratio: 10.25:1. Brake hp: 120 at 3800 rpm. Five main bearings. Hydraulic valve lifters. Carburetor: Rochester one-barrel. Standard rear axle ratio was 3.31:1 in sedans and 3.55:1 in station wagons. Also available with optional 3.55:1 rear axle in sedans and optional 3.73:1 rear axle in station wagons.

TEMPEST "INDY FOUR" OPTIONAL 194-CID FOUR-CYL (PREMIUM FUEL ENGINE WITH AUTOMATIC TRANSMISSION): Inline. Overhead valves. Cast-iron block. Displacement: 194.5 cid. Bore and stroke: 4.06 x 3.75 in. Compression ratio: 10.25:1. Brake hp: 140 at 4400 rpm. Five main bearings. Hydraulic valve lifters. Carburetor: Rochester one-barrel. Standard rear axle ratio was 3.08:1 in sedans and 3.55:1 in station wagons. Also available with optional 3.55:1 rear axle in sedans and optional 3.73:1 rear axle in station wagons.

TEMPEST "INDY FOUR" OPTIONAL 194-CID FOUR-CYL (WITH MANUAL OR AUTOMATIC TRANSMISSION): Inline. Overhead valves. Cast-iron block. Displacement: 194.5 cid. Bore and stroke: 4.06 x 3.75 in. Compression ratio: 10.25:1. Brake hp: 155 at 4800 rpm. Hydraulic valve lifters. Carburetor: Rochester four-barrel. Standard rear axle ratio was 3.55:1. Also available with automatic transmission and optional 3.08:1 rear axle (except station wagon) or with manual transmission and 3.31:1 (except station wagon) or 3.73:1:1 rear axles.

TEMPEST OPTIONAL 215-CID V-8 (WITH AUTOMATIC TRANSMISSION ONLY): Overhead valve. Bore and stroke: 3.50 x 2.80. Displacement: 215 cid. Compression ratio: 8.8:1. Brake hp: 155 at 4600 rpm. Taxable hp: 39.20. Torque: 220 lbs.-ft. at 2400 rpm. Five main bearings. Hydraulic valve lifters. Crankcase capacity: 4 qt. (add 1 qt. for new filter). Cooling system capacity: 11.6 gal. (add 1 gallon with heater). Carburetor: Rochester 7019060 two-barrel. Engine code: XS, YS or XA. Built by Buick. Standard rear axle ratio was 3.55:1. Also available with 3.08:1 rear axle (except station wagon) or 3.73:1:1 rear axle.

CHASSIS

Wheelbase: 112 in. Overall length: 189.3 in. overall width: 72.2 in. Overall height: 53.5 in. Front tread: 56.8 in. Rear tread: 56.8 in. Turning diameter (curb-to-curb): 39.75 ft. Front legroom: (standard models) 44.1 in., (Custom models) 41.9 in. right and 43.4 in. left. Rear legroom: (sedan) 37.8 in., (coupe) 37 in., (sports coupe) 36.8 in., (Safari) 37.5 in. and (Custom coupe) 36.8 in. Front headroom: (sedan) 38.3 in., (coupe) 38.3 in., (Safari) 38.6 in. and (Custom) 38.7 in. Rear headroom: (sedan) 37.1 in., (coupe) 36.8 in., (Safari) 38.0 in. and (Custom) 36.8 in. Front hip room: (sedan and Safari) 58.6 in., (other models) 58.7 in. Rear hip room: (sedan and Safari) 58.2 in., (other models) 57.5 in. Front seat height: (all models except Custom) 10.8 in., (Custom) 11.8 in. Rear seat height: (sedan) 12.4 in., (coupe) 12.8

Four-wheel suspension was supposed to allow the Tempest to remain level, even when the wheels were raised 6 inches.

Paul Zazerine collection

The Tempest showed respectable highway performance in its first year. The base four-cylinder Tempest engine produced 130 hp, and an optional four-barrel carburetor could crank that up to 155 hp.

Paul Zazerine collection

in., (Safari) 12.7 in. and (Custom) 12.8 in. Trunk volume: (coupe and sedan) 27.5 cu. ft. Station wagon cargo compartment length (rear seat up and tailgate closed): 53.1 in. Station wagon cargo area width: (maximum) 56.7 in.; (minimum) 44.1 in. Station wagon cargo compartment maximum height: 30.8 in. Station wagon rear opening width: 49.5 in. Station wagon rear opening height: 29.3 in. Station wagon cargo compartment volume (second seat flat): 72.6 cu. ft. Tires: 6.00 x 15. Fuel tank: 16 gal.

OPTIONS

061 Basic Group, four-cylinder ($172.80). 061 Basic Group, V-8 ($167.42). 062 Protection Group with standard transmission ($41.85). 062 Protection Group with automatic transmission ($39.70). 071 Upper Exterior Décor Group ($32.28). 072 Lower Exterior Décor Group ($12.91). 074 Interior Décor Group, sedans ($69.94). 074 Interior Décor Group, station wagons

($75.32). 432 heavy-duty air cleaner ($4.84). 582 Cool-Pack air conditioner ($318.60). 471 back-up lights with standard transmission ($12.91). 471 back-up lights, with automatic transmission ($10.76). 474 front and rear bumper guards ($16.14). 732 cigar lighter ($2.15). 601 crankcase ventilator, four-cylinder ($4.30). 601 crankcase ventilator V-8 ($5.16). 418 front foam seat cushion ($8.07). Four-cylinder engine with four-barrel carburetor ($26.37). V-8 engine with two-barrel carburetor ($216). 434 oil filter with four-cylinder engine, standard with V-8 ($5.38). 532 all windows tinted glass ($31.20). 534 tinted windshield ($19.91). 384 heater and defroster ($74.24). 472 dual horns ($4.30). 428 padded instrument panel ($16.14). 598 station wagon luggage carrier ($64.56). 612 station wagon luggage compartment mat ($3.23). 441 outside rearview mirror ($4.25). 442 non-glare inside rearview mirror ($4.25). 458 remote-control outside rearview mirror ($11.78). 751 windshield and rear window moldings, sedans ($14.52). 751 windshield and rear

The 1961 Tempest was the first American-built car to feature a transaxle and front-mounted engine.

Paul Zazerine collection

window moldings, station wagon ($12.91). Two-tone paint in standard colors ($12.38). Two-tone paint in special colors ($52.57). Solid paint in special color ($40.19). 498 parking brake light ($4.95). 502 power steering ($75.32). 558 power tailgate window on station wagon ($53.80). 395 manual radio and antenna ($53.80). 396 push-button radio and antenna ($62.41). 541 Deluxe steering wheel ring ($3.77). T02 five 6.00 x 15 four-ply white sidewall tires for sedans without air conditioning ($28.03). T11 five 6.50 x 15 four-ply black sidewall tires for sedans without air conditioning ($8.02). T12 five 6.50 x 15 four-ply white sidewall tires for sedans without air conditioning ($37.32). T12 five 6.50 x 15 four-ply white sidewall tires for sedans with air conditioning and station wagons ($29.70). Tempestorque automatic transmission ($172.80). 731 right-hand inside sun visor ($3.23). 542 Deluxe wheel discs ($15.60). 544 wheel trim rings ($10.76). 408 windshield washer ($13.02). 411 two-speed windshield wipers ($4.84).

OPTION INSTALLATION RATES

Of 100,783 Tempests built, 73.8 percent had automatic transmission, 1.9 percent had a V-8 engine, 98.1 percent had a four-cylinder engine, 64.3 percent had a radio, 95.4 percent had a heater, 6.6 percent had power steering, 0.4 percent had power windows (station wagon rear window only), 7.5 percent had bucket seats, 67.6 percent had white sidewall tires, 43.2 percent had windshield washers, 100 percent had electric windshield wipers, 23.4 percent had a tinted windshield, 31.2 percent had back-up lights, and 2.4 percent had air conditioning.

HISTORICAL FOOTNOTES

Semon E. "Bunkie" Knudsen was general manager at Pontiac Motor Division in 1961. The original Tempest was introduced on November 3, 1959, nearly a month later than other Pontiac products. Model-year production was recorded as 100,783 units or a 1.9

percent share of total U.S. automobile production. Tempests were built in assembly plants in Pontiac, Michigan, and South Gate, California. In the spring of 1961 there was a rash of midyear introductions of new luxury-type economy cars featuring bucket seating and the Pontiac Tempest Le Mans was included along with the Mercury Comet S-22, the Buick Special Skylark, the Ford Falcon Futura, and the Oldsmobile F-85 Cutlass.

Only 7,455 Tempests were built with bucket seats in the 1961 model year and all were Le Mans hardtops. Calendar-year production for 1960 was 32,052 units of which 5,587 were built in October, 13,565 were built in November and 12,900 were built in December. All of these were 1961 Tempests. Calendar-year production for 1961 (which included both late-1961 and early-1962 models) was 115,945. Calendar-year production does not tell you how many cars like yours were produced, but it is important because automakers use calendar-year production for their annual sales figures.

Even before the Tempest hit the market, Pontiac engineers had driven the cars 3,000,000 miles in testing. Nevertheless, on July 1, 1960, Pontiac turned over two pre-production Tempests to a team of teen-agers to test the performance and reliability of the new compact car. The Tempest sedan and Tempest Safari station wagon were driven hard 24 hours a day during the test, which ended on October 15, 1960. Both of the four-cylinder cars traversed 48 states and seven Canadian provinces. The sedan racked up 100,947 miles and the Safari did 101,002 miles. Plugs, points and filters were changed every 12,000-15,000 miles. The brakes were adjusted several times and the tires were changed twice. Repairs done on the sedan included a new starter solenoid at 19,194 miles, a cracked windshield repaired at 20,701 miles, a left back-up light replaced at 40,094 miles, a fuel pump replaced at 62,765 miles, generator brushes replaced at 96,492 miles and a radiator leak repaired at 98,549 miles. The Safari had a light switch replaced at 4,576 miles, a stone chip in the windshield at 16,192 miles, a heater switch connector hose replaced at 51,368

The Tempest's twin-grille styling was a Pontiac trademark.

Paul Zazerine photo

Paul Zazerine collection

The two-door Tempest was the last of the first-year midsize Pontiacs to debut in 1961. The four-door sedan and wagon were in showrooms earlier in the year.

miles, a gas tank pierced by a flying rock at 51,368 miles, generator brushes replaced at 96,527 miles, and a rear wheel bearing replaced at 97,210 miles.

Sales of the original Tempest were strong enough to make Pontiac America's third best-selling automobile for the first time in divisional history. The new compact accounted for 30 percent of all Pontiac sales in 1961! A special 1961 Pontiac Tempest was built for exhibition at new-car shows. The body could be raised up so that spectators could see the Tempest's unique "rope" drive shaft. GM's first "Monte Carlo" was not a Chevrolet, but a 1961 Tempest show car with a sports-car racing motif. Rear-deck headrest pods enhanced its competition look. It also had racing stripes and racing mirrors. Famed GM stylist Bill Mitchell created the Monte Carlo as a Corvair Sebring Spyder companion. It had a blown four-cylinder engine, a racing windshield, chrome body-side windsplits, a tonneau cover, hood louvers, wire wheels and thin-stripe tires. A PMD employee bought the car after it was retired from the show circuit. He modified it for street use. Later it was obtained by the San Antonio, Texas Museum of Transportation, where it was housed for many years.

The Pontiac Tempest Le Mans also started life as a show car that appeared in mid-1961 auto shows. This hardtop coupe had bucket seats, a floor shifter, wire wheels, a louvered hood, and Le Mans fender badges. Stylist sketches of a 1961 Tempest converted into a two-passenger coupe were rendered by a Pontiac designer, but the concept never got past the drawing board stage as far as anyone knows. *Motor Life's* technical editor Chuck Nerpel did a nine-page article on the Tempest in the magazine's October 1960 issue. The Society of Automotive Engineers published several detailed papers on the innovative new car. Paper No. S-263 was "The Pontiac Tempest: A Car Without A Counterpart" by John Z. DeLorean, which G.W. Roberts, of Pontiac Motor Division, presented to Auto Enthusiasts International. It

is a highly detailed 42-page study of the Tempest complete with illustrations and color photos. Paper no. 320A was "The 1961 Tempest Drive Line" by F.F. Timpner of Pontiac Motor Division. It was presented at the 1961 SAE National Automobile Week conference at the Sheraton-Cadillac Hotel in Detroit on March 13-17, 1961. Almost a year later, D.F. Miller of Pontiac Motor Division, documented the Tempest Flexible Drive Line Pre-Production Durability Testing program in a memo dated March 3, 1962. This memo noted that the conception of the flexible drive line took place in October 1956. Initial laboratory fatigue tests were conducted at the GM Technical Center between February and December of 1957.

The first experimental car installation was made in August 1957. This car was once pictured in a small photo in *Motor Trend* magazine. Stress and vibrations analysis and general development work were in process during 1957. Eleven experimental cars completed 325,000 test miles at the GM Proving Ground. In May 1959, the first experimental Tempest XP8-4 prototype was built. Ten prototype Tempests subsequently completed a total of 388,000 test miles at the GM Proving Ground. In January 1960, the first complete Tempest program car was built. Seven Tempests then completed 373,000 test miles. In July 1960, 10 production-design drive lines successfully completed laboratory fatigue tests of 50 million cycles each under test conditions far in excess of any real-world automobile requirements.

From June thru August 1960, the two program Tempests driven by college students on a 24-hour schedule each completed 100,000 test miles on all types of roads throughout the U.S. and Canada. In October 1960, Tempest production began. By that time, GM had completed 1,286,000 miles of durability testing on the flexible drive line design.

Richard Croteau photo

**The 1962 Tempest Custom was a popular and appealing offering for Pontiac.
This convertible came in Cameo Ivory.**

A Tempest convertible and a Tempest Le Mans convertible were headline news for 1962. In one somewhat embarrassing advertisement featuring a black Le Mans convertible with red bucket seat interior, Pontiac included an incorrect phonetic spelling of the French word Le Mans (indicating that it should be pronounced "Luh-manz" instead of "La-Mah"). Pontiac ad copywriters also varied in how they spelled the name. Some ads read Le Mans and some read LeMans. Whatever the pronunciation or spelling, buyers new that the Le Mans represented a small, sporty and luxurious model.

Styling changes for all Tempests included a new wider-spaced split grille theme with a third grille section (incorporating a V-shaped emblem) placed in the center and the addition of bolt-in bright metal fins at the rear. Technical refinements included new upper and lower control arm bushings that gave a softer, more easily controlled ride, new intake manifolding, and a new carburetor designed to give faster warm-ups and better fuel economy. A heater became standard equipment, although it could be deleted and was by .09 percent of all Tempest buyers.

There were five basic models: the sedan, the coupe, the sports coupe (a two-door hardtop), the Safari (station wagon), and the convertible. The sports coupe and convertible could be optioned with the Le Mans trim package, which included high-wing bucket seats in special expanded Morrokide (vinyl), thick pile carpeting and custom hardware and trim pieces.

I.D. NUMBERS

VIN on left front door post. First symbol tells series: 21=Tempest. Second and third symbols tell year: 62=1962. Fourth symbol tells assembly plant: P=Pontiac,

Call it the Tempest LeMans! (Luh-mahnz)

Pontiac's new package of punch...posh...and low price! Convertible or Coupe! A couple of fancy, frisky newcomers. Pull the trigger on a fired-up "4". (Standard power: 110, 115, 120 or 140 h.p. Optional at extra cost: 166-horse "4"; 185 h.p. aluminum V-8; four-speed, floor mounted stick shift.) Plush sports-type bucket seats and full carpeting are part of the package. Plenty more. Front engine balanced by rear transmission. Independent suspension at all four wheels. Big 15-inch wheels and tires (at no extra cost). Get the good word from your Pontiac dealer. He's very high on the car and very low on the price.   PONTIAC MOTOR DIVISION • GENERAL MOTORS CORPORATION

Drive America's only front engine/rear transmission car . . . it's balanced like none of the others!

**A Tempest convertible with the Le Mans option was the top of the Tempest line
for 1962 and came with a starting price tag of $2,742.**

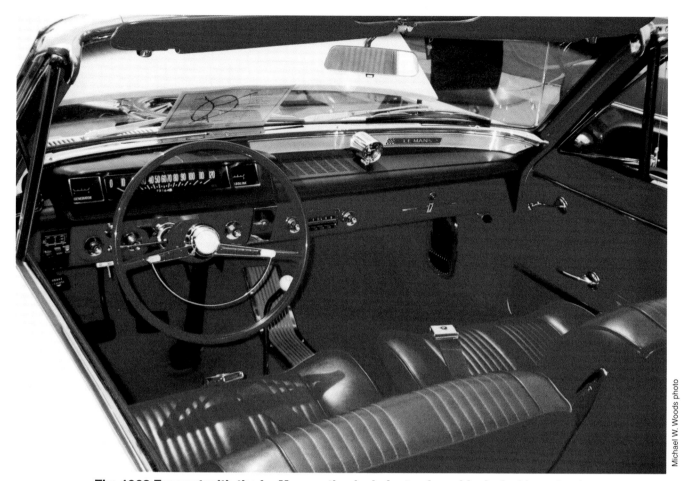

Michael W. Woods photo

The 1962 Tempest with the Le Mans option had plenty of good looks inside and out.

Michigan, S=South Gate, California, and K=Kansas City, Kansas. The remaining symbols in VIN are the sequential production number beginning at 1001 for each factory. Body/style number plate under hood tells manufacturer, Fisher style number, assembly plant, trim code, paint code, accessory codes. Style number consists of 62 (for 1962) prefix and four symbols that appear in second column of charts below. First two symbols indicate series; second two symbols indicate body type. VIN appears on front of engine at right-hand cylinder bank along with an alphanumerical engine production code. Engine production codes included: (195-cid/110-hp four) 89Z/85Z; (195-cid/115-hp four) 79Y; (195-cid/120-cid four) 86Z; (195-cid/140-hp four) 76Y; (195-cid/166-hp four) 77Y/87Z; (215-cid/185-hp aluminum V-8) 91Z/97Z.

COLORS

Paint color codes for 1962 were: A=Regent Black, C=Cameo Ivory, D=Silvermist Gray Poly, E=Ensign Blue Poly, F=Yorktown Blue Poly, H=Kimberly Blue, J=Silverleaf Green Poly, L=Belmar Red Poly, M=Bamboo Cream, N=Burgundy Poly, P=Aquamarine Poly, Q=Seafoam Aqua, R=Yuma Beige, T=Caravan Gold Poly and V=Mandalay Red. Interior trim codes for 1961 were: 201=Blue cloth and vinyl, 206/215=Blue vinyl, 204=Fawn cloth and vinyl, 209/216=Fawn vinyl, 205=Maroon cloth and vinyl, 210/218=Maroon vinyl, 207=Aqua vinyl, 208=Green vinyl, 211=Black vinyl, 213=Red vinyl, 214=Saddle vinyl, and 217=Gray vinyl.

TEMPEST — (FOUR-CYL) — SERIES 21

Standard equipment included: heater and defroster, electric wipers, turn signals, left-hand visors, and five tubeless black sidewall tires. Those delivered in Custom trim level had twin sun visors, a cigarette lighter, a Deluxe steering wheel, custom upholstery and special exterior trim. The Custom convertible sported courtesy lamps. The Tempest sports coupe and the Le Mans sports coupe had a "town car" roof with more formal-looking, angular lines. The rear window on these models was not as wide as the rear window on the regular coupe. All Tempest interiors were plush and practical. The standard sedan and coupe interiors had cloth-and-Morrokide upholstery combinations in choices of Blue, Gold or Red. A Morrokide interior in Gray and Gold or Red and Gray was standard in the Safari station wagon. The convertible featured custom "Jeweltone" Morrokide in Blue, Gold and Beige, or Red and Ivory. Custom interiors in other models also featured Jeweltone Morrokide in Blue, Aqua, Green, Gold and Beige, or Red and Ivory. Le Mans convertible monochromatic interior color choices were Black, Parchment, Red, Saddle, or Blue expanded Morrokide.

Model Number	Body/Style Number	Body Type & Seating	Factory Price	Shipping Weight	Production Total
TEMPEST — (FOUR-CYL) — SERIES 21					
21	19	4d Sedan-6P	$2,240	2,815 lbs.	16,057
21	27	2d Coupe-6P	$2,186	2,785 lbs.	15,473
21	17	2d Hardtop-6P	$2,294	2,800 lbs.	12,319
21	67	2d Convertible-5P	$2,564	2,955 lbs.	5,076
21	35	4d Sta Wagon-6P	$2,511	2,995 lbs.	6,504
TEMPEST CUSTOM — (FOUR-CYL) — SERIES 21 (LE MANS OPTION)					
21	17	2d Hardtop-6P	$2,418	—	39,662
21	67	2d Convertible-5P	$2,742	—	15,599

NOTE 1: 141,535 Tempest fours were built.
NOTE 2: 28,867 Tempest fours had synchromesh; 112,668 had Tempestorque.
NOTE 3: 1,658 Tempest V-8s were built.
NOTE 4: 86 Tempest V-8s had synchromesh and 1,572 had Tempestorque automatic.
NOTE 5: Figures in parenthesis are production of Tempests with Deluxe package.
NOTE 6: Sport coupe and convertible came Custom-only; no Deluxe option.

ENGINES

TEMPEST "INDY FOUR" BASE 194-CID FOUR-CYL (WITH SYNCHROMESH): Inline. Overhead valves. Cast-iron block. Displacement: 194.5 cid. Bore and stroke: 4.06 x 3.75 in. Compression ratio: 8.6:1. Brake hp: 110 at 3800 rpm. Torque: 190 lbs.-ft. at 2000 rpm. Five main bearings. Hydraulic valve lifters. Carburetor: Rochester one-barrel. Standard with standard manual transmission and standard 3.31:1 rear axle.

TEMPEST "INDY FOUR" OPTIONAL 194-CID FOUR-CYL (WITH AUTOMATIC TRANSMISSION): Inline. Four-cylinder. Overhead valves. Cast-iron block. Displacement: 194.5 cid. Bore and stroke: 4.06 x 3.75 in. Compression ratio: 8.6:1. Brake hp: 115 at 4000 rpm. Torque: 195 lbs.-ft. at 2200. Hydraulic valve lifters. Carburetor: One-barrel. With optional automatic transmission and standard 3.08:1 rear axle.

TEMPEST "INDY FOUR" BASE 194-CID FOUR-CYL (PREMIUM FUEL FOUR-CYL WITH MANUAL TRANSMISSION): Inline. Overhead valves. Cast-iron block. Displacement: 194.5 cid. Bore and stroke: 4.06 x 3.75 in. Compression ratio: 10.25:1. Brake hp: 120 at 3800 rpm. Torque: 202 lbs.-ft. at 2000 rpm. Five main bearings. Hydraulic valve lifters. Carburetor: Rochester one-barrel. With standard manual transmission and standard 3.31:1 rear axle.

TEMPEST "INDY FOUR" OPTIONAL 194-CID FOUR-CYL (PREMIUM FUEL FOUR-CYL WITH AUTOMATIC TRANSMISSION): (Tempest "Indy Four") Inline. Overhead valves. Cast-iron block. Displacement: 194.5 cid. Bore and stroke: 4.06 x 3.75 in. Compression ratio: 10.25:1. Brake hp: 140 at 3800 rpm. Torque: 207 lbs.-ft. at 2200 rpm. Five main bearings. Hydraulic valve lifters. Carburetor: Rochester one-barrel. With optional automatic transmission and standard 3.08:1 rear axle.

TEMPEST "INDY FOUR" OPTIONAL 194-CID FOUR-CYL (WITH MANUAL OR AUTOMATIC TRANSMISSION): Overhead valves. Cast-iron block. Displacement: 194.5 cid. Bore and stroke: 4.06 x 3.75 in.

Compression ratio: 10.25:1. Brake hp: 166 at 3800 rpm. Torque: 215 lbs.-ft. at 2800 rpm. Hydraulic valve lifters. Carburetor: Rochester four-barrel. With standard manual or optional automatic transmission and standard 3.55:1 rear axle.

TEMPEST OPTIONAL 215-CID V-8 (HYDRA-MATIC ONLY): Overhead valve. Bore and stroke: 3.50 x 2.80. Displacement: 215 cid. Compression ratio: 10.25:1. Brake hp: 185 at 4800 rpm. Taxable hp: 39.20. Torque: 230 lbs.-ft. at 2800 rpm. Five main bearings. Hydraulic valve lifters. Crankcase capacity: 4 qt. (add 1 qt. for new filter). Cooling system capacity: 11.6 gal. (add 1 gallon with heater). Carburetor: Rochester 4GC model 7020078 four-barrel. Engine code: 97Z. (Built by Buick). With standard automatic transmission and standard 3.08:1 rear axle.

CHASSIS

Wheelbase: 112 in. Overall length: 189.3 in. Overall width: 72.2 in. Overall height: (sedan) 53.6 in., (Safari) 54.8 in., (coupe) 53.2 in. and (convertible) 53.7 in. Front tread: 56.8 in. Rear tread: 56.8 in. Turning diameter (curb-to-curb): 39.75 ft. Front legroom: (all models) 44.1 in. Rear legroom: (sedan) 37.8 in., (coupe) 36.8 in., (sports coupe) 36.8 in., (Safari) 37.5 in. and

The Gas-saving "4" with Pontiac Punch!

ABOVE: 1962 TEMPEST SAFARI STATION WAGON. ALSO AVAILABLE: SEDAN, COUPE, CONVERTIBLE, SPORTS COUPE, LEMANS CONVERTIBLE AND LEMANS COUPE.

New Tempest doesn't rock and roll. It's balanced!

Tempest keeps a level head—even over a chorus of washboards. Two reasons: Each wheel is independently suspended—there are no solid axles to transmit shock from one wheel to another. Each wheel carries equal weight—the front engine is balanced by a *rear* transmission. Solid, too. Body and frame are a single unit. The gas-saving, 4-cylinder engine puts out 110, 115, 120 or 140 horsepower. The extra-cost 4-barrel carburetor makes it 166 and the aluminum V-8 delivers an honest 190 horses. Take a Tempest over a miserable road. You'll like it!

PONTIAC MOTOR DIVISION • GENERAL MOTORS CORPORATION

Drive America's only front engine/rear transmission car . . . it's balanced like none of the others!

Pontiac boasted that the 1962 Tempest line was "balanced" better than the competition with its front engine/rear transmission construction. The ads at the time tempted buyers to "tackle a back road in a Tempest Safari."

(convertible) 36.9 in. Front headroom: (sedan) 38.1 in., (coupe) 38.1 in., (sports coupe) 38.1 in., (Safari) 38.6 in. and (convertible) 38.8 in. Rear headroom: (sedan) 37.2 in., (coupe) 36.7 in., (sports coupe) 36.7 in., (Safari) 37.8 in. and (convertible) 37.2 in. Front hip room: (all models) 58.6 in. Rear hip room: (sedan) 58.3 in., (coupe) 57.4 in., (sports coupe) 57.4 in., (Safari) 58.3 in. and (convertible) 47.4 in. Front seat height: (all models except convertible) 11 in., (convertible) 11.1 in. Rear seat height: (sedan) 12.4 in., (coupe) 12.7 in., (sports coupe) 12.7 in., (Safari) 12.6 in. and (convertible) 12.8 in. Trunk volume: (coupe and sedan) 27.5 cu. ft. Station wagon cargo compartment length (rear seat up and tailgate closed): 53.1 in. Station wagon cargo area width: (maximum) 56.7 in.; (minimum) 44.1 in. Station wagon cargo compartment maximum height: 30.8 in. Station wagon rear opening width: 49.5 in. Station wagon rear opening height: 29.3 in. Station wagon cargo compartment volume (second seat flat): 72.6 cu. ft. Fuel tank: 16 gal. Tires: (sedan, coupe and convertible) 6.00 x 15, (station wagon) 6.50 x 15.

OPTIONS

431 heavy-duty air cleaner ($4.84). 582 Cool-Pack air conditioner ($318.60). 621 Northern areas antifreeze ($3.30). 622 Southern areas antifreeze ($1.70). 471 back-up lights with standard transmission ($12.91). 471 back-up lights, with automatic transmission ($10.76). 474 front and rear bumper guards ($16.14). 752 cigar lighter ($2.15). 604 electric clock ($15.60). 601 crankcase ventilator, four-cylinder ($4.30). 601

The standard Tempest engine was the "Indy Four" with a single carburetor.

Richard Croteau photo

crankcase ventilator V-8 ($5.16). 414 front foam seat cushion ($8.07). Four-cylinder engine with four-barrel carburetor ($38.74). V-8 engine with two-barrel carburetor ($261.36). 434 oil filter with four-cylinder engine, standard with V-8 ($5.38). 531 all windows tinted glass ($31.20). 532 tinted windshield ($19.91). 472 dual horns ($4.30). 424 padded instrument panel ($12.91). 482 glove box lamp ($2.85). 491 courtesy lamps ($4.30 but standard in convertible). 492 ash tray lamp ($3.12). 494 parking brake signal lamp with standard transmission ($4.95). 571 station wagon luggage carrier ($64.56). 762 station wagon luggage compartment mat ($3.23). 454 outside rearview mirror

The 1962 Tempest with the Le Mans option was an appealing package.

Frederick J. Brown photo

($4.25). 442 non-glare inside rearview mirror ($4.25). 444 remote-control outside rearview mirror ($11.78). 541 windshield and rear window moldings, sedans ($14.52). 541 windshield and rear window moldings, station wagon ($12.91). Two-tone paint in standard colors ($12.38). Two-tone paint in special colors ($52.57). Solid paint in special color ($40.19). 501 power steering ($75.32). 552 power tailgate window on station wagon ($53.80). 395 manual radio and antenna ($53.80). 396 push-button radio and antenna ($62.41). 754 Deluxe steering wheel ring ($3.77). 572 spare wheel and tire cover ($2.58). T02 five 6.00 x 15 four-ply white sidewall tires for sedans without air conditioning ($28.03). T11 five 6.50 x 15 four-ply black sidewall tires for sedans without air conditioning ($8.02). T12 five 6.50 x 15 four-ply white sidewall tires for sedans without air conditioning ($37.32). T12 five 6.50 x 15 four-ply white sidewall tires for sedans with air conditioning and station wagons ($29.70). Tempestorque automatic transmission ($172.80). 751 right-hand inside sun visor ($3.23). 462 Deluxe wheel discs ($15.60). 523 wheel trim rings ($13.45). 421 windshield washer ($13.02). 402 two-speed windshield wipers ($4.84). 061 Basic Group includes: push-button radio and antenna, dual-speed windshield wipers, front foam cushion, windshield washer, heavy-duty air cleaner, and oil filter ($80.27-$98.56 depending on model, engine, and other options). 062 Protection Group, includes: tilt-type inside rearview mirror, left-hand outside rearview mirror, back-up lamps, dual horns, and bumper guards ($41.85 with manual transmission or $39.70 with automatic transmission). 071 Upper Exterior Décor Group includes: windshield and rear window moldings, door and center pillar scalp moldings, and fender-top ornament ($19.37 on Custom sports coupe and $32.28 on other models). 072 Lower Exterior Décor Group includes: front crown moldings, front fender windsplits, and fender-top ornament ($34.43). 074 Interior Décor Group includes right-hand inside sun visor, cigarette lighter, front fender top ornament, Custom interior appointments, and luggage mat in station wagons ($69.94 in sedan and $75.32 in station wagon). 073 Exterior Décor Group includes all ingredients of Group 071 and Group 072 ($53.80 in Custom sports coupe and $66.71 on other models except convertible). 088 Le Mans option group includes bucket seats, Lemans nameplates, and power top on convertible ($123.74 for Custom sports coupe and $177.54 for Custom convertible).

OPTION INSTALLATION RATES

Of 143,193 Tempests built, 79.8 percent had automatic transmission, 5.6 percent had a four-speed synchromesh transmission, 1.1 percent had a V-8 engine, 98.9 percent had a four-cylinder engine, 81.6 percent had a radio, 99.1 percent had a heater, 8.7 percent had power steering, 3.6 percent had power windows (station wagon rear window only), 38.6 percent had bucket seats, 80.3 percent had white sidewall tires, 56.5 percent had

A total of 6,504 Tempest Safari wagons were produced in 1962.

Tony Secino photo

This 1962 Tempest Le Mans received aftermarket fender skirts.

windshield washers, 27.9 percent had a tinted windshield, 8.9 percent had all tinted windows, 42.1 percent had back-up lights, 53.4 percent had full wheel covers, and 3.6 percent had air conditioning.

HISTORICAL FOOTNOTES

Elliott M. "Pete" Estes was general manager at Pontiac Motor Division in 1962. The 1962 Tempest was introduced in Pontiac dealer showrooms on September 21, 1961. With increased demand, Pontiac added a third assembly plant in Kansas City, Kansas, to the factories sourcing 1962 Tempest models. Model-year production of Tempests was 143,353 units, including 67,454 two-door sedans, 20,635 convertible coupes, 37,430 four-door sedans and 17,674 four-door two-seat Safari station wagons. Calendar-year production was 145,676 cars and wagons. Body styles 2117 and 2167 came only as Tempest Custom or Tempest Custom with Le Mans option. Pontiac Motor Division won the Grand Prix award in the Pure Oil performance and economy trials at Daytona Beach, Florida, scoring well in the three-phase trials. Retail sales of 1962 Tempests sold by U.S. new-car dealers were counted as 140,744 units or 2.1 percent of the industry total for calendar-year 1962. That compared to 113,543 units or 2.0 percent of industry in 1961. In model-year 1962, only 1,600 Tempests were ordered with the optional V-8.

Pontiac engineering created a car called the 389 Tempest GT that was a Tempest coupe with a 389-cid Pontiac V-8 under its hood. A large air scoop was added to the hood to duct cool air to the engine. Pontiac sent paperwork on this car to the Automobile Competition Committee of the Federation Internationale De L'Autombile (FIA) to certify the model for sports car racing. During 1962, a Pontiac draftsman did a proposal for a 1963 Tempest facelift and the car was called the Ventura. The car featured a louvered hood, a highly styled front radiator grille, and six-bolt wheels, but never went into production. Super-Duty drag racing versions of the early Tempests were built. The concept of dumping the big-block 421-cid Super-Duty V-8 into the small Tempest body shell was actually dreamed up by the late Mickey Thompson for A/FX (Factory Experimental) drag racing competition. Another pair of A/FX class 421 Tempests — a coupe and a Safari station wagon — were campaigned by Pontiac racing driver Arnie Beswick as covered in the 1963 section.

Thomas Glatch photo

There was a lot to like about the 1963 Tempest. Its clean lines, ample options, and competitive price made it a solid performer for Pontiac, and cars from the era remain popular collector vehicles.

Pontiac was third on the automotive industry's best-seller list again in 1963, and the Tempest was the reason for this. Sales of big Pontiacs stayed strong and the Tempest sales were all "plus" business. The 1963 Tempest was nearly 4 inches longer that the 1961-1962 versions. The term "senior compact" was often used to describe the new model. It had the same wheelbase and technical features as earlier Tempests, but it was 2 inches wider and 5 inches longer. Design changes included a slight "Coke bottle" shape, more angular rooflines, creased side panels, longer trunks, split grille styling, wider wheel openings, and dual vertically stacked taillights. The Le Mans trim kit became a luxury series. Topping engineering changes was the inception of a Pontiac-built 260-hp cast-iron V-8 engine (326 cid) derived from the larger 389-cid V-8. It replaced the Buick-built 185-hp aluminum V-8. The cast-iron engine provided a price-versus-power advantage over the aluminum engine. Other refinements included an improved automatic transmission, a widened rear track, and a redesigned rear suspension.

I.D. NUMBERS

VIN on left front door post. First symbol tells series:

21=Tempest. Second and third symbols tell year: 63=1963. Fourth symbol tells assembly plant: P=Pontiac, Michigan; S=South Gate, California; and K=Kansas City, Kansas. (Production of 384 cars in Bloomfield, New Jersey, was reported. These were export units built in other factories and sent to Bloomfield for shipment overseas.) Following symbols are sequential production number starting with 1001 at each assembly plant. Body/style number plate under hood tells manufacturer, Fisher style number, assembly plant, trim code, paint code, accessory codes. Style number consists of 63 (for 1963) prefix and four symbols that appear in second column of charts below. First two symbols indicate series. The second two symbols indicate body type. VIN appears on front of engine at right-hand cylinder bank along with an alphanumerical engine production code. Engine production codes included: (195-cid/115-hp four) 89Z/85Z/79Y. (195-cid/120-hp four) 86Z/83Z. (195-cid/140-hp four) 76Y. (195-cid/166-hp four) 77Y/84Z/87Z. (326-cid/260-hp V-8) 68X/71X/60O/69O. (326-cid/280-hp V-8) 70X/59O.

COLORS

Paint color codes for 1963 were: A=Starlight Black,

Pontiac made the Tempest 2 inches wider for 1963 and aggressively marketed its "wide-track" abilities.

C=Cameo Ivory, D=Silvermist Gray, F=Yorktown Blue Poly, H=Kimberly Blue, J=Silverleaf Green, K=Cordovan Tan, L=Marimba Red, P=Aquamarine, Q=Marlin Aqua, R=Yuma Beige, T=Caravan Gold Poly, V=Grenadier Red and W=Nocturne Blue. Interior trim codes for 1963 included 201=Blue cloth and vinyl, 208/217=Blue vinyl, 202=Aqua cloth and vinyl, 209=Aqua cloth, 204=Fawn cloth and vinyl, 211=Fawn vinyl, 214=Fawn vinyl, 205=Maroon cloth and vinyl, 212/207=Maroon cloth, 213=Black vinyl, 206=Silver vinyl, 210=Green vinyl, 215=Red vinyl, and 216=Bronze vinyl.

TEMPEST — (FOUR-CYL) — SERIES 21

Standard equipment included a heater and defroster, electric wipers, turn signals, a left-hand sun visor and five black tubeless tires. Oversize 6.50 x 15 tires were used on V-8-equipped Tempests and Safaris.

Model Number	Body/Style Number	Body Type & Seating	Factory Price	Shipping Weight	Production Total
21	27	2d Coupe-6P	$2,188	2,810 lbs.	13,307
21	17	2d Hardtop-6P	$2,294	2,820 lbs.	(13,157)
21	19	4d Sedan-6P	$2,241	2,815 lbs.	12,808
					(15,413)
21	67	2d Cus Conv-5P	$2,564	2,955 lbs.	5,012
21	35	4d Sta Wagon-6P	$2,512	2,995 lbs.	4,203
					(5,932)

NOTE 1: 69,831 Series 21 Tempests were built.
NOTE 2: 16,657 Tempests had synchromesh and 53,174 had Tempestorque automatic transmission.
NOTE 3: Figures in parenthesis are Tempests with optional Deluxe trim.

The base four-cylinder Tempest engine for 1963 produced 115 hp.

Thomas Glatch photo

NOTE 4: Production of body style 63-2117 is not broken out separately.

TEMPEST LE MANS — (V-8) — SERIES 22

The Le Mans nameplate was listed as a separate series. As a Pontiac brochure put it, "Styled with spirit and zest, the 1963 Le Mans is offered in a special line of its own for those enthusiasts who demand swiftness and power with a neat, trim design that fits perfectly in any landscape." Standard equipment on the Le Mans included dual sun visors, a deluxe steering wheel, a custom interior, bucket seats, a front seat console, and a power convertible top. Identification features included model badges on front fenders, partially blacked-out grilles, horizontal taillights, and a horizontal décor panel on the deck latch panel.

Model Number	Body/Style Number	Body Type & Seating	Factory Price	Shipping Weight	Production Total
22	17	2d Hardtop-6P	$2,418	2,865 lbs.	45,701
22	67	2d Cus Conv-5P	$2,742	3,035 lbs.	15,957

NOTE 5: 61,659 Le Mans were built.
NOTE 6: 18,034 Le Mans had synchromesh and 43,625 had Tempestorque.
NOTE 7: 23,227 Le Mans sport coupes and 8,744 Le Mans convertibles had four-cylinder engines.
NOTE 8: All other Le Mans were V-8 powered.

ENGINES

TEMPEST "INDY FOUR" BASE 194-CID FOUR-CYL (WITH SYNCHROMESH): Inline. Overhead valves. Cast-iron block. Displacement: 194.5 cid. Bore and stroke: 4.06 x 3.75 in. Compression ratio: 8.6:1. Brake hp: 115 at 4000 rpm. Five main bearings. Hydraulic valve lifters. Carburetor: Rochester one-barrel.

TEMPEST "INDY FOUR" BASE 194-CID FOUR-CYL (WITH HYDRA-MATIC): Inline. Overhead valves. Cast-iron block. Displacement: 194.5 cid. Bore and stroke: 4.06 x 3.75 in. Compression ratio: 10.25:1. Brake hp: 120 at 3800 rpm. Five main bearings. Hydraulic valve lifters. Carburetor: Rochester one-barrel.

TEMPEST "INDY FOUR" OPTIONAL 194-CID FOUR-CYL: Inline. Overhead valves. Cast-iron block. Displacement: 194.5 cid. Bore and stroke: 4.06 x 3.75 in. Compression ratio: 10.25:1. Brake hp: 140 at 3800 rpm.

Five main bearings. Hydraulic valve lifters. Carburetor: Rochester one-barrel.

TEMPEST "INDY FOUR" OPTIONAL 194-CID FOUR-CYL: Inline. Four-cylinder. Overhead valves. Cast-iron block. Displacement: 194.5 cid. Bore and stroke: 4.06 x 3.75 in. Compression ratio: 10.25:1. Brake hp: 166 at 3800 rpm. Hydraulic valve lifters. Carburetor: Rochester four-barrel.

TEMPEST, LE MANS OPTIONAL 326-CID V-8: Overhead valve. Bore and stroke: 3.718 x 3.75. Displacement: 326 cid. Compression ratio: 10.25:1. Brake hp: 260 at 4800 rpm. Taxable hp: 44.4. Torque: 352 lbs.-ft. at 2800 rpm. Five main bearings. Hydraulic valve lifters. Crankcase capacity: 4 qt. (add 1 qt. for new filter). Cooling system capacity: 18.5 gal. (add 1 gallon with heater). Carburetor: Four-barrel. Engine code: 68X, 71X, 60O or 69O.

CHASSIS

Wheelbase: 112 in. Overall Length: 194.3 in. Overall width: 74.2 in. Overall height: 54.2 in. Front tread: 57.3 in. Rear tread: (Tempest) 58 in. Front headroom: 34 in. Rear headroom: 33.7 in. Front legroom: 44.1 in. Rear legroom: 37.8 in. Rear axle road clearance: 6 in. Turning diameter (curb-to-curb): 37.7 ft. Standard tires: (Tempest) 6.00 x 15.

OPTIONS

431 heavy-duty air cleaner ($4.84). 582 Cool-Pack air conditioner ($318.60). 471 back-up lights with standard transmission ($12.91). 471 back-up lights, with automatic transmission ($10.76). 474 front and rear bumper guards ($16.14). 652 cigar lighter ($2.15). 604 electric clock in body styles 2119, 2127 and 2135 ($19.37). 602 console shift in body style 2200, requires automatic transmission ($48.15). 412 front foam seat cushion ($8.07). Four-cylinder engine with one-barrel carburetor and heavy-duty clutch ($26.90). Four-

The '63 Tempest featured an unusual in-dash transmission range selector, rather than an on-the-column or console shifter.

Thomas Glatch photo

The Le Mans nameplate on the front quarter panels was one way to identify the 1963 Tempests with the Le Mans option.

Rich McClean photo

The Custom convertible for 1963 came with a base price of $2,564.

Michael Harrison photo

cylinder engine with four-barrel carburetor and heavy-duty clutch ($65.64). Four-cylinder engine with four-barrel carburetor ($38.74). V-8 engine with two-barrel carburetor ($167.40). 434 oil filter with four-cylinder engine, standard with V-8 ($5.38). 531 all windows tinted glass ($31.20). 532 tinted windshield ($19.91). 472 dual horns ($4.30). 424 padded instrument panel ($16.14). 482 glove box lamp ($2.85). 491 courtesy lamps ($4.30 but standard in convertible). 492 ash tray lamp ($3.12). 494 parking brake signal lamp with standard transmission ($4.95). 571 station wagon luggage carrier ($64.56). 662 station wagon luggage compartment mat ($3.23). 454 outside rearview mirror ($4.25). 441 visor-vanity mirror ($1.45). 442 non-glare inside rearview mirror ($4.25). 444

remote-control outside rearview mirror ($11.78). 541 windshield and rear window moldings, sedans and coupes ($14.52). 541 windshield and rear window moldings, station wagon ($12.91). Two-tone paint in standard colors, except convertible ($12.38). Two-tone paint in special colors, except convertible ($52.57). Solid paint in special color ($40.19). 501 power steering ($75.32). 554 power tailgate window on station wagon ($53.80). 561 power left-hand tilt bucket seat in styles 2119 and 2135 with 074 option group and all 2200 styles ($66.71). Power top on convertible style 2167 (($53.80). 395 manual radio and antenna ($53.80). 396 push-button radio and antenna ($62.41). 624 deluxe front seat belts ($18.83). 562 front bucket seats in body styles

The popular Tempest helped make Pontiac No. 3 among U.S. automakers in 1963.

2119 and 2135 with Group 074 ($134.50). 534 shelf-mounted spare tire in coupes and sedans ($8.50). 634 heavy-duty shock absorbers and springs ($6.24). 414 Custom steering wheel in 2100 styles with Group 074 and all 2200 styles ($8.98), 414 Custom steering wheel in style 2127, 2119 and 2135 with Group 074 ($12.75). 461 steering wheel with Deluxe ring in styles 2119, 2127 and 2135 ($3.77). 572 spare wheel and tire cover ($2.58). 504 rear-door switch ($1.72). 664 tachometer, not available with electric clock ($53.80). Cordova top

The Aqua cloth-and-vinyl interior was far from drab in this 1963 Tempest Custom convertible.

Bill Mawbey photo

This is one of 5,012 Tempest Custom convertibles produced by Pontiac in model year 1963.

Bill Mawbey photo

Greg Walters photo

Even without the Le Mans option, the Tempest Custom was a sporty ride in 1963, and its design is appealing more than four decades later.

on styles 2117 and 2217 ($75.32). T02 five 6.00 x 15 four-ply white sidewall tires for sedans without air conditioning ($28.03). T11 five 6.50 x 15 four-ply black sidewall tires for sedans without air conditioning ($8.02). T12 five 6.50 x 15 four-ply white sidewall tires for sedans without air conditioning ($37.32). T12 five 6.50 x 15 four-ply white sidewall tires for sedans with air conditioning and station wagons ($29.70). Tempestorque automatic transmission ($172.80). Four-speed synchromesh transmission ($189.00). 651 right-hand inside sun visor ($3.23). 462 Deluxe wheel discs ($15.60). 521 Custom wheel discs ($22.60). 402 windshield washer ($17.27). 402 two-speed windshield wipers ($4.84). 061 Basic Group includes push-button radio and antenna, dual-speed windshield wipers, front foam cushion, windshield washer, heavy-duty air cleaner and oil filter for models with bench seats ($103.89-$110.88). 061 Basic Group includes push-button radio and antenna, dual-speed windshield wipers, front foam cushion, windshield washer, heavy-duty air cleaner and oil filter for models with bucket front seats ($95.28-$102.81). 071 Upper Exterior Décor Group includes windshield and rear window moldings, door and center pillar scalp moldings and fender-top ornament ($19.37 on styles 2117 and 2127 Custom Sports Coupe and $32.28 on other styles). 072 Lower Exterior Décor Group includes front crown moldings, front fender windsplits and fender-top ornament ($34.43). 074 Interior Décor Group includes right-hand inside sun visor, cigarette lighter, front fender top ornament, Custom interior appointments and luggage mat in station wagons ($69.94 in sedan and $75.32 in station wagon). 081 Mirror Group ($17.48). 082 Safety Group ($55.41).

OPTION INSTALLATION RATES

Of 131,490 Tempests built, 73.6 percent had automatic transmission, 3.1 percent had a four-speed synchromesh transmission, 38.2 percent had a V-8 engine, 61.8 percent had a four-cylinder engine, 87.7 percent had a radio, 99.1 percent had a heater, 19.7 percent had power steering, 3.1 percent had power brakes, 2.6 percent had power windows (station wagon rear window only), 47.1 percent had bucket seats, 16.4 percent had seat belts, 83 percent had white sidewall tires, 60.6 percent had windshield washers, 29.9 percent had a tinted windshield, 10.9 percent had all tinted windows, 69.2 percent had back-up lights, 63.2 percent had full wheel covers, 2 percent had dual exhausts, and 6 percent had air conditioning.

HISTORICAL FOOTNOTES

The 1963 Tempest was introduced in Pontiac dealer showrooms on October 4, 1962. Production began Sept. 4, 1962. Introductions were on Oct. 4, 1962. Model-year production was 131,490 units including 72,165 two-door sedans, 28,221 four-door sedans, 20,969 convertibles and 10,135 four-door two-seat station wagons. In addition to utilizing the 421 SD V-8, the Super-Duty Tempests came equipped with aluminum front sheet metal and bumpers and a special clutch-operated four-speed transaxle. Super-Duty Tempests were built during the 1962 Christmas holiday and came out just prior to GM's infamous corporate edict against factory participation in racing in January 1963.

The famous Grand Turisimo Omologato (GTO) option package debuted on 1964 Le Mans models.

Jerry Heasley photo

Tempests were among the most completely changed cars for 1964. Pontiac's now mid-sized model was enlarged again and had separate frame construction with conventional drivetrain engineering. Although all of the body sheet metal was new, the Tempest styling motif retained a split grille and a strong Pontiac identity. The greenhouse area of the body was the same used for other GM intermediate cars, but other body panels were distinctively Pontiac in appearance. The Safari station wagon, which was always a strong-selling Tempest model, was even more popular due to its larger carrying capacity. Gone were the four-cylinder engine, the "rope" drive shaft, the rear-mounted transaxle and the swing-axle rear suspension. The independent front and rigid rear axle suspension had a Wide-Track design.

A 215-cid inline six-cylinder engine, assembled by Pontiac Motor _Division from Chevrolet-produced components, was the base power plant. Two versions of the Pontiac 326-cid V-8 were the initial V-8 offerings. These engines came with a choice of two versions of a new two-speed automatic transmission with a torque converter, a three-speed manual transmission, or a four-speed manual transmission.

There were three lines called Tempest, Tempest Custom, and Le Mans, but the real excitement came with the mid-season release of the now legendary GTO option package for the Le Mans. The GTO was the first real American "muscle car" and started a phenomenon that would last from mid-1964 until 1975.

I.D. NUMBERS

VIN on left front door post. First symbol tells engine type: 6=six-cylinder, 8=V-8. Second symbol indicates series: 0=Tempest, 1=Tempest Custom, 2=Le Mans. Third symbol tells year: 64=1964. Fourth symbol tells assembly plant: P=Pontiac, Michigan, K=Kansas City, Kansas, GMAD plant, F=Fremont, California and B=Baltimore, Maryland, Chevrolet assembly plant. Following symbols are sequential production numbers starting with 1001 at each assembly plant. Body/style number plate under hood tells manufacturer, Fisher style number, assembly plant, trim code, paint code, accessory codes. Style number consists of 64 (for 1964) prefix and four symbols that appear in second column of charts below. First two symbols indicate series. The second two symbols indicate body type. The VIN appears on front of engine at right-hand cylinder bank along with an alphanumerical engine production code. Engine production codes included: (215-cid/140-hp six)

The GTO had numerous chassis upgrades and a definite performance car feel.

"GTO" lettering in the lower left-hand grille helped identify the first-year GTO package.

Ace Wilson's Royal Pontiac dealership, located in Royal Oak, Michigan, helped design the special "Royal Bobcat" GTOs, one of which *Car and Driver* used as a test vehicle for a magazine story about the model's durability and performance.

80Z/81Z/85Z/83Y/88Y/89Y. (326-cid/250-hp V-8) 92X/96O. (326-cid/280-hp V-8) 94X/97O. (389-cid/325-hp four-barrel GTO V-8) 78X with synchromesh, 79J with Hydra-Matic. (389-cid/348-hp GTO Tri-Power V-8) 76X with synchromesh, 77J with Hydra-Matic. (Note: Some Pontiac experts claim that a few GTOs were built with factory-installed and/or dealer-installed 421-cid V-8s.)

COLORS

Paint color codes for 1964 were: A=Starlight Black, C=Cameo Ivory, D=Silvermist Gray Poly, F=Skyline Blue, J=Pinehurst Green Poly, L=Marimba Red Poly,

N=Sunfire Red Poly, P=Aquamarine Poly, Q=Gulfstream Aqua Poly, R=Alamo Beige, S=Saddle Bronze Metallic, T=Singapore Gold Poly, V=Grenadier Red, and W=Nocturne Blue Poly. Vinyl top colors were 1=Ivory and 2=Black. Convertible top colors were 1=Ivory, 2=Black, 4=Blue, 5=Aqua, 6=Beige and 7=Saddle. Interior trim codes for 1964 base Tempests were: 201=Blue cloth and vinyl, 202=Aqua cloth and vinyl, 203=Saddle cloth and vinyl, 206=Saddle vinyl, 207=Red vinyl, 204=Maroon cloth and vinyl, and 205=Gray vinyl. Interior trim codes for 1964 Tempest Customs were: 208=Blue vinyl, 209-Aqua vinyl, 212=Maroon vinyl, 211=Saddle vinyl and 210=Olive vinyl. Interior trim codes for 1964 Le Mans were: 214=Black vinyl,

Many enthusiasts will argue that the 1964 GTO was the first true American muscle car.

Jerry Heasley photo

215=Dark Blue vinyl, 216=Saddle vinyl, 217=Dark Aqua vinyl, 218=Medium Red vinyl and 219=Parchment. Interior trim codes for 1964 Le Mans GTOs were: 214=Black vinyl, 215=Dark Blue vinyl, 216=Saddle vinyl, 217=Dark Aqua vinyl, 218=Medium Red vinyl, and 219=Parchment.

TEMPEST — (SIX-CYL) — SERIES 20

The 1964 Tempests were different in many ways. They had three more inches of wheelbase and nine more inches of overall length. The front suspension was by conventional unequal-length A-arms and coil springs with a link-type stabilizer bar between the two lower control arms. All steering linkage was mounted ahead of the front wheels. The new frame was of perimeter design with torque boxes for extra strength and rigidity. A conventional semi-floating, hypoid rear axle was used. It had four rubber-bushed, stamped steel links positioning the axle, which was suspended on a pair of coil springs. Small hubcaps, the absence of upper belt line moldings, and triple windsplits behind front wheel openings identified Series 20 base Tempests were. Cars with optional V-8 power were dressed with front fender badges.

Model Number	Body/Style Number	Body Type & Seating	Factory Price	Shipping Weight	Production Total
20	69	4d Sedan-6P	$2,313	2,970 lbs.	15,516
					(3,911)
20	27	2d Hardtop-6P	$2,259	2,930 lbs.	17,169
					(4,596)
20	35	4d Sta Wagon-6P	$2,605	3,245 lbs.	4,597
					(2,237)

NOTE 1: No brackets=Tempest six production. Brackets=Tempest V-8 production.

TEMPEST CUSTOM — (SIX-CYL) — SERIES 21

Tempest Customs had the same general styling features as base Tempests, but could be easily identified by the bright upper beltline moldings accenting the "Coke-bottle" shape. There were also Tempest Custom nameplates on the rear fenders. Extra standard equipment included all-vinyl upholstery, carpeting, a deluxe steering wheel, and courtesy lamps on convertibles.

Model Number	Body/Style Number	Body Type & Seating	Factory Price	Shipping Weight	Production Total
21	69	4d Sedan-6P	$2,399	2,990 lbs.	15,851
					(14,097)
21	67	2d Convertible-5P	$2,641	3,075 lbs.	4,465
					(3,522)
21	27	2d Hardtop-6P	$2,345	2,955 lbs.	12,598
					(13,235)
21	35	4d Sta Wagon-6P	$2,691	3,260 lbs.	4,254
					(6,442)

NOTE 2: No brackets=Tempest six production. Brackets=Tempest V-8 production.

TEMPEST LE MANS — (SIX-CYL) — SERIES 22

Le Mans series Tempests had distinct styling touches such as: Le Mans nameplates on the rear fender sides, ribbed décor plates for the deck lid latch panel, model badges on the deck lid, simulated slanting louvers ahead of rear wheel cutouts, and Le Mans script plates for the dashboard. Standard equipment in all Le Mans models included: a Circ-L-Aire heater and defroster, bright rocker panel moldings, a 37-amp. Delcotron alternator and voltage regulator, windows with curved side glass, electric windshield wipers, extra-big self-adjusting air-cooled brakes, front and rear armrests with ashtrays, a long-cruise 21 1/2-gallon fuel tank, chromed hubcaps, a glove compartment lock, an interior dome light (except convertible), improved dual interior sun shades, a cigar lighter, plastic kick pads, a vinyl-coated fabric headliner, a full-flow oil filter, 14-in. diameter wheels with big 6.50 x 14 tires, push-button door locks, individually adjustable front bucket seats, luxurious expanded Morrokide interiors, exclusive Le Mans exterior trim, three-bulb horizontal taillights, exclusive instrument panel bright trim, full nylon blend carpeting, a deluxe steering wheels, and a formed foam pad bucket front seat cushion. The Le Mans convertible also had a power-operated top, rear interior lighting in the armrest panels, and an instrument panel courtesy lamp.

The Tempest styling motif on the GTO retained a split grille and a strong Pontiac look for 1964.

Jerry Heasley photo

Model Number	Body/Style Number	Body Type & Seating	Factory Price	Shipping Weight	Production Total
22	27	2d Coupe-5P	$2,491	2,975 lbs.	11,136
					(20,181)
22	37	2d Hardtop-5P	$2,556	2,995 lbs.	7,409
					(23,901)
22	67	2d Convertible-5P	$2,796	3,125 lbs.	5,786
					(11,773)

NOTE 3: No brackets=Tempest six production. Brackets=Tempest V-8 production.

TEMPEST LE MANS GTO — (V-8) — SERIES 22 (WITH GTO OPTION)

The famous Grand Turisimo Omologato (GTO) option package was released for Le Mans models this year. The Italian term used as the model name actually meant Grand Touring Automobile, although the Pontiac GTO was far from a 2+2 closed-body sports car. The real idea behind this package was to circumvent the corporate racing-and-high-performance ban by providing the 389-cid V-8 as an option in the most luxurious intermediate-size Pontiac. This package turned the Le Mans into a "super car" and the term "muscle car" later became the popular label for this breed. The 389-cid V-8 was the standard power plant and came in two versions, both of which were fitted with special high-performance goodies. One featured a single four-barrel carburetor and the other substituted three two-barrel carburetors. GTOs also featured special appearance items in place of some regular Le Mans styling touches. They included G-T-O letters in the left-hand grille opening, G-T-O lettering on the rear fender tips and deck lid, tri-colored (red, white and blue) GTO crests behind the front wheel openings, a special hood stamping with air scoops and cast-aluminum grilles in the scoop openings, a GTO crest on the dashboard, and an engine-turned aluminum trim panel surrounding the instruments. Since the GTO was a sports-type car, it had numerous chassis modifications, including higher-rate springs in the front and rear for a firmer ride. The front stabilizer bar was thicker. Also included in the package were 14 x 6-in. rims (as opposed to standard 14 x 5-in. Tempest rims), and 7.50 x 14

tubeless nylon tires with a thin red stripe. White sidewall tires of the same size, but with conventional rayon construction, were a no-cost option for GTO-optioned cars. The engine block, crankshaft, rods, pistons, and bearings used in the GTO engine were the same as used in other 389-cid Pontiac V-8s, but the cylinder heads and valve train were of special design and construction. The heads were the same ones used on Pontiac's 421 H.O. V-8 and gave a 10.75:1 compression ratio through the use of smaller valve clearance notches in the 389 piston tops. Larger diameter valves (1.92-in. intake and 1.66-in. exhaust) were used in the GTO compared to the standard size (1.88-in. intake and 1.60-in. exhaust) used in other Pontiacs. The H.O. heads also had larger, streamlined valve ports. The GTO's "C" code hydraulic-lifter camshaft was also of a high-lift design for high performance. The hydraulic lifters were also special and provided a high pump-up speed thanks to their longer check-ball travel and the use of dual valve springs. The GTO option also incorporated a heavy-duty radiator, a thermostatically controlled viscous-drive seven-blade 18-in. fan, a dual exhaust system, a heavy-duty starter, and a heavy-duty battery. The base GTO engine featured a single Carter four-barrel carburetor with 1.438-in. primary and 1.688-in. secondary throttle bores. The optional GTO V-8 featured three Rochester two-barrel carburetors with a 1.44-in. bore on the center carburetor and 1.69-in. bores on the others. Three transmissions were offered: a standard three-speed manual, an optional Muncie four-speed manual, and a two-speed automatic with torque converter (also optional). Floor-mounted Hurst gear shifters were used for both manual gearboxes, whether or not a center console was added between the front seats. The shifter for the automatic transmission was on the steering column, except when the console was added, in which case it was moved to the console. A 3.23:1 rear axle was used with the four-barrel V-8 and a 3.55:1 rear was used with the "Tri-Power" engine.

The 389-cid Tri-Power V-8 gave Pontiac drivers
horsepower to burn for 1964.

Floor-mounted shifters were used for both the three-
and four-speed manual gearboxes in 1964.

The 1964 Tempests looked and felt bigger than before, and they were. The cars had 3 inches added to the
wheelbases and 9 inches added to their overall length.

Model Number	Body/Style Number	Body Type & Seating	Factory Price	Shipping Weight	Production Total
22	27	2d Coupe-5P	$2,852	3,106 lbs.	7,384
22	37	2d Hardtop-5P	$2,963	3,126 lbs.	18,422
22	67	2d Convertible-5P	$3,081	3,360 lbs.	6,644

ENGINES

TEMPEST BASE 215-CID SIX-CYL: Inline. Overhead valves. Cast-iron block. Displacement: 215 cid. Bore and stroke: 3.75 x 3.25 in. Compression ratio: 8.6:1. Brake hp: 140 at 4200 rpm. Torque: 206 lbs.-ft. at 2000 rpm. Seven main bearings. Hydraulic valve lifters. Carburetor: Rochester one-barrel. Available with standard manual transmission and standard 3.08:1 rear axle (except 3.36:1 axle standard in station wagon). Also available with optional automatic transmission and standard 2.78:1 rear axle. With the automatic transmission a 2.56:1 economy rear axle was available. A 3.93:1 performance axle was also optionally available for all models except the Tempest sports coupe, Tempest four-door sedan, Tempest Custom four-door sedan, and all Safaris, which offered a standard 2.56:1 axle and an optional 2.93:1 performance axle.

TEMPEST, LE MANS OPTIONAL 326-CID V-8: Overhead valve. Displacement: 326 cid. Bore and stroke: 3.718 x 3.75. Compression ratio: 8.6:1. Brake hp: 250 at 4600 rpm. Taxable hp: 44.4. Torque: 333 lbs.-ft. at 2800. Five main bearings. Hydraulic valve lifters. Crankcase capacity: 4 qt. (add 1 qt. for new filter). Cooling system capacity: 19.5 gal. (add 1 gallon with heater). Carburetor: Two-barrel. Engine code: 92X or 96O.

Available with standard manual transmission and standard 3.23:1 rear axle or optional 3.08:1 economy rear axle. Also available with optional automatic transmission and standard 2.56:1 rear axle or optional 2.93:1 performance rear axle.

TEMPEST, LE MANS OPTIONAL 326-CID V-8: Overhead valve. Bore and stroke: 3.718 x 3.75. Displacement: 326 cid. Compression ratio: 10.5:1. Brake hp: 280 at 4800 rpm. Taxable hp: 44.4. Torque: 355 lbs.-ft. at 3200. Five main bearings. Hydraulic valve lifters. Crankcase capacity: 4 qt. (add 1 qt. for new filter). Cooling system capacity: 19.5 gal. (add 1 gallon with heater). Carburetor: Carter AFB four-barrel. Engine code: 94X or 97O. Available with standard manual transmission and standard 3.36:1 rear axle (except 3.36:1 axle standard in station wagon). Also available with optional automatic transmission and standard 3.23:1 rear axle. Optional 3.87:1, 3.90:1 and 4.30:1 rear axle ratios were available on special order for some models.

GTO BASE 389-CID V-8: Overhead valve. Cast-iron block. Bore and stroke: 4.06 x 3.75. Displacement: 389 cid. Compression ratio: 10.75:1. Brake hp: 325 at 4800 rpm. Taxable hp: 52.80. Torque: 428 lbs.-ft. at 3200 rpm. Five main bearings. Hydraulic valve lifters. Crankcase capacity: 5 qt. (add 1 qt. for new filter). Cooling system capacity with heater: 19.5 qt. Carburetor: Four-barrel. Engine code: 78X or 79J. Available with standard three-speed manual transmission and standard 3.23:1 rear axle. Also available with optional four-speed manual transmission and standard 3.23:1 rear axle. Also

Kenny Lentz photo

A straightforward muscle car: the 1964 GTO with 389-cid four-barrel and four-speed transmission. The fuzzy dice were not standard!

Dick Barrow photo

A mint-condition 1964 Le Mans ragtop with a 326-cid V-8, three-speed, and Yorktown Blue Metallic paint.

available with optional automatic transmission and standard 3.23:1 rear axle.

GTO OPTIONAL 389-CID V-8: Overhead valve. Cast-iron block. Bore and stroke: 4.06 x 3.75. Displacement: 389 cid. Compression ratio: 10.75:1. Brake hp: 348 at 4900 rpm. Taxable hp: 52.80. Torque: 428 lbs.-ft. at 3600 rpm. Five main bearings. Hydraulic valve lifters. Crankcase capacity: 5 qt. (add 1 qt. for new filter). Cooling system capacity with heater: 19.5 qt. Carburetion: Three Rochester two-barrel carburetors. Engine code: 76X or 77J. Available with standard three-speed manual transmission and standard 3.23:1 rear axle. Also available with optional four-speed manual transmission and standard 3.23:1 rear axle. Also available with optional automatic transmission and standard 3.23:1 rear axle. Special-order axle ratios included 3.08:1, 3.36:1, 3.55:1, and 3.90:1. A special radiator, a speedometer adapter, a heavy-duty fan, metallic brake linings, and Safe-T-Track were required with some combinations at extra cost. Air conditioning was not available when certain axles were ordered.

CHASSIS

Wheelbase: 115 in. Overall length: 203 in. Overall width: 73.3 in. Overall height: 53.5 in. Front track: 58 in. Rear track: 58 in. Ground clearance: 6 in. Turning circle (GTO): 41 ft. Turns lock-to-lock: 4 1/2. Front headroom (sedan): 38.1 in. Rear headroom (sedan): 36.8 in. Front legroom (sedan): 42.3 in. Rear legroom (sedan): 35.1 in. Front hiproom (sedan): 60.2 in., Rear hiproom (sedan): 58.8 in. Standard tires: (coupe and sedan) 6.50 x 14 rayon black sidewall, (convertible and Safari) 7.00 x 14 Rayon black sidewall, (GTO) 7.50 x 14 nylon red stripe (7.50 x 14 rayon white sidewall optional at no extra cost).

OPTIONS

581 Tri-Comfort air conditioner ($319). 411 pair of front seat belts. 604 electric clock. 601 front seat center console. 572 spare wheel and tire cover. 412 Custom front foam cushion. 451 remote-control rear deck lid. 541 electric rear window defogger, except convertible. 701 Safe-T-Track differential ($75). 531 Soft-Ray tinted glass in all windows. 532 Soft-Ray tinted glass in windshield only. 382 GTO option for Le Mans coupe, hardtop or convertible ($295). 512 door edge guards. 612 Ride & Handling package. 492 ashtray and cigarette light lamp. 491 courtesy lamp, except convertible. 484 dome and reading lamp, except convertible. 482 glove

box lamp. 494 parking brake on lamp. 404 under-hood lamp. 471 back-up lamp. 631 front floor mats. 632 rear floor mats. 442 non-glare inside day/night rearview mirror. 602 left-hand outside rearview mirror. 444 remote-control left-hand outside rearview mirror. 441 visor-vanity mirror. 424 instrument panel pad. ($16). 502 power brakes. 561 full-width power seat. 501 power steering. 551 power windows. 399 manual radio and electric antenna. 398 manual radio and manual antenna. 393 push-button radio and electric antenna. 392 push-button radio and manual antenna. 401 Separa-Phonic rear speaker, except convertible. 474 Verbra-Phonic amplifier package, except convertible. 624 Custom retractable front seat belts. 622 Superlift rear shock absorbers. 454 tilt-adjustable steering wheel. 524 Custom Sports steering wheel. 452 tachometer, except with transistor ignition ($54); with transistor ignition ($54). T02 6.50 x 14 Rayon white sidewall tires. T03 7.00 x 14 Rayon black sidewall tires. T04 7.00 x 14 Rayon white sidewall tires. 421 dual-speed windshield wipers and washers. 462 deluxe wheel discs. 521 Custom wheel discs. 402 dual-speed electric winshield wipers. 061 Basic Group includes push-button radio and manual antenna, Custom foam front seat cushion, dual-speed windshield wipers and washers, heavy-duty air cleaner and back-up lights. 062 Protection Group, includes instrument panel pad, door edge guards, a rear window defogger, a spare tire wheel cover, Custom retractable front seat belts and front and rear floor mats. 081 Mirror Group, includes visor-vanity mirror, non-glare inside rearview mirror and remote-control left-hand outside rearview mirror. 084 Lamp Group includes under-hood lamp, luggage lamp, glove box lamp, dome and reading lamp, courtesy lamp and parking-brake-on lamp. 984330 traffic hazard warning flasher. 984333 right-hand tailpipe extension. 984334 left-hand tailpipe extension. 984326 vacuum gauge ($48). Power convertible top ($54). Power tilt left bucket seat ($67). Power tailgate window ($54). Bucket seats ($134). Custom steering wheel ($6-$9). Deluxe steering wheel with ring ($4). Cordova top ($75).

OPTION INSTALLATION RATES

Of 235,126 Tempests built, 70.2 percent had automatic transmission, 13.7 percent had a four-speed synchromesh transmission, 58.0 percent had a V-8 engine, 42 percent had a six-cylinder engine, 90.2

When it came to power and style in 1964, it was tough to beat a GTO convertible.

Mike Mueller photo

Daniel B. Lyons photo

The beautiful first-year GTO coupe in Skyline Blue.

percent had a radio, 100 percent had a heater, 41.1 percent had power steering, 18.3 percent had power brakes, 0.2 percent had a power seat, 1.5 percent had power side windows, 3.2 percent had a power station wagon rear window, 50 percent had bucket seats, 1.6 percent had an adjustable steering column, 78.5 percent had white sidewall tires, 64.4 percent had windshield washers, 32.7 percent had a tinted windshield, 15.1 percent had all tinted windows, 75.6 percent had back-up lights, 9.9 percent had air conditioning, 4.8 percent had dual exhausts, 14.1 percent had a limited-slip differential, and 76.8 percent had full wheel covers.

HISTORICAL FOOTNOTES

Elliott M. "Pete" Estes continued as general manager of Pontiac Motor Division. John Z. DeLorean was chief engineer and a moving force behind the creation of the new GTO option. Production started Sept. 3, 1963. Tempest introductions were held Oct. 3, 1963. According to *Ward's 1964 Automotive Yearbook*, "A Gran Turisimo Omologato option for the plush Le Mans two-door hardtop and convertible, bowing in October, included a 389 'cube' V-8 of 325 hp."

Often regarded by automotive enthusiasts as the first true muscle car, in the sense of being a mid-size car with a big-block V-8 engine, the original GTO was not really a car, but an option. Due to General Motor's winter 1963 ban on divisional participation in high-performance marketing, Pontiac was restricted insofar as putting an engine larger than 330 cid into an intermediate-size car. That's why Pontiac's "Young Turk" executives and an ad man named Jim Wangers snuck the GTO into existence as an extra-cost package for the Tempest Le Mans. Late in October of 1963, the Grand Turismo Omologato package was announced for the Le

Mans coupe, hardtop, and convertible as a $295 option. In January 1964, *Motor Trend* magazine found a four-speed GTO convertible capable of doing the quarter mile in 15.8 seconds at 93 mph. The same car's 0 to 60-mph performance was 7.7 seconds and it had a 115-mph top speed. The 348-hp GTO hardtop went 0 to 60 mph in 6.6 seconds and did the quarter-mile in 14.8 seconds. By the year's end, the GTO was considered a huge sales success. Pontiac records show production of 7,384 GTO coupes, 18,422 two-door hardtops and 6,644 convertibles. Some sports car enthusiasts bemoaned Pontiac's brash adaptation of the Ferrari model designation "GTO."

As a result, in March 1964, *Car and Driver* magazine conducted an exhaustive road test of the Pontiac Tempest GTO using two nearly identical cars. Both were coupes and both had been fitted with a special "Bobcat" kit developed and installed by Ace Wilson's Royal Pontiac dealership, located in Royal Oak, Michigan. *Car and Driver* drove one of the cars all over the country. It had manual steering and metallic brake linings and racked up 3,000 miles of use. The second car was driven about 500 miles. The magazine attempted to borrow a Ferrari GTO to race against the Tempest. The writers actually drove two of these Ferraris, but were not able to run either one against the Pontiac GTO on a head-to-head basis. However, the somewhat controversial test reported a 0-to-60 time of 6 seconds for the Pontiac GTO and a 13.1-second quarter-mile run with a terminal speed of 115 mph! *Car and Driver* then concluded that the Tempest with GTO fitted with a NASCAR suspension "will take the measure of any Ferrari other than prototype racing cars or the recently announced 250-L-M." They did admit, however, that the then-$20,000 Ferrari GTO would go around a road racing circuit several seconds faster than the as-tested-$3,377.91 Tempest GTO.

Among the design changes for the 1965 Tempest line (this is a GTO) were stacked headlights and a more recessed grille design.

Jerry Heasley photo

Design refinements characterized the three Tempest lines for 1965 and included vertically stacked headlights, larger wheel openings, crisper body-side sculpturing, and more-deeply-recessed grilles. A two-door hardtop was added to the Tempest Custom series and the Le Mans lineup got a four-door sedan. While the wheelbase was unchanged, overall length grew 3 inches. The GTO remained a hot and hot-selling option package for a second year. Advertising copywriters depicted the Tempest as a Pontiac and the GTO as a "Tiger." Outwardly, the GTO got a grille and rear-end facelift, a new hood (designed to accommodate a dual-quad carburetor option that was canceled), higher horsepower ratings, an optional new Rally cluster gauge package, and optional new Kelsey-Hayes Rally wheels.

I.D. NUMBERS

VIN on left front door post. First symbol indicates GM division: 2=Pontiac. Second and third symbols indicate series: 33=Tempest, 35=Tempest Custom, 37=Tempest Le Mans. Fourth and fifth symbols indicate body style and appear as last two symbols in body/style number column of charts below. Sixth symbol indicates model year: 5=1965. Seventh symbol tells assembly plant: P=Pontiac, Michigan, X=Kansas City, Kansas,

Z=Fremont, California, and B=Baltimore, Maryland. Following symbols are sequential production numbers starting with 100001 at each assembly plant. Body/style number plate under hood tells manufacturer, Fisher style number, assembly plant, trim code, paint code, accessory codes. Style number consists of 65 (for 1965) prefix and four symbols that appear in second column of charts below. First two symbols indicate series. The second two symbols indicate body type. VIN appears on front of engine at right-hand cylinder bank along with an alphanumerical engine production codes included: (215-cid/125-hp six) ZD/ZE. (215-cid/140-hp six) ZK/ZL/ZM/ZN/ZR/ZS. (326-cid/250-hp V-8) WP/YN6O. (326-cid/285-hp V-8) WR/YP. (389-cid/335-hp four-barrel GTO V-8) WT with synchromesh, YS with Hydra-Matic. (389-cid/360-hp GTO Tri-Power V-8) WS with synchromesh, YR with Hydra-Matic.

COLORS

Paint color codes for 1965 were: A=Starlight Black, B=Blue Charcoal, C=Cameo Ivory, D=Fontaine Blue Poly, E=Nightwatch Blue, H=Palmetto Green, K=Reef Turquoise, L=Teal Turquoise, N=Burgundy, P=Iris Mist, R=Montero Red, T=Capri Gold, V=Mission Beige, W=Bluemist Slate and Y=Mayfair Maize. Vinyl top colors were 2=Black and 6=Beige. Convertible top colors were 1=White, 2=Black, 4=Blue, 5=Turquoise and 6=Beige. Interior trim codes for 1965 base Tempests were: 201=Blue cloth and vinyl, 202=Turquoise cloth and vinyl, 205=Turquoise vinyl, 203=Gold cloth and vinyl, 206=Gold vinyl, 204=Red cloth and vinyl, 207=Red vinyl and 208=Silver vinyl. Interior trim codes for 1965 Tempest Customs were: 209=Blue vinyl, 210=Turquoise vinyl, 211=Gold vinyl and 212=Red vinyl. Interior trim codes for 1965 Le Mans were: 265=Blue cloth and vinyl, 298=Burgundy cloth and vinyl, 213=Black vinyl, 214=Turquoise vinyl, 215=Gold vinyl, 216=Red vinyl, 217=Blue vinyl and 218=Parchment vinyl. Interior trim codes for 1965 Le Mans GTOs were: 213=Black vinyl, 214=Turquoise vinyl, 215=Gold vinyl, 216=Red vinyl, 217=Blue vinyl, and 218=Parchment/Black vinyl.

TEMPEST — (SIX-CYL) — SERIES 233

The 1965 Tempest models had the Tempest name in chrome block letters on the sides of the rear fenders. Styling features included stacked headlights, a split grille with two horizontal members in each half, the Pontiac name in the left-hand grille, and an arrowhead-shaped Pontiac badge in the center. Base models in the 233 Series were identified by the absence of upper beltline moldings and plainer interior trims. Vinyl rubber floor mats were used. Standard equipment included a heater and defroster, electric wipers, seat belts, turn signals, and five black tubeless tires. Safari station wagons came with 7.35 x 14 oversized tires as regular equipment.

Model Number	Body/Style Number	Body Type & Seating	Factory Price	Shipping Weight	Production Total
233	69	4d Sedan-6P	$2,263	2,963 lbs.	15,705
233	27	2d Coupe-6P	$2,211	2,943 lbs.	18,198
233	35	4d Sta Wagon-6P	$2,549	3,237 lbs.	5,622

NOTE 1: 39,525 Tempests were built.
NOTE 2: 9,255 had synchromesh and 30,270 had automatic attachments.

TEMPEST CUSTOM — (SIX-CYL) — SERIES 235

Tempest Custom models had bright upper beltline moldings to accent the venturi-shaped body styling. Chrome scalp moldings decorated the bottom edges of the roof. Accenting the rocker panels were bright metal moldings running between the wheel openings. Standard extras included all vinyl upholstery, carpeting, and a deluxe steering wheel. The Custom convertible had courtesy lamps.

Model Number	Body/Style Number	Body Type & Seating	Factory Price	Shipping Weight	Production Total
235	69	4d Sedan-6P	$2,496	3,021 lbs.	25,242
235	27	2d Coupe-6P	$2,295	2,965 lbs.	18,367
235	37	2d Hardtop-6P	$2,359	2,983 lbs.	21,906
235	67	2d Convertible-6P	$2,584	3,064 lbs.	8,346
235	35	4d Sta Wagon-6P	$2,633	3,250 lbs.	10,792

NOTE 3: 84,653 Tempest Customs were built.
NOTE 4: 10,630 had synchromesh and 74,023 had automatic attachments.

TEMPEST LE MANS — (SIX-CYL) — SERIES 237

Special identifying features seen on the Tempest Le Mans models included: grilled-over taillights, Le Mans front fender nameplates, Le Mans lettering on the sides of rear fenders, and simulated louvers behind front wheel cutouts on two-door models. All features found on Tempest Customs were considered standard equipment, as well as vinyl interior trim, custom foam front seat cushions, front bucket seats on two-door styles, and a power-operated folding top on the Le Mans convertible.

Model Number	Body/Style Number	Body Type & Seating	Factory Price	Shipping Weight	Production Total
237	69	4d Sedan-6P	$2,496	3,021 lbs.	14,227
237	27	2d Coupe-5P	$2,437	2,996 lbs.	18,881
237	37	2d Hardtop-5P	$2,501	3,014 lbs.	60,548
237	67	2d Convertible-5P	$2,736	3,107 lbs.	13,897

Pontiac claimed it had a "tiger" under the hood of both its 1965 Le Mans (left) and GTO (right).

The 1965 GTO got a new grille, hood, and rear end.

Jerry Heasley photo

The base power plant for GTO in 1965 was the 389-cid Tri-Power V-8, which produced 335 bhp. A 360-hp version was optional.

Jerry Heasley photo

Wider 7.75 x 14 Red Line tires were optional on the 1965 GTO.

Jerry Heasley photo

TEMPEST LE MANS GTO — (V-8) — SERIES 237 WITH GTO OPTION

The GTO was not yet a separate series, although special identification features on GTOs replaced some items regularly seen on Tempest Le Mans models. These included: GTO lettering for the left-hand grille, the rear fender sides and the rear deck lid, a single hood scoop and horizontally elongated V-shaped badges behind the front wheel openings. The GTO's redesigned grille was made of heavy die-cast metal and had an Argent Silver grille surround with a thin stainless-steel molding snapped into its leading edge. Black-finished thin horizontal bars filled the cavities and "GTO" letters identical to the 1964 letters were mounted towards the outboard end of the left-hand grille opening. A body-color one-piece vertical panel decorated with a Pontiac arrowhead badge separated the grilles. The hood incorporated a large center air scoop sculptured into the sheet metal with a swept-back front opening. A die-cast metal ornament with ribbed inserts was bolted to the hood. Both the front and rear bumpers were revised. The rear had a full-width rear panel with six chrome ribs and black background finish running between the taillights, which continued the same basic design around the body corners. The Pontiac name was block-lettered in the center of this ribbed rear panel. The roofline on coupe and hardtop models was the same as in 1964. GTO convertibles were available with White, Black, Blue, Turquoise, and Beige tops. A vinyl Cordova top was optional on coupes and hardtops and came in a choice of Black or Beige colors. The GTO body sides had only minor changes, such as notches in the rear fenders for new wraparound taillight lenses. Badges that read "GTO 6.5-LITRE" were placed behind the front wheel openings in the same location as in 1964. On the rear body sides,

Jerry Heasley photo

A 1965 GTO with the parchment vinyl interior.

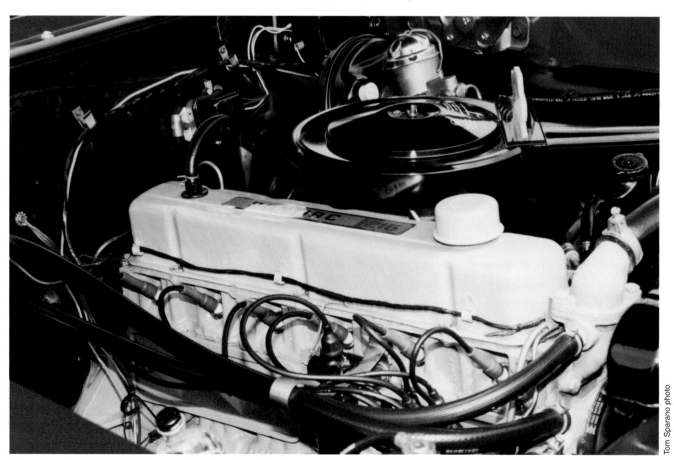

Tom Sparano photo

The standard 215-cid Tempest inline six-cylinder engine delivered 140 hp. Manual transmission was standard.

The Parchment/Black vinyl interior combination makes a bold statement in this 1965 Tri-Power GTO.

Jerry Heasley photo

the GTO lettering was lowered a few inches to bumper-top height. A four-pod instrument cluster was carried over, but the engine-turned insert of 1964 was replaced with a wood-grained insert. A deluxe steering wheel similar to that used in the Le Mans was standard. Instrumentation was the same as last season, but a new AM/FM radio was optional. The standard GTO Trophy V-8 gained 10 hp for 1965. The cylinder heads were re-cored to remove restrictions and abrupt changes in cross section. The engine had a revised camshaft and improved intake manifolds with different runners. The GTO was also available with a 360-hp Tri-Power V-8. Stick-shift cars with the Tri-Power engine now used a mechanical progressive linkage, while cars with the Tri-Power V-8 and automatic transmission retained the vacuum-operated linkage used in 1964. Chrome valve covers and a chrome air cleaner were included. The extra horses went to good use, as the car was 3.1 inches longer and 340 lbs. heavier. Stiff springs and shock absorbers were part of the package and a Ride & Handling kit was available on top of that. Wider 7.75 x 14 red line or rayon whitewall tires were optional at the base price. The standard GTO transmission was a three-speed, all-synchromesh manual gearbox with a floor-mounted Hurst shifter. A heavy-duty three-speed (actually Ford's "top-loader") was available starting in March. Wide- and close-ratio four-speed manual transmissions were optional, along with a two-speed automatic transmission.

Model Number	Body/Style Number	Body Type & Seating	Factory Price	Shipping Weight	Production Total
237	27	2d Coupe-5P	$2,787	3,478 lbs.	8,319
237	37	2d Hardtop-5P	$2,855	3,478 lbs.	55,722
237	67	2d Convertible-5P	$3,093	3,700 lbs.	11,311

NOTE 5: 182,905 Le Mans Tempests were built including cars with the GTO option.
NOTE 6: 75,756 had synchromesh attachments and 107,149 had automatic.
NOTE 7: 75,352 GTOs are included in these totals.
NOTE 8: 56,378 had synchromesh and 18,974 had automatic.
NOTE 9: Four-speed gearboxes were in 18.8 percent of all 1965 Tempests.

ENGINES

TEMPEST, TEMPEST CUSTOM, LE MANS BASE 215-CID SIX-CYL: Inline. Overhead valves. Cast-iron block. Displacement: 215 cid. Bore and stroke: 3.75 x 3.25 in. Compression ratio: 8.6:1. Brake hp: 140 at 4200 rpm. Seven main bearings. Hydraulic valve lifters. Carburetor: Rochester model 7025167 one-barrel.

TEMPEST, TEMPEST CUSTOM, LE MANS BASE 326-CID V-8: Overhead valve. Bore and stroke: 3.718 x 3.75. Displacement: 326 cid. Compression ratio: 9.2:1. Brake hp: 250 at 4600 rpm. Taxable hp: 44.4. Torque: 333 lbs.-ft. at 2800 rpm. Five main bearings. Hydraulic valve lifters. Crankcase capacity: 4 qt. Cooling system capacity with heater: 20.5 qt. (add 1 qt. for new filter). Carburetor: Two-barrel. Engine code: WP, WX, YN or XF.

TEMPEST, TEMPEST CUSTOM, LE MANS OPTIONAL 326-CID V-8: Overhead valve. Displacement: 326 cid. Bore and stroke: 3.718 x 3.75. Compression ratio: 10.5:1. Brake hp: 285 at 5000 rpm. Taxable hp: 44.4. Torque: 359 lbs.-ft. at 3200 rpm. Five main bearings. Hydraulic valve lifters. Crankcase capacity: 4 qt. Cooling system capacity with heater: 20.5 qt. (add 1 qt. for new filter). Carburetor: Carter AFB four-barrel Model 3899-S. Engine code: WR, YP or XG.

GTO BASE 389-CID V-8: Overhead valve. Cast-iron block. Bore and stroke: 4.06 x 3.75. Displacement: 389 cid. Compression ratio: 10.75:1. Brake hp: 335 at 5000 rpm. Taxable hp: 52.80. Torque: 431 lbs.-ft. at 3200 rpm. Five main bearings. Hydraulic valve lifters. Crankcase capacity: 5 qt. (add 1 qt. for new filter). Cooling system capacity with heater: 20.5 qt. Carburetor: Four-barrel. Engine code: WT, WW, YS or XE. A 3.23:1 rear axle was standard with manual or automatic transmission. A 3.08:1 rear axle was standard on GTOs with automatic transmission and air conditioning. Special order axle ratios available with the four-barrel GTO V-8 and specific equipment combinations included 3.36:1,

3.55:1, 3.90:1 and 4.33:1.

GTO OPTIONAL 389-CID V-8: Overhead valve. Cast-iron block. Bore and stroke: 4.06 x 3.75. Displacement: 389 cid. Compression ratio: 10.75:1. Brake hp: 360 at 5200 rpm. Taxable hp: 52.80. Torque: 424 lbs.-ft. at 3600 rpm. Five main bearings. Hydraulic valve lifters. Crankcase capacity: 5 qt. (add 1 qt. for new filter). Cooling system capacity with heater: 20.5 qt. Carburetion: Three Rochester two-barrel carburetors. Engine code: WS, WV. XS or YR. A 3.55:1 rear axle was standard with manual or automatic transmission. A 3.08:1 rear axle was standard on GTOs with automatic transmission and air conditioning. Special order axle ratios available with the Tri-Power GTO V-8 and specific equipment combinations included 3.36:1, 3.90:1, and 4.33:1.

CHASSIS

Wheelbase: 115 in. Overall length: (Tempest Safaris) 204.4 in., (Tempest passenger cars) 206.2 in. Front tread: 58 in. Rear tread: 58 in. Overall width: 73.4 in. Overall height: 53.6 in. Turning diameter (GTO): 40.9 ft. Turns lock-to-lock: (GTO with power steering) 4.2. Driveshaft: open, one-piece. Wheels: (Tempest) 14 x 5 in, (GTO) 14 x 6 in. Standard tires: (Tempest) 6.95 x 14, (GTO) 7.75 x 14.

OPTIONS

591 speedometer gear adapter ($11.30). 431 heavy-duty air cleaner ($4.84). 582 Tri-Comfort air conditioner ($345.60). 471 back-up lights with manual transmission ($12.91). 471 back-up lights with automatic transmission ($10.76). 651 heavy-duty battery, standard with air conditioning or GTO ($3.55). 522 floor carpet with base sports coupe or sedan ($19.37). 604 electric clock, not available in cars with a tachometer ($19.37). Heavy-duty clutch with six-cylinder engine ($4.52). 601 center console in Le Mans sport coupe, two-door hardtop or convertible ($48.15). 572 spare wheel and tire cover, except Safari station wagon ($2.58). 412 front foam cushion in base or Custom models ($8.07). 451 remote-control rear deck lid, except Safari ($10.76). 541 rear wind deflector on Safari station wagon ($26.30). 541 rear window defogger in coupes and sedans ($21.52). 701 Safe-T-Grip non-slip differential ($37.66). 534 heavy-duty engine fan ($3.12). 326-cid two-barrel V-8 ($108.00). 326-cid four-barrel V-8 ($173.31). 389-cid Tri-Power V-8 in Le Mans with GTO option ($115.78). 511 dual exhausts with V-8 engine only ($30.88). 422 tailpipe extensions all Custom and Le Mans models except Safari station wagon ($21.30). 531 tinted glass in all windows ($31.20). 532 tinted windshield ($19.91). 382 Grand Turisimo Omologato option for Le Mans sports coupe, hardtop and convertible ($295.90). 512 door edge guards for two-door models ($4.84). Door edge guards for four-door models ($8.34). 621 Ride & Handling package ($16.14). 584 heater deletion, not available in cars with air conditioning ($73 credit). 472 dual horns ($4.30). 671 transistor ignition, with air conditioning ($75.27). 671 transistor ignition, without air conditioning ($64.51). 424 padded instrument panel ($16.14). 482 glove box lamp ($2.85). 491 courtesy lamps ($4.30, except standard in convertibles). 492 ash tray lamp ($3.12). 494 parking-brake-on signal lamp ($4.95). 481 luggage lamp ($3.55). 404 under-hood lamp ($3.55). 571 Safari station wagon luggage carrier ($64.56). 631 front floor mat ($6.24). 632 rear floor mats ($5.81). 602 outside rearview mirror ($4.25). 441 visor-vanity mirror ($1.45). 442 non-glare inside rearview mirror ($4.25). 444 remote-control outside rearview mirror ($11.78). Standard color two-tone paint, except convertible or Safari station wagon ($31.74). Special color two-tone paint, except convertible or Safari station wagon ($71.93). Special color solid paint ($40.19). Standard color two-tone paint on Safari station wagon ($12.38). Special color two-tone paint on Safari station wagon ($52.57). 504 Rally gauge cluster with tachometer

The Le Mans came with a base six-cylinder, but could be had with a 326-cid V-8, like this four-door model.

Paul Zazerine collection

($86.08). 391 power antenna, except Safari station wagon ($29.75). 502 power brakes ($42.50). 561 power seat in all base, all Custom, and Le Mans sedan models ($71.02). 501 power steering ($96.84). 554 Safari station wagon power tailgate window ($26.90). 564 left-hand tilt bucket seat ($71.02). 434 Tempest Custom convertible power top ($53.80). 551 power side windows ($102.22). 432 heavy-duty radiator with 326-cid two-barrel or 326-cid four-barrel H.O. V-8s ($15.06). 432 heavy-duty radiator with 215-cid six-cylinder engine ($12.91). 398 manual-tune radio and antenna ($53.80). 392 push-button radio and antenna ($62.41). 394 AM/FM push-button radio and manual antenna ($136.65). 401 rear seat radio speaker for coupes and sedans ($14.15). 474 Verbra-Phonic "reverb" type rear radio speaker for coupes and sedans ($53.80). 662 transistorized ignition regulator ($10.76). 624 Custom retractable front seat belts ($7.53). 414 seat belts deletion ($11.00 credit). 622 Superlift rear shock absorbers ($40.35). 634 Safeguard speedometer ($16.14). 654 heavy-duty front and rear springs for base coupe and sedan and Custom sedan ($15.06). 524 Custom sport steering wheel in base Tempest with Décor Group, Tempest Custom, or Le Mans ($39.27). 524 Custom sport steering wheel in base Tempest without Décor Group ($43.04). 461 steering wheel with deluxe horn ring in base Tempest models ($3.77). 454 tilt-adjustable steering wheel, requires power steering ($43.04). 612 quick-ratio steering, except in cars with power steering ($10.76). 611 rear doorjamb switches, except two-door models ($3.23). 581

Daniel B. Lyons photo

The vertically stacked headlights were one of the main changes to the 1965 Tempest/GTO lineup.

automatic temperature control, requires air conditioning ($64.56). Cordova top, except Safari or convertible ($71.93). Cordova top on Le Mans four-door sedan ($86.08). Cordova top on Tempest Custom coupes and Le Mans coupe ($75.32). AB five 6.95 x 14 white sidewall tires, except Safari station wagons and cars with 326-cid V-8 ($29.05). BA five 7.35 x 14 black sidewall tires, except standard on Safari station wagon or cars with 326-cid V-8 ($7.53). BB five 7.35 x 14 white sidewall tires, except Safari station wagon or cars with 326-cid V-8 ($39.81). BB five 7.35 x 14 white sidewall tires on Safari station wagon or cars with 326-cid V-8 ($32.28). CA five 7.75 x 14 black sidewall tires on Safari station wagons or cars with 326-cid V-8 ($15.06). CB five 7.75 x 14 white sidewall tires on Safari station wagons or cars with 326-cid V-8 ($47.34). Four-speed manual synchromesh transmission ($188.30). Automatic transmission with six-cylinder engine ($188.30). Automatic transmission with V-8 engine ($199.06). 614 positive crankcase ventilation ($5.38). 411 wire wheel discs with Décor Group or Sports Option ($53.80). 411 wire wheel discs with Décor Group or Sports Option ($71.02). 521 Custom wheel discs with Décor Group or Sports Option ($19.90). 521 Custom wheel discs without Décor Group or Sports Option ($37.12). 462 deluxe wheel discs ($17.22). 691 Rally wheels without Décor Group ($52.72). 691 Rally wheels with Décor Group ($35.50). 421 two-speed windshield wipers and washers ($17.27). 061 Basic Group includes: push-button AM radio, front foam seat cushions, two-speed windshield wipers and washers, heavy-duty air cleaner and back-up lights in base Tempest or Tempest Custom with six-cylinder or base 326-cid V-8 engine and manual transmission ($105.50). 061 Basic Group includes: push-button AM radio, front foam seat cushions, two-speed windshield wipers and washers, heavy-duty air cleaner and back-up lights in base Tempest or Tempest Custom with six-cylinder or base 326-cid V-8 engine and automatic transmission ($103.35). 061 Basic Group includes push-button AM radio, front foam seat cushions, two-speed windshield wipers and washers, heavy-duty air cleaner and back-up lights in base Tempest or Tempest Custom with 326-cid H.O. V-8 engine and manual transmission ($100.66). 061 Basic Group includes: push-button AM radio, front foam seat cushions, two-speed windshield wipers and washers, heavy-duty air cleaner and back-up lights in base Tempest or Tempest Custom with 326-cid H.O. V-8 engine and automatic transmission ($98.51). 061 Basic Group includes: push-button AM radio, front foam seat cushions, two-speed windshield wipers and washers, heavy-duty air cleaner and back-up lights in Le Mans with six-cylinder or base 326-cid V-8 engine and manual transmission ($97.43). 061 Basic Group includes: push-button AM radio, front foam seat cushions, two-speed windshield wipers and washers, heavy-duty air cleaner and back-up lights in Le Mans with six-cylinder or base 326-cid V-8 engine and automatic transmission ($95.28). 061 Basic Group includes: push-button AM radio, front foam seat cushions, two-speed windshield wipers and washers, heavy-duty air cleaner and back-up lights in Le Mans with 326-cid H.O. V-8 engine and

The 1965 Tempests lacked the distinctive badging and trim of the GTO and Le Mans models from the same year.

manual transmission ($92.59). 061 Basic Group includes: push-button AM radio, front foam seat cushions, two-speed windshield wipers and washers, heavy-duty air cleaner and back-up lights in Le Mans with 326-cid H.O. V-8 engine and automatic transmission ($90.44). 062 Protection Group includes padded instrument panel, door edge guards, rear window defogger, floor mats, spare tire cover and retractable seat belts in two-door models except convertible ($64.66). 062 Protection Group includes: padded instrument panel, door edge guards, rear window defogger, floor mats, spare tire cover and retractable seat belts in four-door models except Safari station wagon ($68.16). 062 Protection Group includes: padded instrument panel, door edge guards, rear window defogger, floor mats, spare tire cover and retractable seat belts in Safari station wagon ($44.06). 062 Protection Group includes: padded instrument panel, door edge guards, rear window defogger, floor mats, spare tire cover and retractable seat belts in convertible ($43.14). 064 Décor Group includes: deluxe steering wheel, deluxe wheel discs and décor moldings on base Tempest sports coupe ($40.36); on

The base Tempest two-door sedan carried a price tag of $2,211. This car had the optional 326-cid V-8, which was either $108 or $173.31 extra, depending on whether it had a two- or four-barrel carburetor.

base Tempest Safari ($42.51); on base Tempest four-door sedan ($39.28); on Tempest Custom sports coupe or hardtop ($36.59); on Tempest Custom Safari ($38.74), and on Tempest Custom four-door sedan ($35.51). 071 Mirror Group includes: visor-vanity mirror, inside glare-proof mirror and remote-control left-hand outside rearview mirror ($17.48). 074 Lamp Group includes: under-hood lamp, luggage compartment lamp, lighted glove box, roof rail and reading lights, ash tray light and parking-brake-on warning light in all except Safari or convertible ($22.32); in base Tempest or Tempest Custom Safari ($18.77); in Tempest Custom or Le Mans convertible ($18.02).

OPTION INSTALLATION RATES

Of 307,083 Tempests built, 68.9 percent had automatic transmission, 18.8 percent had a four-speed synchromesh transmission, 77.1 percent had a V-8 engine, 22.9 percent had a six-cylinder engine, 93.6 percent had a radio, 99.2 percent had a heater, 54.7 percent had power steering, 25.4 percent had power brakes, 0.9 percent had a power seat. 1.7 percent had power side windows. 2.6 percent had a station wagon power rear window only, 54.9 percent had bucket seats, 97.5 percent had seat belts, 76.7 percent had white sidewall tires, 77.6 percent had windshield washers, 34.3 percent had a tinted windshield, 18.7 percent had all tinted windows, 81.3 percent had back-up lights, 14.9 percent had air conditioning, 27.8 percent had dual exhausts, 19.2 percent had a limited-slip differential, 76.4 percent had full wheel covers, 8.7 percent had a vinyl top, 2.8 percent had a power antenna, and 1.6 percent had a moveable steering column.

HISTORICAL FOOTNOTES

Production started Aug. 24, 1964. Introductions were done on Sept. 24, 1964. *Ward's 1966 Automotive Yearbook* said, "The amazing metamorphosis of the Tempest over a period of five years (from its '61 intro as a four-cylinder engine compact through its move into the intermediate-size class with a V-8 GTO option and a standard overhead camshaft six) again tops the Pontiac success story of 1965." The 1 millionth Tempest was built late in the year and the nameplate had a 28.2 percent gain in sales popularity—the best of any GM car. Calendar-year output was 326,054. Model-year output was 307,083 for a 3.5 percent share of the U.S. industry total. Of these, 158,213 Tempests were made in Pontiac, Michigan, 39,150 were built in Fremont, California, 57,782 were constructed in Baltimore, Maryland, and 51,983 left the GM assembly plant in Kansas City, Kansas. Franchised Pontiac dealers reported selling 312,692 Tempests in the 1965 calendar year, or 3.5 percent of total domestic model sales. The 335-hp GTO convertible went 0 to 60 mph in 7.2 seconds and did the quarter-mile in 16.1 seconds.

Pontiac fans could get a GTO record and poster for 25 cents, and these are collector's items today. Late in the year, Pete Estes moved to Chevrolet and John Z. DeLorean became the general manager of Pontiac Motor Division.

Daniel B. Lyons photo

1965 GTOs in this condition are definite collector prizes.

Jerry Heasley photo

The Tempest series was fully redesigned for 1966. The cars featured smoother, rounder bodies, stacked headlights, and distinctive ornamentation. The GTOs, the one shown here is a convertible with 389-cid Tri-Power, were again the high-performance machines of the series.

Pontiac marked its 40th birthday in 1966, while the Tempest marked its sixth. The year's new Tempests were completely restyled with smoother bodies, rounder contours, wider wheel openings, recessed split grilles, and stacked headlights. Each of the four series now had completely distinctive ornamentation. The really big news was under the hood, where a unique overhead camshaft six-cylinder engine was now employed as the base power plant for all models except GTOs. The high-performance GTO was in its own series. An undetermined number of cars in each of the lower three series were built with a sporty Sprint OHC-6 option package. Two-door Tempests with the Sprint option had horizontal racing stripes between the wheel openings.

I.D. NUMBERS

VIN on left front door post. First symbol indicates GM division: 2=Pontiac. Second and third symbols indicate series: 33=Tempest, 35=Tempest Custom, 37=Le Mans, 52=Catalina, 56=Star Chief, 62=Bonneville, 66=Grand Prix. Fourth and fifth symbols indicate body style and appear as last two symbols in body/style number column of charts below. Sixth symbol indicates model year: 6=1966. Seventh symbol tells assembly plant: P=Pontiac, Michigan, Z=Fremont, California, B=Baltimore, Maryland, K=Kansas City, Missouri, G=Framingham, Massachusetts. Following symbols are sequential production number starting with 100001 at each assembly plant. Body/style number plate under hood tells manufacturer, Fisher style number, assembly plant, trim code, paint code, accessory codes. Style number consists of 66 (for 1966) prefix and four symbols that appear in second column of charts below. The first two symbols indicate series. The second two symbols indicate body type. VIN appears on front of engine at right-hand cylinder bank along with an alphanumerical engine production code. Engine production codes included: (230-cid/155-hp OHC six) ZF/ZG. (230-cid/165-hp OHC six) ZK/ZS/ZN/ZM. (230-cid/207-hp OHC six) ZD/ZE. (326-cid/250-hp V-8) WP/WX/YN/XF. (326-cid/285-hp V-8) WR/YP/XG. (389-cid/335-hp four-barrel GTO V-8) WT/WW with synchromesh, YS/XE with Hydra-Matic. (389-cid/360-hp GTO Tri-Power V-8) WS/WV with synchromesh, XS/YR with Hydra-Matic.

COLORS

Paint codes for 1966 Tempests were: A=Starlight Black, B=Blue Charcoal, C=Cameo Ivory, D=Fontaine Blue, E=Nightwatch Blue, H=Palmetto Green, K=Reef Turquoise, L=Marina Turquoise, N=Burgundy, P=Barrier Blue, R=Montero Red, T=Martinique Bronze, V=Mission Beige, W=Platinum and Y=Candlelite Cream. Vinyl top colors for 1966 Tempests were: 1=Ivory, 2=Black and 6=Beige. Convertible top colors for 1966 Tempests were: 1=White, 2=Black, 4=Blue, 5=Turquoise and 6=Beige. Interior trim codes for base Tempests were: 201=Blue cloth and vinyl, 202=Turquoise cloth and vinyl, 207=Turquoise vinyl, 203=Fawn cloth and vinyl, 208=Fawn vinyl, 204=Red cloth and vinyl, 209=Red vinyl, 205=Black vinyl and 210=Slate vinyl.. Interior Trim Codes for Tempest Customs were: 213=Blue vinyl, 214=Turquoise vinyl, 215=Fawn vinyl and 216=Red vinyl. Interior trim codes for Le Mans were: 228=Black cloth and vinyl, 223/231=Black vinyl, 219/232=Blue vinyl, 220=Turquoise vinyl, 221/233=Fawn vinyl, 222=Red vinyl and 224=Parchment vinyl. GTO Trim codes included: 219=Dark Blue vinyl, 220=Dark Turquoise vinyl, 221=Fawn vinyl, 222=Medium red vinyl, 223=Black vinyl, and 224=Parchment vinyl.

STANDARD TEMPEST — (SIX-CYL) — SERIES 233

Standard Tempest trim appointments included windsplit moldings behind the front wheel openings, Tempest rear fender scripts, and nylon-faced fabric upholstery with Jeweltone Morrokide accents. All Tempests featured a swept-hip perimeter design frame with a box section structure, 14 x 5J steel disc wheels. Tire sizes varied. Six-cylinder coupes and sedans came standard with 6.95 x 14 tires. Six-cylinder convertibles and V-8 coupes and sedans substituted 7.35 x 14 low-pressure tires. All Safari station wagons shared 14 x 6J wheels and 7.75 x 14 tires with the GTO. The ball-joint front suspension had upper and lower control arms that pivoted on rubber bushings. The lower control arms had dual-rate rubber

The '66 GTOs had twin slotted taillights.

Pin striping came with certain colors in 1966, as shown here on this white GTO.

Dan Lucht photo

The Tempest Custom had thin accent moldings and chrome window and lower-body moldings to go with its new "Coke bottle" shape.

bushings. Double-acting shock absorbers were mounted inside the front coil springs. A four-link rear suspension included angle-mounted upper and lower control arms, angle-mounted shock absorbers and large-diameter low-rate coil springs. Steering was a link-parallelogram design with a re-circulating ball-bearing gear. The steering ratio was 24:1 manual, 20:1 quick-rate manual, and 17.5:1 power. Drum brakes were used all around. The standard transmission was a fully synchronized three-speed manual. Options included a heavy-duty three-speed manual, close- or wide-ratio four-speed manuals and the two-speed automatic. The automatic transmission gear shifter went on the column in all models (including GTOs) unless a front seat console was ordered. The new 230-cid/165-hp inline overhead camshaft six-cylinder engine was standard in all Tempest, Tempest Custom, and Le Mans models. Engine options included the 207-hp six, the 326-cid/250-hp two-barrel V-8, and the 285-hp H.O. version of the 326. When the 207-hp six was ordered, it came with a Hurst floor shifter, specially valved shock absorbers, a stabilizer bar, a high-performance exhaust system, a chromed low-restriction air cleaner, and a performance rear axle ratio. Base Tempest interiors were covered with Parcrest pattern cloth and trimmed Morrokide upholstery. Tempests had wedge-shaped taillights rather than the slat-type used on GTOs.

Model Number	Body/Style Number	Body Type & Seating	Factory Price	Shipping Weight	Production Total
233	69	4d Sedan-6P	$2,331	3,075 lbs.	17,392
233	07	2d Coupe-6P	$2,278	3,040 lbs.	22,266
233	35	4d Sta Wagon-6P	$2,624	3,340 lbs.	4,095

NOTE 1: 43,753 standard Tempests were built.
NOTE 2: 10,610 standard Tempests had synchromesh and 33,143 had automatic.

TEMPEST CUSTOM — (OHC SIX-CYL) — SERIES 235

Tempest Custom trimmings included thin moldings accenting the smooth new "Coke-bottle" shape, Tempest Custom script/badge identification on the rear fenders, chrome windshield and window moldings and chrome moldings on the lower body-side feature line. Deluxe steering wheels and carpets were other standard features. Convertibles sported courtesy lamps and Morrokide trims. Customs had all-Morrokide upholstery and full molded floor carpeting. The Tempest Custom line included all body styles in the base Tempest series, plus two- and four-door hardtops and a convertible.

Model Number	Body/Style Number	Body Type & Seating	Factory Price	Shipping Weight	Production Total
235	69	4d Sedan-6P	$2,415	3,100 lbs.	23,988
235	39	4d Hardtop-6P	$2,547	3,195 lbs.	10,996
235	07	2d Coupe-6P	$2,362	3,060 lbs.	17,182
235	17	2d Hardtop-6P	$2,426	3,075 lbs.	31,322
235	67	2d Convertible-6P	$2,655	3,170 lbs.	5,557
235	35	4d Sta Wagon-6p	$2,709	3,355 lbs.	7,614

NOTE 3: 96,659 Tempest Customs were built.
NOTE 4: 13,566 Tempest Customs had synchromesh and 83,093 had automatic.

TEMPEST LE MANS — (OHC SIX-CYL) — SERIES 237

Le Mans models had special trim features that set them apart. They included simulated louvers on the forward edge of front fenders, engine call-outs behind the front wheel openings, and Le Mans lettering on the rear fender sides. A new "shadow box" roofline was seen on the two-door hardtop coupe. Standard equipment included Morrokide-and-cloth trim combinations in four-door hardtops and all-Morrokide in others. Convertibles, hardtops, and sport coupes (two-door sedans) came with the choice of bucket or notchback front seats with folding armrest. All Le Mans had carpeting, front foam seat cushions, an ashtray, a cigarette lighter lamp, a glove box lamp, and a power top on convertibles. Convertible tops came in White, Black, Blue, Turquoise, and Beige.

Model Number	Body/Style Number	Body Type & Seating	Factory Price	Shipping Weight	Production Total
237	39	4d Hardtop-6P	$2,701	3,195 lbs.	13,897
237	07	2d Coupe-6p	$2,505	3,090 lbs.	16,654
237	17	2d Hardtop-6P	$2,568	3,125 lbs.	78,109
237	67	2d Convertible-6P	$2,806	3,220 lbs.	13,080

NOTE 5: 121,740 Le Mans were built.
NOTE 6: 22,862 Le Mans had synchromesh and 98,878 had automatic attachments.

TEMPEST GTO — (V-8) — SERIES 242

GTO line was now a separate series with distinctive trim on the new Tempest sheet metal. The trademark split grille was of an all-new design and was made of plastic. Pontiac was the first automaker to introduce such a grille on the '66 GTO and Grand Prix models. A wire mesh "egg-crate" style grille insert was used. Both grilles incorporated rectangular parking/directional lamps on the outboard side and a GTO nameplate was mounted inboard of the rectangular lamp on the left-hand side. A body-color vertical panel again separated the grilles, but it no longer carried a Pontiac arrowhead badge. Instead, such a badge was mounted above it, on the peak of the hood. Circular Guide T-3 headlights were stacked vertically on each side of the grille. A massive new front bumper was fitted. The hood, except for the new badge on its nose, was identical with the 1965 hood. A single scoop appeared on the hood and was closed at the front, unless an optional Ram Air package was ordered. Elongated V-shaped badges were mounted behind the front wheel openings. GTO lettering appeared on the deck lid and rear fenders. The upper beltline contour was pin striped when certain colors were ordered. Horizontal twin-slot taillights were used. Standard equipment included all Le Mans items plus a special 389-cid four-barrel V-8, walnut grain dash panel inserts, dual exhausts, heavy-duty shock absorbers, heavy-duty springs, a fat stabilizer bar, and 7.75 x 14 red line or white sidewall tires. The rear end no longer carried a full-width decorative panel between the taillights. The Pontiac name was in the center, below the round trunk lock cylinder. The taillights consisted of three slats on each side. Each slat carried a thin, bright metal trim molding. The gas filler was behind the license plate in the center of the massive rear bumper. The 1966 GTO interiors came in Black, Parchment, Red, Turquoise, Bronze, and Blue Morrokide and were a bit fancier than before. A new instrument panel was also fitted. It had a wood veneer insert panel and large circular gauges. An optional Rally gauge cluster was again available. There were few major mechanical changes for the 1966 GTO. When Tri-Power was added, the center carburetor was a

Carl Dickson photo

This pristine 1966 Goat was outfitted with a three-speed and Black exterior with Dark Turquoise interior. It also came with positraction and three two-barrel carburetors.

This Platinum 1966 GTO was equipped with Tri-Power and a four-speed.

Bill Rouch photo

larger one than used in the past. It was now the same size as the front and rear carburetors. This required revisions to the Tri-Power intake manifold as well. An air scoop package was again optional and at midyear a new Ram Air V-8 (code XS) was introduced. It included the Air Scoop package, a hotter cam, and beefier valve springs. A limited number of cars were fitted with this engine.

Model Number	Body/Style Number	Body Type & Seating	Factory Price	Shipping Weight	Production Total
242	07	2d Coupe-5P	$2,783	3,445 lbs.	10,363
242	17	2d Hardtop-5P	$2,847	3,465 lbs.	73,785
242	67	2d Convertible-5P	$3,082	3,555 lbs.	12,798

ENGINES

TEMPEST, TEMPEST CUSTOM, LE MANS BASE OHC 230-CID SIX-CYL: Inline. Overhead valves. Overhead camshaft. Cast-iron block. Displacement: 230 cid. Bore and stroke: 3.75 x 3.25 in. Compression ratio: 9.0:1. Brake hp: 165 at 4700 rpm. Torque: 216 lbs.-ft. at 2600 rpm. Hydraulic valve lifters. Carburetor: Rochester model 7026167 one-barrel.

TEMPEST, TEMPEST CUSTOM, LE MANS "SPRINT" OHC 230-CID SIX-CYL: Inline. Overhead valves. Overhead camshaft. Cast-iron block. Displacement: 230 cid. Bore and stroke: 3.75 x 3.25 in.

Jerry Heasley photo

The single hood scoop was closed at the front of the GTOs, unless the Ram Air package was ordered.

Jeffrey L. Smith photo

This 1966 GTO sported an attractive combination of Mission Beige paint and a Fawn vinyl interior.

Compression ratio: 10.5:1. Brake hp: 207 at 4200 rpm. Torque: 228 lbs.-ft. at 3800 rpm. Hydraulic valve lifters. Carburetor: Rochester four-barrel.

TEMPEST, TEMPEST CUSTOM, LE MANS BASE 326-CID V-8: Overhead valve. Bore and stroke: 3.718 x 3.75. Displacement: 326 cid. Compression ratio: 9.2:1. Brake hp: 250 at 4600 rpm. Taxable hp: 44.4. Torque: 333 lbs.-ft. at 2800. Five main bearings. Hydraulic valve lifters. Crankcase capacity: 5 qt. (add 1 qt. for new filter). Cooling system capacity with heater: 20.5 qt. Carburetor: Two-barrel. Engine code: WP, WX, YN, or XF.

TEMPEST, TEMPEST CUSTOM, LE MANS OPTIONAL 326-CID V-8: Overhead valve. Bore and stroke: 3.718 x 3.75. Displacement: 326 cid. Compression ratio: 10.5:1. Brake hp: 285 at 5000 rpm. Taxable hp: 44.4. Torque: 359 lbs.-ft. at 3200. Five main bearings. Hydraulic valve lifters. Crankcase capacity: 5 qt. (add 1 qt. for new filter). Cooling system capacity with heater: 20.5 qt. Carburetor: Four-barrel. Engine code: WR, YP or XG.

GTO BASE 389-CID V-8: Overhead valve. Cast-iron block. Bore and stroke: 4.06 x 3.75. Displacement: 389

The spec's on the 1966 Tempest GTO hardtop: 206.4 inches long, 115-inch wheelbase, 3,465 lbs., and a 389-cid/335-hp V-8 standard under the hood.

53

The 1966 389-cid GTO Tri-Power V-8 was rated at 360 hp.

capacity with heater: 20 qt. Carburetor: Four-barrel. Engine code: WT, WW, YS or XE.

GTO OPTIONAL 389-CID V-8: Overhead valve. Cast-iron block. Bore and stroke: 4.06 x 3.75. Displacement: 389 cid. Compression ratio: 10.75:1. Brake hp: 360 at 5200 rpm. Taxable hp: 52.80. Torque: 424 lbs.-ft. at 3600 rpm. Five main bearings. Hydraulic valve lifters. Crankcase capacity: 5 qt. (add 1 qt. for new filter). Cooling system capacity with heater: 20 qt. Carburetion: Three Rochester two-barrel carburetors. Engine code: WS, WV, XS or YR.

CHASSIS

Wheelbase: 115 in. Overall length: (Safari) 203.6 in., (passenger cars) 206.4 in. Overall width: 74.4 in. Overall height: (four-door sedan) 54 in.; (sports coupe) 53.2 in.; (hardtop) 53.2 in; (four-door hardtop) 54 in.; (convertible) 53.1 in. and (Safari) 55.4 in. Front legroom: (Tempest sedan and sports coupe) 41.2 in.; (Tempest and Tempest Custom Safari) 41.0 in; (Tempest Custom cars) 41.4 in.; (Le Mans four-door hardtop) 41.4; (other Le Mans models and all GTOs) 41.8 in. Rear legroom: (Tempest and Tempest Custom sedan, Tempest Safari and Le Mans four-door hardtop) 35.7 in.; (Tempest, Tempest Custom sports coupe, Tempest Custom coupe and Tempest Custom convertible) 33.1;

cid. Compression ratio: 10.75:1. Brake hp: 335 at 5000 rpm. Taxable hp: 52.80. Torque: 431 lbs.-ft. at 3200 rpm. Five main bearings. Hydraulic valve lifters. Crankcase capacity: 5 qt. (add 1 qt. for new filter). Cooling system

The 1966 GTO was recognized by its elongated V-shaped badges behind the front wheel openings, GTO lettering on the deck lid and rear fenders, and single hood scoop.

Mike Mueller photo

This '66 Tri-Power Goat was resplendent in Barrier Blue.

(all other models) 32.3 in. Front headroom: (Tempest sedan, Tempest Custom sedan, Tempest Custom and Le Mans four-door hardtop and convertible and GTO convertible) 38.1 in.; (Tempest sports coupe) 37.4 in.; (Tempest Custom sports coupe and hardtop) 37.2 in.; (Lemans and GTO sports coupe and hardtop) 37.5 in. and (Tempest and Tempest Custom Safari) 37.87 in. Rear headroom: (Tempest sedan) 37.3 in.; (Tempest Custom sedan) 37.2 in.; (Tempest sports coupe) 36.3 in.; (all other sports coupes and hardtops) 36.1 in.; (four-door hardtops) 37.1 in.; (all convertibles) 36.6 in. and (all safaris) 38.3 in. Luggage volume: (Tempest Safari) 85.3 cu. ft.; (Tempest Custom safari) 84.5 cu. ft.; (all other four-door models) 29.2 cu. ft.; (all two-door models) 30.4 cu. ft. Front tread: 58 in. Rear tread: 58 in. Standard tires: (convertible and hardtop) 7.35 x 14, (other models) 6.95 x 14.

OPTIONS

582 Custom air conditioner. 612 Air Injector Reactor (AIR) exhaust control, for California cars only. 674 heavy-duty 55-amp alternator. 631 front and rear Custom seat belts. 651 heavy-duty aluminum front brake drums. 444 electric clock. 472 front seat center console. SVT Cordova top. 372 spare wheel and tire cover. 422 remote control rear deck lid release. 374 rear window defogger. 731 Safe-T-Track differential. 326-cid two-barrel V-8 ($108.00). 326-cid four-barrel V-8 ($173.31). 482 tailpipe extensions with dual exhausts. 531 tinted glass in all windows. 532 tinted windshield. 382 door edge guards for two-door models. 571 right- and left-hand headrests. 584 heater deletion, not available in cars with air conditioning. 514 heavy-duty seven-blade de-clutching fan with air conditioning. Rally gauge instrument panel cluster with tachometer. Walnut four-speed gear shifter knob. 402 glove box lamp. 411 courtesy lamps, except standard in convertible. 412 ashtray lamp. 414 parking-brake-on signal lamp. 401 luggage lamp ($3.55). 421 under-hood lamp. 404 roof rail reading lamp, except convertible. 522 red fender liners. 631 front floor mats. 632 rear floor mats. 394 non-glare inside rearview mirror. 392 visor-vanity mirror. 394 remote-control left-hand outside rearview mirror. SPS

special solid color paint. STT special two-tone paint, except convertible. RTT standard color two-tone paint except convertible. 614 positive crankcase ventilation. 502 Wonder Touch power brakes. 501 Wonder Touch power steering. 564 left-hand power bucket seat. 551 power side windows. 681 heavy-duty radiator without air conditioning, four-barrel engine only. 349 manual radio with electric antenna. 348 manual-tune radio and manual antenna. 343 push-button radio and electric antenna. 342 push-button radio and manual antenna, 344 AM/FM push-button radio and manual antenna. 345 push-button AM/FM radio and electric antenna. 351 Separa Phonic rear speaker, not available with convertible or reverb. 352 Verbra-Phonic "reverb" type rear radio speaker for coupes and sedans. 664 transistorized ignition regulator. 621 Ride & Handling package. 574 headrests and right-hand reclining seat.

634 Superlift rear shock absorbers. 438 front seat shoulder harness. 628 Soft Ride springs and shocks. 441 Safeguard speedometer. 471 Custom Sports steering wheel. 511 quick-ratio 20:1 steering with power steering. 504 tilt-adjustable steering wheel with power steering and floor shift. CC 7.75 x 14 Nylon red line tires. CB 7.75 x 14 rayon white sidewall tires. 521 hazard warning indicator switch. 642 trailer towing provisions. 671 transistor ignition system. 784 four-speed synchromesh transmission. 782 automatic transmission. 785 heavy-duty three-speed manual transmission with floor shift, 458 Custom wheel discs. 461 deluxe wheel discs. 452 wire wheel discs. 454 Rally wheels with 7.75 x 14 tires. 061 Basic Group includes: push-button AM radio, front foam seat cushions, two-speed windshield wipers and washers, heavy-duty air cleaner and back-up lights in base Tempest or Tempest Custom with six-cylinder or

Daniel B. Lyons photo

Fontaine Blue with red pin striping and a white top made for a striking combination on this 1966 GTO.

base 326-cid V-8 engine and automatic transmission. 062 Protection Group includes: padded instrument panel, door edge guards, rear window defogger, floor mats, spare tire cover and retractable seat belts in two-door models except convertible ($64.66). 062 Protection Group includes: padded instrument panel, door edge guards, rear window defogger, floor mats, spare tire cover and retractable seat belts in four-door models except Safari station wagon. 071 Mirror Group includes: visor-vanity mirror, inside non-glare mirror and remote-control left-hand outside rearview mirror. 074 Lamp Group includes under-hood lamp, luggage compartment lamp, lighted glove box, roof rail and reading lights, ashtray light and parking-brake-on warning light. 622 heavy-load springs and shocks. 642 Trailer Towing Group includes heavy-load springs and shocks, constant-rate directional signal flasher and trailer wiring harness. 661 heavy-duty frame on convertible. 681 includes heavy-duty radiator and 7.75 x 14 tires. Special order axles. 484 metallic brake linings. 731 Safe-T-Track rear axle. 591 speedometer adapter. Special order close-ratio four-speed manual transmission. Special order Stratobench seats.

OPTION INSTALLATION RATES

Of 359,098 Tempests built, 69.8 percent had automatic transmission, 18.3 percent had a four-speed synchromesh transmission, 74.7 percent had a V-8 engine, 25.3 percent had a six-cylinder engine, 94.3 percent had a radio, 99.3 percent had a heater, 63.5 percent had power steering, 1.7 percent had a moveable steering column, 29.7 percent had power brakes, 0.9 percent had a power seat, 1.9 percent had power side windows, 1.7 percent had a station wagon power rear window only, 56.9 percent had bucket seats, 17.2 percent had a vinyl top, 74.9 percent had white sidewall tires, 36.7 percent had a tinted windshield, 21.9 percent had all tinted windows, 19.2 percent had air conditioning, 29.2 percent had dual exhausts, 20.3 percent had a limited-slip differential, 76.3 percent had full wheel covers, 4 percent had a power antenna, and 28.8 percent had a non-glare rearview mirror.

HISTORICAL FOOTNOTES

John Z. DeLorean was general manager of Pontiac in 1966. Tempest model introductions took place September 24, 1965. Model-year production was 384,794 units. Of these, 150,484 were reported built in Pontiac, Michigan, 54,382 were reported built in Kansas City, Missouri, 41,608 were reported built in Fremont, California, 63,205 were reported built in Baltimore, Maryland, and 48,795 were reported built in Framingham, Massachusetts. Tempest production showed an overall increase of 18 percent, from 326,054 in 1965 to 384,794 in 1966. Tempest customer deliveries increased by 16.8 percent over those of the previous record year—365,165 versus 312,692. Full-size Pontiac sales slipped a bit, but the Tempest increase gave the company a one percent overall boost in a year that many automakers were down. Pontiac earned an over 10 percent share of market for the first time ever. To top it off, in June of 1966, Pontiac built the 11 millionth car in its 40 year history.

The biggest Tempest news of the year was the introduction of the overhead cam six. The 207-hp Tempest Sprint could go 0-to-60 mph in 8.2 seconds and do the quarter-mile in 16.7 seconds at 82 mph. *Car Life* magazine (May 1966) asked for and almost got a "standard" GTO to test drive. Pontiac supplied a sport coupe with the 389-cid/335-hp four-barrel engine, four-speed manual gearbox, a console, tinted glass, rally gauges, a tachometer, rally wheels, a radio, a remote rearview mirror, and air conditioning. It booked out at $3,589, a bit more than the sport coupe's base price of $2,763. The car had a 3.08:1 rear axle and a dual reverse-flow exhaust system with mufflers and resonators. The 389-cid V-8 had 335 hp at 5000 rpm and 431 ft.-lbs. of torque at 3200 rpm.

Car Life's 3,950-pound GTO carried 11.6 pounds per horsepower and delivered outstanding performance. It went from 0 to 60 mph in 6.8 seconds and did the quarter mile in 15.4 seconds at 92 mph. Another publication test drove a heavier '66 GTO convertible with the 360-hp Tri-Power V-8 and did not do any better, running 0 to 60 mph in the same 6.8 seconds and using 15.5 seconds to cover the quarter mile at 93 mph.

One of the most famous Pontiac drag racing teams was the "Tin Indian Racing Team" sponsored by Pontiac dealer Bill Knaefel. Working in conjunction with Pontiac's legendary "back door" driver Arlen Vanke and mechanic Bill Abraham, as well as Larry "Doc" Dixon, the Knaefel team racked up more regional, national and world championships than any other combo in the history of the sport. A pair of "Tin Indian" GTO coupes took the 1966 National Hot Rod Association and NASCAR stock eliminator championships.

Jerry Heasley photo

The GTO had a few exterior changes in 1967, one year after a major redesign. The rocker panel moldings were wider and twin pin stripes were seen along the upper beltline.

All Tempests were mildly face-lifted, with grille and rear panel treatments varying by series. Last year's plastic "egg crate" grille was replaced by two different grilles. The Tempest, Tempest Custom and Le Mans lines shared a split grille with six distinct groupings of short vertical blades with negative space between each group of five vertical members. It looked nice and so did the handsome wire mesh GTO grille insert, which again carried left-hand inboard GTO letters and rectangular outboard park/signal lights. The Tempest's new taillights had single, wide-and-thin rectangular lenses that carried a almost square, white back-up light lens in the center on Tempest and Le Mans models. The GTO had four slats arranged two on top and two on the bottom. The edge of the rear deck lid was flattened a bit. Interior and exterior trim on each of the same four series was distinctive.

All Tempests had a number of new standard GM safety devices, such as: front seat shoulder belt anchors, a padded instrument panel, padded sun visors, a four-way hazard warning flasher, a dual master cylinder brake system with a warning light, dual-speed windshield wipers, windshield washers, back-up lights, a left-hand outside rearview mirror, tire safety rims, front and rear push-button seat belt buckles (also on Safari station wagon third-position seats), soft low-profile window control knobs and coat hooks, safety door latches and hinges, a thick-laminate windshield, passenger-guard door locks on all doors, folding seat back latches on two-door models, an inside day/night rearview mirror with shatter-resistant vinyl-edged glass and a breakaway support, directional signals that incorporated a lane-change feature, corrosion-resistant brake lines, an energy-absorbing steering wheel, an energy-absorbing instrument panel with smooth contoured knobs and levers, front seat belt retractors, a uniform (PRNDL) shift quadrant, a reduced-glare instrument panel, reduced-glare windshield wiper arms, and reduced-glare windshield wiper blades.

The 165-hp OHC six-cylinder engine remained base equipment for the Tempest, but the Sprint version of the OHC-6 was upped to 215 hp. For GTOs, the venerable 389-cid V-8 was bored out to 400 cid and got some

Jerry Heasley photo

The 1967 GTO came with the 335-hp V-8, but the Ram Air option could jack the horsepower up to 360.

The 1967 LeMans with the Sprint option was easily identified by the Sports striping on the lower body sides.

improvements, but a Tri-Power option was not on the list.

I.D. NUMBERS

VIN on left front door post. First symbol indicates GM division: 2=Pontiac. Second and third symbols indicate series: 33=Tempest, 35=Tempest Custom, 37=Le Mans, 39=Tempest Safari, 42=GTO. Fourth and fifth symbols indicate body style and appear as last two symbols in body/style number column of charts below. Sixth symbol indicates model year: 7=1967. Seventh symbol tells assembly plant: P=Pontiac, Michigan, Z=Fremont, California, B=Baltimore, Maryland, K=Kansas City, Missouri, U=Framingham, Massachussetts. Following symbols are sequential production number starting with 100001 at each assembly plant. Body/style number plate under hood tells manufacturer, Fisher style number,

assembly plant, trim code, paint code, accessory codes. Style number consists of 67 (for 1967) prefix and four symbols that appear in second column of charts below. First two symbols indicate series. Second two symbols indicate body type. VIN appears on front of engine at right-hand cylinder bank along with an alphanumerical engine production code. Engine production codes included: (230-cid/155-hp OHC six) ZF/ZG. (230-cid/165-hp OHC six) ZK/ZS/ZN/ZM. (230-cid/215-hp OHC six) ZD/ZE/ZR/ZL. (326-cid/250-hp V-8) WP/WX/YN/XF/WH/WC/YJ/XL. (326-cid/285-hp V-8) WK/WO/WR/YM/YP/-XG/XO/XR. (400-cid/260-hp V-8) YB. (400-cid/265-hp V-8) WA/YA/YB/WB. (400-cid/290-hp) YC/YD. (400-cid/293-hp V-8) XC. (400-cid/325-hp V-8) YE/YF/YT/WI/WQ/WZ/WU/XN. (400-cid/333-hp V-8) WE/WD/XZ/XY/XH. (400-cid/350-hp V-8) XZ/XY/XJ. (400-cid/255-hp two-barrel GTO V-8, automatic only) XL/XM. (400-cid/335-hp four-barrel special GTO V-8)

WT/WW with synchromesh, YS with Turbo-Hydra-Matic. (400-cid/360-hp GTO special V-8) WS/WV with synchromesh, XP/XS/YR/YZ with Hydra-Matic.

COLORS

Paint codes for 1967 Tempests were: A=Starlight Black, C=Cameo Ivory, D=Montreux Blue, E=Fathom Blue, F=Tyrol Blue, G=Signet Gold, H=Linden Green, K=Gulf Turquoise, L=Marina Turquoise, M=Plum Mist, N=Burgundy, P=Silverglaze, R=Regimental Red, S=Champagne and T=Montego Cream. Vinyl top colors for 1967 Tempests were: 1=Ivory, 2=Black and 7=Cream. Convertible top colors for 1967 Tempests were: 1=Ivory White, 2=Black, 4=Blue, 5=Turquoise and 7=Cream. Interior trim codes for base Tempests were: 201=Blue cloth and vinyl, 202=Turquoise cloth and vinyl, 203=Gold cloth and vinyl, 205=Black cloth and vinyl and 210=Black vinyl. Interior Trim Codes for Tempest Customs were: 213=Blue vinyl, 214=Turquoise vinyl, 215=Gold vinyl, 217=Black vinyl and 218=Red vinyl. Interior trim codes for Le Mans were: 228=Black cloth and vinyl, 229=Blue cloth and vinyl, 219/232=Blue vinyl, 220=Turquoise vinyl, 221/233=Gold vinyl, 223/235=Black vinyl, 224/236=Parchment vinyl and 225=Red vinyl. GTO Trim codes included: 219=Dark Blue vinyl, 220=Dark Turquoise vinyl, 221=Medium Gold vinyl, 223=Black vinyl, 224=Parchment vinyl, 225=Medium Red vinyl, 235=Black vinyl with front bench seat, and 236=Parchment vinyl with front bench seat.

TEMPEST — (SIX-CYL) — SERIES 233

Pontiac copywriters described the 1967 base Tempest as a "car that could warm Scrooge's heart, yet be unmistakably a Pontiac." The base models had new molded plastic grille bars arranged vertically, in groups of five, with wide spaces between them. Three block-shaped taillight lenses set into rectangular frames were seen. The Tempest name appeared behind the front wheel opening and the rear fender had three horizontal slits on the side that housed side markers. All GM safety features were standard, plus the 165-hp OHC six-cylinder engine, a vinyl floor covering, a cigar lighter, armrests, a heater and defroster, five black sidewall tubeless tires and a standard type steering wheel. Inside, the seats were upholstered in Panharra pattern cloth and Morrokide vinyl, or you could order a beautiful all-black all-Morrokide interior on the sports coupe model at no extra cost. The Sprint option was available even for cars in this low-priced line. The heart of the Sprint option was the new 215-hp overhead-cam six, which carried a four-barrel Quadrajet carburetor topped with a special chromed low-restriction air cleaner. Sprint owners also received heavy-duty front shocks, heavy-duty front springs, a front stabilizer bar, an all-synchro floor-mounted stick shift, a special 3.55:1 axle ratio (3.23:1 with automatic transmission), chromed wheel openings, distinctive sports striping on all coupe models, and the word "Sprint" in the striping just behind the front wheel openings.

Model Number	Body/Style Number	Body Type & Seating	Factory Price	Shipping Weight	Production Total
233	69	4d Sedan-6P	$2,388	3,140 lbs.	13,136
233	07	2d Coupe-6P	$2,341	3,110 lbs.	17,978
233	35	4d Sta Wagon-6P	$2,666	3,370 lbs.	3,495

NOTE 1: A total of 34,609 standard Tempests were built.
NOTE 2: 7,154 standard Tempests had synchromesh and 27,455 had automatic.

TEMPEST CUSTOM — (SIX-CYL) — SERIES 235

Added opulence outside and in were the hallmarks of the 1967 Tempest Custom models. Standard equipment on these cars included all features included on the base Custom, plus (or in place of) special all-Morrokide interior trim, dual-speed windshield wipers, windshield washers, a padded dashboard, padded sun visors, armrests, courtesy lamps, a cigar lighter, a ball-bearing ashtray, special exterior trim, nylon-blend carpeting, a deluxe steering wheel, and panel courtesy lamps on convertibles. There were no horizontal slits on the rear fender sides and the nameplate behind the front wheel opening carried Tempest Custom lettering. Upper beltline and wheel opening moldings were used. The rocker panels had wide bright metal moldings with matching lower front and rear fender extensions. The Sprint option described above could also be added to Tempest Custom models.

Model Number	Body/Style Number	Body Type & Seating	Factory Price	Shipping Weight	Production Total
235	69	4d Sedan-6P	$2,482	3,145 lbs.	17,445
235	39	4d Hardtop-6P	$2,608	3,240 lbs.	5,493
235	07	2d Coupe-6P	$2,434	3,130 lbs.	12,469
235	17	2d Hardtop-6P	$2,494	3,140 lbs.	30,512
235	67	2d Convertible-6P	$2,723	3,240 lbs.	4,082
235	35	4d Sta Wagon-6P	$2,760	3,370 lbs.	5,324

NOTE 3: A total of 75,325 Tempest Customs were built.
NOTE 4: 8,302 Tempest Customs had synchromesh and 67,023 had automatic.

TEMPEST LE MANS — (SIX-CYL) — SERIES 237 & 239

When the name Le Mans appeared on the back fenders, Tempest buyers got all the features of the lower models, plus (or in place of) front foam seat cushions and lamps for the ashtray, a cigar lighter, and a glove box as standard equipment. Buyers of two-door models in this line found three vertical air slots on rear fenders. The four-door hardtop did not have these, but came with short slanting chrome slashes on the rear roof pillar. The Le Mans convertible, hardtop and sports coupe offered a choice of bucket seats (in Blue, Turquoise. Gold, Black, Parchment or Red) or a front notchback bench seat with center armrests (in Parchment or Black) at no extra cost. In the four-door hardtop you could pick between Prevue pattern cloth and expanded Morrokide bench seats (in Black or Blue), or a notchback front bench seat with center armrest (in Black, Blue or Gold). A special station wagon with wood-grained exterior paneling was called the Series 239 Tempest Safari and was generally finished in Le Mans-level trim and appointments. The Sprint option described above for the base Tempest

The hood tachometer was an $84.26 option in 1967.

Jerry Heasley photo

Jerry Heasley photo

Dark Blue vinyl was one of eight different interior choices on the 1967 GTO.

could also be added to Le Mans models.

Model Number	Body/Style Number	Body Type & Seating	Factory Price	Shipping Weight	Production Total
TEMPEST LE MANS — (SIX-CYL) — SERIES 237					
237	39	4d Hardtop-6P	$2,771	3,265 lbs.	8,424
237	07	2d Coupe-5P	$2,586	3,155 lbs.	10,693
237	17	2d Hardtop-5P	$2,648	3,155 lbs.	75,965
237	67	2d Convertible-5P	$2,881	3,250 lbs.	9,820
TEMPEST SAFARI — (SIX-CYL) — SERIES 237 & 239					
239	35	4d Sta Wagon-6P	$2,936	3,390 lbs.	4,511

NOTE 5: 104,902 Le Mans passenger cars were built.
NOTE 6: 14,770 Le Mans passenger cars had synchromesh and 90,132 had automatic.
NOTE 7: 129 Tempest Safari wagons had synchromesh and 4,382 had automatic.

TEMPEST GTO — (V-8) — SERIES 242

The GTO's new wire mesh grille and four-lens taillight treatment were distinguishing marks of the 1967 model. The rocker panel moldings were made wider and now covered the body sides as well as the lower edge of the doors, the front fenders and the rear quarters. The trim along the center grille divider now went from one side of the car to the other, with a dip around the center divider. V-shaped fender badges behind the front wheel opening were eliminated. Like the Grand Prix, the GTO had twin pin stripes along the upper beltline and bright metal wheel opening moldings. Rectangular front grille parking lamps were still used in front and the new taillights now took the form of four thin rectangles at each side. All Le Mans features were standard, plus walnut-grain dash inserts, bucket seats, paint pin striping, heavy-duty shocks, springs and stabilizer bars, redline or white sidewall tires, dual exhausts, and the new 335-hp four-barrel 400-cid V-8. This engine featured new cylinder heads that were reworked for improved volumetric flow. They carried push rod guides, screw-in studs, and larger diameter valves. GM's corporate de-emphasis of performance brought a ban on multi-carburetor setups,

Jerry Heasley photo

Front-end changes in 1967 included rectangular parking lights and a new wire mesh grille.

Mike Mueller photo

This beautiful GTO convertible was one of 9,517 made for 1967.

so Tri-Power carburetion was no longer available. However, there was an H.O. (high-output) 400 using the Rochester Quadrajet four-barrel carburetor. In addition to raising the rocker panel moldings, Pontiac moved the GTO's engine call-outs (which said "6.5 Litre") onto the rocker panel molding just behind the front wheel cutouts. In addition to the new engine, the old two-speed automatic transmission was replaced by a specially modified three-speed Turbo-Hydra-Matic (THM 400), with a steering-column-mounted shifter as standard equipment. A new option was a Hurst Dual Gate shifter that was exclusive to the GTO. The driver could use this like a regular automatic by leaving the shifter in drive or could move the shifter to the right and shift through the gears like a manual transmission. A factory Ram Air option was also offered at midyear. The 1967 GTOs continued to use the same hood panel used in 1965-1966, but when the Ram Air package was installed an ornament was added to the scoop. This was supposed to be used only in good weather and was removed and replaced by the regular closed ornament when the weather got bad. A special block with four-bolt main bearings, Moraine 400 bearings, forged rods and pistons, swirl-polished valves, stiffer valve springs, and a 301/313-degrees camshaft was part of the Ram Air option. Pontiac rated the Ram Air 400 for 360 hp at 5400 rpm and 438 ft.-lbs. of torque at 3800 rpm so as not to shake up the GM brass.

Model Number	Body/Style Number	Body Type & Seating	Factory Price	Shipping Weight	Production Total
242	07	2d Coupe-5P	$2,871	3,425 lbs.	7,029
242	17	2d Hardtop-5P	$2,935	3,430 lbs.	65,176
242	67	2d Convertible-5P	$3,165	3,515 lbs.	9,517

NOTE 8: 81,722 GTOs were built.
NOTE 9: 39,128 GTOs had synchromesh and 42,594 had automatic.

ENGINES

TEMPEST, TEMPEST CUSTOM, LE MANS BASE OHC 230-CID SIX-CYL: Inline. Overhead valves. Overhead camshaft. Cast-iron block. Displacement: 230 cid. Bore and stroke: 3.85 x 3.25 in. Compression ratio: 9.0:1. Brake hp: 165 at 4700 rpm. Torque: 216 lbs.-ft. at 2600 rpm. Hydraulic valve lifters. Carburetor: Rochester model 7027167 one-barrel.

TEMPEST, TEMPEST CUSTOM, LE MANS OPTIONAL OHC 230-CID "SPRINT" SIX-CYL: Overhead valves. Overhead camshaft. Cast-iron block. Displacement: 230 cid. Bore and stroke: 3.85 x 3.25 in. Compression ratio: 10.5:1. Brake hp: 215 at 5200 rpm. Torque: 240 lbs.-ft. at 3800 rpm. Hydraulic valve lifters. Chrome low-restriction air cleaner. Carburetor: Rochester four-barrel Quadrajet.

TEMPEST, TEMPEST CUSTOM, LE MANS BASE 326-CID V-8: Overhead valve. Bore and stroke: 3.718 x 3.75. Displacement: 326 cid. Compression ratio: 9.2:1. Brake hp: 250 at 4600 rpm. Taxable hp: 44.40. Torque: 333 lbs.-ft. at 2800. Five main bearings. Hydraulic valve lifters. Crankcase capacity: 6 qt. (add 1 qt. for new filter). Cooling system capacity with heater: 18.5 qt. Carburetor: Two-barrel. Engine code: WP, WX, YN, XF, WH, WC, XJ and XL.

GTO OPTIONAL 400-CID "ECONOMY" V-8 (AUTOMATIC TRANSMISSION): Overhead valve. Cast-iron block. Bore and stroke: 4.12 x 3.75. Displacement: 400 cid. Compression ratio: 8.6:1. Brake hp: 255 at 4400 rpm. Taxable hp: 54.3. Torque: 397 lbs.-ft. at 2400 rpm. Five main bearings. Hydraulic valve lifters. Crankcase capacity: 6 qt. (add 1 qt. for new filter). Cooling system capacity with heater: 17.75 qt. Carburetor: Two-barrel. Engine code: YB.

TEMPEST, TEMPEST CUSTOM, LE MANS OPTIONAL H.O. V-8: Overhead valve. Bore and stroke: 3.718 x 3.75. Displacement: 326 cid. Compression ratio: 10.5:1. Brake hp: 285 at 5000 rpm. Taxable hp: 44.40. Torque: 359 lbs.-ft. at 3200 rpm. Five main bearings. Hydraulic valve lifters. Dual exhaust system. Crankcase capacity: 6 qt. (add 1 qt. for new filter). Cooling system capacity with heater: 18.5 qt. Carburetor: Four-barrel. Engine code: WK, WO, WR, YM, YP, XG, XO and XR.

GTO BASE 400-CID V-8: Overhead valve. Cast-iron block. Bore and stroke: 4.12 x 3.75. Displacement: 400 cid. Compression ratio: 10.75:1. Brake hp: 335 at 5000 rpm. Taxable hp: 54.3. Torque: 441 lbs.-ft. at 3400 rpm. Five main bearings. Hydraulic valve lifters. Chrome air cleaner. Chrome rocker covers. Chrome oil filler cap. Crankcase capacity: 6 qt. (add 1 qt. for new filter). Cooling system capacity with heater: 17.75 qt. Carburetor: Four-barrel. Engine code: WT, WW and YS.

GTO OPTIONAL V-8: Overhead valve. Cast-iron block. Bore and stroke: 4.12 x 3.75. Displacement: 400 cid. Compression ratio: 10.75:1. Brake hp: 360 at 5100 rpm. Taxable hp: 54.3. Torque: 438 lbs.-ft. at 3600 rpm. Five main bearings. Hydraulic valve lifters. Chrome low-restriction air cleaner. Chrome rocker covers. Chrome oil filler cap. Special dual exhausts. High-output camshaft and valve train. De-clutching fan. Crankcase capacity: 6 qt. (add 1 qt. for new filter). Cooling system capacity with heater: 17.75 qt. Carburetor: Four-barrel. Engine code: WS, WV, XP, XS, YR and YZ.

GTO OPTIONAL "RAM AIR" V-8: Overhead valve. Cast-iron block. Bore and stroke: 4.12 x 3.75. Displacement: 400 cid. Compression ratio: 10.75:1. Brake hp: 360 at 5400 rpm. Taxable hp: 54.3. Torque: 438 lbs.-ft. at 3800 rpm. Five main bearings. Hydraulic valve lifters. Chrome low-restriction air cleaner. Chrome rocker covers. Chrome oil filler cap. Special dual exhausts. High-output camshaft and valve train. De-clutching fan. Crankcase capacity: 6 qt. (add 1 qt. for new filter). Cooling system capacity with heater: 17.75

qt. Carburetor: Four-barrel. Engine code: WS, WV, XP, XS, YR and YZ.

CHASSIS

Wheelbase: 115 in. Overall length: (Tempest station wagon) 203.4 in., (Tempest and GTO passenger cars) 206.6 in. Overall width: (Le Mans and GTO) 74.4 in.; (Others) 74.7 in. Overall height: (four-door sedan) 55 in., (sports coupe) 54.2 in. except GTO 53.7 in., (two-door hardtop) 54.2 in. except GTO 53.7 in., (four-door hardtop) 55 in., (convertible) 54.1 in. except GTO 53.6 in., (Safari) 55.4 in. Front legroom: (Tempest four-door sedan and sports coupe) 40.2 in., (Tempest Safari) 40.3 in., (all Tempest Custom and Le Mans four-door hardtop) 40.6 in., (Le Mans sport coupe, four-door hardtop and convertible and all GTO) 41.1 in. Rear legroom: (Tempest and Tempest Custom four-door sedan, Tempest Custom Safari and Le Mans four-door hardtop) 35.7 in. (Tempest sport coupe and Tempest Custom sport coupe, two-door hardtop and convertible) 33.1 in., (Le Mans and GTO sport coupe, two-door hardtop and convertible) 32.3 in. Front headroom: (Tempest and Tempest Custom four-door sedan, Tempest Custom and Le Mans four-door hardtop and Le Mans and GTO convertible) 38.1 in., (Tempest sports coupe) 37.4 in., (Tempest Custom sports coupe and two-door hardtop) 37.2 in., (Tempest Custom convertible and Tempest and Tempest Custom Safari) 38.1 in. and (other models) 37.5 in. Rear headroom: (Tempest four-door sedan) 37.3 in., (Tempest sports coupe) 36.3 in., (all Safaris) 38.3 in., (Tempest Custom, Le Mans, and GTO all coupes) 36.1 in., (all four-door hardtops) 37.1 in. and (all convertibles) 36.6 in. Total luggage compartment volume: (all four-door sedans and hardtops) 29.1 cu. ft., (all coupes and convertibles) 30.4 cu. ft., (Tempest Safari) 85.3 cu. ft. and (all other Safaris) 84.5 cu. ft. Front tread: 58 in. Rear tread: 59 in. Standard tires: (Tempest, Tempest Custom, Le Mans) 7.75 x 14, (GTO) F70 x 14.

The Series 239 Tempest Safari featured wood-grain exterior panels.

Paul Zazerine collection

There were only 3,495 of the base Tempest Safari wagons built in 1967.

Paul Zazerine collection

OPTIONS

591 speedometer gear adapter ($11.06). 361 dual-stage air cleaner ($9.45). 582 Custom air conditioner ($343.20). 612 Air Injection Reactor exhaust system control, positive crankcase ventilation required ($44.76). 678 heavy-duty battery for base Tempest, Tempest Custom, Le Mans and Tempest Safari without air conditioning ($3.48). 572 floor carpets for base Tempest ($18.96). 44 electric clock ($18.96) 514 heavy-duty clutch and fan for all models except GTO without options 582, 684 or 688 ($15.80). 514 heavy-duty clutch and fan in GTO without options 582, 684 or 688 ($3.05). 472 console in GTO with Hydra-Matic transmission ($68.46). 472 front seat center console in Le Mans, except four-door hardtop, and in GTO with stick shift ($52.66). 441 cruise control ($52.66). 371 front foam seat cushions ($7.90). 492 remote-control deck lid, except Safari ($12.64). 378 Safari rear window deflector ($26.33). 374 rear window defogger, all models except Safari and convertible ($21.06). 731 Safe-T-Track differential ($42.13). 731 heavy-duty Safe-T-Track differential, in all cars with 74H, 74K, 74P or 74S axles ($63.19). 521 front disc brakes ($104.79). 481 dual exhausts on Tempest, Tempest Custom or Le Mans V-8s, except Safaris ($30.23). 482 tailpipe extensions on Tempest, Tempest Custom or Le Mans V-8s, except Safaris with Sprint option package ($10.53). 482 tailpipe extensions on Tempest, Tempest Custom or Le Mans V-8s, except Safaris without Sprint option package ($20.85). 482 tailpipe extensions on all GTOs ($20.85). 531 tinted glass in all windows ($30.54). 532 tinted windshield only ($21.06). 382 door edge guards on two-door models ($4.74). 382 door edge guards on four-door models ($8.16). 572 bench seat with headrests applied in all models ($42.13). 571 headrests applied to Le Mans two-door models and all GTOs ($52.66). 584 heater deletion, not available when air conditioning was used ($71.76 credit). 494 dual horns in base Tempest ($4.21). 671 capacitor ignition system with air conditioning ($114.80). 671 capacitor ignition system without air conditioning ($104.26). 524 Custom gearshift knob for all with three- or four-speed floor shift ($3.69). 402 glove box lamp all Tempests and Tempest Customs ($2.79). 422 ignition switch light ($2.06). 401 luggage compartment lamp, except Safaris ($3.48). 404 roof rail and reading lamp, except convertibles ($13.59). 421 under-hood lamp ($3.38). 412 ashtray and cigar lighter lamp Tempest and Tempest Custom ($3.05). 411 dash panel courtesy lamps Tempest and Tempest Custom except convertible ($4.21). 522 red fender liners Tempest and Tempest Custom except Safari without Sprint option ($34.65). 522 red fender liners Tempest and Tempest Custom except Safari with Sprint option, plus all Le Mans and GTO models ($26.33). 512 station wagon luggage carrier ($63.19). 362 vinyl luggage compartment mat ($7.90). 631 front floor mat ($6.11). 632 rear floor mat, requires front floor mats ($5.69). 391 visor-vanity mirror ($1.68). 394 remote-control outside rearview mirror ($7.37). SPS special color solid paint ($83.20). STT special color two-tone paint, except Safaris and convertibles ($114.27). STT special color two-tone paint on Safari ($95.32). RTT standard color two-tone paint, except Safaris and convertibles ($31.07). RTT standard color two-tone paint on Safari ($12.12). 444 Rally gauge cluster with tachometer ($84.26), 341

power antenna, except Safari ($29.12). 502 power brakes ($41.60). 561 4-Way power bench seat ($69.51). 501 power steering ($94.79). 542 power station wagon tailgate window ($26.33). 564 4-Way left-hand power bucket seat in all models with bucket seats ($69.51). 544 power top on Tempest Custom convertible ($52.66). 551 power windows ($100.05). 681 heavy-duty radiator without air conditioning ($14.74). 348 manual radio and antenna ($52.66). 342 push-button radio and antenna ($61.09). 344 AM/FM push-button radio and antenna ($133.76). 351 rear seat speaker in Safari ($20.80). 351 rear seat speaker in all except Safari ($15.80). 352 Verbra-Phonic reverb speaker in all except Safari ($52.66). 664 transistorized ignition without air conditioning ($10.53). 431 front and rear Custom seat belts, in two-door models ($6.32); in four-door models ($10.53). 432 rear center seat belt for cars with 431 Custom seat belts option ($7.90). 432 rear center seat belt for cars without 431 Custom seat belts option ($6.32). 578 reclining right-hand bucket seat with headrests in two-door Le Mans or GTO ($84.26). 654 heavy-duty front and rear seats for base Tempests with front foam cushion option 371 ($14.74). 634 Superlift rear shocks ($39.50). 434 front shoulder belts for cars with Custom seat belt option ($26.33). Front shoulder belts for cars without Custom seat belt option ($15.80). 621 Ride & Handling package for Tempest, Tempest Custom or Le Mans without Sprint package ($9.32). 621 Ride & Handling package for GTO and Tempest, Tempest Custom, or Le Mans with Sprint package ($3.74). 622 heavy-load springs and shocks for Tempest, Tempest Custom, and Le Mans ($6.11); for GTO ($3.74). 471 Custom sports steering wheel for base Tempest with 064 Décor option and all other Tempest Custom, Le Mans and GTO ($30.02). 471 Custom sports steering wheel for base Tempest without 064 Décor option ($42.13). 462 deluxe steering wheel in base Tempest ($12.11). 504 tilt steering wheel, power steering required ($42.13). 662 quick steering, all except with power steering ($10.53). 534 rear doorjamb switches ($3.16). 354 stereo tape player ($128.49). TCB 7.75 x 14 white sidewall tires, except GTO ($31.60). TMD F70 x 14 white sidewall nylon tires, all except GTO with Ride & Handling suspension ($65.30). TMD F70 x 14 white sidewall nylon tires for GTO (no cost). TCC 7.75 x nylon red stripe tires, except GTO ($54.77). TCL 7.75 x 14 white sidewall nylon tires except GTO ($54.77). TCL 7.75 x 14 white sidewall nylon tires on GTO ($49.51). TMC F70 x 14 red stripe nylon tires, all except GTO with Ride & Handling option ($65.30). TMC F70 x 14 red stripe nylon tires on GTO (no cost). SVT Cordova vinyl top for two-door coupes and hardtops ($84.26). 77C three-speed manual transmission with four-barrel OHC six without Sprint package ($42.13). 77C three-speed manual transmission with four-barrel OHC six with Sprint package (no cost). 77S three-speed manual transmission in GTO (no cost). 77Z three-speed manual transmission with one-barrel OHC six (no cost). 77S column-shifted three-speed manual transmission on V-8 models without a console (no cost). 77S full-synchro three-speed manual transmission on all models except GTO ($84.26). 776 four-speed manual transmission on cars with Sprint option, not available on Safari or GTO ($184.31). 778 four-speed manual transmission on GTO only ($184.31). 77W four-speed manual transmission on all cars except those with one-barrel OHC six ($184.31). 77D automatic transmission with 326-cid V-8 and air conditioning, except GTO ($194.84). 77Y automatic transmission for all models with the one-barrel OHC six ($184.31). 77X Turbo Hydra-Matic automatic transmission for GTO with 400-cid two-barrel V-8 ($226.44). 77J Turbo Hydra-Matic automatic transmission for GTO with 400-cid four-barrel V-8 ($226.44). 77L automatic transmission with Sprint package, not available in safari or GTO ($184.31). 77R automatic transmission for all models with the 326-cid two-barrel V-8 ($194.84). 77T automatic transmission for all models with the 326-cid four-barrel V-8 ($194.84). 77N automatic transmission for all models with the one-barrel OHC six and air conditioning ($184.31). 614 positive crankcase ventilation ($5.27). 458 Custom wheel discs for Tempest or Tempest Custom with Décor Group 064 ($19.48). 458 Custom wheel discs without Décor Group ($36.33). 461 Deluxe wheel discs for all models ($16.85). 452 wire wheel discs for Tempest and Tempest Custom with Décor group 064 ($52.66). 452 wire wheel discs for all without Décor Group 064 ($69.51). 454 Rally I wheels for all without 064 Décor Group ($56.87). Rally I wheels for Tempest and Tempest Custom with 064 Décor Group ($40.02). 453 Rally II wheels for all without Décor Group 064 ($72.67). 453 Rally II wheels for Tempest and Tempest Custom with 064 Décor Group ($55.81). 451 aluminum hubs and drums for all without 064 Décor Group ($100.05). 451 aluminum hubs and drums for Tempest and Tempest Custom with 064 Décor Group ($83.20). 061 Basic Group includes push-button radio, front foam seat cushion (standard in Le Mans and GTO), electric clock and dual-stage air cleaner in Tempest, Tempest Custom and Tempest Safari ($97.38); in Le Mans and GTO ($89.48). 064 Décor Group includes: deluxe steering wheel, deluxe wheel discs, and décor moldings (price

Paul Zazerine collection

**The 1967 Tempest line included
a four-door hardtop version.**

GM Media Archives photo

The Series 239 Safari wagons had Le Mans level trim.

ranged from $16.85 on the Tempest Custom convertible to $58.45 on the Tempest Safari). 074 Lamp Group includes: luggage lamp (except Safari), roof rail and reading lamps (except convertible), glove box lamp, ashtray and cigar lighter lamp, parking brake lamp, under-hood lamp and ignition switch lamp (price ranged from $9.02 in Le Mans and GTO convertible to $29.18 in Tempest and Tempest Custom Safaris). 071 Mirror Group includes visor-vanity mirror and remote-control driver's outside rearview mirror ($9.05). 062 Protection Group includes: rear window defogger (except Safari and convertible), door edge guards, front and rear Custom seat belts, front and rear floor mats and Safari rear window deflector (price ranged from $22.86 on Tempest Custom, Le Mans and GTO convertibles to $56.82 on all Safaris). 332 Sprint package includes: stabilizer shaft, four-barrel OHC six, three-speed manual transmission with floor shift, sport-type shock absorbers, front fender emblems, wheel opening moldings on 23307, 23507, 23517 and 23567 models, plus side Sprint stripes on coupes and convertibles (price ranged from $105.60 on

the Le Mans four-door hardtop to $126.72 on models 23307, 23507, 23517 and 23567.)

(ENGINES FOR MANUAL TRANSMISSION CARS): Code WP 326-cid two-barrel V-8 without A.I.R. option 612, for all models except GTO ($95.04). Code WR 326-cid four-barrel V-8 without A.I.R. option 612, for all models except Safaris and GTOs ($159.14). Code WS 400-cid four-barrel H.O. V-8 without A.I.R. option 612 ($76.89). Code WX 326-cid two-barrel V-8 with A.I.R. option 612, in all models except GTO ($95.04). 400-cid four-barrel H.O. V-8 with A.I.R. option 612, in GTO ($76.89). 400-cid four-barrel V-8 with A.I.R. option 612, in GTO series (no cost). Code XR 326-cid four-barrel V-8 with A.I.R. option 612 in base Tempest, Tempest Custom, and Le Mans except Safaris ($159.14). Code XR-S 400-cid Ram Air four-barrel V-8 with or without A.I.R. option 612 ($263.30). Code ZD-R 230-cid OHC six with four-barrel carburetor with or without A.I.R. option 612 in Tempest, Tempest Custom and Le Mans (except Safaris) with 332 Sprint option package (no charge). ZS-

K 230-cid OHC six with one-barrel carburetor with or without A.I.R. option 612 in all except GTO (no cost). ZD-R 230-cid OHC six with four-barrel carburetor, with or without A.I.R. option 612 in all models without the Sprint package except GTOs ($57.93).

(ENGINES FOR AUTOMATIC TRANSMISSION CARS): Code YN 326-cid two-barrel V-8 without A.I.R. option 612, for all models except GTO ($95.04). Code YP 326-cid four-barrel V-8 without A.I.R. option 612, for all models except Safaris and GTOs ($159.14). Code XF 326-cid two-barrel V-8 with A.I.R. option 612 in all models except GTO ($95.04). Code XG 326-cid four-barrel V-8 with A.I.R. option 612, for all models except Safaris and GTOs ($159.14). Code XL-M 400-cid two-barrel V-8 with or without A.I.R. option 612, GTO only (no cost). Code YS 400-cid four-barrel V-8 in GTO (no cost). Code XP 400-cid four-barrel "Ram Air" V-8 in GTO series only ($263.30). Code YZ 400-cid four-barrel H.O. V-8 in GTO only ($76.89). Code ZE-L 230-cid OHC six with or without A.I.R. option 612 in all except GTO without Sprint option ($57.58). Code ZE-L 230-cid OHC six with or without A.I.R. option 612 in all with Sprint option, except station wagons (no cost). ZM-N 230-cid OHC six with one-barrel carburetor, with or without A.I.R. option 612 in all models except GTOs (no cost).

OPTION INSTALLATION RATES

Of 301,069 Tempests built, 76.9 percent had automatic transmission, 13.6 percent had a four-speed synchromesh transmission, 78.5 percent had a V-8 engine, 21.5 percent had a six-cylinder engine, 91.4 percent had an AM radio, 27.5 percent had air conditioning, 1.9 percent had a movable steering column, 73.8 percent had power steering, 31.3 percent had power drum brakes, 2.4 percent had disc brakes, 0.9 percent had a 4-Way power seat, 2.1 percent had power windows, 2.6 percent had a power tailgate window, 56.1 percent had bucket seats, 28.5 percent had a vinyl top, 74.3 percent had white sidewall tires, 37.5 percent had a tinted windshield only, 25.9 percent had all tinted glass, 29 percent had dual exhausts, 16 percent had a limited-slip differential, 76.5 percent had full wheel covers, 1.5 percent had a speed-regulating device, 8.9 percent had a power antenna, 3.4 percent had an AM/FM radio, and 29.5 percent had a clock.

HISTORICAL FOOTNOTES

John Z. DeLorean was general manager on Pontiac in 1967. It was a great season for the company, as Pontiac sold more passenger cars than in any other year in its history. It was also the only U.S. automaker to have both increased sales and market penetration in every year since 1962. The division's share of the domestic market, excluding overseas sales, rose to 11.1 percent from 10 percent in 1966 and 9.4 percent in 1965. The 1967 sales total included 295,847 Tempests. Pontiac remained America's third best-selling brand of cars. However, the division was unable to maintain its unbroken years of steady production gains and actually built 10,000 less cars in the model-year than it had previously. Stretched model-year production totals for the Tempest were 301,069 cars manufactured versus 359,098 in 1966. Model-year production of Tempests by assembly plant included 116,792 made at Pontiac, Michigan, 52,264 made at Kansas City, Missouri, 34,648 made at Fremont, California, 53,146 made at Baltimore, Maryland, 43,571 made at Framingham, Massachusetts, and 648 made elsewhere and shipped overseas from a GM facility in Bloomfield, New Jersey. The Pontiac Tempest's percentage of total domestic production declined to 3.9 percent from 4.2 percent the previous model year.

Interesting conversions of 1967 Pontiacs include the Dean Jeffries-built "Monkeemobile" GTO phaeton (made for "The Monkees" TV show). New features included the 400-cid, the Turbo Hydra-Matic transmission, and the Hurst Dual-Gate shifter option. The Tempest Sprint option was more heavily emphasized in sales literature this year, but installations of this package dropped to 21.4 percent from an even 24 percent the previous season.

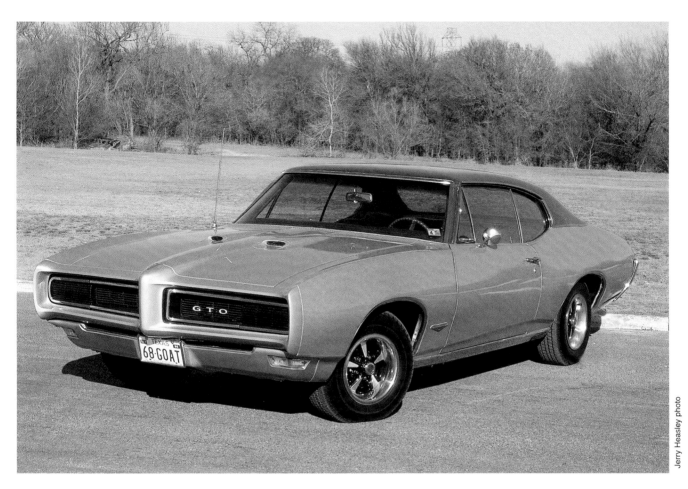

Jerry Heasley photo

Certainly the most notable change in the 1968 GTO was the innovative Endura front end.

Intent on regaining its production momentum, as well as maintaining its positive sales trends, Pontiac Motor Division concentrated on innovations to make its 1968 Tempest models more exciting to the car-buying public. For the first time, the Tempest, Tempest Custom, and Le Mans models were offered with different wheelbases for two- and four-door models.

The GTO had a revolutionary new "Endura" energy-absorbing bumper. The bumper's Endura plastic construction was the combination of a special synthetic compound backed with a heavy-gauge steel reinforcement that functioned as an energy-absorbing system. The synthetic front cushion was painted to match the car's body color and was said to be mar-resistant. Under most circumstances, when the bumper was hit, it would depress and then rebound to its original form nearly instantaneously. Pontiac also claimed that if

the Endura bumper was damaged in a very severe accident that a Pontiac dealer could repair, rather than replace it.

The 1968 OHC six had larger displacement and a new 12-counterweight crankshaft. The V-8 engine options now included an "RF" (regular-fuel) version of the 350-cid motor with a two-barrel carburetor and 9.2:1 compression ratio. Halfway through the model year, Pontiac issued a revised Ram Air option for the GTO. It was good for 360 hp and had new round exhaust ports. Pontiac's 1968 changes, especially those for Tempest models, were well received and pushed annual sales to a new record.

I.D. NUMBERS

VIN on left side of dashboard, visible through the

69

windshield. First symbol indicates GM division: 2=Pontiac. Second and third symbols indicate series: 33=Tempest, 35=Tempest Custom, 37=Le Mans, 39=Tempest Safari, 42=GTO. Fourth and fifth symbols indicate body style and appear as last two symbols in body/style number column of charts below. Sixth symbol indicates model year: 8=1968. Seventh symbol tells assembly plant: P=Pontiac, Michigan, C=South Gate, California, R=Arlington, Texas, Z=Fremont, California, B=Baltimore, Maryland, K=Kansas City, Missouri, G=Framingham, Massachussetts. Following symbols are sequential production number starting with 100001 at each assembly plant. Body/style number plate under hood tells manufacturer, Fisher style number, assembly plant, trim code, paint code, accessory codes. Style number consists of 68 (for 1968) prefix and four symbols that appear in second column of charts below. First two symbols indicate series. Second two symbols indicate body type. VIN appears on front of engine at right-hand cylinder bank along with an alphanumerical engine production code. Engine production codes included:

(250-cid/175-hp OHC six) ZK/ZN. (250-cid/215-hp OHC six) ZD/ZE/ZO. (350-cid/265-hp V-8) WP/YN/WD/WC/YJ. (350-cid/320-hp V-8) WR/YM/YP/WK. (400-cid/265-hp two-barrel GTO V-8, automatic only) XM. (400-cid/350-hp four-barrel special GTO V-8) WT/WW with synchromesh, YS with Turbo Hydra-Matic. (400-cid/350-hp GTO special V-8) WT manual transmission only. (400-cid/360-hp special GTO V-8) WS/XS with synchromesh, YZ/XP Hydra-Matic.

COLORS

Paint codes for 1968 Tempests were: A=Starlight Black, C=Cameo Ivory, D=Alpine Blue, E=Aegena Blue, F=Nordic Blue, G=April Gold, I=Autumn Bronze, K=Meridian Turquoise, L=Aleutian Blue, N=Flambeau Burgundy, P=Springmist Green, Q=Verdoro Green, R=Solar Red, T=Primavera Beige, V=Nightshade Green, and Y=Mayfair Maize. Vinyl top colors for 1968 Tempests were: 1=Ivory White, 2=Black, 5=Teal, and 8=Gold. Convertible top colors for 1968 Tempests were: 1=Ivory-

The 1968 Tempest Safari wagon came with a standard six-cylinder engine and wood-grained interior and exterior paneling.

White, 2=Black, 5=Teal, and 8=Gold. Interior trim codes for 1968 Tempests were: 201=Blue cloth and vinyl, 202=Turquoise cloth and vinyl, 203=Gold cloth and vinyl, and 206=Black vinyl. Interior trim codes for 1968 Tempest Customs were: 213=Blue vinyl, 214=Turquoise vinyl, 215=Gold vinyl, 217=Black vinyl and 218=Red vinyl. Interior trim codes for 1968 Le Mans were 219=Teal Vinyl, 220=Turquoise vinyl, 221=Gold vinyl, 223=Black vinyl, 224=Parchment vinyl, 225=Red vinyl, 228=Black cloth and vinyl, 231=Black vinyl, 232=Teal vinyl, 233=Parchment vinyl, 235=Black vinyl, and 236=Parchment vinyl. Interior trim codes for 1968 GTOs were: 219=Teal vinyl, 220=Turquoise vinyl, 221=Gold vinyl, 223=Black vinyl, 224=Parchment vinyl, 225=Red vinyl, 235=Black vinyl front bench seat, and 236=Parchment vinyl front bench seat.

TEMPEST — (SIX-CYL) — SERIES 233

Two new A-body shells were introduced for Pontiac intermediate-size series in 1968. Two-door models were now built on a 112-inch wheelbase, while four-door models and station wagons were on a 116-inch stance. The Wide-Track also grew even wider to 60 inches front and rear. On the two-door cars, the length was approximately 6 inches less than in 1967. The styling emphasis was on the long hood/short deck motif that was popular at the time. A look of aesthetic unity was created by blending the bodies and roofs together with unbroken styling lines. A peripheral bumper grille was used and taillights were placed in the bumper. The front end and hood had a "ship's prow" look that maintained Pontiac's trademark split grille and side-by-side round headlights. The rear featured a broad, wraparound rear bumper with large, rectangular taillights embedded into it on either side of a center section that held the license plate in a recess. Regular equipment on standard Tempests included GM safety features, a 250-cid/175-hp overhead cam six-cylinder engine, a heater and defroster, armrests, and rocker panel moldings. The Tempest name was on the front fender sides, ahead of the wheel opening. Engine call-outs appeared on the front of the rocker panel moldings. The code 342 Sprint option package was available for all Tempests without air conditioning, except station wagons. It included a front stabilizer bar, the four-barrel OHC-6 engine, a three-speed manual transmission with floor shifter, sport-type shock absorbers, wheel opening moldings, and Sprint stripes on two-door models. The price of the 1968 Sprint option varied from $105.65 to $126.75 depending upon series and body style. It was more expensive for two-door models because they had side stripes. The Sprint package cost less for Le Mans models because the Le Mans trim level already included the cost of wheel opening moldings.

Model Number	Body/Style Number	Body Type & Seating	Factory Price	Shipping Weight	Production Total
233	69	4d Sedan-6P	$2,509	3,307 lbs.	11,590
233	27	2d Coupe-6P	$2,461	3,242 lbs.	19,991

NOTE 1: 31,581 standard Tempests were built.
NOTE 2: 5,876 had synchromesh and 25,705 had automatic.

TEMPEST CUSTOM — (SIX-CYL) — SERIES 235

Tempest Customs had all the features found on 233 models, plus special interior and exterior trim, carpeting, a deluxe steering wheel, armrests with ashtrays, a cigarette lighter, an ignition buzzer alarm, front and rear body-side marker lights, and dual horns. In addition to rocker panel moldings, the Tempest Custom had rear quarter panel extension moldings. The Tempest name appeared on the front fender sides, ahead of the wheel opening, and a Custom plaque was placed under the model name. The Tempest Custom also had wheel opening moldings. Station wagons and convertibles had all-Morrokide seats and carpeting, with panel courtesy lamps on convertibles. Tempest lettering along with custom badges appeared at tips of front fenders. The Tempest Custom station wagon featured all-Morrokide upholstery. The Sprint option was also available on Tempest Custom models.

Model Number	Body/Style Number	Body Type & Seating	Factory Price	Shipping Weight	Production Total
235	69	4d Sedan-6P	$2,602	3,297 lbs.	17,304
235	39	4d Hardtop-6P	$2,728	3,382 lbs.	6,147
235	27	2d Coupe-6P	$2,554	3,252 lbs.	10,634
235	37	2d Hardtop-6P	$2,614	3,277 lbs.	40,574
235	67	2d Convertible-6P	$2,839	3,337 lbs.	3,518
235	35	4d Sta Wagon-6P	$2,906	3,667 lbs.	8,253

NOTE 3: 75,325 Custom Tempests were built.
NOTE 4: 8,302 had synchromesh and 67,023 had automatic.

TEMPEST LE MANS — (SIX-CYL) — SERIES 237 AND SERIES 239

Standard in Le Mans were all GM safety features, plus disappearing wipers, dual horns, and an all-Morrokide interior. Two-door models came with a choice of bucket or notchback armrest seats at the same price. The four-door hardtop had cloth and Morrokide upholstery and a choice of a notchback or bench front seat. A deluxe steering wheel, carpeting, a cigar lighter, armrests and ashtrays, an ignition alarm, panel courtesy lamps, an ashtray lamp, and a glove box lamp were also featured. The Le Mans convertible had a power top and special courtesy lights. The series 239 Safari was generally appointed in Le Mans level trim with wood-grained interior and exterior paneling. The word Le Mans was on the rear fender of each Le Mans. The word Safari was on the front of the wood-trimmed station wagons. Pontiac had considered adding louvers to the front fender tips of the 1968 Le Mans and a prototype version with this feature was photographed, but the louvers did not make it on production cars. The Sprint option was also available on Tempest Le Mans models.

Model Number	Body/Style Number	Body Type & Seating	Factory Price	Shipping Weight	Production Total
TEMPEST LE MANS — (SIX-CYL) — SERIES 237					
237	39	4d Hardtop-6P	$2,916	3,407 lbs.	9,002
237	27	2d Coupe-6P	$2,724	3,287 lbs.	8,439
237	37	2d Hardtop-6P	$2,786	3,302 lbs.	110,036
237	67	2d Convertible-6P	$3,015	3,377 lbs.	8,820

The 1968 Tempest line, this is a GTO, featured a large rear bumper with large rectangular taillights.

The GTO again featured distinct badging and styling.

Badging was found behind the front wheel openings on the 1968 GTO. The Endura nose was billed as safer and more durable than anything previously used by Pontiac.

TEMPEST SAFARI — (SIX-CYL) — SERIES 239

Model Number	Body/Style Number	Body Type & Seating	Factory Price	Shipping Weight	Production Total
239	35	4d Sta Wagon-6P	$3,017	3,677 lbs.	4,414

NOTE 5: 136,297 Le Mans cars were built.
NOTE 6: 12,233 Le Mans cars had synchromesh and 124,074 had automatic transmission.
NOTE 7: 122 Le Mans Safaris had synchromesh and 4,292 had automatic transmission.

GTO — (V-8) — SERIES 242

The GTO was down to two models for 1968. Both the hardtop coupe and the convertible were built on the shorter two-door Tempest wheelbase. The true distinction of the 1968 GTO was its Endura front end. This was truly a Pontiac innovation, as no other GM car had it at the time. It was also a look into the future. Although the early Endura plastic had its teething problems (paint discoloration issues) it would not be long before other models and makes were wearing similar frontal treatments. Since the Endura treatment was so radical at the time, Pontiac offered GTO buyers the option of getting their car with the standard chrome Tempest grille, since there was a shortage of Endura bumpers. In addition to the body-color nose, the GTO also came standard with hidden windshield wipers. Hidden headlights were also a very popular GTO option. The standard grille was comprised of four groups of eight short horizontal fins stacked on each other with the characteristic GTO lettering on the left-hand grille. If the car did not have Hide-Away (hidden) headlights, the twin round lights were outboard of the grille. On cars with the optional Hide-Away headlights, when the lights were "parked" in the hidden position, the rear of the unit faced the front and extended the grille with three

additional stacks of eight short fins. A new hood was used on the 1968 GTO. It had twin air scoops flowing out of the cowl. The hood air scoops had bolted-on, closed ornaments. However, the Ram Air package included open ornaments that had to be paint matched. Owners were advised to use the closed ornaments in rainy weather. A large bulge ran up the center of the hood and came to a point at the ship's prow nose. Standard in GTOs were: all GM safety features, dual exhausts, a three-speed manual transmission with Hurst shifter, sports-type springs and shock absorbers, redline tires, bucket or notchback armrest seats, a cigar lighter, carpeting, an ignition alarm, disappearing windshield

A deluxe steering wheel and Hurst shifter were among the standard features on the 1968 GTO.

Ads for the 1968 GTO boasted that there was only one "Great One."

The 400-cid V-8 was standard on the 1968 GTO.

Jerry Heasley photo

wipers, panel courtesy lights, an ashtray lamp, a glove box lamp, a deluxe steering wheel, and a 350-hp/400-cid four-barrel V-8 (or two barrel 400-cid regular fuel V-8). GTOs had the twin hood scoops, GTO grille badges, right-hand deck lid badges, a V-shaped badge behind each front wheel opening, a Pontiac arrowhead nose emblem, and distinct taillights.

Model Number	Body/Style Number	Body Type & Seating	Factory Price	Shipping Weight	Production Total
242	37	2d Hardtop-5P	$3,101	3,506 lbs.	77,704
242	67	2d Convertible-5P	$2,996	3,346 lbs.	9,980

NOTE 8: 87,684 GTOs were built.
NOTE 9: 36,299 had synchromesh and 51,385 had automatic.

ENGINES

TEMPEST, TEMPEST CUSTOM, LE MANS BASE OHC 250-CID SIX-CYL: Inline. Overhead valves. Cast-iron block. Displacement: 250 cid. Bore and stroke: 3.875 x 3.531 in. Compression ratio: 9.0:1. Brake hp: 175 at 4800 rpm. Torque: 240 lbs.-ft. at 2600 rpm. Hydraulic valve lifters. Crankcase capacity with oil filter: 5 qt. Cooling system capacity with heater: 12 qt. Carburetor: Rochester model 7028065 one-barrel.

TEMPEST, TEMPEST CUSTOM, LE MANS OPTIONAL OHC 250-CID SIX-CYL: Inline. Overhead valves. Cast-iron block. Displacement: 250 cid. Bore and stroke: 3.875 x 3.531 in. Compression ratio: 10.5:1. Brake hp: 215 at 4800 rpm. Torque: 255 lbs.-ft. at 3800 rpm. Hydraulic valve lifters. Crankcase capacity with oil filter: 5 qt. Cooling system capacity with heater: 12 qt. Carburetor: Rochester Quadrajet four-barrel.

TEMPEST, TEMPEST CUSTOM, LE MANS OPTIONAL REGULAR FUEL (RF) 350-CID V-8: Overhead valves. Cast-iron block. Displacement: 350 cid. Bore and stroke: 3.875 x 3.75 in. Compression ratio: 9.2:1. Brake hp: 265 at 4600 rpm. Torque: 355 lbs.-ft. at 2800 rpm. Hydraulic valve lifters. Crankcase capacity with oil filter: 5 qt. Cooling system capacity with heater: 19 1/2 qt. Carburetion: Rochester model 7028071 two-barrel.

GTO OPTIONAL "ECONOMY" 400-CID V-8: Overhead valves. Cast-iron block. Displacement: 400 cid. Bore and stroke: 4.125 x 3.75 in. Compression ratio: 8.6:1. Brake hp: 265 at 4600 rpm. Torque: 397 lbs.-ft. at 2400 rpm. Five main bearings. Hydraulic valve lifters. Crankcase capacity with oil filter: 5 qt. Cooling system capacity with heater: 19 1/2 qt. Carburetor: two-barrel.

TEMPEST, TEMPEST CUSTOM, LE MANS OPTIONAL H.O. 350-CID V-8: Overhead valves. Cast-iron block. Displacement: 350 cid. Bore and stroke: 3.875 x 3.75 in. Compression ratio: 10.5:1. Brake hp: 320 at 5100 rpm. Torque: 380 lbs.-ft. at 3200 rpm. Hydraulic valve lifters. Crankcase capacity with oil filter: 5 qt. Cooling system capacity with heater: 17 3/4 qt. Carburetion: Rochester four-barrel.

GTO BASE 400-CID V-8: Overhead valves. Cast-iron block. Displacement: 400 cid. Bore and stroke: 4.125 x 3.75 in. Compression ratio: 10.75:1. Brake hp: 350 at 5000 rpm. Torque: 445 lbs.-ft. at 3000 rpm. Five main bearings. Hydraulic valve lifters. Crankcase capacity with oil filter: 5 qt. Cooling system capacity with heater: 17 3/4 qt. Carburetor: Rochester model 7028266 four-barrel.

GTO OPTIONAL H.O. 400-CID V-8: Overhead valves. Cast-iron block. Displacement: 400 cid. Bore and stroke: 4.125 x 3.75 in. Compression ratio: 10.75:1. Brake hp: 360 at 5100 rpm. Torque: 445 lbs.-ft. at 3600 rpm. Five main bearings. Hydraulic valve lifters. Crankcase capacity with oil filter: 5 qt. Cooling system capacity with heater: 17 3/4 qt. Carburetor: Rochester Quadrajet four-barrel.

EARLY 1968 GTO OPTIONAL RAM AIR 400-CID V-8: Overhead valves. Cast-iron block. Displacement: 400 cid. Bore and stroke: 4.125 x 3.75 in. Compression ratio: 10.75:1. Brake hp: 360 at 5400 rpm. Torque: 445 lbs.-ft. at 3600. Five main bearings. Hydraulic valve lifters. Crankcase capacity with oil filter: 5 qt. Cooling system capacity with heater: 17 3/4 qt. Carburetor: Rochester Quadrajet four-barrel.

1968 1/2 GTO OPTIONAL RAM AIR 400-CID V-8: Overhead valves. Cast-iron block. Displacement: 400 cid. Bore and stroke: 4.125 x 3.75 in. Compression ratio: 10.75:1. Brake hp: 370 at 5500 rpm. Torque: 445 lbs.-ft. at 3900. Five main bearings. Hydraulic valve lifters. The later Ram Air V-8 featured tunnel-port cylinder heads, a 308/320-degree hydraulic camshaft, 1.50-to-1 rocker arms and lighter-weight valves. Carburetor: Rochester Quadrajet four-barrel.

CHASSIS

Wheelbase: (Tempest two-door) 112 in., (Tempest four-door) 116 in. Overall length: (Tempest station wagons) 211 in., (Tempest two-door) 200.7 in., (Tempest four-door) 204.7 in. Front tread: 60 in. Rear tread: 60 in. Turning diameter curb-to-curb: 40.9 ft. Fuel tank capacity: 21.5 gal.

OPTIONS

591 speedometer gear adapter ($11.59). 731 heavy-duty air cleaner ($9.48). 582 custom air conditioner ($360.20). 701 heavy-duty battery, included with all Tempest having four-barrel V-8; for others with OHC-6 without air conditioning ($4.21). 701 heavy-duty battery in all V-8s except base Tempest ($6.32). 511 Custom floor carpet in base Tempest ($18.96). 474 electric clock ($18.96). 514 heavy-duty seven-blade radiator fan in base Tempest without air conditioning or other Tempest V-8s without air conditioning ($15.80). 472 front seat console in base Tempest without contour bench seat ($50.55). 472 center console in GTO with Hydra-Matic ($68.46). 472 front seat console in Le Mans, except four-door hardtop, and GTO without Hydra-Matic ($52.66). 414 GTO retractable headlight covers ($52.66). 441 cruise control, requires V-8 and automatic transmission ($52.66). 401 foam front seat cushion, all Tempest, Tempest Custom, and Tempest Safari ($8.43). 392 remote-control deck lid release, except Safari ($13.69). 408 rear window air deflector on Safari ($26.33). 404 rear window defogger, all except Safari and convertible ($21.06). 361 Safe-T-Track differential ($42.13). 361 Safe-T-Track differential with H-K-P-S code axles ($63.19). 521 front disc brakes, requires option 502 power brakes on Safaris ($63.19). 342 Sprint OHC-6 with four-barrel carburetor, without air conditioning, includes three-speed manual transmission with floor shift, OHC-6 Sprint emblems, left- and right-hand body sill moldings and F70 x 14 black sidewall Wide-Oval tires ($116.16). 343 "RF" 350-cid two-barrel V-8, all except GTO ($105.60). 344 350-cid H.O. four-barrel V-8, all except GTO and Tempest Custom station wagon

($170.02). 342 400-cid four-barrel Ram Air V-8 in GTO only, not available with air conditioning ($342.29). 348 400-cid four-barrel H.O. V-8 in GTO ($76.88). 481 dual exhausts on base Tempest with "FR" V-8 or other Tempest/Le Mans models except the Tempest Custom station wagon, all with V-8s ($30.54). 482 exhaust extension for single exhaust V-8s ($10.53). 482 exhaust extension for dual exhaust V-8s ($21.06). 444 Rally Gauge cluster with tachometer ($84.26). 484 Rally Gauge cluster and clock ($50.55). 531 all windows tinted, except base Tempest ($34.76); base Tempest ($30.54). 532 tinted windshield, except base Tempest ($25.28); base Tempest ($21.06). 412 door edge guards on two-door models ($6.24); on four-door models ($10.41). 571 bucket seats, Le Mans sports coupe, hardtop and convertible and all GTOs ($84.26). 572 front bench seat ($42.13). 578 right-hand reclining bucket seat Le Mans two-door models and all GTOs ($84.26). 414 dual horns in base Tempest ($4.21). 524 custom gear shifter knob with all three- or four-speed manual transmission with floor shifter ($4.21). 671 under-hood lamp ($3.16). 664 glove box lamp, all Tempest and Tempest Customs ($3.16). 672 ignition switch lamp ($2.11). 652 luggage compartment lamp, except station wagon ($3.16). 651 cornering lamps ($33.70). 662 ashtray lamp in base Tempest and Tempest Custom ($3.16). 661 dash panel courtesy lamps in Tempest and Tempest Custom except convertibles ($4.21). 512 station wagon luggage carrier ($63.19). 631 front floor mats ($6.85). 632 rear floor mats ($6.32). 422 right- and left-hand visor-vanity mirrors, except convertibles ($4.21). 421 right-hand visor-vanity mirror ($2.11). 424 remote-control left-hand outside rearview mirror ($9.48). SPS special solid paint ($83.20). STT special color two-tone paint, except Safari and convertible ($123.22). STT special color two-tone paint on Safari ($99). RTT standard color two-tone paint, except Safari and convertible ($40.02). RTT standard color two-tone paint on Safari ($15.80). 502 power brakes ($42.13). 561 4-Way full-width power front seat ($69.51). 501 power steering ($94.79). 542 station wagon power tailgate window ($31.60). 564 left-hand 4-Way power front bucket seat ($69.51). 544 power convertible top, Tempest Custom convertible ($52.66). 551 power windows ($100.05). 381 power antenna, except Safaris ($29.49). 388 AM/FM stereo radio with manual antenna ($239,08). 394 stereo tape player, not available with rear seat speaker or reverb ($133.76). 382 push-button AM radio and antenna ($61.09). 384 push-button AM/FM radio with manual antenna ($133.76). 391 rear seat speaker in Safari ($21.06). 391 rear seat speaker, other models ($15.80). 392 rear seat reverb speaker, except Safari ($52.66). 494 Rally stripes on all GTOs ($10.53). 431 front and rear Custom seat belts in two-doors ($9.48). 431 front and rear Custom seat belts in four-doors ($13.69). 432 rear seat shoulder belts with options 431 and 754 only ($26.33) 754 front seat shoulder belts with Custom seat belts only ($26.33). 754 front shoulder belts without Custom seat belt option ($23.17). 634 Superlift rear shock absorbers ($42.13). 702 collapsible spare tire ($15.80). 442 Safeguard speedometer ($15.80). 621 Ride & Handling package, base Tempest without option 345 and others, except GTO, without option 342 ($9.48). 621 Ride & Handling package, base Tempest with option 345, GTO, and other models with option 342 ($4.21). 471 Custom Sports steering wheel in base Tempest with option 324 and all Tempest Custom, Le Mans and GTOs ($30.54). 471 Custom Sports steering wheel in base Tempest without option 324 ($45.29). 462 deluxe steering wheel in base Tempest ($14.74). 504 tilt-adjustable steering column, power steering required ($42.13). 434 hood-mounted tachometer ($63.19). 402 spare tire and wheel cover, except Safari or convertible ($5.27). SVT cordova top, except Safari or convertible ($94.79). 351 Turbo Hydra-Matic transmission in GTO ($236.97). 352 automatic transmission in other models ($194.84). 354 four-speed manual transmission with floor shift without option 341 or 37S axle ($184.31). 355 heavy-duty three-speed manual transmission with floor shift, all non-Sprint Tempests, except GTO, with option 341 ($42.13). 358 close-ratio four-speed manual transmission with floor shift, GTO with 37P axle ($184.31). 534 Custom trim pedal plates, all Tempest and Tempest Custom models ($5.27). 534 black coated-fabric pedal trim for Tempest with trim code 206 ($27.38). 458 Custom wheel discs for Tempest, Tempest Custom and Le Mans with option 324 ($20.01); without option 324 ($41.07). 461 deluxe wheel discs ($21.06). 452 wire wheel discs for Tempest and Tempest Custom and Le Mans with option 324 ($52.66);

without option 324 ($73.72). 453 Rally wheel rims for Tempest, Tempest Custom and Le Mans with option 324 ($63.19); without option 324 ($84.26). 411 recessed windshield wipers for Tempest and Tempest Custom ($18.96). 321 Basic Group including push-button radio, front foam cushion, electric clock, and heavy-duty air cleaner on Tempest, Tempest Custom, and Tempest Safari ($97.96); on Le Mans and GTO ($89.53). 324 Décor Group includes deluxe steering wheel, deluxe wheel discs, décor moldings, recessed windshield wipers and Custom pedal trim plates ($21-$83 depending on series and body style). 332 lamp group includes luggage lamp on passenger cars, panel courtesy lamps, except on convertible, glove box lamp, ashtray lamp and ignition switch lamp ($2.11-$15.80 depending on series and body style). 331 mirror group includes right- and left-hand visor-vanity mirrors, except convertible and remote-control left-hand outside rearview mirror ($9.45-$13.65 depending on model and body style). 322 Protection Group includes door edge guards, Custom seat belts, front and rear floor mats, rear window air deflector on Safaris, rear window defogger except in Safaris and convertibles and a spare wheel and tires cover ($34.10-$63.60 depending on model and body style). 342 Sprint option package includes front stabilizer, four-barrel OHC-6, three-speed manual transmission with floor shift, sport type shock absorbers, wheel opening moldings and Sprint stripes on two-door

This 1968 GTO sported Solar Red paint and a white convertible top.

Photo courtesy of Greg Walters

models ($105.65-$126.75 depending upon series and body style). TCB 7.75 x 14 rayon white sidewall tires ($31.66). TDA 8.25 x 14 rayon black sidewall tires ($14.75). TDB 8.25 x 14 rayon white sidewall tires ($40-$54.75 depending on model). TPC G70 x 14 nylon red line tires (no charge GTO, $67-$82 on other models). TPD G70 x 14 nylon white sidewall tires (no charge GTO, $67-$82 on other models). TRC G77 x 14 nylon red line tires on GTO (no charge). TRD G77 x 14 nylon white sidewall tires on GTO (no charge). TSM 205R x 14 rayon white sidewall tires ($10.50 on GTO, $82-$96 on other models).

OPTION INSTALLATION RATES

Of 346,406 Tempests built, 82.4 percent had automatic transmission, 10.6 percent had a four-speed synchromesh transmission, 84.7 percent had a V-8 engine, 15.3 percent had a six-cylinder engine, 90.3 percent had a AM radio, 37 percent had an air conditioner, 4 percent had a movable steering column, 84.3 percent had power steering, 38.3 percent had power drum brakes, 3.2 percent had front disc brakes, 1.1 percent had a power seat, 2.7 percent had power side windows, 2.4 percent had power station wagon rear window, 56.7 percent had bucket seats, 77.5 percent had white sidewall tires, 32.6 percent had a tinted windshield only, 33.4 percent had all tinted windows, 27.4 percent had dual exhausts, 12.7 percent had a limited-slip differential, 71.8 percent had full wheel discs, 0.6 percent had a speed regulating device, 4.99 percent had an AM/FM radio, 3.4 percent had a stereo tape player and 30.5 percent had a clock.

HISTORICAL FOOTNOTES

John Z. Delorean remained as general manager of Pontiac at the start of 1968, but F.J. McDonald replaced him at the end of the year. Production started Aug. 21, 1967.

The model introductions were Sept. 21, 1967. It turned out to be Pontiac's sixth straight year of increased sales. The delivery of 334,259 Tempests was a 13 percent increase from the previous year's 295,857. It represented 3.9 percent of total domestic auto sales for the second year in a row. On October 31, 1968, Pontiac assembled its 13,000,000 car, which was a 1969 Grand Prix. Model-year production of Tempests was 346,406 units compared to 301,069 the year earlier. Broken down by factory, the total included 135,514 cars built in Pontiac, Michigan; 17,114 cars built in Kansas City, Missouri; 39,668 cars made in Fremont, California, 43,618 cars made in Arlington, Texas, 51,169 cars built in Baltimore, Maryland, 59,203 cars made in Framingham, Massachusetts, and 120 cars built in one or more of these factories and shipped overseas from a GM facility in Bloomfield, New Jersey.

The GTO Endura nose was a feature that was standard on GTOs and optional on some Tempest models.. This was the first year for two wheelbases in the Tempest series, with four-doors on the longer chassis.

The 360-hp GTO hardtop did 0 to 60 mph in 6.6 seconds and the quarter-mile took 15.5 seconds. Pontiac and Sun Electric Corporation adapted diagnostic technology from the aircraft industry in 1968. This Sercon system permitted simultaneous checking of all the electrical systems in each Pontiac, which was said to involve three miles of wiring. Pontiac mechanics could plug a special instrument into the car to display system malfunctions in colored lights.

Also new were two anti-theft measures—the ignition key buzzer and visible-through-the-windshield VINs. Pontiac won *Motor Trend* magazine's "Car of the Year" award for the fourth time since 1959, and this honor was due largely to the innovations seen on the 1968 GTO.

Jerry Heasley photo

"The Judge" was originally planned as a no-frills muscle car, but by the time it debuted it was a flashy, unmistakable attention grabber, either in convertible or hardtop form.

The 1969 Tempest continued the basic styling introduced in 1968 with a new basket-weave grille insert, but without vent windows in hardtops and convertibles. The ship's prow nose protruded further out from the redesigned bottom bumper bar and the basket-weave pattern filled the enlarged openings in the sides of the nose. The Pontiac name was lettered across the left-hand grille insert and the twin side-by-side headlights, though still round in shape, were carried in square-shaped surrounds with rounded corners.

Base Tempest models still featured the 175-hp OHC-6. The Tempest Custom was renamed the Custom S and was designed to look expensive, but sell at a price the same as competitors without as much standard equipment. The LeMans was still one step up the equipment scale and the GTO was Pontiac's muscle car. Before 1969 was over, Pontiac came through with a surprise GTO model that was announced for a 1969 1/2 introduction. This high-performance "The Judge" was a version of the "Goat" that came as a hardtop coupe or a convertible It had a black grille, exposed headlights,

Pontiac produced 100,001 LeManses for 1969. The sporty midsize cars were available in convertible, coupe and four-door hardtop body styles.

functional Ram Air hood scoops, and a tri-color Rally stripe. The standard engine was a 366-hp Ram Air V-8, with a 370-hp version as an option.

I.D. NUMBERS

VIN on left top of instrument panel, visible through windshield. First symbol indicates GM division: 2=Pontiac. Second and third symbols indicate series: 33=Tempest, 35=Tempest Custom, 37=LeMans, 39=Tempest Safari, 42=GTO. Fourth and fifth symbols indicate body style and appear as last two symbols in body/style number column of charts below. Sixth symbol indicates model year: 9=1969. Seventh symbol tells assembly plant: A=Atlanta, Georgia, P=Pontiac, Michigan, R=Arlington, Texas, Z=Fremont, California, B=Baltimore, Maryland, K=Kansas City, Missouri, G=Framingham, Massachusetts. Following symbols are sequential production number starting with 100001 at each assembly plant. Body/style number plate under hood tells manufacturer, Fisher style number, assembly plant, trim code, paint code, accessory codes. Style number consists of 69 (for 1969) prefix and four symbols that appear in second column of charts below. First two

symbols indicate series. Second two symbols indicate body type. VIN appears on front of engine at right-hand cylinder bank along with an alphanumerical engine production code. Engine production codes included: (250-cid/175-hp one-barrel OHC six) ZC/ZF/ZK/ZN, (250-cid/230-hp four-barrel OHC six, passenger cars only) ZH/ZD, (350-cid/265-hp two-barrel regular-fuel V-8) WU/YU/XS/XR/YN/WP/WM YE XB/WC XL YJ, (350-cid/330-hp H.O. four-barrel V-8) WV/XU, (400-cid/265-hp two-barrel GTO regular-fuel V-8) XM/XX/YA/YB/YF, (400-cid/350-hp four-barrel GTO V-8) WT/YS, (400-cid/366-hp GTO four-barrel Ram Air V-8) WS/WW/YZ, and (400-cid/370-hp GTO four-barrel Ram Air IV V-8) XP.

COLORS

Paint codes for 1969 Tempests were: 10=Starlight Black, 50=Cameo White, 51=Liberty Blue, 52=Matador Red, 53=Warwick Blue, 55=Crystal Turquoise, 57=Midnight Green, 59=Limelight Green, 61=Expresso Brown, 63=Champagne, 65=Antique Gold, 67=Burgundy, 69-Palladium Silver, 73=Vedoro Green, and 87=Windward Blue. Vinyl top colors for 1969 Tempests were: 2=Black,

3=Dark Blue, 5=Parchment, 8=Dark Fawn and 9=Dark Green. Convertible top colors for 1969 Tempests were: 1=Ivory-White, 2=Black, 3=Dark Blue and 9=Dark Green. Interior trim codes for 1969 Tempests ands Tempest Customs were: 231= Blue cloth and vinyl, 232=Gold cloth and vinyl, 236=Green cloth and vinyl, 241=Blue vinyl, 242=Gold vinyl, 246=Green vinyl, 248=Black vinyl and 249=Black vinyl. Interior trim codes for 1969 LeMans were 250=Blue vinyl, 252=Gold vinyl, 254=Red vinyl, 256=Green vinyl, 257=Parchment vinyl, 258=Black vinyl, 260=Blue vinyl, 262=Gold vinyl, 266=Green vinyl, 267=Parchment vinyl, and 268=Black vinyl. Interior trim codes for 1969 GTOs were 250=Blue vinyl, 252=Gold vinyl, 254=Red vinyl, 256=Green vinyl, 257=Parchment vinyl, 258=Black vinyl, 267=Parchment vinyl with front bench seat, and 268=Black vinyl with front bench seat.

TEMPEST — (SIX-CYL) — SERIES 233

Standard equipment on base models included all GM safety features, carpets, Morrokide accented upholstery trims, and the 175-hp OHC-6. A Tempest script was placed on the leading edge of front fenders. The Tempest had rocker panel moldings and attractive Morrokide trimmed cloth upholstery. Artwork in the sales catalog depicted wheel lip moldings, but these were optional or available as part of other packages such as the Décor option or the Sprint option. The Sprint option, though not as heavily promoted in 1969, was still offered. It cost $126.72 to add it to the base Tempest sedan and $132 to add it to the base Tempest sports coupe. The package included the 230-hp OHC-6 with a four-barrel carburetor and chrome low-restriction air cleaner, a three-speed manual transmission with a floor-mounted gear shifter, a front stabilizer shaft, sport-type shock absorbers, wheel opening moldings, and Sprint side stripes on two-door models. The Sprint option was not available on cars with air conditioning.

Model Number	Body/Style Number	Body Type & Seating	Factory Price	Shipping Weight	Production Total
233	69	4d Sedan-6P	$2,557	3,250 lbs.	9,741
233	27	2d Coupe-6P	$2,510	3,180 lbs.	17,181

NOTE 1: 26,922 standard Tempests were built.
NOTE 2: 4,450 had synchromesh and 22,472 had automatic transmission.

TEMPEST CUSTOM S — (SIX-CYL) — SERIES 235

The one-step-up series was now called the Custom S series and front fender scripts used on all models carried this designation. Standard equipment included all

The convertible Judge had a starting price of $4,212. It included special paint, stripes and decals, heavy-duty suspension, Rally II wheels, and wide-tread tires.

Jerry Heasley photo

Tempest features, plus all-Morrokide upholstery, concealed windshield wipers, dual horns, an ignition buzzer, and panel courtesy lamps on convertibles. Small hubcaps were a regular feature. The Tempest Custom S could also be ordered with the Sprint option that was $126.72 on the four-door hardtop and $132 on sport coupes, two-door hardtops and convertibles (to cover the extra cost of the Sprint side stripes used on two-door models). The contents of the Sprint package were the same as for the base Tempest.

Model Number	Body/Style Number	Body Type & Seating	Factory Price	Shipping Weight	Production Total
235	69	4d Sedan-6P	$2,651	3,235 lbs.	16,532
235	39	4d Hardtop-6P	$2,777	3,315 lbs.	3,918
235	27	2d Coupe-6P	$2,603	3,210 lbs.	7,912
235	37	2d Hardtop-6P	$2,663	3,220 lbs.	46,886
235	67	2d Convertible-6P	$2,888	3,265 lbs.	2,379
235	35	4d Sta Wagon-6P	$2,956	5,696 lbs.	6,963

NOTE 3: 84,590 Tempest Custom S models were built.
NOTE 4: 4,045 Tempest S had synchromesh and 80,545 had automatic transmission.

TEMPEST LEMANS — (SIX-CYL) — SERIES 237 & 239

LeMans models incorporated all Custom S equipment, plus a deluxe three-spoke steering wheel, "pulse" windshield wipers, lamp packages, and several seating arrangement choices. LeMans block lettering appeared on the front fender tips and there were bright metal window and wheel opening moldings. Two-door models were available with bucket or notchback seats, four-door hardtop buyers had a choice of bench or notchback seats with center armrests. LeMans convertibles had power tops and Safaris had wood-grained exterior paneling and concealed headlights. The Sprint option was available for all LeMans models without air conditioning, except the Safari station wagon. The price was $110.88 on the four-door hardtop and $116.16 on any of the two-door body styles. The reason it cost less to make a LeMans into a Sprint is that wheel lip moldings were already included on the LeMans standard equipment list. The wood-trimmed Tempest Safari station wagon had Safari fender scripts. The Safari was not called a LeMans, but was close to a LeMans in its overall level of trim.

Model Number	Body/Style Number	Body Type & Seating	Factory Price	Shipping Weight	Production Total
237	69	4d Hardtop-6P	$2,965	3,360 lbs.	6,475
237	27	2d Coupe-6P	$2,773	3,225 lbs.	5,033
237	37	2d Hardtop-6P	$2,835	3,245 lbs.	82,817
237	67	2d Convertible-6P	$3,064	3,290 lbs.	5,676
TEMPEST SAFARI — (SIX-CYL) — SERIES 239					
239	36	4d Sta Wagon-6P	3,198	3,690	4,115

NOTE 5: 100,001 LeMans passenger cars were built.
NOTE 6: 6,303 LeMans passenger cars had synchromesh and 93,698 had automatic transmission.
NOTE 7: 86 Tempest Safaris had synchromesh and 4,029 had automatic transmission.

This parchment-and-black color combination made for a suitably eye-catching interior on the Judge.

Jerry Heasley photo

GTO — (V-8) — SERIES 242

GTOs were based on the LeMans, with additional standard equipment features. For 1969, the body styling was left pretty much alone, with only minor refinements, but a lot of exciting things took place under the hood. At midyear an exciting new model-option aimed at young performance buyers was introduced. Standard GTO equipment included a 400-cid/350-hp V-8, dual exhausts, a 3.55:1 rear axle ratio, a heavy-duty clutch, a three-speed gearbox with floor shifter, a Power-Flex cooling fan, sports type springs and shock absorbers, redline Wide-Oval tires, carpeting, a deluxe steering wheel, and a choice of bucket or notchback seats. An egg crate pattern grille insert with horizontal divider bars appeared and hidden headlights were again an option. The cover doors matched the grille pattern and worked by vacuum or could also be dropped by hand. This year every GTO was built with the body-color Endura rubber bumper and a chrome bumper was no longer an option. No Pontiac arrowhead emblem was carried on the nose this year. A fiberglass valance below the bumper wrapped around the body sides. GTOs used the same hood as last year. Cars with the Ram Air III V-8 wore "Ram Air" hood scoop decals; cars with the more powerful V-8 had "Ram Air IV" decals. Neither GTO model had ventipanes this year. GTO lettering was seen, on the lower left-hand grille, on the right-hand side of the deck lid and behind the front wheel openings. The lettering in the latter locations replaced the wedge-shaped emblems that had been on every previous GTO. However, the rear quarter panels carried side-marker lights that resembled the old emblem in shape and were distinct from the side-marker lights used on other Tempest models. The GTO taillights were no longer completely surrounded by bumpers and carried lenses with bright metal trim moldings. The twin narrow rectangular taillight lenses appeared to "float" between the bumper and the rear deck lid. The 400-cid H.O. V-8 was gone, but a 366-hp Ram Air option took its place as a factory option. It utilized the H.O. camshaft, but produced six additional horsepower. This engine became known as the Ram Air III V-8. It featured D-shaped cylinder head ports, special free-flowing exhaust manifolds, and a 308/320-degrees cam with 87 degrees of overlap. There was also a new Ram Air IV option that was very conservatively rated at 370 hp. This engine had large round exhaust port heads, redesigned exhaust manifolds, a chrome low-restriction air cleaner with an air tub, chrome rocker covers, a chrome oil filler cap, and a Power-Flex fan. It came only with 3.90:1 or 4.33:1 rear ends. A heavy-duty radiator and a limited-slip differential were mandatory options.

"The Judge" package was identified by decals in several locations, including the airfoil.

Model Number	Body/Style Number	Body Type & Seating	Factory Price	Shipping Weight	Production Total
242	37	2d Hardtop-5P	$2,831	3,080 lbs.	58,126
242	67	2d Convertible-5P	$3,382	3,553 lbs.	7,328

GTO "THE JUDGE" — (V-8) — SERIES 242

A special high-performance "The Judge" option (RPO

The hood tachometer was on the options list for the GTO. The Ram Air engine was identified by a hood badge.

Jerry Heasley photo

554 UPC WT1) was released Dec. 19, 1968. It included one of two available Ram Air V-8s as standard equipment as well as many other muscle car features. Though more expensive than base GTOs, a "The Judge" was the least expensive of several cars now on the market with comparable equipment. The "The Judge" started as a project to build a no-frills muscle car similar to the Plymouth Road Runner. It was originally planned as a 1969-only model and as sort of a spoof on muscle car with all the gimmicks. It was named for the popular "Here come de Judge" skits on the Rowan & Martin "Laugh-In" television comedy show. However, in its final form, Pontiac's "Judge" option was more expensive than it was first supposed to be. (In fact, the GT-37 of the early '70s was truer to the initial "Judge" concept.). Released as a $332.07 option package for the GTO hardtop or convertible, "The Judge" included the Ram Air III V-8, special paint colors, special emblems and stripes, a 60-in. wide rear deck air foil, a heavy-duty suspension, Rally II wheels and G70 x 14 Wide Tread fiberglass-belted black sidewall tires. The Judge was introduced in December 1968, but full-scale production began in January 1969 when the first of the initial batch of 2,000 Carousel Red cars was built. Due to a supplier not getting emblems to PMD in time, these cars did not have "The Judge" emblems on their glove box doors. When F.J. McDonald took over at Pontiac, it was decided to offer "The Judge" GTOs in other colors. A "The Judge" emblem was placed ahead of the front wheel cutouts and bold tri-color stripes decorated the beltline. The original Carousel Red cars had red, blue, and yellow stripes. Later Carousel Red cars had black, red, and yellow stripes. The Judge models painted Limelight Green, Midnight Green, Verdoro Green, or Mayfair Maize had white, yellow, and green stripes. Those painted Starlight Black, Cameo White, Warwick Blue, Liberty Blue, Crystal Turquoise, Palladium Silver, or Carousel Red had the red, yellow, and blue stripes. Cars done in Expresso Brown, Antique Gold, Burgundy, Matador Red, or Champagne had white, red, and black stripes. However, the factory was willing to produce cars that varied from these recommended combinations, so anything was possible. As with other GTOs, "The Judge" models with the 366-hp V-8 had "Ram Air" decals and those with the 370-hp V-8 had "Ram Air IV" decals. The airfoil used on the rear of the cars was slightly different for hardtops and convertibles, due to variances in the body panels of each model.

Model Number	Body/Style Number	Body Type & Seating	Factory Price	Shipping Weight	Production Total
242	37	2d Hardtop-5P	$3,161	NA	6,725
242	67	2d Convertible-5P	$4,212	NA	108

NOTE 8: 72,287 GTOs and "The Judge" optioned GTOs were built.
NOTE 9: 31,433 GTOs and Judges had synchromesh and 40,854 had automatic transmission.
NOTE 10: 8,491 GTOs and Judges (including 362 convertibles) had Ram Air III V-8s.
NOTE 11: Ram Air III engines were coded "YZ" or "WS".
NOTE 12: 759 GTOs and Judges (including 59 convertibles) had Ram Air IV V-8s.
NOTE 13: Ram Air IV engines were coded "XP" (automatic) or "WW" (synchromesh).

ENGINES

TEMPEST, TEMPEST CUSTOM, LEMANS BASE OHC 250-CID SIX-CYL: Inline. Overhead valves. Cast-

This Judge featured the 400-cid/366-hp Ram Air III engine. A 370-hp Ram Air IV was also available.

Jerry Heasley photo

iron block. Displacement: 250 cid. Bore and stroke: 3.875 x 3.531 in. Compression ratio: 9.0:1. Brake hp: 175 at 4800 rpm. Torque: 240 lbs.-ft. at 2600 rpm. Hydraulic valve lifters. Crankcase capacity with oil filter: 5 qt. Cooling system capacity with heater: 12 qt. Carburetor: Rochester model 7028065 one-barrel.

TEMPEST, TEMPEST CUSTOM, LEMANS OPTIONAL OHC 250-CID SIX-CYL: Inline. Overhead valves. Cast-iron block. Displacement: 250 cid. Bore and stroke: 3.875 x 3.531 in. Compression ratio: 10.5:1. Brake hp: 230 at 5400 rpm. Torque: 260 lbs.-ft. at 3600 rpm. Hydraulic valve lifters. Crankcase capacity with oil filter: 5 qt. Cooling system capacity with heater: 12 qt. Crankcase capacity with oil filter: 5 qt. Cooling system capacity with heater: 12 qt. Carburetor: Rochester one-barrel.

TEMPEST, TEMPEST CUSTOM, LEMANS OPTIONAL REGULAR FUEL (RF) 350-CID V-8: Overhead valves. Cast-iron block. Displacement: 350 cid. Bore and stroke: 3.875 x 3.75 in. Compression ratio: 9.2:1. Brake hp: 265 at 4600 rpm. Torque 355 lbs.-ft. at 2800 rpm. Hydraulic valve lifters. Crankcase capacity

The 1969 GTO didn't lack speed, styling, or creature comforts.

with oil filter: 5 qt. Cooling system capacity with heater: 19.5 qt. Carburetion: Rochester two-barrel.

TEMPEST, TEMPEST CUSTOM, LEMANS OPTIONAL H.O. 350-CID V-8: Overhead valves. Cast-iron block. Displacement: 350 cid. Bore and stroke: 3.875 x 3.75 in. Compression ratio: 10.5:1. Brake hp: 330 at 5100 rpm. Torque: 380 lbs.-ft. at 3200 rpm. Hydraulic valve lifters. Crankcase capacity with oil filter: 5 qt. Cooling system capacity with heater: 19.5 qt. Carburetion: Four-barrel.

GTO OPTIONAL "ECONOMY" 400-CID V-8: Overhead valves. Cast-iron block. Displacement: 400 cid. Bore and stroke: 4.125 x 3.75 in. Compression ratio: 8.6:1. Brake hp: 265 at 4600 rpm. Torque: 397 lbs.-ft. at

2400 rpm. Five main bearings. Hydraulic valve lifters. Crankcase capacity with oil filter: 5 qt. Cooling system capacity with heater: 19 1/2 qt. Carburetor: Four-barrel.

GTO BASE 350-CID V-8: Overhead valves. Cast-iron block. Displacement: 400 cid. Bore and stroke: 4.125 x 3.75 in. Compression ratio: 10.75:1. Brake hp: 350 at 5000 rpm. Torque: 445 lbs.-ft. at 3000 rpm. Five main bearings. Hydraulic valve lifters. Crankcase capacity with oil filter: 5 qt. Cooling system capacity with heater: 19 1/2 qt. Low-back-pressure dual exhausts. Power-Flex fan. Chrome air cleaner. Chrome rocker covers. Chrome oil filler cap. Carburetor: Rochester model 7028266 four-barrel.

GTO OPTIONAL RAM AIR III 400-CID V-8: V-8.

Overhead valves. Cast-iron block. Displacement: 400 cid. Bore and stroke: 4.125 x 3.75 in. Compression ratio: 10.75:1. Brake hp: 366 at 5100 rpm. Torque: 445 lbs.-ft. at 3600 rpm. Five main bearings. Hydraulic valve lifters. Crankcase capacity with oil filter: 5 qt. Cooling system capacity with heater: 19 1/2 qt. Special dual exhausts. High-output camshaft and valve train. Chrome low-restriction air cleaner with air trap. Chrome rocker covers. Chrome oil filler cap Power-Flex fan. Carburetor: Rochester four-barrel.

GTO OPTIONAL RAM AIR IV 400-CID V-8: Overhead valves. Cast-iron block. Displacement: 400 cid. Bore and stroke: 4.125 x 3.746 in. Compression ratio: 10.75:1. Brake hp: 370 at 5500 rpm. Torque: 445 lbs.-ft. at 3900 rpm. Five main bearings. Hydraulic valve lifters. Crankcase capacity with oil filter: 5 qt. Cooling system capacity with heater: 19 1/2 qt. Low-back-pressure dual exhausts. Special functional air scoop induction system. High-output long-overlap camshaft. Heavy-duty valve springs. Chrome low-restriction air cleaner with air trap attachment. Chrome rocker covers. Chrome oil filler cap. Carburetor: Rochester four-barrel. Mandatory options with the Ram Air IV V-8 included a Turbo Hydra-Matic automatic transmission or a four-speed manual transmission, a heavy-duty radiator, and a limited-slip differential.

CHASSIS

Wheelbase: (Tempest two-door) 112 in., (Tempest four-door) 116 in. Overall Length: (all Tempest station wagons) 211 in., (Tempest two-door) 201.5 in., (Tempest four-door) 205.5 in. Width: 75.8 in. Height: (Tempest) 52.7 in.; (LeMans) 52.1 in. Front headroom: (Tempest) 38.5 in., (LeMans) 37.5 in. Rear headroom: (Tempest) 37.1 in, (LeMans) 36.2 in. Front legroom: (Tempest) 42.3 in., (LeMans) 42.5 in. Rear legroom: (Tempest) 34.8 in., (LeMans) 31.6 in. Front hiproom: (Tempest) 59.8 in., (LeMans) 59.7 in. Rear hiproom: (Tempest) 59.1 in., (LeMans) 58.8 in. Trunk capacity: 14.6 cu. ft. Turn circle: 38.6 ft. Front tread: 61 in. Rear tread: 61 in. (Note: All height, width, interior space and luggage space dimensions are for four-door sedan.)

OPTIONS

591 speedometer gear adapter ($11.59). 731 heavy-duty air cleaner, not available with H.O. or Ram Air V-8s ($9.48). 582 Custom air conditioner, not available with Sprint option or H.O. V-8 ($375.99). 444 auxiliary gauge panel ($36.86). 362 special order axle ($2.11) 364-368 economy or performance axles ($2.11) 672 heavy-duty battery with OHC six or Sprint six, not available with air conditioning ($4.21). 672 heavy-duty battery in Tempest V-8 ($6.32). 522 Custom floor carpets in base Tempest ($18.96). 492 electric clock, not available with Rally gauge cluster and included with auxiliary gauge panel ($18.96). 472 front seat center console, all LeMans except four-door hardtop and all GTO without Turbo Hydra-Matic transmission ($55.82). 472 front seat center console in GTO with Turbo Hydra-Matic

transmission ($71.62). 441 cruise control, with V-8 only ($57.93). 401 front seat foam cushion, except GTO ($8.43). 492 remote-control rear deck lid, except Safari ($14.70). 404 rear window defogger, except Safari and convertible ($22.15). 361 Safe-T-Track differential ($42.13-$63.19). 481 dual exhausts for Tempest V-8s except GTO and Tempest Custom Safari ($30.54). 341 OHC six-cylinder engine (no charge). 343 350-cid regular-fuel two-barrel V-8 (($110.59). 344 350-cid H.O. four-barrel V-8 all except GTO and Tempest Custom Safari, includes dual exhausts and requires Ride & Handling package ($175.35). 345 400-cid two-barrel GTO economy V-8 (no charge). 346 400-cid regular-fuel

The 1969 Tempest featured a front end with a slightly bigger nosepiece and a redesigned bumper with basket-weave grille pattern.

The LeMans had bright metal window and wheel opening moldings.

two-barrel V-8 in GTO with Turbo Hydra-Matic transmission (no charge). 347 400-cid Ram Air IV four-barrel V-8, requires Ride & Handling package, not available with air conditioning or heavy-duty three-speed manual transmission ($558.26). 482 exhaust extensions with single exhaust ($10.50); with dual exhaust ($21.05). 691 heavy-duty seven-blade fan and clutch, not available with OHC six, Sprint, Ram Air IV or air conditioning ($15.80). 692 heavy-duty variable-pitch fan, not available with OHC six, Sprint, Ram Air IV or air conditioning ($10.53). 534 Custom gearshift knob with three- or four-speed manual transmission ($5.27). 531

Hidden headlights debuted in 1968, and were carried over to the 1969 GTO.

Daniel B. Lyons photo

Soft-Ray tinted glass ($36.86). 532 Soft-Ray tinted windshield ($26.33). 412 door edge guards on two-door ($6.32); four-doors ($10.53). 414 dual horns on base Tempest ($4.21). 694 Instant Aire, not available with Ram Air IV V-8 ($15.80). 662 ashtray lamp ($3.16). 651 cornering lamp ($33.70). 664 glove box lamp ($3.16). 652 luggage compartment lamp ($3.16).661 instrument panel courtesy lamp, standard in convertibles ($4.21). 671 under-hood lamp ($4.21). 524 luggage carrier, Tempest Safari ($63.19). 631 pair of front floor mats ($6.85). 632 pair of rear floor mats ($6.32). 732 luggage compartment throw mats, except Safaris ($8.43). 431/432 right- or left-hand visor-vanity mirrors ($2.11). 424 remote-control left-hand outside rearview mirror ($10.53). 494 wheel opening moldings for Tempest and Tempest Custom models ($15.80). RTT standard two-tone paint, all except convertible and Safari ($40.02). STT special two-tone paint except Safari and convertible ($152.71). SPS special color solid paint all models except convertibles or with cordova top ($115.85). SPS special color solid paint on convertible or models with cordova top ($100.05). 381 rear power antenna, all except Safari ($31.60). 502 Wonder Touch power brakes, all except GTO, included in front disc brakes ($42.13). 511 front disc brakes, includes Wonder Touch power brakes ($64.25). 541 power door locks on two-door ($45.29); on four-door ($68.46). 4-Way power full bench front seat ($73.72) 564 4-Way power left-hand front bucket seat ($73.72). 501 Wonder Touch power steering, except GTO ($100.05); GTO ($115.85). 544 power convertible top on Tempest Custom convertible ($52.66). 542 power tailgate window ($34.76). 551 power windows ($105.32). 382 push-button AM radio with manual front antenna ($61.09). 383 AM/FM radio with manual front antenna ($133.76). 391 rear speaker, except Safari ($15.85). 392 reverb rear speaker ($52.65). 444 Rally gauge cluster and tachometer, not available with Safeguard speedometer or Rally gauges with clock ($84.20). 484 Rally gauge cluster and clock, not available with Safeguard speedometer or Rally gauge cluster with tachometer ($50.55). 494 Rally stripes for GTO ($13.65). 414 retractable headlamp covers for GTO ($52.60). 442 Safeguard speedometer, not available with Rally gauge clusters ($15.80). 431 deluxe front and rear seat belts and front shoulder belts ($12.64-$36.86 depending on model). 432 deluxe front and rear seat belts and front and rear shoulder belts ($38.97-$63.19 depending on model). 434 deluxe front and rear seat belts in convertible ($10.53). 438 deluxe front shoulder belts in convertibles ($23.16). 578 right-hand reclining bucket seats ($42.15). 621 Ride & Handling package on Tempest, Tempest Custom, and LeMans with Sprint option and all GTOs ($4.21). 621 Ride & Handling package on Tempest, Tempest Custom, and LeMans without Sprint option ($9.48). 461 deluxe steering wheel, in base Tempest ($15.80). 462 Custom steering wheel, in base Tempest with Sprint option ($34.76); without Sprint option ($50.55). 504 tilt steering with power steering ($45.29). 544 dual-hinge tailgate on Tempest Custom Safari ($42.13). 471 hood-mounted tachometer, without Rally gauge cluster with tachometer ($63.19). TCB 7.75 x 14 white sidewall tires ($31.60). TDA 8.25 x 14 black sidewall tires ($14.74, but no charge on some models). TDB 8.25 x 15 white sidewall tires ($40.02-$54.77 depending on model). TRC/D G78 x 14 red line or white line tires ($50.35-$65.30 depending on model and no charge on GTO). TRT/RR G78 x 14 red line or white line fiberglass-belted tires (from $26.33 on GTO to $91.63 on other models). TPT/PR G70 x 14 red line or white line fiberglass-belted tires (from $57.93 on

1967 LeMans convertibles were equipped with power tops.

Paul Zazerine collection

Daniel B. Lyons photo

The Judge package may have grabbed the headlines in 1969, but the standard GTOs were also fabulous cars.

GTO to $112.69 on other models). 704 Space-Saver spare tire (no charge to $15.80 depending on model). 402 spare tire and wheel cover ($5.27). SVT cordova top, except Safari and convertible ($100.05). 352 automatic transmission in Tempest with OHC six ($174.24); in Tempest with 350-cid regular-fuel two-barrel V-8 ($184.80). 354 four-speed manual transmission in Tempest V-8 without 37S or 37P axle ($184.80). 355 heavy-duty three-speed manual transmission with floor-mounted gear shifter, except ($84.25); in GTO (no charge). 356 three-speed manual transmission with floor-mounted gear shifter in Tempest with OHC six, option 472 required and included in Sprint option ($42.13). 358 close-ratio four-speed manual transmission in Tempests except GTO with 37P or 37S axle teamed with 350-cid H.O. V-8 and all GTOs with 37P or 37S axle ($184.80). 351 Turbo Hydra-Matic transmission in Tempests with 350-cid regular-fuel V-8 teamed with air conditioning, or H.O. V-8, and all GTOS ($227.04). 359 Turbo Hydra-Matic in Tempest with OHC six ($195.36); in Tempest with 350-cid regular-fuel V-8 and no air conditioning ($205.92). 514 brake pedal trim package in Tempest and Tempest Custom ($5.27). Black coated fabric trim in models 23327 and 23360 with trim code 49 ($27.38). 588 power flow-thru ventilation ($42.44-$57.95 depending on model). 451 deluxe wheel covers on base Tempest ($21.06). 452 Custom wheel covers (($20.01-$51.61 depending on model and other equipment). 453 wire wheel covers ($52.66-($73.72 depending on model and other options). 454 Rally II wheels ($63.19-$84.26 depending on model and other options). 408 Safari rear window air deflector ($26.33). 521 Artic windshield wiper blades ($6.32). 411 recessed windshield wipers on Tempest and Tempest Custom models ($18.96). 321 Basic Group includes: push-button radio, front foam seat cushion, visor-vanity mirror, remote-control left-hand outside rearview mirror, electric clock, remote control deck lid, and heavy-duty air cleaner, unless standard ($107.43-$150.61 depending on model and other equipment). 322 lamp group includes cornering lamps, luggage lamp on passenger cars, panel courtesy lamps, except on convertible, glove box lamp, ashtray lamp, and ignition switch lamp ($37.91-$51.60 depending on model). 324 Décor Group includes: recessed windshield wipers if not standard, deluxe wheel discs, deluxe steering wheel, décor moldings and brake pedal trim package ($21.06-$91.63, depending upon model and other equipment). 331 Power Assist Group includes: Turbo Hydra-Matic transmission, power steering, and front disc brakes ($359.66-$396.61 depending on model and other equipment). 334 Rally Group includes: Rally II wheels, Custom sport steering wheel, Rally gauge cluster, and Ride & Handling package ($152.71-$194.84, depending on model and other equipment). 342 Sprint option package includes: front stabilizer, four-barrel OHC six-cylinder engine, three-speed manual transmission with floor shift, sport-type shock absorbers, wheel opening moldings, and Sprint stripes on two-door models, not available with air conditioning ($110.88-$132.00, depending upon model). 332 Turnpike Cruise Group, includes cruise control, tilt-adjustable steering column, 4-Way power bench seat or 4-Way power left-hand front bucket seat ($176.90-$208.50, depending on model and other equipment). 554 GTO "The Judge" option package included the Ram Air III V-8, special paint colors, special decals and stripes, a 60-inch-wide rear deck air foil, heavy-duty suspension, Rally II wheels, and G70 x 14 Wide Tread fiberglass-belted black sidewall tires ($332.07).

OPTION INSTALLATION RATES

Of 284,244 Tempests built, 83.9 percent had automatic transmission, 10.5 percent had a four-speed synchromesh transmission, 25.1 percent had a standard V-8 engine, 63.1 percent had a standard V-8 engine, 11.8 percent had a six-cylinder engine, 89.7 percent had a AM radio, 5.2 percent had an AM/FM radio, 3.4 percent had a stereo tape player, 3.5 percent had a power antenna, 88.9 percent had power steering, 22.5 percent had power drum brakes, 26.7 percent had front disc brakes, 0.4 percent had power door locks, 1.1 percent had a power seat, 2.7 percent had power side windows, 2.8 percent had power station wagon tailgate window, 45.4 percent had an air conditioner, 3.3 percent had a movable steering column, 54.2 percent had bucket seats, 44.9 percent had a vinyl roof, 79.1 percent had white sidewall tires, 31.3 percent had a tinted windshield only, 40.1 percent had all tinted windows, 27 percent had dual exhausts, 13.8 percent had a limited-slip differential, 66.4 percent had optional full-wheel discs, 0.5 percent had a speed regulating device, 1.3 percent had a station wagon luggage rack, 0.5 percent had reclining front seats, and 25.2 percent had a clock.

HISTORICAL FOOTNOTES

F.J. McDonald took over from John Z. DeLorean at the end of 1968 and was the general manager at Pontiac Motor Division during calendar-year 1969. DeLorean was in inspiration behind the flamboyant GTO "The Judge" option, which symbolized the end of his tenure at Pontiac Motor Division. DeLorean became the general manager of Chevrolet, which represented a promotion at General Motors.

Production of 1969 Tempests began on August 26, 1968. Dealer introductions took place exactly a month later. This was to be Pontiac's last year as America's third-ranking automaker in the 1960s and it was not a good one for the Tempest, either. Sales of the Pontiac intermediate declined by 19.5 percent to 269,177 units, which represented a 3.18 percent share of market. Tempest production in the U.S. dropped more than 20 percent from 352,878 units in 1968 to 287,915 cars for 1969. Production included 22,084 cars manufactured in Pontiac, Michigan; 32,957 Tempests assembled in Fremont, California; 37,526 A-bodies built in Atlanta, Georgia; 41,886 intermediates made in Arlington, Texas, 65,358 units produced in Framingham, Massachusetts and 88,104 built-in-Baltimore cars. An additional 12,139 Tempests were built in Canada and shipped to the U.S.

The 370-hp GTO Judge hardtop could do 0 to 60 mph in 6.2 seconds and the quarter-mile in 14.5 seconds. The 1969 GTO was the official car of the U.S. Ski Team.

Daniel B. Lyons photo

The GTO Judge package came in a wide variety of color combinations. This striking 1970 Judge is decked out in Palisade Green with bright tri-color accents.

With a lineup of 15 models in six series now named Tempest, Tempest T-37, Tempest GT-37, LeMans, LeMans Sport, and GTO, the Pontiac intermediate models sported new Firebird-like bumper grilles, wraparound front parking lights, wraparound taillights, crease sculptured side styling, body-color nose panels, and a new standard overhead-valve six-cylinder engine. The V-8 engine offerings included 350- and 400-cid

options and, for the GTO, a big 455-cid power plant. All models were equipped with glass-belted tires and side guard door beams.

I.D. NUMBERS

VIN on top of dash at left, viewable through windshield. First symbols tell GM division: 2=Pontiac. Second and third symbols tell series: 33=Tempest/T-37, 35=LeMans, 37=LeMans Sport, 42=GTO. Fourth and fifth symbols indicate body style and appear as last two digits of body/style number in charts below. Sixth symbol indicates model year: 0=1970. Seventh symbol indicates assembly plant: B=Baltimore, Maryland, P=Pontiac, Michigan, R=Arlington, Texas, Z=Fremont, California, 1=Oshawa, Ontario Canada. Remaining symbols are sequential unit production numbers at factory, starting with 100001. Fisher Body plate on cowl tells style number: (model year prefix 70, plus number in second column of charts below), body number, trim code, paint code and other data. Six-cylinder engine code stamped on distributor mounting on right side of block. V-8 engine code on front of block below right cylinder head. Engine production codes for 1970 were: (250-cid/155-hp six) CG/RF/ZB/ZG, (350-cid/255-hp V-8) WU/YU/W7/X7, (400-cid/265-hp V-8) XX/YB, WE/YD. (400-cid/330-hp V-8) WT/YS/XV/XZ, (400-cid/350-hp V-8) WT/YS, (400-cid/366-hp V-8) WS/YZ, (400-cid/370-hp V-8) WW/XP, and (455-cid/360-hp V-8) YA/WA.

COLORS

Paint codes for 1970 Tempests were: 10=Polar White, 14=Palladium Silver, 19=Starlight Black, 25=Bermuda Blue, 26=Lucerne Blue, 28=Atoll Blue, 34=Mint Turquoise, 43=Keylime Green, 45=Palisade Green, 47=Verdoro Green, 48=Pepper Green, 50=Sierra Yellow, 51=Goldenrod Yellow, 53=Coronado Gold, 55=Baja Gold, 58=Granada Gold, 63=Palomino Copper, 67=Castillian Bronze, 75=Cardinal Red, 78=Burgundy, and 60=Orbit Orange. Vinyl top colors for 1970 Tempests were: 1=White, 2=Black, 5=Sandalwood, 7=Dark Gold, and 9=Dark Green. Convertible top colors for 1970 Tempests were: 1=White, 2=Black, 5=Sandalwood, and 7=Dark Gold. Interior trim codes for Tempests and T-37s were: 239=Black cloth and vinyl, 230=Black cloth and vinyl, 232=Ivory vinyl, 231=Dark Blue cloth and vinyl, 236=Dark Jade cloth, 236=Dark Jade vinyl, 237=Sandalwood cloth or vinyl, 238=Sandalwood vinyl. Interior trim codes for LeMans models were 241=Dark Blue cloth and vinyl, 245=Dark Jade cloth and vinyl, 247=Sandalwood cloth and vinyl, 249=Black cloth and vinyl, 251=Dark Blue vinyl, 252=Ivory vinyl, 253=Dark saddle vinyl, 256=Dark Jade vinyl, 257=Sandalwood vinyl, 259=Black vinyl bucket seats, 261=Dark Blue vinyl bucket seats, 262=Ivory vinyl bucket seats, 263=Dark Saddle vinyl bucket seats, 264=Dark Sienna vinyl bucket seats, 266=Dark Jade vinyl bucket seats, 267=Sandalwood vinyl bucket seats, and 269=Black vinyl bucket seats. Interior trim codes for GTO models were 254=Dark Red, 261=Dark Blue vinyl bucket seats, 262=Ivory vinyl bucket seats, 263=Dark Saddle vinyl bucket seats, 264=Dark Sienna vinyl bucket seats, 266=Dark Jade vinyl bucket seats, 267=Sandalwood vinyl bucket seats, 269=Black vinyl bucket seats, 277=Sandalwood vinyl notchback or 60/40 seat, and 279=Black vinyl notchback or 60/40 seat.

The interior of the 1970 GTO in Dark Red with deluxe steering wheel.

Jerry Heasley photo

TEMPEST — (SIX-CYL) — SERIES 233

Standard equipment included: front door armrests, panel courtesy lamps, an ashtray lamp, a cigar lighter lamp, a 37-amp Delcotron, dome lamps, automatic interior lamp switches, an in-the-windshield hidden antenna, wraparound side reflex markers, cloth-and-Morrokide upholstery, fiberglass-belted black sidewall tires, and side guard door beams. Tempest lettering was carried behind the front wheel openings.

Model Number	Body/Style Number	Body Type & Seating	Factory Price	Shipping Weight	Production Total
233	69	4d Sedan-6P	$2,670	3,295 lbs.	20,883
233	37	2d Hardtop-6P	$2,750	3,360 lbs.	Note 1
233	27	2d Coupe-6P	$2,623	3,225 lbs.	Note 2

NOTE 1: Total production of Tempest, T-37 and GT-37 two-door hardtops combined was 9,187.
NOTE 2: Total production of Tempest and Tempest GT-37 two-door coupes combined was 11,977.

TEMPEST T-37 — (SIX-CYL) — SERIES 233 (MIDYEAR ADDITION)

In February 1970, the cut-price Tempest T-37 hardtop coupe was introduced. According to Pontiac's Official Historian John Sawruk, the T-37 was an attempt to have a Pontiac that was less expensive than a Chevrolet. It was "de-contented" to have less standard equipment than a base Tempest. The T-37 was, in fact, the lowest-priced General Motors hardtop at the time it was offered. John Sawruk describes the car as a "big mistake," but credits it with siring the GT-37. The "T" stood for "Tempest" and "37" was the Fisher body style designation for a two-door hardtop. Standard equipment on the T-37 included cloth-and-Morrokide front and rear bench seats, a vinyl floor covering, a deluxe steering wheel, upper-level ventilation, a black-grained instrument panel, door-operated dome lamp switches, conventional roof drip moldings, conventional windshield and rear window reveal moldings, dual-speed parallel-action windshield wipers, front disc brakes, E78-14 black sidewall tires, and the 250-cid six-cylinder engine.

Model Number	Body/Style Number	Body Type & Seating	Factory Price	Shipping Weight	Production Total
T-37	37	2d Hardtop Cpe-6P	$2,683	3,250 lbs.	Note 1

NOTE 1: Total production of Tempest, T-37 and GT-37 two-door hardtops combined was 9,187.

TEMPEST GT-37 — (V-8) — SERIES 233 (MIDYEAR ADDITION)

The 1970 1/2 Tempest T-37 hardtop coupe was followed by the appearance of the GT-37 two-door hardtop and coupe. A GT-37 represented the "stripper" muscle car that Pontiac's "The Judge" first set out to be. Standard GT-37 extras included vinyl accent stripes, Rally II wheels less trim rings, G70 x 14 white letter tires, dual exhausts with chrome extensions, a heavy-duty three-speed manual transmission with a floor-mounted gear shifter, hood-locking pins, and GT-37 decal.

Model Number	Body/Style Number	Body Type & Seating	Factory Price	Shipping Weight	Production Total
GT-37	37	2d Hardtop Cpe-6P	$2,920	3,360 lbs.	Note 1
GT-37	27	2d Coupe-6P	$2,907	3,300 lbs.	Note 2

NOTE 1: Total production of Tempest, T-37 and GT-37 two-door hardtops combined was 9,187.
NOTE 2: Total production of Tempest and Tempest GT-37 two-door coupes combined was 11,977.
NOTE 3: 1,419 GT-37s (hardtops and coupes) were built.
NOTE 4: 42,047 Tempests of all types were built.
NOTE 5: 5,148 Tempests had synchromesh and 36,899 had automatic transmission.

LEMANS — (SIX-CYL) — SERIES 235

LeMans nameplates were now attached to the mid-priced Tempests, which were formerly called Custom of Custom S models. Added extras included loop-pile carpets, Morrokide seats and sides, day/night rearview mirrors, and rear armrests with ashtrays. Styling included body décor moldings, LeMans rear fender lettering and LeMans block letters on the right-hand edge of the deck lid.

Model Number	Body/Style Number	Body Type & Seating	Factory Price	Shipping Weight	Production Total
235	69	4d Sedan-6P	$2,782	3,315 lbs.	15,255
235	39	4d Hardtop-6P	$2,921	3,385 lbs.	3,872
235	27	2d Coupe-6P	$2,735	3,240 lbs.	5,656
235	37	2d Hardtop-6P	$2,795	3,265 lbs.	52,304
235	35	4d Sta Wagon-6P	$3,092	3,585 lbs.	7,165

NOTE 6: 84,252 LeMans were made.
NOTE 7: 2,315 LeMans had synchromesh and 81,937 had automatic transmission.

LEMANS SPORT — (SIX-CYL) — SERIES 237

The "high-rung" Tempest line was now identified as the LeMans Sport series and had a "Sport" script below the rear fender model lettering. Standard equipment included all LeMans features plus: four short horizontal chrome slashes behind the front wheel openings, glove compartment and ashtray lamps, front foam cushions, knit and expanded Morrokide trim, and padded wood-grained dashboards. Four-door hardtops had notch-back seats, while hardtop coupes and convertibles had bucket seats or notch-back bench seats. The LeMans Sport Safari had exterior wood trim.

Model Number	Body/Style Number	Body Type & Seating	Factory Price	Shipping Weight	Production Total
237	39	4d Hardtop-6P	$3,083	3,405 lbs.	3,657
237	27	2d Coupe-6P	$2,891	3,265 lbs.	1,673

A 1970 Judge convertible in Sierra Yellow.

Jerry Heasley photo

Jerry Heasley photo

This Judge was a later-production 1970 model, as evidenced by the "eyebrows" above the wheel openings.

237	37	2d Hardtop-6P	$2,953	3,290 lbs.	58,356
237	67	2d Convertible-6P	$3,182	3,330 lbs.	4,670
237	36	4d Sta Wagon-6P	$3,328	3,775 lbs.	3,872

NOTE 8: 72,179 LeMans Sports were built.
NOTE 9: 3,413 LeMans Sports had synchromesh and 68,766 had automatic transmission.

GTO — (V-8) — SERIES 242

The GTO utilized Tempest sheet metal combined with a standard Endura rubber nose. Twin oval cavities housed recessed grilles with GTO letters on the left-hand insert. There was also GTO lettering behind the front wheel openings and flared, crease-sculptured fenders. The twin, side-by-side headlights again had round lenses in round-cornered square housings. Rectangular parking lights were under the headlights in either end of a bumper valance that had twin air openings (one on either side of a center divider to which the front license plate was affixed). At the rear end the wraparound taillights, which were embedded in the bumper, were narrow and wide enough to stretch from the bumper corners to the center-located license plate recess. The 400-cid two-barrel "economy" V-8 was dropped. The standard engine was again the 400-cid four-barrel, now rated at 350 hp. In addition to the optional Ram Air III and Ram Air IV V-8s, buyers could order a 455-cid V-8 with 500 lbs.-ft. of torque. This engine was fast off the line, but could not match the top speed of the 400-cid V-8. Standard equipment included bucket seats, a vinyl

trimmed padded dashboard, a twin-air scoop hood (the same as the 1969 hood), a heavy-duty clutch, sports-type springs and shock absorbers, carpeting, a glove box lamp, an ashtray lamp, panel courtesy lamps, dual exhausts, a deluxe steering wheel, a three-speed manual floor shift, G78 x 14 black sidewall fiberglass-belted tires and, for the first time on a GTO, a rear suspension sway bar. Coupe and convertible models were offered again. The Ram Air options were available and came in a package that included other items and appropriate hood scoop decals. GTOs could also be ordered with an optional striping package that was modified during the model year. Early cars had stripes much like those used on 1970 GTOs with "The Judge" option. Later cars had "eyebrows" above the wheel openings. Interiors were only slightly changed from 1969. Firestone, Goodyear, or U.S. Royal tires were standard equipment and came in a choice of single- or dual-white-stripe designs.

Model Number	Body/Style Number	Body Type & Seating	Factory Price	Shipping Weight	Production Total
242	37	2d Hardtop-5P	$3,267	3,641 lbs.	32,737
242	67	2d Convertible-5P	$3,492	3,691 lbs.	3,615

GTO "THE JUDGE" — (V-8) — SERIES 242 + WT-1

A Code 332-WT1 "The Judge" option was again available at $337 over base model price. It included the 400-cid

Ram Air V-8, Rally II wheels less trim rings, G70 x 14 fiberglass black sidewall tires, rear deck air foil, side stripes, Judge stripes and decals, black textured grilles, and T-handle shifters (on cars with manual gearboxes). GTOs with the 1971 "The Judge" package were available in all regular colors as well as a special Orbit Orange hue introduced at midyear. GTOs with "The Judge" option finished in Palomino Copper, Baja Gold, Palisade Green, Pepper Green, Verdoro Green, Sierra Yellow, or Granada Gold had green, yellow, and white tri-tone striping. GTOs with "The Judge" option finished in Burgundy or Cardinal Red had yellow, black, and red tri-tone striping. GTOs with "The Judge" option finished in Bermuda Blue, Atoll Blue, Mint Turquoise, or Orbit Orange had blue, orange, and pink tri-tone striping. GTOs with "The Judge" option finished in Starlight Black, Polar White, or Palladium Silver had yellow, blue, and red tri-tone striping. Factory variations from these recommended color combinations were possible and there were also variations in the way the rear deck lid airfoil was finished. Some air foils were done in body color, some were painted black and others had striping. Some, but not all, Judges also had a front "baby bib" spoiler. "The Judge" decals appeared behind the front wheel openings and on the passenger side of the rear deck lid. A "The Judge" emblem was affixed to the glove compartment door. Flat black finish was used on the hood scoop ornaments. Initial engine choices were the standard Ram Air III V-8 or the optional Ram Air IV V-8. Late in the model year the 455-cid V-8 was made available.

Model Number	Body/Style Number	Body Type & Seating	Factory Price	Shipping Weight	Production Total
242	37	2d Hardtop-5P	$3,604	—	3,629
242	67	2d Convertible-5P	$3,829	—	168

NOTE 10: 40,149 GTOs and Judges were built in 1970.
NOTE 11: 16,033 GTOs and Judges had synchromesh and 24,116 had automatic transmission.
NOTE 12: 366-hp Ram Air III V-8s were installed in 4,356 GTO and GTO Judge hardtops.
NOTE 13: 366-hp Ram Air III V-8s were installed in 288 GTO and GTO Judge convertibles.
NOTE 14: 370-hp Ram Air IV V-8s were installed in 767 GTO and GTO Judge hardtops.
NOTE 15: 370-hp Ram Air IV V-8s were installed in 37 GTO and GTO Judge convertibles.

ENGINES

TEMPEST, LEMANS, LEMANS SPORT BASE 250-CID SIX-CYL: Inline. Overhead valve. Bore and stroke: 3.88 x 3.53. Displacement: 250 cid. Compression ratio: 8.50:1. Brake hp: 155 at 4200 rpm. Torque: 235 lbs.-ft. at 1600 rpm. Seven main bearings. Hydraulic valve lifters. Crankcase capacity: 4 qt (add 1 qt. for new filter). Cooling system capacity with heater: 13 qt. Carburetor: Rochester Model 7040071 one-barrel.

Jerry Heasley photo

"The Judge" was hard to miss from any angle.

Carburetor: four-barrel. Engine code: YS, XV and XZ.

GTO BASE 400-CID V-8: Overhead valve. Cast-iron block. Bore and stroke: 4.12 x 3.75. Displacement: 400 cid. Compression ratio: 10.25:1. Brake hp: 350 at 5000 rpm. Taxable hp: 54.3. Torque: 445 lbs.-ft. at 3000 rpm. Five main bearings. Hydraulic valve lifters. Crankcase capacity: 5 qt. (add 1 qt. for new filter). Cooling system capacity with heater: (GTO) 18.5 qt.; (Grand Prix) 18.6 qt. Carburetor: Rochester four-barrel Model 7040263. Engine code: WT and YS.

GTO OPTIONAL RAM AIR III 400-CID V-8: Overhead valve. Cast-iron block. Bore and stroke: 4.12 x 3.75. Displacement: 400 cid. Compression ratio: 10.50:1. Brake hp: 366 at 5100 rpm. Taxable hp: 54.3. Torque: 445 lbs.-ft. at 3600 rpm. Five main bearings. Hydraulic valve lifters. Crankcase capacity: 5 qt. (add 1 qt. for new filter). Cooling system capacity with heater: 18.5 qt. Carburetor: four-barrel. Engine code: WS and YZ.

GTO OPTIONAL RAM AIR IV 400-CID V-8: Overhead valve. Cast-iron block. Bore and stroke: 4.12 x 3.75. Displacement: 400 cid. Compression ratio: 10.50:1. Brake hp: 370 at 5500 rpm. Taxable hp: 54.3. Torque: 445 lbs.-ft. at 3900 rpm. Five main bearings. Hydraulic valve lifters. Crankcase capacity: 5 qt. (add 1 qt. for new filter). Cooling system capacity with heater: 18.5 qt. Carburetor: four-barrel. Engine code: WW and XP.

GTO OPTIONAL 455 FOUR-BARREL V-8: Overhead valve. Cast-iron block. Bore and stroke: 4.15 x 4.210. Displacement: 455 cid. Compression ratio: 10.00:1. Brake hp: 360 at 4300 rpm. Torque: 500 lbs.-ft. at 2700 rpm. Five main bearings. Hydraulic valve lifters. Crankcase capacity: 5 qt. (add 1 qt. for new filter). Cooling system capacity with heater: 18.5 qt. Carburetor: four-barrel. Engine code: WA/YA.

CHASSIS

Wheelbase: (Tempest two-door) 112 in., (Tempest four-door) 116 in. Overall length: (All Tempest station wagons) 210.6 in., (Tempest two-door) 202.5 in., (Tempest four-door) 206.5 in. Width: 76.7 in. Height: 52.6 in. Front headroom: 38.5 in. Rear headroom: (Tempest and LeMans) 37.1 in. Front legroom: (Tempest) 42.3 in.; (LeMans) 42.4 in. Rear legroom: (Tempest and LeMans) 34.8 in. Front hiproom: (Tempest and LeMans) 59.4 in. Rear hip room: (Tempest and LeMans) 59.4 in. Trunk capacity: 14.6 cu. ft. Turn circle: 37.4 ft. Front tread: 61 in. Rear tread: 61 in. (Note: All height, width, interior space, and luggage space dimensions are for four-door sedan.)

OPTIONS

591 speedometer gear adapter ($11.59). 724 heavy-duty air cleaner, not available with H.O. or Ram Air V-8s ($9.48). 582 Custom air conditioner, not available with six-cylinder Tempest or heavy-duty battery teamed with Tempest six-cylinder ($375.99). 362 special order axle

This is the way fun is going to be.

Whether you go for economy, or prefer tooling up and down the coast with a fine road machine. It's Pontiac's new LeMans Sport. A 250-cube, 155-hp six is standard. That's economy. Or you can order up to a 400-cuber with 330 V-8 ponies. That's performance, baby.

With all that engine talk, we don't want you to forget luxury. We didn't. Like that convertible below. Buckets in knit vinyl and expanded Morrokide. Wall-to-wall nylon-blend carpeting. Very spiffy.

Go ahead and forget the wipers. They're in hiding. Forget the radio antenna, too. It's been exiled to the windshield. Just to keep this all-new cars styling clean. Wild.

You say driving's your sport? LeMans Sport. That's the way it's going to be.

Pontiac's new LeMans Sport

GM (We take the fun of driving seriously.)

A total of 72,179 LeMans Sports were built for 1970. The Sports were considered the "high-rung" cars of the Tempest line.

TEMPEST, LEMANS, LEMANS SPORT OPTIONAL 350-CID V-8: Overhead valve. Cast-iron block. Bore and stroke: 3.88 x 3.75. Displacement: 350 cid. Compression ratio: 8.80:1. Brake hp: 255 at 4600 rpm. Taxable hp: 48. Torque: 355 lbs.-ft. at 2800 rpm. Five main bearings. Hydraulic valve lifters. Crankcase capacity: 5 qt. (add 1 qt. for new filter). Cooling system capacity with heater: (Firebird) 19.5 qt.; (others) 18 qt. Carburetor: Rochester two-barrel Model 7040071. Engine code: WU, YU, W7 and X7.

TEMPEST, LEMANS, LEMANS SPORT OPTIONAL 400-CID V-8: Overhead valves. Cast-iron block. Bore and stroke: 4.125 x 3.75 in. Displacement: 400 cid. Compression ratio: 8.80:1. Brake hp: 265 at 4600 rpm. Taxable hp: 54.3. Torque: 397 lbs.-ft. at 2400 rpm. Five main bearings. Hydraulic valve lifters. Crankcase capacity: 5 qt. (add 1 qt. for new filter). Cooling system capacity with heater: 18.5 qt. Carburetor: two-barrel. Engine code: XX and YB.

TEMPEST, LEMANS, LEMANS SPORT OPTIONAL 400-CID V-8: Overhead valves. Cast-iron block. Bore and stroke: 4.125 x 3.75 in. Displacement: 400 cid. Compression ratio: 10.0:1. Brake hp: 330 at 4800 rpm. Taxable hp: 54.3. Torque: 445 lbs.-ft. at 2900 rpm. Five main bearings. Hydraulic valve lifters. Crankcase capacity: 5 qt. (add 1 qt. for new filter). Cooling system capacity with heater: (Pontiac) 18 qt.; (LeMans) 18.5 qt.

($2.11) 364-368 economy or performance axles ($2.11) 692 heavy-duty battery with Tempest six without air conditioning ($4.21). 692 heavy-duty battery Tempest V-8 ($6.32). 431 deluxe front and rear seat belts and front shoulder belts ($12.64-$36.86 depending on model). 432 deluxe front and rear seat belts and front and rear shoulder belts ($38.97-$63.19 depending on model). 434 deluxe front and rear seat belts in convertible ($10.53). 524 Custom floor carpets in base Tempest ($18.96). 492 electric clock, not available with Rally gauge cluster and included with auxiliary gauge panel ($18.96). 494 front seat center console, all LeMans except four-door hardtop and all GTO without Turbo Hydra-Matic ($55.82). 494 front seat center console in GTO with Turbo Hydra-Matic ($71.62). 424 spare tire cover ($5.27). 481 cruise control, with V-8 only ($57.93). 421 front seat foam cushion, except GTO ($8.43). Safari rear window deflector ($26.33). 404 rear window defogger, except Safari and convertible ($26.33). 534 electric rear window defroster ($52.66). 361 Safe-T-Track differential ($42.13-$63.19). 481 dual exhausts for Tempest V-8s except GTO and Tempest Custom Safari ($30.54). 341 155-hp six-cylinder engine (standard). 343 350-cid regular-fuel two-barrel V-8 (($110.59). 344 400-cid H.O. four-barrel V-8, including three-speed manual transmission with column shift and dual exhausts for GTO, not available with "The Judge" option or four-speed manual transmission and Ride & Handling package required ($57.95). 344 400-cid H.O. four-barrel V-8, including three-speed manual transmission with column shift and dual exhausts for Tempests except GTO with Turbo Hydra-Matic transmission ($210.64). 346 400-cid two-barrel regular-fuel V-8 on all Tempests with Turbo Hydra-Matic transmission, except GTO ($163.25). 347 400-cid Ram Air IV four-barrel V-8, including hood Ram Air inlet equipment, chrome rocker covers, chrome oil cap, dual exhausts, heavy-duty battery and F70-14 fiberglass-belted redline or white line Wide-Oval tires in Tempest two-door hardtop with Turbo Hydra-Matic transmission or close-ratio four-speed manual transmission without Lamp Group ($905.75). 347 400-cid Ram Air IV four-barrel V-8, including hood Ram Air inlet equipment, chrome rocker covers, chrome oil cap, dual exhausts, heavy-duty battery and F70-14 fiberglass-belted redline or white line Wide-Oval tires in Tempest two-door convertible with Turbo Hydra-Matic transmission or close-ratio four-speed manual transmission without Lamp Group ($889.95). 347 400-cid Ram Air IV four-barrel V-8, including hood Ram Air inlet equipment, chrome rocker covers, chrome oil cap, dual exhausts, heavy-duty battery and F70-14 fiberglass-belted red line or white line Wide-Oval tires in all GTOs with the WT-1 "The Judge" option, includes air-inlet hood, requires Ride & Handling package and not available with air conditioning ($389.68). 347 400-cid Ram Air IV four-barrel V-8 including hood Ram Air inlet equipment, chrome rocker covers, chrome oil cap, dual exhausts, heavy-duty battery and F70-14 fiberglass-belted redline or white line Wide-Oval tires in all GTOs without the WT-1 "The Judge" option ($558.20). 348 400-CID H.O. V-8 includes chrome air cleaner, chrome rocker covers, chrome oil filler cap, dual exhausts, F70-14 fiberglass-belted redline or white line Wide-Oval tires and three-speed manual transmission with floor shift on Tempest two-door hardtop with Turbo Hydra-Matic, four-speed manual or close-ratio four-speed manual

This 1970 GTO was factory-fresh and outfitted in Cardinal Red.

GM photo

Jerry Heasley photo

Pontiac produced 3,797 Judges for 1970. This coupe was decked out in Starlight Black with blue and red tri-tone striping.

transmissions ($424.44). 348 400-CID H.O. V-8 includes chrome air cleaner, chrome rocker covers, chrome oil filler cap, dual exhausts, F70-14 fiberglass-belted redline or white line Wide-Oval tires and three-speed manual transmission with floor shift on Tempest two-door convertible with Turbo Hydra-Matic, four-speed manual or close-ratio four-speed manual transmissions ($408.64). 348 400-CID H.O. V-8 includes: chrome air cleaner, chrome rocker covers, chrome oil filler cap, dual exhausts, F70-14 fiberglass-belted redline, or white line Wide-Oval tires and three-speed manual transmission with floor shift on Tempest two-door hardtop without Turbo Hydra-Matic, four-speed manual or close-ratio four-speed manual transmissions ($508.70). 348 400-CID H.O. V-8 includes chrome air cleaner, chrome rocker covers, chrome oil filler cap, dual exhausts, F70-14 fiberglass-belted redline or white line Wide-Oval tires and three-speed manual transmission with floor shift on Tempest two-door convertible without Turbo Hydra-Matic, four-speed manual, or close-ratio four-speed manual transmissions ($492.90). 349 400-cid four-barrel Ram Air III V-8 in GTO without WT-1 "The Judge" option, includes air-inlet hood, requires Ride & Handling package ($168.51). 34P 455-cid V-8 in Tempest except GTO with Turbo Hydra-Matic, dual exhausts required ($279.10). 34P 455-cid V-8 in GTO ($57.93). 711 evaporative emissions system, required on all California cars ($36.86). 611 driver-controlled exhaust on GTO, not available with Ram Air V-8s ($63.19). 534 Custom gearshift knob with three- or four-speed manual transmission ($5.27). 531 Soft-Ray tinted glass ($36.86). 532 Soft-Ray tinted windshield ($26.33). 684 door edge guards on two-door ($6.32); four-doors ($10.53). 672 headlight delay ($12.64). 601 air-inlet hood for GTO with 400 H.O. V-8, standard with Ram Air III and Ram Air IV V-8s ($84.26). 414 dual horns on base Tempest ($4.21). 694 Instant Aire, not available with Ram Air IV V-8 ($15.80). 661 rear compartment courtesy lamp in Safari ($10.53). 662 ash tray lamp ($3.16). 651 cornering lamp ($33.70). 654 dome reading lamp, except convertible ($13.69). 664 glove box lamp ($3.16). 652 luggage compartment lamp ($3.16). 671 under-hood lamp ($4.21). 541 luggage carrier, Tempest Safari ($63.19). 521 pair of front floor mats ($6.85). 522 pair of rear floor mats ($6.32). 441 right- or left-hand visor-vanity mirrors ($2.11). 424 remote-control left-hand outside rearview mirror ($10.53). 694 wheel opening moldings for Tempest and Tempest Custom models ($15.80). 754 Mountain Performance group for all Tempest except GTO with 350-cid V-8 teamed with automatic or Turbo Hydra-Matic transmission without air conditioning ($16.85). 754 Mountain Performance group for all Tempest except GTO with 350-cid V-8 teamed with automatic or Turbo Hydra-Matic transmission with air conditioning ($2.11). RTT standard two-tone paint, all except Safari ($40.02). RTT standard two-tone paint on Safari ($15.80). STT special two-tone paint on Safari ($131.65). STT special two-tone paint on Tempests except Safari ($155.87). SPS special color solid paint all models except convertibles or with cordova top ($115.85). SPS special color solid paint on convertible or models with cordova top ($100.05). 511 Wonder Touch power brakes, all except GTO, included in front disc brakes ($42.13). 502 front disc brakes, includes Wonder Touch power brakes ($64.25). 541 power door locks and seat back locks on two-door ($68.46). 554 remote-control deck lid, except Safari ($14.74). 552 power door locks only, in four-door models ($68.46). 734 power door locks only in two-door models ($45.29). 4-Way power full bench front seat ($73.72). 564 4-Way power left-hand front bucket seat ($73.72).

Variable-ratio power steering ($105.32). 542 power tailgate window ($34.76). 551 power windows ($105.32). 401 push-button AM radio with windshield antenna ($61.09). 402 AM/FM radio with windshield antenna ($133.76). 404 AM/FM stereo radio with windshield antenna ($239.08). 411 rear speaker, except Safari ($15.80). 411 rear speaker for Safari ($21.06). 412 stereo tape player ($133.76). 482 Rally gauge cluster and clock, not available with Safeguard speedometer or Rally gauge cluster with tachometer ($50.55). 484 Rally gauge cluster with tachometer, not available with six-cylinder engine, Rally gauge cluster with clock, hood-mounted tachometer or electric clock ($84.26). 634 rear

Daniel B. Lyons photo

Only 168 Judge convertibles were produced in 1970.

lamp monitor, except Safari and convertible ($26.33). 482 Safeguard speedometer, not available with Rally gauge clusters ($15.80). 571 reclining right-hand bucket seat ($42.13). 621 Ride & Handling package on Tempest, Tempest Custom, and LeMans with Sprint option and all GTOs ($4.21). 621 Ride & Handling package on Tempest, Tempest Custom, and LeMans without Sprint option ($9.48). 461 deluxe steering wheel in base Tempest ($15.85). 462 Custom steering wheel in base Tempest with Sprint option ($34.50); without Sprint option ($50.85). 464 Formula steering wheel in Tempests without the Décor Group option ($57.93). 464 Formula steering wheel in Tempests with the Décor Group option ($42.13). 504 tilt steering with power steering ($45.29). 544 dual-hinge tailgate on Tempest Custom Safari ($42.13). 491 hood-mounted tachometer, not available with six-cylinder engine or Rally Gauge Cluster with tachometer ($63.19). SVT cordova top, except Safari and convertible ($100.05). 352 automatic transmission in Tempest with six-cylinder engine without air conditioning or console ($163.68); in Tempest with 350-cid regular-fuel two-barrel V-8 without console ($174.20). 351 Turbo Hydra-Matic transmission in Tempests with six-cylinder engine or 350-cid regular-fuel V-8 ($227.04). 354 four-speed manual transmission in Tempest V-8 without 37S or 37P axle ($184.80). 355 heavy-duty three-speed manual transmission with floor shift, except ($84.24). 356 three-speed manual transmission with floor shift in Tempest with six-cylinder engine, option 472 required and included in Sprint option ($42.13). 358 close-ratio four-speed manual transmission in Tempests except GTO with 37P or 37S axle teamed with 350-cid H.O. V-8 and all GTOs with 37P or 37S axle ($184.80). 359 Turbo Hydra-Matic in Tempest with six-cylinder ($195.36); in Tempest with 350-cid regular-fuel V-8 and no air conditioning ($205.92). Black coated fabric trim in models 23327 and 23360 with trim code 49 ($27.38). 514 brake pedal trim package in Tempest and Tempest Custom ($5.27). 471 deluxe wheel covers on base Tempest ($21.06). 472 Custom wheel covers ($20.01-$51.61 depending on model and other equipment). 473 wire wheel covers ($52.66-$73.72) depending on model and other options. 454 Rally II wheels ($63.19-$84.26 depending on model and other options). 432 recessed windshield wipers on Tempest and Tempest Custom models ($18.96). TDR H78-14 white sidewall tires ($33.70). TGR F78-14 white sidewall tires ($28.44). TRF G78-14 black sidewall tires ($14.74). TRR G78-14 white sidewall tires ($30.54-$45.29 depending on model). TPR G70 x 14 white sidewall tires ($66.35). TPL G70 x 14 white letter tires ($51.61). TSF H78-15 black sidewall tires on two-door hardtop and convertible, standard with air conditioning, otherwise ($17.90 extra). 704 Space-Saver spare tire ($15.80). 321 Basic Group includes: push-button radio, front foam seat cushion, visor-vanity mirror, remote-control left-hand outside rearview mirror, electric clock, remote control deck lid, and heavy-duty air cleaner, unless standard ($107.43-$125.34 depending on model and other equipment). 324 Décor Group includes: recessed windshield wipers if not standard, deluxe wheel discs, deluxe steering wheel, décor moldings, and brake

pedal trim package ($123.32-$124.28 depending upon model and other equipment). 322 lamp group includes cornering lamps, luggage lamp on passenger cars, panel courtesy lamps, except on convertible, glove box lamp, ashtray lamp and ignition switch lamp ($7.37-$27.38 depending on model). 331 Power Assist Group includes: Turbo Hydra-Matic transmission, power steering and front disc brakes ($364.93-$396.61 depending on model and other equipment). 334 Rally Group includes: Rally II wheels, Custom Sport steering wheel, Rally gauge cluster, Ride & Handling package ($157.98-$194.84 depending on model and other equipment). 332-WT1 GTO "The Judge" option package included the 400-cid Ram Air III V-8, special paint colors, special "The Judge" decals and stripes, black texture in grille, T-handle shifter with manual transmission, a 60-in.-wide rear deck air foil, heavy-duty suspension, Rally II wheels less trim rings, and G70 x 14 wide-tread fiberglass-belted black sidewall tires ($337.02).

OPTION INSTALLATION RATES

Of 213,239 Tempests built 88.7 percent had automatic transmission, 6.8 percent had a four-speed synchromesh transmission, 17.4 percent had a standard V-8 engine, 75.4 percent had a standard V-8 engine, 7.2 percent had a six-cylinder engine, 87.8 percent had a AM radio, 7.3 percent had an AM/FM radio, 3.3 percent had a stereo tape player, 92 percent had power steering, 23.5 percent had power drum brakes, 30.9 percent had front disc brakes, 0.7 percent had power door locks, 1.1 percent had a power seat, 2.7 percent had power side windows, 3.9 percent had power station wagon tailgate window, 57.5 percent had an air conditioner, 2.4 percent had a movable steering column, 42.8 percent had bucket seats, 42.5 percent had a vinyl roof, 85.2 percent had white sidewall tires, 32.7 percent had a tinted windshield only, 44.5 percent had all tinted windows, 19 percent had dual exhausts, 9.7 percent had a limited-slip differential, 65.1 percent had optional full wheel discs, 23.1 percent had optional styled wheels, 1 percent had a speed regulating device, 2.1 percent had a station wagon luggage rack, 0.3 percent had reclining front seats and 20.9 percent had a clock.

HISTORICAL FOOTNOTES

James McDonald was general manager of Pontiac Motor Division. Calendar-year sales of new "Tempests" by registered Pontiac dealers came to 184,913 units for a 2.6 percent share of the domestic industry total. Model-year production was 213,239 units for a slightly better 2.8 percent share of industry output. By factory, the totals included 75,483 cars built in Pontiac, Michigan, 38,354 cars made in Fremont, California, 50,194 cars made in Arlington, Texas and 49,208 cars made in Baltimore, Maryland. The 1970 GTO with the 400-cid/366-hp V-8 was capable of 0 to 60 mph in 6 seconds flat. It did the quarter-mile in 14.6 seconds. The 455-cid/360-hp GTO hardtop registered 6.6 seconds 0 to 60 mph and a 14.8-second quarter-mile.

The 1971 GTO had a new wire-mesh grille and long scoops on the hood. "The Judge" was again the top gun of the Tempest line.

Jerry Heasley photo

1971

Pontiac intermediates for 1971 included the T-37, the LeMans, the LeMans Sport, the GT-37, the GTO, and the GTO Judge. There were 17 models. All had restyled front ends and hoods. All but the GTO had a new blade front bumper. A fiberglass panel between the hood and the bumper surrounded the dual headlamps and grille. The GTO featured a new wire-mesh grille protected by a restyled Endura bumper and long air scoops in its hood. To give young buyers a cheaper GTO-like alternative, Pontiac made the Endura styling option available for LeMans Sport models. The $73.72 package included the GTO hood, GTO Endura bumper, and the GTO headlamp assembly.

I.D. NUMBERS

VIN on top of dash at left, viewable through windshield. First symbol tells GM division: 2=Pontiac. Second and third symbols tell series: 33=Tempest/T-37, 35=LeMans, 37=LeMans Sport, 42=GTO. Fourth and fifth symbols indicate body style and appear as last two digits of body/style number in charts below. Sixth symbol indicates model year: 1=1971. Seventh symbol indicates assembly plant: A=Atlanta, Georgia, B=Baltimore, Maryland, P=Pontiac, Michigan, R=Arlington, Texas, Z=Fremont, California. Remaining symbols are sequential unit production number at factory, starting with 100001. Fisher body plate on cowl tells style number: (Model year prefix 71, plus number in second column of charts below), body number, trim code, paint code and other data. Six-cylinder engine code stamped on distributor mounting on right side of block. V-8 engine code on front of block below right cylinder head. Engine production codes for 1971 were: (250-cid/155-hp six) ZB/CAA/ZG/CAB. (350-cid/250-hp V-8) WR/WU/-XU/XR/WN/WP/YN/-YP. (400-cid/265-hp V-8) WS/WX/-

XX/YX. (400-cid/300-hp V-8) WT/WK/YS. (455-cid 260-hp V-8) WG/YG. (455-cid 335-hp V-8) WJ/YC/WL/WC/YE/YA.

COLORS

Paint codes for 1971 were: 11/C=Cameo White, 13/P=Nordic Silver, 19/A=Starlight Black, 24/D=Adriatic Blue, 26/F=Lucerne Blue, 42/H=Limekist Green, 43/L=Tropical Green, 49/M=Laurentian Green, 53/Y=Quezal Gold, 59/Z=Axtec Gold, 61/B=Sandalwood, 62/T=Canyon Copper, 67/S=Castillian Bronze and 75/R=Cardinal Red. Vinyl top colors for 1971 were: 1=White, 2=Black, 5=Sandalwood, 7=Dark Brown, and 9=Dark Green. Convertible top colors for 1971 were: 1=White, 2=Black, 5=Sandalwood, and 9=Dark Green. Interior trim codes for Tempests and T-37s were: 239=Black cloth and vinyl, 230=Black cloth and vinyl, 232=Ivory vinyl, 231=Dark Blue cloth and vinyl, 236=Dark Jade cloth, 236=Dark Jade vinyl, 237=Sandalwood cloth or vinyl, 238=Sandalwood vinyl. Interior trim codes for LeMans models were: 241=Dark Blue cloth and vinyl, 245=Dark Jade cloth and vinyl, 247=Sandalwood cloth and vinyl, 249=Black cloth and vinyl, 251=Dark Blue vinyl, 252=Ivory vinyl, 253=Dark saddle vinyl, 256=Dark Jade vinyl, 257=Sandalwood vinyl, 259=Black vinyl bucket seats, 261=Dark Blue vinyl bucket seats, 262=Ivory vinyl bucket seats, 263=Dark Saddle vinyl bucket seats, 264=Dark Sienna vinyl bucket seats, 266=Dark Jade vinyl bucket seats, 267=Sandalwood vinyl bucket seats and 269=Black vinyl bucket seats. Interior trim codes for GTO models were 261=Dark Blue vinyl bucket seats, 262=Ivory vinyl bucket seats, 263=Dark Saddle vinyl bucket seats, 264=Dark Sienna vinyl bucket seats, 266=Dark Jade vinyl bucket seats, 267=Sandalwood vinyl bucket seats, 269=Black vinyl bucket seats, 277=Sandalwood vinyl notchback or 60/40 seat, and 279=Black vinyl notchback or 60/40 seat.

T-37 — (SIX-CYL) — SERIES 233

Pontiac T-37 lettering was seen behind the front wheel wells of the lowest-priced A-body models. Standard equipment included cloth-and-Morrokide bench seats, a vinyl floor covering, a deluxe steering wheel, upper level ventilation in hardtops, a black-grained instrument panel, door-operated dome lamp switches, conventional roof drip moldings, conventional windshield moldings, conventional rear window reveal moldings, dual-action parallel-sweep windshield wipers, front disc brakes, and E78-14 black sidewall tires. Pillared coupes and sedans also had chrome-edged ventipanes. The GTO-type Endura nose was now a $74 option for all LeMans models, including the Safari station wagon.

Jerry Heasley photo

The Judge for 1971 was still available in a variety of color schemes. The Cameo White models were trimmed with yellow, blue, and red striping. Airfoils on the white cars could be black or body color.

Model Number	Body/Style Number	Body Type & Seating	Factory Price	Shipping Weight	Production Total
233	27	2d Sedan-6P	$2,747	3,189 lbs.	7,184
233	69	4d Sedan-6P	$2,795	3,219 lbs.	29,466
233	37	2d Hardtop-6P	$2,807	3,194 lbs.	8,336

NOTE 1: 5,525 T-37s had synchromesh and 39,461 had automatic transmission.

GT-37 — (V-8) — SERIES 233 + WU-2

The GT-37 was available again and was advertised as "The GTO For Kids Under 30." This option (code 334) was offered in just hardtop versions. It included vinyl accent stripes, Rally II wheels (less trim rings), G70-14 tires (white-lettered), dual exhausts with chrome extensions, heavy-duty three-speed manual transmission with floor shift, body-colored outside mirrors (left-hand remote control), hood locking pins, and GT-37 nameplates. It was designed to provide buyers with a low-cost high-performance option. A "post coupe" version of the GT-37 could be ordered in 1970 and appeared on the order sheet again in 1971. However, no such cars were ever made due to the fact that the dual sport mirrors, which were standard on 1971 GT-37s, would have interfered with the ventipanes (vent windows) used on the coupe body. De-contenting the T-37 got as intense as using only one plastic coat hook in the car and removing the grille nameplate, even though the holes were not filled. This resulted in an extremely lightweight car that could be turned into a real "factory hot rod" with the right engine and drive train options. The "eyebrow" style stripes used in 1971 were similar to those used on The Judge models. A second 1971 1/2 design, with "sword-style stripes," was reflective.

Model Number	Body/Style Number	Body Type & Seating	Factory Price	Shipping Weight	Production Total
233 + WU-2	37	2d Hardtop-6P	$2,928	3,450 lbs.	Note 5

NOTE 5: A combined total of 5,802 GT-37s were built as 1971 and 1971 1/2 models.

LEMANS — (SIX-CYL) — SERIES 235

LeMans models had the word "Pontiac" on the left-hand grille. They carried vertical slash louvers behind the

The GT-37 option was a low-cost, high-performance package billed by Pontiac as "The GTO For Kids Under 30."

wheel wells and LeMans lettering under the rear fender crease lines. Extra features on LeMans models included richer upholstery, loop-pile carpets, safety rear armrests with integral ashtrays, a wood-grained dashboard, concealed windshield wipers, rocker panel moldings, a hood rear edge molding, side window reveal moldings on coupes and vent windows on four-door styles. Station wagons had two-way tailgates and power front disc brakes.

Model Number	Body/Style Number	Body Type & Seating	Factory Price	Shipping Weight	Production Total
235	27	2d Sedan-6P	$2,877	3,199 lbs.	2,734
235	69	4d Sedan-6P	$2,025	3,229 lbs.	11,979
235	39	4d Hardtop-6P	$3,064	3,314 lbs.	3,186
235	37	2d Hardtop-6P	$2,938	3,199 lbs.	40,966
235	36	4d Sta Wagon-6P	$3,353	3,765 lbs.	6,311
235	46	4d Sta Wagon-9P	$3,465	3,825 lbs.	4,363

NOTE 6: 1,231 LeMans had synchromesh and 67,948 had automatic transmission.

LEMANS SPORT — (SIX-CYL) — SERIES 237

Standard equipment in LeMans Sport models included all items found in LeMans models plus dual horns, pedal trim plates, ashtray and glove box lamps, courtesy lamps on convertibles, carpeted lower door panels, a custom cushion steering wheel and wheel well moldings. Buyers of two-door hardtops and convertibles had a choice of knit-vinyl bucket seats or notchback bench seats and the four-door hardtop used knit vinyl bench seats. LeMans Sport model nameplates were seen on the sides of rear fenders. GTO-type Endura rubber noses were a $74 styling option for all LeMans Sport models, including station wagons. This front end was also marketed as part of the code 602 LeMans Sport Endura styling option that included the GTO hood, GTO Endura bumper, and GTO headlight assembly.

Model Number	Body/Style Number	Body Type & Seating	Factory Price	Shipping Weight	Production Total
237	39	4d Hardtop-6P	$3,255	3,314 lbs.	2,451
237	37	2d Hardtop-6P	$3,125	3,199 lbs.	34,625
237	67	2d Convertible-6P	$3,359	3,289 lbs.	3,865

NOTE 7: 1,229 LeMans Sports had synchromesh and 39,712 had automatic transmission.

GTO — (V-8) — SERIES 242

A new Endura nose piece identified the 1971 GTO. It had larger twin grille cavities, round parking lamps below the side-by-side headlights, and integral body-colored bumpers. The headlight lenses were round and housed in shiny, square housings with rounded corners. GTO fenders differed from other LeMans fenders. Other characteristics included: twin air slots at the front of the hood scoop, GTO lettering on the lower part of the left-hand grille opening, GTO lettering on the front fender sides, and GTO letters on the right-hand edge of the rear deck lid. The grille had a diagonal crosshatch insert. The taillights were wide, thin wraparound units. The 1971 instrument panel had the same motifs as the 1970 type.

The instrument panel facing was no longer wood veneer, but a grained panel. Strato-bucket seats with all-Morrokide expanded vinyl trim were standard. A notchback bench seat was optional. Standard equipment included all items found on LeMans models, plus: an engine-turned aluminum dash insert, dual exhausts with extensions through the rear bumper valance panel, a Power-Flex cooling fan, heavy-duty stabilizer bars, heavy-duty shock absorbers, heavy-duty springs, and G70-14 black sidewall tires. The biggest revisions to the 1971 GTO were under the hood. A 400-cid/300-hp V-8 was standard. Two 455-cid V-8s were optional. The first had a four-barrel carburetor and 325 hp. The second was the 455 H.O. engine with round-port exhausts, special exhaust manifolds, an aluminum intake and 335 hp. The 455 H.O. was available with a Ram Air package. The 1971 air-inlet hood was designed to keep the weather out and was not driver controlled.

Model Number	Body/Style Number	Body Type & Seating	Factory Price	Shipping Weight	Production Total
242	37	2d Hardtop-5P	$3,446	3,619 lbs.	9,497
242	67	2d Convertible-5P	$3,676	3,664 lbs.	661

GTO "THE JUDGE" — (V-8) — SERIES 242 + 332

For $395 extra "The Judge" option was available (for the last time) this year. It was discontinued in January 1971. This option (code 332) included a 455-cid four-barrel H.O. V-8, Rally II wheels (less trim rings), a hood air-inlet system, a T-handle gearshift control (with manual transmission), a rear deck lid air foil, specific side stripes, "The Judge" decals, Ram Air decals, and a black-textured grille. Since the option was being dropped, not all cars this year had every item in the package. If a non-critical part ran out, Pontiac built the car without it. A "The Judge" emblem appeared on the lower right-hand corner of the glove box. A large "The Judge" decal was placed behind each front wheel opening. An even larger decal was on the right end of the rear deck lid. Multi-color "eyebrow" decal stripes were placed above the wheel arches. The airfoil was painted body color, but could be had in black on white cars. It carried 455 H.O. decals on its sides. Recommended body color and stripe combinations included: blue, orange and pink striping with cars done in Adriatic Blue, Lucerne Blue, Castillion Bronze, or Canyon Copper. Cars painted Sandalwood, Rosewood, Cardinal Red, or Quezal Gold got yellow, black, and red stripes. Cars finished in Limekist Green, Tropical Lime or Laurentian Green had green, yellow, and white stripes. Finally, cars painted Starlight Black, Cameo White, or Nordic Silver were decorated with yellow, blue and red striping. "The Judge" came with one of three types of G70-14 tires, Firestone Wide-Oval, Goodyear Polyglas GT, or Uniroyal Tiger Paws. G60-15 tires were optional.

Model Number	Body/Style Number	Body Type & Seating	Factory Price	Shipping Weight	Production Total
242	37	2d Hardtop-5P	$3,840	—	357
242	67	2d Convertible-5P	$4,070	—	17

NOTE 8: 2,587 of all GTOs had synchromesh and 7,945 had automatic transmission.

Thomas Glatch photo

At a base price of $3,359, the convertible was the most expensive of the LeMans Sport models for 1971. The Sport was also available in two- and four-door hardtop models.

ENGINES

TEMPEST, LEMANS, LEMANS SPORT BASE 250-CID SIX-CYL: Inline. Overhead valve. Bore and stroke: 3.88 x 3.53. Displacement: 250 cid. Compression ratio: 8.50:1. Brake hp: 145 at 4200 rpm. Torque: 230 lbs-ft. at 1600 rpm. Seven main bearings. Hydraulic valve lifters. Crankcase capacity: 4 qt (add 1 qt. for new filter). Cooling system capacity with heater: 13 qt. Carburetor: Rochester Model 7040071 one-barrel carburetor. Engine code: ZB, ZG, CAA and CAB.

T-37, LEMANS, LEMANS SPORT (TWO- & FOUR-DOOR) OPTIONAL 350-CID V-8: Overhead valve. Cast-iron block. Bore and stroke: 3.88 x 3.75. Displacement: 350 cid. Compression ratio: 8.00:1. Brake hp: 250 at 4400 rpm. Net hp: 165 at 4200 rpm. Taxable hp: 48. Torque: 350 lbs.-ft. at 2400 rpm. Net torque: 275 lbs.-ft. at 2200 rpm. Five main bearings. Hydraulic valve lifters. Crankcase capacity: 5 qt. (add 1 qt. for new filter). Cooling system capacity with heater: 18 qt. Carburetor: Rochester two-barrel. Engine code: WR, WU, YU, XR, WN, WP, YN and YP.

T-37, LEMANS, LEMANS SPORT (TWO- & FOUR-DOOR) OPTIONAL 400-CID V-8: Overhead valves. Cast-iron block. Bore and stroke: 4.125 x 3.75 in. Displacement: 400 cid. Compression ratio: 8.2:1. Brake hp: 265 at 4400 rpm. Net hp: 180 at 3800 rpm. Taxable hp: 54.3. Torque: 400 lbs.-ft. at 2400 rpm. Net torque: 320 lbs.-ft. at 2200 rpm. Five main bearings. Hydraulic valve lifters. Crankcase capacity: 5 qt. Cooling system capacity with heater: 18.5 qt. (add 1 qt. for new filter). Carburetor: Two-barrel. Engine code: WS, WX, XX, and XY.

GTO BASE V-8; T-37, LEMANS, LEMANS SPORT (TWO- & FOUR-DOOR) OPTIONAL 400-CID V-8: Overhead valve. Cast-iron block. Bore and stroke: 4.12 x 3.75. Displacement: 400 cid. Compression ratio: 8.2:1. Brake hp: 300 at 4800 rpm. Net hp: 255 at 4400 rpm. Taxable hp: 54.3. Torque: 400 lbs.-ft. at 3600 rpm. Net torque: 340 lbs.-ft. at 3200 rpm. Five main bearings. Hydraulic valve lifters. Crankcase capacity: 5 qt. (add 1 qt. for new filter). Cooling system capacity with heater: 18.6 qt. Carburetor: Rochester four-barrel. Engine code: WT, WK and YS.

T-37, LEMANS, LEMANS SPORT, GTO (NON-"JUDGE") OPTIONAL 455-CID FOUR-BARREL V-8: Overhead valve. Cast-iron block. Bore and stroke: 4.15 x 4.21. Displacement: 455 cid. Compression ratio: 8.2:1. Brake hp: 325 at 4400 rpm. Net hp: 260 at 4000 rpm. Taxable hp: 54.5. Torque: 455 lbs.-ft. at 3200 rpm.

Net torque: 360 lbs.-ft. at 2800 rpm. Five main bearings. Hydraulic valve lifters. Crankcase capacity: 5 qt. (add 1 qt. for new filter). Cooling system capacity with heater: 17.25 qt. Carburetor: Rochester four-barrel. Engine code: WJ and YC.

LEMANS SPORT (TWO-DOOR), GTO, GTO "THE JUDGE" OPTIONAL 455-CID H.O. V-8: Overhead valve. Cast-iron block. Bore and stroke: 4.15 x 4.21. Displacement: 455 cid. Compression ratio: 8.4:1. Brake hp: 335 at 4800 rpm. Taxable hp: 54.5. Torque: 480 lbs.-ft. at 360 rpm. Five main bearings. Hydraulic valve lifters. Crankcase capacity: 5 qt. (add 1 qt. for new filter). Cooling system capacity with heater: 17.25 qt. Carburetor: Rochester Quadrajet four-barrel. Engine code: WL, WC, YE and YA.

CHASSIS

Wheelbase: (Tempest two-door) 112 in., (Tempest four-door) 116 in. Overall length: (all Tempest station wagons) 210.9 in., (Tempest two-door) 202.3 in., (Tempest four-door) 206.8 in. Width: 76.7 in. Height: 52.6 in. Front headroom: (T-37 and LeMans) 38.5 in. Rear headroom: (T-37 and LeMans) 37.1 in. Front legroom: (Tempest) 42.3 in.; (LeMans) 42.4 in. Rear

GM photo

Only 661 GTO convertibles were built for 1971.

Judge decals could be seen on the deck lid, with the 455 H.O. identification on the right side of the airfoil.

Jerry Heasley photo

legroom: (T-37 and LeMans) 34.8 in. Front hiproom: (T-37) 59.8 in.; (LeMans) 59.4 in. Rear hiproom: (Tempest and LeMans) 54.9 in. Trunk capacity: 14.6 cu. ft. Turn circle: 38.6 ft. Front tread: 61 in. Rear tread: 61 in. (Note: All height, width, interior space, and luggage space dimensions are for four-door sedan.)

OPTIONS

422 heavy-duty air cleaner, not available with 455-cid H.O. V-8 ($9.48). 582 manual air conditioning, not available with two-speed automatic transmission ($407.59). 362 special order axle without Mountain Performance option ($10.53). 362 special order axle with Mountain Performance option (no charge). 368 performance axle ($10.53). 364 economy axle without Mountain Performance option ($10.53). 364 economy axle with Mountain Performance option (no charge). 692 heavy-duty battery, not available with Delco

Maintenance-Free battery ($10.53). 654 Delco Maintenance-Free battery, requires 455-cid four-barrel V-8 or 455-cid H.O. four-barrel V-8 ($26.33). 451 Custom front and rear seat and front shoulder belts, closed passenger cars ($15.80). 451 Custom front and rear seat and front shoulder belts, convertible ($40.02). 451 Custom front and rear seat and front shoulder belts, Safari ($18.96). 452 Custom front and rear seat and shoulder belts, closed passenger cars ($42.13). 452 Custom front and rear seat and shoulder belts, convertible ($66.35). 452 Custom front and rear seat and shoulder belts, Safari ($45.29). 524 Custom floor carpets in T-37 ($21.06). 524 Custom load floor carpets in Safari ($52.66). 572 Safari luggage carrier ($63.19). 722 electric clock, not available with Rally gauge cluster ($18.96). 431 front seat console in LeMans Sport two-door or GTO models ($61.09). 424 spare wheel and tire cover ($5.27). 711 cruise control with two-speed automatic or Turbo Hydra-Matic transmissions without

Thomas Glatch photo

**All the Pontiac intermediates for 1971 had restyled hoods and front ends.
This LeMans Sport was one of 3,865 convertibles made.**

air-inlet hood ($63.19). 534 rear window air deflector ($26.33). 541 rear window defogger, except Safari and convertible ($31.60). 541 rear window defogger, Safari ($36.86). 534 rear window defroster, except Safari and convertible ($63.19), Safe-T-Track differential, except with code 37P or 37S rear axle ($46.34). 34A 250-cid six-cylinder engine (standard). 34D 350-cid two-barrel V-8, in all models except GTO and not available with Turbo Hydra-Matic or close-ratio four-speed manual transmissions ($121.12). 34G 400-cid two-barrel V-8 in all models except GTO with Turbo Hydra-Matic transmission ($173.78). 34K 400-cid four-barrel V-8, in all models except GTO with heavy-duty three-speed manual transmission with floor shifter, four-speed manual transmission, close-ratio four-speed manual transmission or Turbo Hydra-Matic transmission ($221.17). 34L 400-cid four-barrel V-8 (standard in GTO). 34P 455-cid four-barrel V-8, all models except GTO with Turbo Hydra-Matic and dual exhausts required at extra cost ($279.10). 34P 455-cid four-barrel V-8 in GTO, not available with GTO "The Judge" option ($57.93). 34U 455-cid H.O. four-barrel V-8 in T-37, LeMans and LeMans Sport coupes and convertibles, requires dual exhausts and Ride & Handling package and

not available with transmissions 35A, 35E, 35J, or 35K ($358.09). 34U 455-cid H.O. four-barrel V-8 in GTO without "The Judge" option ($136.92). 34U 455-cid H.O. four-barrel V-8 in GTO with "The Judge" option (standard equipment). 682 dual exhausts, on all V-8 models except GTO ($30.54). 531 all tinted glass ($43.18). 532 tinted windshield only ($30.54). 692 door edge guards, on two-door models ($6.32). 692 door edge guards on four-door models ($10.53). 731 front bumper guards, except GTO or cars with Endura Styling option ($15.80). 732 rear bumper guards ($15.80). 601 air-inlet hood on GTO with 455 H.O. V-8 ($84.26, but standard with "The Judge" option). 681 dual horns, except LeMans Sport and GTO ($4.21). 672 ashtray lamp, except LeMans Sport and GTO ($3.16). 664 instrument panel courtesy lamp on T-37 and LeMans group except convertible ($4.21) 662 Safari rear compartment courtesy lamp ($10.53). 661 dome reading lamp ($13.69). 674 glove box lamp ($3.16). 662 luggage compartment lamp ($3.16). 691 rechargeable utility lamp ($12.64). 671 under-hood lamp ($4.21). 521 front floor throw mats ($7.37). 522 rear floor throw mats ($6.32). 434 dual body-color rearview mirrors, left-hand remote control ($26.33). 444 remote-control left-hand

107

outside rearview mirror ($12.64). 441 right- or left-hand visor-vanity mirror ($3.16). 724 rocker panel moldings on T-37 ($10.53). 481 roof drip scalp moldings, standard with vinyl top, without vinyl top on T-37 and LeMans coupe and four-door sedan ($13.69). 482 side window reveal moldings on T-37 coupe ($21.06). 482 side window reveal moldings on other T-37 models and Safari ($31.60). 491 wheel opening moldings on T-37 and LeMans group except Safaris ($15.80). 704 Mountain Performance option with 350-cid two-barrel V-8 with automatic or Turbo Hydra-Matic transmission or 400-cid four-barrel V-8 with Turbo Hydra-Matic transmission and without manual air conditioning ($31.60). 704 Mountain Performance option with 350-cid two-barrel V-8 with automatic or Turbo Hydra-Matic transmission or 400-cid four-barrel V-8 with Turbo Hydra-Matic transmission and with manual air conditioning ($10.53). SPS special solid color paint on all models except convertibles without vinyl top ($115.85). SPS special solid color paint on all models except convertibles with vinyl top ($100.05). STT special two-tone paint on LeMans Safari ($137.97). STT special two-tone paint on T-37 and LeMans except Safari ($155.87). RTT standard two-tone paint on LeMans Safari ($22.12). RTT standard

Mike Butts photo

It didn't have quite the muscle or mystique of the GTO, but the '71 LeMans Sport was plenty appealing.

Mike Mueller photo

1971 GTOs that were painted Sandalwood were trimmed with yellow, black, and red stripes.

two-tone paint on T-37 and LeMans group except Safari ($40.02). 502 power front disc brakes on T-37 and LeMans group except Safari, includes Wonder Touch power brakes ($69.51). 511 Wonder Touch power brakes on T37 and LeMans group except Safari and standard on GTO ($47.39). 421 power remote-control deck lid release, except Safari ($14.74). 554 power door locks in two-door models ($45.29). 554 power door locks on four-door models ($68.46). 552 power door locks and seat back locks, on two-door models ($68.46). 561 Four-way power full bench seat in T-37 and LeMans group with bench seat ($78.99). 564 power left front bucket seat ($78.99). 501 power steering ($115.85). 544 Safari power tailgate window ($34.76). 701 heavy-duty radiator, not available with air conditioning ($21.06). 401 AM push-button radio ($66.35). 403 AM/FM radio ($139.02). 405 AM/FM stereo radio ($239.08). 411 rear seat speaker in LeMans group, except Safari, with AM push-button radio or AM/FM stereo radio ($18.96). 411 rear seat speaker in LeMans Safari with AM push-button radio or AM/FM stereo radio ($21.06). 412 stereo 8-track

tape player, requires 401, 403 or 405 radio ($133.76). 414 stereo cassette tape player, requires 401, 403 or 405 radio ($133.76). 714 Rally gauge cluster with tachometer, includes electric clock ($84.26). 718 Rally gauge cluster and clock, not available with 250-cid six, Rally gauge cluster with tachometer or 722 electric clock ($47.39). 571 front foam cushion in T-37 and LeMans group ($8.43). 621 Ride & Handling package on LeMans group except GTO and station wagons, and required with 455-cid H.O. V-8 ($9.48). 621 Ride & Handling package on GTO and required with 455-cid H.O. V-8 or "The Judge" option ($4.21). 461 Custom cushion steering wheel in T-37 or LeMans ($15.80). 462 Custom sport steering wheel in T-37 or LeMans ($57.93). 462 Custom sport steering wheel in LeMans Sport or GTO ($42.13). 464 Formula steering wheel in T-37 or LeMans with power steering ($57.93). 464 Formula steering wheel in LeMans Sport or GTO with power steering ($42.13). 504 tilt steering, requires power steering ($45.29). 614 vinyl stripes on T-37 or LeMans two-door, not available with "The Judge" option or vinyl body side moldings ($31.60). 721 hood-mounted tachometer on T-37 or LeMans with V-8, not available with Rally gauge cluster with tachometer ($63.19). SVT cordova top on T-37 and LeMans except convertible ($100.05). 35A three-speed manual transmission with column shift (standard, except GTO). 35C heavy-duty three-speed manual transmission with floor-mounted gear shifter in GTO (standard). 35C heavy-duty three-speed manual transmission with floor-mounted gear shifter in T-37 or LeMans except Safari ($84.26). 35E four-speed manual transmission in T-37 or LeMans ($195.36). 35G heavy-duty close-ratio four-speed manual transmission in T-37 or LeMans with 455-cid H.O. V-8 ($237.60). 35G heavy-duty close-ratio four-speed manual transmission in T-37 or LeMans with 400-cid four-barrel V-8 or 455-cid H.O. V-8 teamed with 37P or 37S axle ($237.60). 35J two-speed automatic transmission in T-37, LeMans or LeMans Sport with 250-cid six-cylinder engine and no air conditioning ($179.52). 35J two-speed automatic transmission in T-37, LeMans or LeMans Sport with 350-cid two-barrel V-8 ($190.08). 35K Turbo Hydra-Matic in T-37 and LeMans with 350-cid two-barrel V-8 ($221.76). 35K Turbo Hydra-Matic in T-37 and LeMans with 250-cid six-cylinder engine ($211.20). 35L Turbo Hydra-Matic in T-37 and LeMans group, except with 250-cid six-cylinder engine or 350-cid two-barrel V-8 ($242.88). Trim-coated fabric in T-37 coupe and four-door sedan with Trim no. 38 or 39 and T-37 four-door hardtop with Trim no. 32, 38 or 39 ($27.38). 514 pedal trim package for T-37 or LeMans with automatic transmission ($5.27). Custom wheel covers for T-37 and LeMans group ($31.60). 473 wire wheel covers for T-37 or LeMans group ($84.26). 474 Rally II wheels with trim rings on T-37 or LeMans ($89.52). 487 honeycomb wheels on T-37 or LeMans, except Safari without "The Judge" option ($126.38). 432 concealed windshield wipers on T-37 only ($18.96). 602 Endura styling option, including: GTO hood, GTO Endura bumper, and GTO headlight assembly for

GM Media Archives photo

At less than $2,900 new, the T-37 two-door coupes (a hardtop and sedan were both available) were a relative bargain.

LeMans Sport ($73.72). 334 GT option, including: vinyl accent stripes, Rally II wheels less trim rings, G70-14 white-lettered tires, dual exhausts with chrome extensions, heavy-duty three-speed manual transmission with floor-mounted gear shifter, four-speed manual transmission with floor-mounted gear shifter or three-speed Turbo Hydra-Matic transmission, body-color manual right-hand and remote-control left-hand mirror, hood locking pins, GT decals, and GT-37 nameplate for T-37 two-door hardtop with V-8 ($236.97). 332 "The Judge" option includes: 455-cid H.O. V-8, Rally II wheels less trim rings, air-inlet hood, T-handle shifter with manual transmission, rear deck lid air foil, specific body side stripes, "The Judge" decals, Ram Air decals, and black texture in the grille ($394.95). TDR H78-14 white sidewall tires on LeMans Safari ($35.81). TGF F78-14 black sidewall tires on T-37 with 250-cid six-cylinder engine ($14.74, but no charge with V-8). TGR F78 x 14 white sidewall tires on T-37 with 250-cid six-cylinder engine ($45.29). TGR F78 x 14 white sidewall tires on T-37 with V-8 engine ($30.54). TGR F78 x 14 white sidewall tires on LeMans and LeMans Sport, except Safari, with 250-cid six-cylinder engine ($30.54). TGR F78 x 14 white sidewall tires on LeMans and LeMans Sport, except Safari, with V-8 or air conditioning ($30.54). THR E78-14 white sidewall tires on T-37 with six-cylinder engine ($28.44). TPL G70-14 white letter tires on T-37, except Safari, with six-cylinder engine ($93.73). TPL G70-14 white-letter tires on T-37, except Safari, with V-8 or GT option ($78.99). TPL G70-14 white-letter tires on LeMans and LeMans Sport, except Safari, with V-8 without air conditioning ($78.99). TPL G70-14 white-letter tires on LeMans and LeMans Sport, except Safari, with V-8 and air conditioning ($64.25). TPL G70-14 white-letter tires on GTO ($43.18). TPR G70-14 white sidewall tires on T-37 with six-cylinder engine ($83.20). TPR G70-14 white sidewall tires on T-37 with V-8 engine ($68.46). TPR G70-14 white sidewall tires on LeMans and LeMans Sport, except Safari, with V-8 and no air conditioning ($68.46). TPR G70-14 white sidewall tires on LeMans and LeMans Sport, except Safari, with V-8 and air conditioning ($53.71). TPR G70-14 white sidewall tires on GTO ($32.65). TRR G78 x 14 white sidewall tires on T-37 with six-cylinder engine ($62.14). TRR G78 x 14 white sidewall tires on T-37 with V-8 engine ($47.39). TRR G78 x 14 white sidewall tires on LeMans and LeMans Sport, except Safari, with V-8 and without air conditioning ($47.39). TRR G78 x 14 white sidewall tires on LeMans and LeMans Sport, except Safari, with V-8 and air conditioning ($32.65). TXL G60-15 white-letter tires on GTO convertible with Rally II or Honeycomb wheels only ($74.78). TRF G78-14 black sidewall tires on T-37, except Safari, with six-cylinder engine ($29.49). TRF G78-14 black sidewall tires on T-37, except Safari, with V-8 engine ($14.74). TRF G78-14 black sidewall tires on LeMans or LeMans Sport, except Safari, with V-8 engine and air conditioning ($14.74).

OPTION INSTALLATION RATES

Of 165,638 Tempests built, 93.6 percent had automatic transmission, 2.1 percent had a four-speed synchromesh transmission, 6.4 percent had a standard V-8 engine, 85.7 percent had a standard V-8 engine, 7.9 percent had a six-cylinder engine, 87.6 percent had a AM radio, 5.3 percent had an AM/FM radio, 3.2 percent had a stereo tape player, 94.7 percent had power steering, 21.7 percent had power drum brakes, 6.4 percent had standard front disc brakes, 28 percent had optional front disc brakes, 0.8 percent had power door locks, 0.9 percent had a power seat, 5.3 percent had power side windows, 60.7 percent had an air conditioner, 2.1 percent had a movable steering column, 28.4 percent had bucket seats, 39.7 percent had a vinyl roof, 83.8 percent had white sidewall tires, 32.8 percent had a tinted windshield only, 42.5 percent had all tinted windows, 11.2 percent had dual exhausts, 5.3 percent had a limited-slip differential, 61.4 percent had optional full wheel discs, 23 percent had styled wheels, 0.7 percent had a speed regulating device, and 18.9 percent had a clock.

HISTORICAL FOOTNOTES

James F. McDonald was general manager of Pontiac Motor Div. Pontiacs were introduced September 23, 1970. Sales were good enough to put Pontiac back in third place on the charts in 1971. Pontiac built its 15 millionth car on July 6, 1971. Unfortunately, calendar-year sales of new "Tempests" by registered Pontiac dealers actually declined and came to just 181,588 units for a 2.1 percent share of the domestic industry total. Model-year production was only 165,638 units for a slightly better 2.3 percent share of industry output. By factory, the totals included 81,113 cars built in Pontiac, Michigan, 39,688 cars made in Fremont, California, 23,056 cars made in Lakewood, Georgia, and 21,781 cars made in Framingham, Massachusetts. A 60-day-long UAW strike had a negative effect on Pontiac's model-year production.

Mike Mueller photo

Only 5,807 of the LeMans coupes and two-door hardtops built were fitted with the GTO option.

The General Motors A-body cars, including the Pontiac "LeMans" models, had been scheduled for a major overhaul for the 1972 model year, but a 1970 United Auto Worker strike upset the plan and only minor changes were possible for 1972 models. The Luxury LeMans was a new addition to the Pontiac intermediate line. This new series offered two- and four-door hardtops. Both models included distinctive features like a special grille, a chromed front valance panel, fender skirts, special moldings and special interiors.

The standard LeMans was available in six models that featured a new split grille with each side also divided horizontally. The grille was flanked by side-by-side dual headlamps. The interiors were revamped and promoted as being "better looking." The GTO reverted to option status this year. GTO models again had a distinctive Endura nose treatment. The GTO grille was the same shape as the 1971 grille, but the grille inserts were deeply recessed, instead of flush. The grille texture had a square crosshatch pattern, instead of a diagonal one. New engine air extractor openings appeared on the front fender sides, behind the wheel openings. "The Judge" option package was no longer available. Engine choices were the same as in 1971, but gross horsepower ratings were not advertised. Horsepower ratings were now expressed in net horsepower (nhp).

I.D. NUMBERS

VIN on top of dash at left, viewable through windshield. First symbol tells GM division: 2=Pontiac. Second symbol tells series: D=LeMans, G=Luxury LeMans. Third and fourth symbols indicate body style and appear as last two letters of body/style number in charts below. Fifth symbol indicates engine. Sixth symbol indicates model year: 2=1972. Seventh symbol indicates assembly plant: A=Atlanta, Georgia, G=Framingham, Massachusetts, P=Pontiac, Michigan, and Z=Fremont, California Remaining symbols are sequential unit production number at factory, starting with 100001. Fisher body plate on cowl tells style number: Model year prefix 72, plus (this year only) 1971 type body/style number codes, body number, trim code, paint code and other data. Six-cylinder engine code stamped on distributor mounting on right side of block. V-8 engine code on front of block below right cylinder head. Engine production codes for 1972 were: (250-cid/110-nhp six) W6/CBJ/Y6/CBG/CBA/CBC. (350-cid/160-nhp V-8) WR/YU/YV/YR. (400-cid/180-nhp V-8) YX/ZX. (400-cid/200-nhp) WS/WK/YS/ZS. (400-cid/250-nhp) YY. (455-cid/190-nhp) YH/ZH. (455-cid/220-nhp) YC/YA. (455-cid/300-nhp) YB/YE. (455-cid/210-nhp) n.a. (455-cid/240-nhp) n.a. (455-cid/200-nhp) U.

COLORS

Paint codes for 1972 were: 11=Cameo White, 14=Revere Silver, 18=Antique Pewter, 19=Starlight Black, 24=Adriatic Blue, 26=Lucerne Blue, 28=Cumberland Blue, 36=Julep Green, 43=Springfield Green, 48=Wilderness Green, 50=Brittany Beige, 53=Quetzel Gold, 54=Arizona Gold, 55=Shadow Gold, 56=Monarch Yellow, 57=Brasilia Gold, 62=Spice Beige, 63=Anaconda Gold, 65=Sundance Orange, 69=Cinnamon Bronze, and 75=Cardinal Red. Vinyl top colors for 1972 were: 1=White, 2=Black, 4=Pewter, 6=Beige and 7=Tan. Interior trim codes for Tempests and T-37s were: 241=Blue cloth-and-vinyl bench seat, 244=Green cloth-and-vinyl bench seat, 245=Beige cloth-and-vinyl bench seat, 253=Saddle vinyl bench seat, 254=Green vinyl bench seat, 252=White vinyl bench seat, 256=Black vinyl bench seat, 270=Pewter vinyl Strato bucket seat,

272=White vinyl Strato bucket seat, 274=Green vinyl Strato bucket seat, and 276=Black vinyl Strato bucket seat.

BASE LEMANS — (SIX-CYL) — SERIES 2D

Standard equipment included: bench seats with cloth-and-Morrokide trim, front and rear foam seats, rear ashtrays in armrests (except coupe), loop-pile carpet (except coupe), a deluxe steering wheel, upper level ventilation (hardtop coupe), teakwood dash accents, in-the-windshield radio antenna, concealed windshield wipers (except coupe), ventipanes (except hardtop coupe), chrome valance panel and bright moldings on the roof gutters, windshield, rear window, and body sills on most styles. Station wagons had: all-Morrokide seats, under-floor cargo compartments, vinyl cargo floor coverings, two-way tailgates with built-in steps, power brakes with front discs, and power tailgate windows on nine-passenger jobs. Standard tires were H78-14 size on Safaris and F78-14 size on other styles. The WW-4 option was available on LeMans style numbers 2027 and 2037 and included: a 400-cid four-barrel V-8, a four-speed manual transmission with floor-mounted gear shifter, a heavy-duty Safe-T-Track differential, front power disc brakes, custom carpet (coupe only), and the Ride & Handling package. The WW-5 option was available on LeMans style numbers 2027 and 2037 and included: a choice of Turbo Hydra-Matic or close-ratio four-speed manual transmission, a 455-cid four-barrel H.O. V-8, a heavy-duty Safe-T-Track differential, body-color outside mirrors (left-hand remote control), a Formula steering wheel, roof drip moldings and carpeting (in coupe only), a Rally gauge cluster with tachometer, the Ride & Handling package, a Ram Air hood, and a unitized ignition system. The GTO-style Endura styling option was available on most LeMans models this year, including Safari station wagons. However, it could not be ordered in cars with the 250-cid six-cylinder engine and was not available on three-seat Safari with option 424 or on the two-seat Safari, or with the GT package. Also available for $231 extra was the LeMans GT package for the two-door hardtop or the LeMans Sport convertible. The GT option included: a heavy-duty three-speed manual transmission with floor shift, G70-14 fiberglass-belted raised white-letter tires, a

Mark Black photo

The 1972 LeMans came in coupe and hardtop models. A four-door sedan and station wagon were also available.

manual right-hand body-color outside rearview mirror, a remote-control left-hand outside rearview mirror, Rally II wheels (less trim rings), vinyl body side stripes, dual exhausts with side splitters, and GT decals. It was not available with the 250-cid inline six-cylinder engine or the 455-cid H.O. V-8, or teamed with the GTO option or the Endura styling option.

Model Number	Body/Style Number	Body Type & Seating	Factory Price	Shipping Weight	Production Total
BASE LEMANS — (SIX-CYL) — 2D SERIES					
2D	27	2d Coupe-6P	$2,722	3,294 lbs.	6,721
2D	36	4d Sta Wagon-6P	$3,271	3,799 lbs.	8,332
2D	37	2d Hardtop-6P	$2,851	3,234 lbs.	74,710
2D	46	4d Sta Wagon-9P	$3,378	3,839 lbs.	5,266
2D	69	4d Sedan-6P	$2,814	3,269 lbs.	19,463

NOTE 1: 9,601 LeMans had synchromesh and 110,698 had automatic transmission (including cars with the GTO option).

NOTE 2: A code 737 LeMans Sport hardtop option was available on style number 2D37 and included bucket seats, custom door and rear quarter trim, a custom rear seat, and special front fender nameplates. This car was not part of the LeMans Sport series, which included only one convertible model.

LEMANS SPORT — (SIX-CYL) — SERIES D67

The LeMans convertible was in a convertible sub-series called the LeMans Sport line. This model carried special "Sport" signature scripts and had standard bucket seats. Many sources list this style with the LeMans series, but the factory broke it out separately in calculating production totals. The code 332 LeMans GT package was available and included a three-speed heavy-duty manual transmission, G70 x 14 white-letter tires, body-color mirrors, Rally II wheels (less trim rings), vinyl tape stripes, dual exhausts with side splitters, and "GT" decals.

Model Number	Body/Style Number	Body Type & Seating	Factory Price	Shipping Weight	Production Total
2D	67	2d Convertible-5P	$3,228	3,284 lbs.	3,438

NOTE 3: 317 LeMans Sport "sport convertibles" made with synchromesh and 3,121 made with automatic transmission.

LUXURY LEMANS — (V-8) — SERIES 2G

A distinctive grille treatment with twin cavities divided by bright horizontal blades was used on Luxury LeMans models. Twin-ribbed full-length body-side moldings, fender skirts, and roof pillar letter badges were additional external distinctions. The standard equipment list was the same as for LeMans styles, plus a V-8 engine and all-Morrokide bucket seats in hardtop coupes or a notchback bench seats in any body style. Interior trim features included: all-Morrokide or cloth and Morrokide upholstery combinations, carpeted lower door panels with reflectors, a custom cushion steering wheel, pedal trim plates, front door assist straps, bright armrest accents, an ashtray lamp, and a glove box lamp.

Model Number	Body/Style Number	Body Type & Seating	Factory Price	Shipping Weight	Production Total
2G	37	2d Hardtop-5P	$3,196	3,488 lbs.	8,641
2G	39	4d Hardtop-6P	$3,319	3,638 lbs.	37,615

NOTE 4: 269 Luxury LeMans had synchromesh and 45,987 had automatic transmission.

GTO — (V-8) — SERIES D OPTION

Flat black paint finished the GTO's new egg-crate grille. The recessed section of the grille was painted Argent Silver and had decorative bright-metal moldings. As usual, a GTO nameplate was positioned in the left-hand grille. This year it was off to the far left side at about the middle. (LeMans models with the Endura option had a "Pontiac" nameplate instead.) The GTO was no longer a separate series. The new code 334 GTO option package was available for the style number 2D37 LeMans hardtop coupe and the 2D27 LeMans two-door coupe. It included: a 400-cid/250-net hp four-barrel V-8 with dual exhausts, a three-speed heavy-duty manual floor shift transmission, G70-14 black sidewall tires, body-color mirrors, the Endura styling option, a special twin air-slot hood, functional front fender air extractors, firm shock absorbers, front and rear stabilizer bars, and GTO identification. The price of the GTO option package was $344 over base model costs. A pair of 455-cid V-8 engines was optional. The first was a 250-nhp job with a four-barrel carburetor, dual exhausts, and an 8.2:1 compression ratio. The second was a 300-nhp job with a four-barrel carburetor, dual exhausts, and an 8.4:1 compression ratio. When the 300-hp engine was ordered at the factory, "GTO 455 H.O." decals were placed on the rear quarter panels at bumper-top height. Both models had bright rocker panel moldings and the hardtop had bright roof drip moldings (an option for the coupe). The 1972 taillights were slightly different and had thin vertical division bars and a reflector to serve as a side marker light on the wraparound portion. No 1972 GTO convertibles are known to have been built. Only 5,807 GTOs left the factory and body style breakouts are not available. (Note: These cars are included in the LeMans production totals given above). Only two GTOs are known to have had a rear deck lid spoiler that was listed as an option in early Pontiac literature. The option was later canceled, but these cars (and possibly others) snuck through with it. GTOs were available with either the base LeMans interior or the LeMans Sport interior. The Ram Air package or air-inlet hood (RPO 601) was available. It could be ordered separately with the 400-cid V-8 or with either of the 455-cid V-8s. It also came standard as part of the WW5 performance package.

Model Number	Body/Style Number	Body Type & Seating	Factory Price	Shipping Weight	Production Total
LEMANS GTO — (V-8) — 2D SERIES + RPO334					
2D	27	2d Coupe-6P	$3,066	—	134
2D	37	2d Hardtop-6P	$2,851	—	5,673

NOTE 5: Only 5,807 of the LeMans coupes and two-door hardtops built were fitted with the GTO option.

ENGINES

LEMANS, LEMANS SPORT BASE 250-CID SIX-CYL: Inline. Overhead valve. Bore and stroke: 3.88 x 3.53. Displacement: 250 cid. Compression ratio: 8.50:1. Net hp: 110 at 3800 rpm. Net torque: 185 lbs.-ft. at 1600 rpm. Seven main bearings. Hydraulic valve lifters. Crankcase capacity: 4 qt (add 1 qt. for new filter).

Cooling system capacity with heater: 13 qt. Carburetor: Rochester one-barrel carburetor. Engine code: D.

LUXURY LEMANS BASE V-8; LEMANS, LEMANS SPORT OPTIONAL 350-CID V-8: Overhead valve. Cast-iron block. Bore and stroke: 3.88 x 3.75. Displacement: 350 cid. Compression ratio: 8.50:1. Net hp: 160 at 4400 rpm. Taxable hp: 48.00. Net torque: 270 lbs.-ft. at 2000 rpm. Five main bearings. Hydraulic valve lifters. Crankcase capacity: 5 qt. (add 1 qt. for new filter). Cooling system capacity with heater: (Firebird) 19.4; (LeMans) 20.2. Carburetor: Rochester two-barrel. Single exhaust. VIN code: M.

LEMANS, LEMANS SPORT, LUXURY LEMANS OPTIONAL 350-CID V-8: Overhead valve. Cast-iron block. Bore and stroke: 3.88 x 3.53. Displacement: 350 cid. Compression ratio: 8.0:1. Net hp: 175 at 4400 rpm. Taxable hp: 48.00. Torque: 275 lbs.-ft. at 2000 rpm. Five main bearings. Hydraulic valve lifters. Carburetor: Rochester two-barrel. Crankcase capacity: 5 qt. (add 1 qt. for new filter). Cooling system capacity with heater: 20.2. Carburetor: Rochester four-barrel. Dual exhaust. VIN code: N.

LEMANS, LEMANS SPORT, LUXURY LEMANS OPTIONAL 400-CID V-8: Overhead valve. Cast-iron block. Bore and stroke: 4.12 x 3.75. Displacement: 400 cid. Compression ratio: 8.2:1. Taxable hp: 54.30. Net hp: 175 at 4000 rpm. Net torque: 310 lbs.-ft. at 2400 rpm. Five main bearings. Hydraulic valve lifters. Crankcase capacity: 5 qt. (add 1 qt. for new filter). Cooling system capacity with heater: 18.6. Carburetor: Rochester two-barrel. Single exhaust. VIN code: R.

LEMANS, LEMANS SPORT, LUXURY LEMANS OPTIONAL 400-CID V-8: Overhead valve. Cast-iron block. Bore and stroke: 4.12 x 3.75. Displacement: 400 cid. Compression ratio: 8.2:1. Net hp: 200 at 4000 rpm. Taxable hp: 54.30. Net torque: 325 lbs.-ft. at 2400 rpm. Five main bearings. Hydraulic valve lifters. Crankcase capacity: 5 qt. (add 1 qt. for new filter). Cooling system capacity with heater: 18.6. Carburetor: Rochester two-barrel. Dual exhaust. VIN code: P.

LEMANS, LEMANS SPORT, LUXURY LEMANS OPTIONAL 400-CID V-8: Overhead valve. Cast-iron block. Bore and stroke: 4.12 x 3.75. Displacement: 400 cid. Compression ratio: 8.2:1. Net hp: 200 at 4000 rpm. Taxable hp: 54.30. Net torque: 295 lbs.-ft. at 2800 rpm. Five main bearings. Hydraulic valve lifters. Crankcase capacity: 5 qt. (add 1 qt. for new filter). Cooling system capacity with heater: 18.6. Carburetor: Rochester four-barrel. Single exhaust. VIN code: S.

The Luxury LeMans was a much fancier car than its 1960s predecessors, whether in two- or four-door configurations.

LEMANS, LEMANS SPORT, LUXURY LEMANS, GTO OPTIONAL 455-CID V-8: Overhead valve. Cast-iron block. Bore and stroke: 4.15 x 4.21. Displacement: 455 cid. Compression ratio: 8.2:1. Net hp: 230 at 4400 rpm. Taxable hp: 55.20. Net torque: 360 lbs.-ft. at 2800 rpm. Five main bearings. Hydraulic valve lifters. Crankcase capacity: 5 qt. (add 1 qt. for new filter). Cooling system capacity with heater: 17.9. Carburetor: Rochester four-barrel. Dual exhaust.

GTO BASE V-8; LEMANS, LEMANS SPORT, LUXURY LEMANS OPTIONAL 400-CID V-8: Overhead valve. Cast-iron block. Bore and stroke: 4.12 x 3.75. Displacement: 400 cid. Compression ratio: 8.2:1. Net hp: 250 at 4400 rpm. Taxable hp: 54.30. Taxable hp: 55.20. Net torque: 325 lbs.-ft. at 3200 rpm. Five main bearings. Hydraulic valve lifters. Crankcase capacity: 5 qt. (add 1 qt. for new filter). Cooling system capacity with heater: 18.6. Carburetor: Rochester four-barrel. Dual exhaust. VIN code: T.

LEMANS, LEMANS SPORT, LUXURY LEMANS, GTO OPTIONAL 455-CID FOUR-BARREL V-8: Overhead valve. Cast-iron block. Bore and stroke: 4.15 x 4.21. Displacement: 455 cid. Compression ratio: 8.2:1. Net hp: 250 at 3600 rpm. Taxable hp: 55.20. Net torque: 370 lbs.-ft. at 2400 rpm. Five main bearings. Hydraulic valve lifters. Crankcase capacity: 5 qt. (add 1 qt. for new filter). Cooling system capacity with heater: 17.9. Carburetor: Rochester four-barrel. Dual exhaust. VIN code: Y.

LEMANS, LEMANS SPORT, LUXURY LEMANS, GTO OPTIONAL 455-CID H.O. V-8: Overhead valve. Cast-iron block. Bore and stroke: 4.15 x 4.21. Displacement: 455 cid. Compression ratio: 8.4:1. Net hp: 300 at 4000 rpm. Taxable hp: 55.20. Net torque: 415 lbs.-ft. at 3200 rpm. Five main bearings. Hydraulic valve lifters. Crankcase capacity: 5 qt. (add 1 qt. for new filter). Cooling system capacity with heater: 17.9. Carburetor: Rochester four-barrel. Dual exhaust. VIN code: X.

CHASSIS

Wheelbase: (two-door) 112 in., (four-door) 116 in. Overall length: 207.2 in. Width: 76.7 in. Height: 52.6 in. Front headroom: 38.5 in. Rear headroom: 37.1 in. Front legroom: 42.4 in. Rear legroom: 34.9 in. Front hiproom: 59.5 in. Rear hiproom: 59.1 in. Trunk capacity: 14.6 cu. ft. Turn circle: 38.6 ft. Front tread: 61 in. Rear tread: 61 in. (Note: All height, width, interior space and luggage space dimensions are for LeMans four-door sedan.)

OPTIONS

422 heavy-duty air cleaner ($9). 582 manual air conditioning ($397). 362 special order axle without Mountain Performance option ($10.53). 611 rear spoiler for LeMans coupe or two-door hardtop $46 (only two GTOs are known to have been built with this option, which was cancelled before the model year began). 368 performance axle ($10). 364 economy axle ($10). 361 Safe-T-Track differential with 37K or 37W axles ($45). 361 heavy-duty Safe-T-Track differential with 37K or 37W axle ($66). 691 Delco X Maintenance-Free battery and required with 455-cid four-barrel V-8s ($26). 692 heavy-duty battery, not available with Delco Maintenance-Free battery ($10). 451 Custom front and rear seat and front shoulder belts, in closed passenger cars ($15). 451 Custom front and rear seat and front shoulder belts, in convertible ($39). 451 Custom front and rear seat and front shoulder belts, in Safari ($18). 454 Custom front and rear seat belts in convertible ($13). 522 Custom floor carpets in LeMans without 702 or 704 ($21). 524 Custom load floor carpets in Safari ($51). 722 electric clock ($18). 431 front seat console in LeMans Sport two-door or GTO models, except with three-speed manual column-shift or two-speed automatic transmissions ($59). 424 spare wheel and tire cover ($5). 711 cruise control with two-speed automatic or Turbo Hydra-Matic transmissions ($62). 421 remote

The GTO was available in coupe and hardtop varieties in 1972. It received a new egg-crate grille. Two optional 455-cid engines were available.

Charles Bates photo

Full-length body-side moldings and fender skirts helped distinguish the 1972 Luxury LeMans.

deck lid release, except Safari ($14). 534 Safari rear window air deflector ($26). 541 rear window defogger in cars ($31). 541 rear window defogger in safari ($36). 534 electric rear window defroster, except Safaris ($62). 602 Endura styling option, for standard LeMans, except with 250-cid six-cylinder engine and not available on three-seat Safari with option 424 or with two-seat Safari and option 332, standard with code 334 GTO package ($41). 591 California assembly line emission test ($15). 34D 250-cid one-barrel six-cylinder engine in all models except Luxury LeMans and not available with GTO option or in California cars with air conditioning (standard). 34H 350-cid two-barrel V-8 in Luxury LeMans (standard). 34H 350-cid two-barrel V-8 in LeMans or LeMans Sport ($118). 34R 400-cid two-barrel V-8 in Luxury LeMans with Turbo Hydra-Matic transmission ($51). 34R 400-cid two-barrel V-8 in LeMans or LeMans Sport with Turbo Hydra-Matic transmission ($169). 34S 400-cid four-barrel V-8 in Luxury LeMans with heavy-duty three-speed or any four-speed or 35L Turbo Hydra-Matic transmission required ($97). 34S 400-cid four-barrel V-8 in standard LeMans without WW4 or GTO option and heavy-duty three-speed or any four-speed or 35L Turbo Hydra-Matic transmission required ($215). 34W 455-cid four-barrel V-8, requires 35L Turbo Hydra-Matic transmission and dual exhausts, except on Safari, for base LeMans without WW4 or GTO options and LeMans Safari ($272). 34W 455-cid four-barrel V-8, requires 35L Turbo Hydra-Matic transmission and dual exhausts, in GTO (standard). 34W 455-cid four-barrel V-8, requires 35L Turbo Hydra-Matic

transmission and dual exhausts in Luxury LeMans ($154). 34X 455-cid H.O. four-barrel V-8 in base LeMans coupe or hardtop or LeMans Sport convertible without WW4 or GTO option, requires heavy-duty four-speed manual or 35L Turbo Hydra-Matic transmission, Endura styling option, performance axle, dual exhausts, and air-inlet hood ($349). 34X 455-cid H.O. four-barrel V-8 in base LeMans coupe or hardtop or LeMans Sport convertible with WW4 or GTO option, requires heavy-duty four-speed manual or 35L Turbo Hydra-Matic transmission, Endura styling option, performance axle, dual exhausts and air-inlet hood ($134). (Note: the 34X V-8 was included with the WW5 option.) 531 all tinted glass ($42). 532 tinted windshield only ($30). 492 door edge guards, on two-door models ($6). 692 door edge guards on four-door models ($9). 731 front bumper guards, except GTO or cars with Endura Styling option ($15). 732 rear bumper guards, except Safari ($5). 601 air-inlet hood on LeMans and LeMans Sport coupes and convertibles with the 455-cid H.O. V-8 ($56). 681 dual horns on base LeMans ($4). 672 ash tray lamp, base LeMans except standard in convertible ($4). 662 rear compartment lamp in Safari ($10). 661 dome reading lamp ($13). 671 under-hood lamp ($4). 674 glove box lamp in base LeMans ($3). 521 front floor throw mats ($7). 522 rear floor throw mats ($6). 434 dual body-color rearview mirrors, left-hand remote control ($26). 441 right-hand visor-vanity mirror ($3). 441 left-hand visor-vanity mirror ($3). 444 remote-control left-hand outside rearview mirror ($12). 494 body-side moldings ($31). 481 roof drip moldings on base LeMans except two-door hardtop and LeMans Sport convertible ($13). 491 wheel opening moldings on base LeMans group except Safaris ($15). 482 side window reveal moldings on base LeMans coupes ($21). 482 side window reveal moldings on base LeMans four-door sedan ($26). 651 hood rear edge molding on base LeMans, included in Décor Group ($5). SPS special solid color paint on all models except convertibles without vinyl top ($113). SPS special solid color paint on LeMans Sport convertible or all base LeMans or Luxury LeMans with vinyl top ($97). STT special two-tone paint on LeMans Safari ($134). STT special two-tone paint on all LeMans except Safari ($152). RTT standard two-tone paint on LeMans Safari ($22). RTT standard two-tone paint on LeMans group

except Safari ($39). 514 pedal trim package on base LeMans ($5). 502 power front disc brakes on LeMans group except Safari, includes Wonder Touch power brakes ($68). 511 Wonder Touch power brakes on LeMans group except Safari and standard with WW4, WW5 or GTO ($46). 554 power door locks in two-door models ($44). 554 power door locks on four-door models ($67). 552 power door locks and seat back locks, on two-door models ($67). 561 4-Way power full bench seat in LeMans group with bench seat ($77). 501 power steering ($113). 542 Safari power tailgate window ($34). 701 heavy-duty radiator, standard with air conditioning ($21). 401 AM push-button radio ($65). 403 AM/FM radio ($135). 405 AM/FM stereo radio ($233). 411 rear

Mike Mueller photo

1972 GTOs equipped with the 455-cid H.O. engines had identifying decals placed on the rear quarter panels.

seat speaker in LeMans group, except Safari, with AM push-button radio or AM/FM stereo radio ($18). 411 rear seat speaker in LeMans Safari with AM push-button radio or AM/FM stereo radio ($21). 412 stereo 8-track tape player, requires 401, 403, or 405 radio ($130). 414 stereo cassette tape player, requires 401, 403 or 405 radio ($130). 714 Rally gauge cluster with tachometer, includes electric clock ($82). 718 Rally gauge cluster and clock, not available with 250-cid six, Rally gauge cluster with tachometer, or 722 electric clock ($49). 571 front foam cushion in base LeMans ($8). 621 Ride & Handling package on LeMans group except when standard ($9). 473 wire wheel covers on Luxury LeMans ($61). 473 wire wheel covers on base LeMans without Décor Group, not available with Custom Trim Group ($82). 473 wire wheel covers on base LeMans with Décor Group, not available with Custom Trim Group ($56). 478 honeycomb wheels on LeMans coupe or convertible with option 332 GT package ($62). 478 honeycomb wheels on LeMans Group with décor package ($92). 474 Rally II wheel rims on Luxury LeMans ($61). 474 Rally II wheel rims on base LeMans with Décor Group ($56). 474 Rally II wheel rims on base LeMans without Décor Group ($87). 471 chrome wheel trim rings ($26). 432 recessed windshield wipers on base LeMans coupe ($18). Wood-grained "Safari" paneling on LeMans Safari, except with Endura styling option or optional body-side moldings ($154). 721 Décor Group, including: Custom cushioned steering wheel, deluxe wheel discs, wheel opening moldings, except Safaris, pedal trim package and hood rear edge molding on base LeMans, except Safaris, without GT option package, WW4, WW5 options, or Custom trim group ($66). 721 Décor Group including: Custom cushioned steering wheel, deluxe wheel discs, wheel opening moldings on all but Safaris, pedal trim package, and hood rear edge molding on base LeMans coupe, sport coupe or convertible with GT option, WW4 option or Custom trim group ($35). 721 Décor Group including Custom cushioned steering wheel, deluxe wheel discs, wheel opening moldings on all but Safaris, pedal trim package and hood rear edge molding on base LeMans coupe, sport coupe, or convertible with WW5 option ($20). 721 Décor Group including: Custom cushioned steering wheel and deluxe wheel discs on Safaris ($51). 332 GT package for LeMans two-door hardtop or LeMans Sport convertible, including heavy-duty three-speed manual transmission with floor shift, G70-14 fiberglass-belted raised white-letter tires, manual right-hand body-color outside rearview mirror, remote-control left-hand outside rearview mirror, Rally II wheels less trim rings, vinyl body side stripes, dual exhausts with side splitters and GT decals, not available with six-cylinder engine, 455-cid H.O. V-8, GTO option or Endura styling option ($231). 334 GTO option for

The 1972 LeMans convertible was its own separate line, called the LeMans Sport.

Paul Zazerine collection

LeMans two-door hardtop, coupe, or LeMans Sport convertible, including: 400-cid four-barrel V-8, heavy-duty three-speed manual transmission with floor shift, G70-14 fiberglass-belted black sidewall tires, dual exhausts with side splitters, Endura styling option, special hood with dual air scoops, front fender air extractors, firm shock absorbers, front and rear stabilizer bars, and GTO identification, not available with six-cylinder engine, 350-cid V-8, 400-cid two-barrel V-8, or GT option package ($344). 724 handling package for base LeMans coupe or two-door hardtop without GTO option, WW4 option, WW5 option, or GT package ($236). 724 handling package for base LeMans coupe or two-door hardtop with GTO option without WW4 or WW5 option ($186). 724 handling package for base LeMans two-door hardtop with GT package ($159). 621 Ride & Handling package for standard LeMans coupe, required with GTO option ($4). 461 Custom cushion steering wheel in base LeMans ($15). 462 Custom Sport steering wheel in base LeMans without WW5 option and without Décor Group ($56). 462 Custom Sport steering wheel in Luxury LeMans ($41). 462 Custom Sport steering wheel in base LeMans without WW5 option, but with Décor Group ($41). 464 Formula steering wheel in base LeMans without WW5 option and without Décor Group ($56). 464 Formula steering wheel in base LeMans without WW5 option and with Décor Group ($41). 464 Formula steering wheel in Luxury LeMans ($41). 504 tilt steering, requires power steering ($44). 614 vinyl stripes on LeMans two-door, not available with GT option or vinyl body-side moldings ($31). SVT cordova top on LeMans group, except convertible and Safari ($97). 35A three-speed manual transmission with column shift (standard with 250-cid six-cylinder engine or 350-cid two-barrel V-8). 35C heavy-duty three-speed manual transmission with floor shift in LeMans except with 350-cid two-barrel V-8 or 34S 400-cid four-barrel V-8 ($82). 35E four-speed manual transmission in LeMans, except Safari with 350-cid two-barrel V-8 or 34S 400-cid four-barrel V-8 ($190). 35G heavy-duty close-ratio four-speed manual transmission in LeMans with 455-cid or 455-cid H.O. V-8 without WW4 ($231). 35G heavy-duty close-ratio four-speed manual transmission in LeMans with 455-cid or 455-cid H.O. V-8 with WW4 ($41). 35J two-speed automatic transmission in LeMans with 250-cid six-cylinder engine and no air conditioning ($174). 35J two-speed automatic transmission in LeMans with 350-cid two-barrel V-8 ($185). 35K Turbo Hydra-Matic in LeMans with 350-cid two-barrel V-8 ($215). 35L Turbo Hydra-Matic in LeMans group, except with WW4, not available with 250-cid six-cylinder engine or 350-cid two-barrel V-8 ($236). 35L Turbo Hydra-Matic in LeMans group, with WW4, not available with 250-cid six-cylinder engine or 350-cid two-barrel V-8 ($46). Vinyl interior trim in LeMans two-door models ($27). 654 Custom Trim bucket seats in GTO ($160). 634 Unitized ignition system in LeMans two-door models with 455-cid H.O. V-8 ($77). 476 deluxe wheel covers for LeMans group, except with Custom Trim Group ($31). TDR H78-14 white sidewall tires on LeMans Safari ($35). TGR F78 x 14 white sidewall tires on LeMans, except Safari, with 250-cid six-cylinder engine or 350-cid two-barrel V-8

($30). TPL G70-14 white letter tires on LeMans, except Safari, with V-8 or GT option ($77). TPL G70-14 white letter tires on LeMans and LeMans Sport, except Safari, with V-8 without air conditioning ($77). TPL G70-14 white letter tires on LeMans and LeMans Sport, except Safari, with V-8 and air conditioning ($63). TPL G70-14 white letter tires on GTO ($42). TRF G78-14 black sidewall tires on LeMans or LeMans Sport, except Safari, with V-8 engine and air conditioning ($14). TRF G78-14 black sidewall tires on T-37, except Safari, with six-cylinder engine ($29). TRR G78-14 white sidewall tires on T-37 with V-8 engine ($46). TXL G60-15 white letter tires on GTO convertible with Rally II or Honeycomb wheels only ($75).

OPTION INSTALLATION RATES

Of 213,239 Tempests built, 88.7 percent had automatic transmission, 6.8 percent had a four-speed synchromesh transmission, 17.4 percent had a standard V-8 engine, 75.4 percent had a standard V-8 engine, 7.2 percent had a six-cylinder engine, 87.8 percent had a AM radio, 7.3 percent had an AM/FM radio, 3.3 percent had a stereo tape player, 92 percent had power steering, 23.5 percent had power drum brakes, 30.9 percent had front disc brakes, 0.7 percent had power door locks, 1.1 percent had a power seat, 2.7 percent had power side windows, 3.9 percent had power station wagon tailgate window, 57.5 percent had an air conditioner, 2.4 percent had a movable steering column, 12.8 percent had bucket seats, 42.5 percent had a vinyl roof, 85.2 percent had white sidewall tires, 32.7 percent had a tinted windshield only, 44.5 percent had all tinted windows, 19 percent had dual exhausts, 9.7 percent had a limited-slip differential, 65.1 percent had optional full wheel discs, 23.1 percent had optional styled wheels, 1 percent had a speed regulating device, 2.1 percent had a station wagon luggage rack, 0.3 percent had reclining front seats, and 20.9 percent had a clock.

HISTORICAL FOOTNOTES

Production startup date was August 12, 1971. Factory introductions were held September 23, 1971. Among U.S. automakers, Pontiac Motor Division ranked in fifth place. F.J. McDonald was Pontiac general manager for most of the year. On October 1, 1972, Martin J. Caserio took over as general manager. Sales of LeMans intermediate rose 9 percent and came to 198,969 units. Model-year production was 169,993 units. By factory, the totals included 93,552 cars built in Pontiac, Michigan, 14,165 cars made in Fremont, California, 47,928 cars made in Lakewood, Georgia, and 14,348 cars made in Framingham, Massachusetts. The 1972 GTO hardtop with 300 net hp was tested at 7.1 seconds 0 to 60 mph and 15.4 seconds in the quarter-mile. The 1972 Firebird Esprit did 0 to 60 mph in 9.9 seconds and the quarter-mile in 17.6 seconds. The GTO returned to option status this year and Pontiac made the Turbo Hydra-Matic and disc brakes standard on all models.

The new Grand Ams didn't get the 455-cid Super-Duty engine that some enthusiasts were hoping for in 1973, but they were still eye-catching cars that were very well received.

GM Media Archives photo

Pontiac's A-body intermediate line had highly revised "Buck Rogers" styling this season. Design characteristics included V-shaped hoods, split rectangular grilles, single headlamps mounted in square housings, highly sculptured fenders and "Colonnade" style rooflines. The Colonnade styling provided heavier roof pillars to meet federal rollover standards with large window openings cut deep into the beltline in limousine style. This styling combined with a dramatic-looking frontal treatment characterized an all-new Grand Am model that was a direct derivative of the LeMans series. Enthusiasts got a bit excited when they saw press photos of two-door A-body Pontiacs with the SD-455 V-8 and

noticed this engine listed in the 1973 sales literature for all models except the Luxury LeMans. But alas, the Super-Duty coupes were all prototypes and the SD-455 V-8 never made it into production in an A-body car.

I.D. NUMBERS

VIN on top of dash at left, viewable through windshield. First symbol tells GM division: 2=Pontiac. Second symbol tells series: D=LeMans, F=LeMans Sport, G=Luxury LeMans, H=Grand Am. Third and fourth symbols indicate body style and appear as last two digits of body/style number in charts below. Fifth symbol indicates engine. Sixth symbol indicates model year: 3=1973. Seventh symbol indicates assembly plant: A=Lakewood (Atlanta), Georgia, G=Framingham, Massachusetts, P=Pontiac, Michigan, Z=Fremont, California, and 1=Oshawa, Canada. Remaining symbols are sequential unit production number at factory, starting with 100001. Fisher body plate on cowl tells style number: Model year prefix 73, plus new type body/style number codes, body number, trim code, paint code and other data. Six-cylinder engine code stamped on distributor mounting on right side of block. V-8 engine code on front of block below right cylinder head. Engine production codes for 1973 were: (250-cid/100-nhp six) CCC-CCD-CCA-CCB-CDR-CDS-CAW. (350-cid/150-nhp V-8) YL-Y2-YR-Y7-YV-XR-XV-ZR-ZV-XC. (350-cid/175-nhp V-8) WV-ZB-ZD-WD-XC-X2-WF-WA-XF-WC-WL-WN-YW. (400-cid/170-nhp V-8) YP-Y4-YX-Y1-ZX-ZK-YZ. (400-cid/185-nhp V-8) P. (400-cid/200-nhp V-8) S. (400-cid/230-nhp V-8) WK-WS-WP-YS-Y3-YN-YT. (400-cid/250-nhp V-8) X4-X1-X3-XH-W5-Y6-YF-YG-XN-XX-X5-XZ-XK. (455-cid/215-nhp V-8) W. (455-cid/250-nhp V-8) WW-WT-YC-YA-ZC-ZZ-ZE-XE-XA-XJ-XL-XO-XT-X7-XY-XM. (455-cid/310-nhp Super-Duty V-8) ZJ-XD-W8-Y8 (believed to have been used in only one pre-production Grand Am coupe).

COLORS

Paint codes for 1973 were: 11=Cameo White, 24=Porcelain Blue, 26=Regatta Blue, 29=Admiralty Blue, 42=Verdant Green, 44=Slate Green, 46=Golden Olive, 48=Brewster Green, 56=Desert Sand, 60=Valencia Gold, 64=Ascot Silver, 66=Burnished Amber, 68=Burma Brown, 74=Florentine Red, and 81=Mesa Tan. Vinyl top colors for 1973 were: 1=White, 2=Black, 3=Beige, 4=Chamois, 5=Green, 6=Dark Burgundy, and 7=Blue. Interior trim codes for LeMans were: 251=Blue vinyl bench seat, 252=White vinyl bench seat, 253=Saddle vinyl bench seat, 256=Black vinyl bench seat, 257=Burgundy vinyl bench seat, 258=Chamois vinyl bench seat, 261=Blue cloth-and-vinyl bench seat, 264=Green cloth-and-vinyl bench seat, 265=Beige cloth-and-vinyl bench seat, 271=Blue vinyl bench seat, 272=White vinyl bench seat, 273=Saddle vinyl bench seat, 274=Green vinyl bench seat, 275=Beige vinyl bench seat, 276=Black vinyl bench seat, 277=Burgundy vinyl bench seat, 281=Blue cloth-and-vinyl bench seat, 284=Green cloth-and-vinyl bench seat, 285=Beige cloth-and-vinyl bench seat, 286=Black cloth-and-vinyl bench seat, 292=White vinyl bucket seat, 293=Chamois vinyl bucket seat, 296=Burgundy vinyl bucket seat, and 297=White vinyl bucket seat.

LEMANS — (SIX-CYL) — SERIES 2AD

Base LeMans models had a split grille assembly with 23 vertical fins in each grille section framed by a bright-metal surround molding. Both grilles were mounted in a full-width, body-colored front-end panel. This panel had a pointed "nose" at it center bearing the Pontiac "Arrowhead" crest. At the outboard end of each grille were headlights with round lenses in bright square

housings with rounded corners. A massive new front bumper was required to meet new government crashworthiness standards. A body-color filler panel was above the bumper and rubber bumper impact strips were optional. The parking lights were in the bumper, directly below the headlights. LeMans lettering appeared behind the front wheel opening and thin body sill moldings were used. Station wagons were officially called Safaris again. Available options on the LeMans included the GT and GTO packages. The new LeMans body had "pontoon" style rear fenders and heavy sculpturing. The taillights were narrow rectangles with a small, square back-up lens in their center. All-new LeMans interiors were seen. Seating options included the standard split bench seat or a notchback bench seat and bucket seats in some models. The dashboard was a single integral unit surrounding the instrument panel on the left and dipped down over the glove box on the right. The underside also surrounded the instrument panel before sweeping upwards to the right-hand door. A cushioned two-spoke steering wheel was standard equipment. By 1973, a long list of safety and anti-theft features were installed on all General Motors (GM) cars, including Pontiac LeMans models. These were also used on all cars made in subsequent years, with some upgrades over the years. GM occupant safety features promoted in 1973 Pontiac literature included: front driver and passenger single-buckle seat belts, front shoulder belts, a front safety belt warning system, push-button buckles for all passenger positions, front headrests, an energy-absorbing steering column, passenger-guard door locks with forward-mounted lock buttons, safety door latches and hinges, folding seat back latches, and energy-absorbing padded instrument panel and padded front and intermediate seat back tops, a thick-laminate windshield, padded sun visors, safety armrests, a safety steering wheel, Cargo-Guard, side-guard beam doors, fuel tank impact security, glove box door security, console door latch impact security, smooth-contoured door and window regulator handles, soft low-profile window control knobs and coat hooks, front and rear automatic locking seat belt retractors, shoulder belt anchorages for outboard passengers, a Roto-Safe radiator cap, high-strength front and rear seat construction and retention and at least one stamped steel door hinge per door. GM accident prevention features promoted in 1973 were comprised of side marker lights and reflectors, parking lamps that illuminated with the headlights, four-way hazard flashers, back-up lights, directional signals with a lane-change function, a defroster, dual-speed windshield wipers and washers, a left-hand outside rearview mirror, a dual brake master cylinder with monitor light, dual-action safety hood hinges, headlight aiming access provisions, a low-glare instrument panel surface, low-glare windshield wipers, low-glare steering wheel metal parts, safety wheel rims, a uniform shift quadrant, self-adjusting brakes with corrosion-resistant lines and wheel nuts, and covers without protrusions. GM also promoted anti-theft features in its 1973 models, such as an anti-theft ignition key with warning buzzer, an anti-theft steering column lock, multiple key combinations, visible-through-the-windshield VINs and a tamper-resistant odometer with a telltale feature. Other standard LeMans equipment included: bench seats with cloth-and-vinyl trim, molded foam seat cushions and backs with integral springs, nylon-blend loop-pile carpeting, improved acoustical insulation, an inside hood-latch release, improved instrument panel serviceability, high-low ventilation, a deluxe steering wheel, new improved front and rear impact-resistant bumpers, fixed rear quarter windows, an in-the-windshield radio antenna, concealed windshield wipers, frameless door glass, standard hubcaps, a heavy-duty perimeter frame, improved body mounts, a four-wheel coil spring suspension, improved shock absorbers, front disc brakes, and F78-14 black sidewall tires. The LeMans Safari station wagon featured all-Morrokide upholstery, a deluxe two-spoke steering wheel, rear armrests, a rear-facing third seat in the D45 model, a textured steel cargo floor covered with special vinyl paint, an under-the-floor stowage compartment, concealed windshield wipers, swing-out rear quarter vents on the D45 model, vertical tailgate rub strips, a lift-type tailgate (with electric tailgate release on the D45 model), front disc brakes, and extra bright-metal body moldings.

Model Number	Body/Style Number	Body Type & Seating	Factory Price	Shipping Weight	Production Total
2AD	29	4d Hardtop-6P	$2,918	3,605 lbs.	26,554
2AD	37	2d Hardtop-6P	$2,920	3,579 lbs.	67,736
2AD	45	4d Sta Wagon-9P	$3,429	3,993 lbs.	6,127
2AD	35	4d Sta Wagon-6P	$3,296	3,956 lbs.	10,446

LEMANS SPORT COUPE — (SIX-CYL) — SERIES 2AF

The LeMans Sport convertible was discontinued and replaced by the Series 2AF LeMans Sport Coupe. This model constituted a separate sub-series. It had the same grille as the LeMans. The LeMans Sport Coupe came standard with bucket seats and louvered rear quarter window styling. Available options on the LeMans Sport Coupe included the GT and GTO packages. In addition to standard LeMans features, the LeMans Sport Coupe also offered no-cost all-vinyl upholstery options, a front notchback bench seat with folding center armrest or bucket seats, special interior door panels, solid foam seat backs and cushions, fixed louvered rear quarter windows, concealed windshield wipers, computer-selected springs and LeMans Sport emblems behind the front wheel openings and on the right-hand side of the rear deck lid.

Model Number	Body/Style Number	Body Type & Seating	Factory Price	Shipping Weight	Production Total
2AF	37	2d Hardtop-5P	$3,008	3,594 lbs.	46,193

GTO OPTION — (V-8) — SERIES 2AD AND SERIES 2AF + W62 GTO

The GTO option was available on the LeMans two-door hardtop or the LeMans Sport Coupe. The grille had a flat textured finish on the GTO. There was GTO lettering on

The 1973 LeMans came standard with a six-cylinder engine, but four different V-8 mills were also available.

The first-year Grand Am was designed to be a direct competitor to the European touring cars, but at a price the average buyer could stomach. The cars featured a distinctive grille and nosepiece.

John Gunnell photo

the far left-hand edge of the grille. The base LeMans with the GTO option had a conventional quarter window treatment, while the LeMans Sport version had the louvered quarter window treatment. The option package also included the 400-cid four-barrel V-8, a special hood with twin "NASA" hood scoops, Wide-Oval tires, dual exhausts, a heavy-duty three-speed manual gearbox, a floor-mounted gear shifter, firm shock absorbers, front and rear rear sway bars, baby moon hubcaps, 15 x 7-in. wheel rims, specific body striping and suitable GTO decal identification. The Ram Air option was never released for production build.

Model Number	Body/Style Number	Body Type & Seating	Factory Price	Shipping Weight	Production Total
LEMANS GTO — (V-8) — SERIES 2AD AND SERIES 2AD + W62 GTO					
2AD	37	2d Hardtop-5P	$3,288	3,810 lbs.	494
LEMANS GTO — (V-8) — SERIES 2D AND SERIES 2AF + W62 GTO					
2AF	37	2d Hardtop-5P	$3,376	3,810 lbs.	4,806

LUXURY LEMANS — (V-8) — SERIES 2AG

Luxury LeMans models also featured Colonnade styling, but with higher-level interior and exterior appointments, plus standard V-8 power. Styling features included wide beauty moldings running the full width of the body at about mid-wheel height, fender skirts with chrome edge moldings, rear deck beauty panels between the taillights, a die-cast metal grille with vertical blades and vertical chrome division moldings, deluxe wheel covers and

"Luxury" signatures above the LeMans fender lettering. Luxury LeMans upholstery combinations were patterned after those seen in Grand Villes and featured a monogram on the center armrest. The two-door model came with all-vinyl front bucket seats or a notchback bench seat with a choice of all-vinyl or cloth-and-vinyl trim. Other standard extras on the Luxury LeMans included added sound insulation, rear seat ashtrays in the armrests, a wood-grain vinyl inlay on the glove box door, front door assist straps, an ashtray lamp, a glove box lamp, rear fender skirts, body-color door handle inserts and bright metal moldings on the roof gutters, bright rear deck lid moldings, a bright rear-edge-of-hood molding, front wheel opening moldings, bright quarter window moldings, and taillight moldings.

Model Number	Body/Style Number	Body Type & Seating	Factory Price	Shipping Weight	Production Total
LUXURY LEMANS — (V-8) — SERIES 2AG					
2AG	29	4d Hardtop-6P	$3,344	3,867 lbs.	9,377
2AG	37	2d Hardtop-6P	$3,274	3,799 lbs.	33,916

GRAND AM — (V-8) — SERIES 2AH

One of the most distinctive cars offered in the sales sweepstakes this model year was the original Pontiac Grand Am. This A-body intermediate had an international flavor. It was designed to try to steal sales away from luxurious European touring cars like the

Mercedes-Benz 300 SEL 6.3, the BMW, and the Jaguar. It had "Euro" touches like a stalk-mounted headlight dimmer (most U.S. cars still had their dimmer switch on the floor at this time) and bucket seats available in the four-door sedan version (only a few domestic sedans had ever offered bucket seats). The name of the car was intended to carry the message that it was part Trans Am (sports car) and part Grand Prix (personal-luxury car). The fact that it was LeMans based meant that Pontiac could offer the Grand Am at less than half the price of the European competitors. As a yardstick, the Mercedes-Benz 300 SEL 6.3 was a $16,000 car, the BMW 3.0 CSA was a $10,000 car, and the Jaguar XJ6 was an $8,300 car in 1973. The most startling thing about the 1973 Grand Am was its front-end appearance, which featured a three-piece nose section made of injection-molded urethane plastic. The center panel was a "ship's prow" nosepiece bearing a small, red Pontiac arrowhead crest. On either side of center were grille sections with three wide vertical slots, each filled with five vertical bright-metal fins. The headlight openings were at the outboard ends of the grilles. The single headlights had round lenses in bright square housings with rounded corners. A small "Pontiac" nameplate was placed above the left-hand grille. Standard equipment for the Grand Am included: wide-wale corduroy or all-vinyl upholstery trimmed in leather-like Morrokide vinyl, a three-spoke custom sport steering wheel with a large padded center, a distinctive instrument panel with an African crossfire mahogany inlay, an electric clock, an oil pressure gauge, a water-temperature indicator, a voltmeter, a fuel gauge, a trip odometer, plug-in instrument panel components, high-low ventilation, a front seat console with floor-mounted gear shifter and mahogany trim, an ashtray lamp, a courtesy lamp, a glove box lamp, a headlamp dimmer switch on the steering column instead of the floor, reclining front bucket seats with adjustable lower back supports, nylon-blend loop-pile carpeting, pedal trim plates, pull straps on all doors, concealed windshield wipers, custom finned wheel covers, exclusive taillight styling, dual horns, an in-the-windshield radio antenna, rear window moldings, side windowsill moldings, wheel lip moldings, a molding on the rear edge of the hood, black-accented rocker panel moldings, a 1.12-in. front stabilizer bar, a 0.94-in. rear stabilizer bar, variable-ratio power steering, power front disc/rear drum brakes, GR70-15 steel-belted radial black sidewall tires, a four-wheel coil spring suspension, firm shock absorbers, computer-selected springs, a heavy-gauge perimeter frame, a Power-Flex cooling fan, dual exhausts, 7-in.-wide wheels, and a standard 400-cid two-barrel V-8 with Turbo Hydra-Matic transmission and a 3.08:1 rear axle ratio. Early pre-production versions of the Grand Am coupe that appeared in factory photos and were even tested by the motoring press carried the rare LS2 Super-Duty 455 V-8 that featured a Quadrajet carburetor, forged connecting rods, TRW pistons, Ram Air induction, and 310 hp. With this engine, it was reported that the Grand Am could do the quarter-mile in 15 seconds flat at 94 mph. This engine was also listed as an option for the Grand Am two-door model in Pontiac sales literature and in early Pontiac advertisements.

Unfortunately, this engine was not EPA-certified for A-body Pontiacs and never made it into production-line models. Documentation exists that states the Grand Am was originally planned to be the GTO.

Model Number	Body/Style Number	Body Type & Seating	Factory Price	Shipping Weight	Production Total
2AH	29	4d Hardtop-6P	$4,353	4,018 lbs.	8,691
2AH	37	2d Hardtop-6P	$4,264	3,992 lbs.	34,445

ENGINES

LEMANS, LEMANS SPORT BASE 250-CID SIX-CYL: Inline. Overhead valve. Bore and stroke: 3.88 x 3.53. Displacement: 250 cid. Compression ratio: 8.50:1. Net hp: 100 at 3600 rpm. Net torque: 175 lbs.-ft. at 1600 rpm. Seven main bearings. Hydraulic valve lifters. Crankcase capacity: 4 qt (add 1 qt. for new filter). Cooling system capacity with heater: 13 qt. Carburetor: Rochester one-barrel carburetor. Engine code: D.

LUXURY LEMANS BASE V-8; LEMANS, LEMANS SPORT OPTIONAL 350-CID V-8: Overhead valve. Cast-iron block. Bore and stroke: 3.88 x 3.53. Displacement: 350 cid. Compression ratio: 7.6:1. Net hp: 150 at 4000 rpm. Taxable hp: 48.00. Net torque: 270 lbs.-ft. at 2000 rpm. Five main bearings. Hydraulic valve lifters. Crankcase capacity: (Ventura) 4 qt., (others) 5 qt. (add 1 qt. for new filter). Cooling system capacity with heater: (Ventura, Firebird) 19.5 qt., (others) 20.2 qt. Carburetor: Rochester two-barrel. Engine code M.

GRAND AM BASE V-8; LEMANS, LEMANS SPORT, LUXURY LEMANS OPTIONAL 400-CID V-8: Overhead valve. Cast-iron block. Bore and stroke: 4.12 x 3.75. Displacement: 400 cid. Compression ratio: 8.00:1. Net hp: 170 at 3600 rpm. Taxable hp: 54.30. Net torque: 320 lbs.-ft. at 2000 rpm. Five main bearings. Hydraulic valve lifters. Crankcase capacity: 5 qt. (add 1 qt. for new filter). Cooling system capacity with heater: 18.6 qt. Carburetor: Rochester two-barrel. Engine code R.

GTO BASE V-8, LEMANS, LEMANS SPORT, LUXURY LEMANS OPTIONAL 400-CID V-8: Overhead valve. Cast-iron block. Bore and stroke: 4.12 x 3.75. Displacement: 400 cid. Compression ratio: 8.00:1. Net hp: 230 at 4400 rpm. Taxable hp: 54.30. Net torque: 325 lbs.-ft. at 3200 rpm. Five main bearings. Hydraulic valve lifters. Crankcase capacity: 5 qt. (add 1 qt. for new filter). Cooling system capacity with heater: 18.6 qt. Carburetor: Rochester two-barrel. Engine code T.

GTO OPTIONAL 455-CID V-8 (WITH TURBO HYDRA-MATIC ONLY): Overhead valve. Cast-iron block. Bore and stroke: 4.15 x 4.21. Displacement: 455 cid. Compression ratio: 8.00:1. Net hp: 250 at 4000 rpm. Taxable hp: 55.20. Net torque: 370 lbs.-ft. at 2800 rpm. Five main bearings. Hydraulic valve lifters. Crankcase capacity: 5 qt. (add 1 qt. for new filter). Cooling system capacity with heater: 18 qt. Dual exhaust. Carburetor: Rochester four-barrel. Code Y engine.

NOTE 1: The above engine data is based on research by Pontiac's official historian, John Sawruk, and is from factory documents dated March 15, 1973. It varies from engine information printed in Pontiac's early 1973 sales literature and from engine charts published in the October 1972 issue of *Motor Trend* magazine.

NOTE 2: Pontiac engineers developed a way to shut off the EGR system in cars after 53 seconds. This allowed Pontiacs to get through EPA testing before the EGR system was shut off and improved real-world engine performance. However, the EPA became aware of this and required the removal of the EGR shutdown system by March 15, 1973. Engines made thereafter were painted darker blue. They had no EGR solenoid and two thermal valves were added to their intake manifold, ahead of the carburetor. As a result, there is a difference in the performance of early- and late-production engines, even though the advertised horsepower and torque ratings did not change

CHASSIS

Wheelbase: (LeMans, LeMans Sport Coupe, Luxury LeMans and Grand Am two-door) 112 in., (LeMans, Luxury LeMans, Grand Am four-door and all LeMans Safari four-door station wagons) 116 in. Overall Length: (LeMans, LeMans Sport Coupe, Luxury LeMans and Grand Am two-door) 207.4 in., (LeMans, Luxury LeMans and Grand Am four-door) 211.4 in., (LeMans Safari) 213.3 in. Overall width: (All) 77.7 in. Overall height: (LeMans, LeMans Sport, Luxury LeMans and Grand Am two-door) 52.9 in., (LeMans, Luxury LeMans and Grand Am four-door) 54.3 in. (Safari) 55 in. Front headroom: (LeMans, LeMans Sport Coupe, Luxury LeMans and Grand Am two-door) 37.8 in., (LeMans, Luxury LeMans, Grand Am four-door) 38.5 in. Rear headroom: (LeMans, LeMans Sport Coupe, Luxury LeMans and Grand Am two-door) 36.9 in., (LeMans, Luxury LeMans, Grand Am four-door) 37.2 in. Front legroom: (LeMans, LeMans Sport Coupe, Luxury LeMans and Grand Am two-door) 42.4 in., (LeMans, Luxury LeMans and Grand Am four-

The Grand Am was very successful in its first year with more than 43,000 cars produced. The four-door model was not nearly as popular with buyers as the two-door coupe.

Paul Zazerine collection

The 1973 two-door LeMans Sport Coupe with Colonnade hardtop in Regatta Blue.

door) 42.4 in. Rear legroom: (LeMans, LeMans Sport Coupe and Luxury LeMans two-door) 33.7 in., (Grand Am two-door) 33.5 in., (LeMans and Luxury LeMans four-door) 38.4 in., (Grand Am four-door) 38.6 in. Front shoulder room: (LeMans, LeMans Sport Coupe, Luxury LeMans and Grand Am two-door) 59.6 in., (LeMans, Luxury LeMans and Grand Am four-door) 59.6 in. Rear shoulder room: (LeMans, LeMans Sport Coupe, Luxury LeMans and Grand Am two-door) 57.5 in., (LeMans, Luxury Lemans and Grand Am four-door) 58.9 in. Trunk capacity: (all cars) 15.1 cu. ft. Top of front seat back to closed tailgate length: (Safari) 82.9 in. Rear opening width at floor: (Safari) 61.2 in. Maximum cargo height: (Safari) 30.1 in. Total cargo volume: (Safari) 85.1 cu. ft. Front tread: (All except Grand Am) 61.5 in., (Grand Am) 61.9 in. Rear tread: (all except Grand Am) 60.7 in., (Grand Am) 61.1 in.

OPTIONS

542 heavy-duty dual-stage air cleaner. 582 Custom air conditioning. 651 Automatic Level Control. 691 Delco Maintenance-Free battery. 692 heavy-duty battery. 502 power front disc brakes. 711 electric clock. 431 front seat center console with automatic transmission. 431 front seat center console with manual transmission. 562 cruise control. 511 Custom pedal trim. 564 rear deck lid

release. 541 rear window defogger. 534 electric rear window defroster. 682 dual exhausts. 712 Rally gauge cluster with clock. 714 Rally gauge cluster with instrument panel tachometer. 531 Soft-Ray tinted glass. 731 front bumper guards. 743 rubber bumper impact strips. 732 rear bumper guards. 681 dual horns. 661 dome reading lamp. 662 rear compartment courtesy lamp. 554 electric door locks without seat back lock for two-door models. 554 eletric door locks without seat back lock for four-door models. 552 electric door locks and seat back lock for two-door models. 552 electric door lock and seat back lock for four-door models. 621 front floor mats. 622 rear floor mats. 444 remote-controlled left-hand outside rearview mirror. 422 left-hand visor-vanity mirror. 441 right-hand visor-vanity mirror. 434 dual body-colored outside rearview mirrors. 481 bright metal roof drip moldings. 701 heavy-duty radiator. 411 AM radio. 413 AM/FM radio. 415 AM/FM stereo ($233). 419 AM/FM stereo with tape player. 371 Safe-T-Track differential. 451 Custom front and rear seat belts and front shoulder belts. 561 power left-hand front bucket seat. 561 6-Way power front bench seat. 652 Superlift shock absorbers. 454 spare wheel and tire cover. 421 rear radio speaker. 462 Custom Sport steering wheel. 504 tilt-adjustable steering column. 501 quick variable-ratio power steering. 694 unitized ignition system. 631 vinyl accent stripes. 476 14-in. deluxe wheel covers. 478 honeycomb wheels. 474 Rally II wheels ($87). 551 power windows ($103). 341 The Original and Most Famous GTO option, including black-textured grille, special hood with dual NASA-style air scoops, firm shock absorbers, GTO decal identification, G60-15 black sidewall tires, an extra-large heavy-duty front stabilizer bar, an extra-large heavy-duty rear stabilizer bar, baby moon hubcaps, performance dual exhausts with chrome extensions, a 400-cid four-barrel V-8, a heavy-duty three-speed manual transmission, and 15 x 7-in.-diameter wheels ($368). Custom Safari option package ($317). LeMans Ride & Handling package ($188). LeMans GT option ($237). Electric sunroof for A-body models ($325), LeMans vinyl top ($97).

OPTION INSTALLATION RATES

Of 248,785 Tempests built, 96.7 percent had automatic transmission, 1 percent had a four-speed synchromesh transmission, 34.7 percent had a standard V-8 engine, 63.6 percent had a standard V-8 engine, 1.7 percent had a six-cylinder engine, 66.5 percent had a AM radio, 16.3 percent had an AM/FM radio, 10.2 percent had a stereo radio, 8.1 percent had a stereo tape player, 98.3 percent had power steering, 94.6 percent had power front disc/rear drum brakes or four-wheel disc brakes, 5.6 percent had manual disc brakes, 4 percent had power door locks, 3.5 percent had a power seat, 10.2 percent had power side windows, 38.3 percent had bucket seats, 42 percent had a vinyl roof, 1.1 percent had a sun roof, 17.3 percent had steel-belted radial tires, 18.6 percent had a tinted windshield only, 68.9 percent had all tinted windows, 1.1 percent had Automatic Temperature Control, 78.3 percent had an air conditioner, 13.6 percent had a movable steering column, 5.7 percent had a limited-slip differential, 4.8 percent had dual exhausts, 12.0 percent had standard wheel covers, 35.7 percent had optional wheel covers, 45.3 percent had optional styled wheels, 17.3 percent had a standard clock, 22.6 percent had an optional clock, 3.4 percent had a speed regulating device, 9.7 percent had a rear window defogger, and 74.6 percent had a remote-control outside rearview mirror.

HISTORICAL FOOTNOTES

Martin J. Caserio was general manager of Pontiac Motor Division in 1973. Model-year production of LeMans and Grand Am models included 4,141 six-cylinder-powered LeMans models and 244,644 V-8-powered LeMans and Grand Am models (these 248,785 cars included 16,185 LeMans cars built in Canada for the U.S. market). U.S.-only model-year production included 3,375 LeMans sixes, 99,039 LeMans V-8s, 169 LeMans Sport sixes, 46.947 LeMans Sport V-8s, 39,333 Luxury LeMans V-8s and 43,137 Grand Ams. The U.S.-only model-year production total of 232,600 A-bodies included 30,930 cars made in Fremont, California, 65,320 cars made in Lakewood, Georgia, 34,974 cars made in Framingham, Massachusetts and 101,376 cars made in Pontiac, Michigan. Domestic calendar-year production of 866,598 Pontiacs of all types was also recorded for a 9.5 percent company market share. The LeMans series contributed 205,135 cars or 23.7 percent to the company's calendar-year production total. (This figure does not include the LeMans models assembled in Canada for sale here.) Overall, LeMans calendar-year sales, including those of the all-new Grand Am, increased by 9.9 percent over 1972.

Motor Trend magazine featured the new Grand Am in its September 1972 issue in an article emphasizing its goal to compete with luxury imports like the Mercedes-Benz, BMW, and Jaguar at about half the price. Author Chuck Koch described the Grand Am as the best of the Grand Prix mated with the best of the Trans Am and incorrectly indicated that the coupe version would be produced with the 310-hp SD-455 V-8. This engine eventually made it into the Formula Firebird and Trans Am, but was never installed in a production A-body car. In October 1972, *Motor Trend* followed up with an article on all the 1973 Pontiacs and pictured the GTO and other intermediate cars. This article by Eric Dahlquist reiterated the availability of SD-455 option for the Grand Am two-door. It correctly pointed out that the SD-455 was not an option for the GTO. However, an engine chart on page 76 of the same issue incorrectly shows the SD-455 as a Grand Am and LeMans option. On page 134 of the same issue, there is even a road test of the SD-455 Grand Am. A 0 to 60-mph time of 7.4 seconds was reported. However, the car tested was a pre-production pilot model. *Motor Trend's* December 1972 issue again features the Grand Am in an article by Eric Dahlquist entitled "General Motors versus Mercedes-Benz."

On Nov. 27, 1972, a blue 1973 Catalina sedan became the 16th millionth Pontiac ever made, which has nothing to do with the LeMans in particular, but underscores the fact that 1973 was a good year for sales of all models.

Stephen McKenzie photo

The Grand Am featured a distinct vertically segmented grille for 1974. The base engine was a 400-cid V-8 that generated 175 hp.

The 1974 LeMans models had new front bumpers with rubber-faced protective guards, more angular front fender corner sections, twin rectangular grilles accented by bright horizontal division bars, and substantially revised vertically curved taillights with new rear bumpers. Minor refinements characterized the 1974 Grand Am. The redesigned grille had six vertical slots on either side of a smaller "nose" and vertical taillights were used this year. This year the GTO package was an option for the Ventura coupe or hatchback coupe, rather than the LeMans. It was available with standard or Custom interior trim.

I.D. NUMBERS

VIN on top of dash at left, viewable through windshield. First symbol tells GM division: 2=Pontiac. Second symbol tells series: Y=Ventura, Z=Ventura Custom, D=LeMans, F=LeMans Sport, G=Luxury LeMans, H=Grand Am. Third and fourth symbols indicate body style and appear as last two digits of body/style number in charts below. Fifth symbol indicates engine: D=250-cid one-barrel six-cylinder, J=350-cid four-barrel V-8 with single exhaust, K=350-cid four-barrel V-8 with dual exhausts, M=350-cid two-barrel V-8 with single exhaust, N=350-cid two-barrel V-8 with dual exhausts, P=400-cid two-barrel V-8 with single exhaust, R=400-cid two-barrel V-8 with dual exhausts, S=400-cid four-barrel V-8 with single exhaust, T=400-cid four-barrel V-8 with dual exhausts and Y=455-cid four-barrel V-8 with dual exhausts. Sixth symbol indicates model year: 4=1974. Seventh symbol indicates assembly plant: (LeMans) A=Atlanta (Lakewood), Georgia, G=Framingham, Massachusetts, P=Pontiac, Michigan, Z=Fremont, California and 1=Oshawa, Canada. (Ventura) L=Van Nuys, California and W=Willow Run, Michigan. Remaining symbols are sequential unit production number at factory, starting with 100001. Fisher body plate on cowl tells style number (model year prefix 74, plus "2" for Pontiac and body/style number from charts below), plus body number, trim code, paint code and other data. Six-cylinder engine code stamped on distributor mounting on right-hand side of block. V-8 engine code on front of block below right-hand cylinder head. Engine production codes for 1974 were: (250-cid/100-nhp six) CCR-CCX-CCW. (350-cid/155-nhp V-8) WA-WB-YA-YB-YC-AA-ZA-ZB. (350-cid/170-nhp V-8) WN-WP-YN-YP-YS-ZP. (400-cid/175-nhp V-8) YH-YJ-AH-ZH-ZJ. (400-cid/200-nhp V-8) WT-YT-AT-ZT-YZ. (455-cid/215-nhp V-8) YY-YU-YX-AU-ZU-ZX-YW-ZW-YR.

COLORS

Paint codes for 1974 were: 11=Cameo White, 19=Starlight Black, 24=Porcelain Blue, 26=Regatta Blue, 29=Admiralty Blue, 36=Gulfmist Aqua, 40=Fernmist Green, 44=Lakemist Green, 46=Limefire Green, 49=Pinemist Green, 50=Carmel Beige, 51=Sunstorm Yellow, 53=Denver Gold, 55=Colonial Gold, 59=Crestwood Brown, 64=Ascot Silver, 66=Fire Coral Bronze, 69=Shadowmist Brown, 74=Honduras Maroon, and 75=Buccaneer Red. Vinyl top colors for 1974 were: 1=White, 2=Black, 3=Beige, 4=Russet, 5=Green, 6=Burgundy, 7=Blue, 8=Brown, 9=Saddle, and 0=Taupe. Interior trim combinations for 1974 were: (LeMans four-door) 201S=standard Blue cloth-and-vinyl, 204S=standard Green cloth-and-vinyl, 211S=standard Blue vinyl, 213S=standard Saddle vinyl, 214S=standard Green vinyl, 217S=standard burgundy vinyl, 238C=Custom Blue cloth-and-vinyl, 239C=Custom Green cloth-and-vinyl, 243C=Custom Beige cloth-and-vinyl, 247C=Custom Blue vinyl, 259C=Custom Saddle vinyl, 266C=Custom Green vinyl, 268C=Custom Beige vinyl, 295S=standard Beige cloth-and-vinyl, 588C=Custom Burgundy vinyl and 589C=Custom Burgundy cloth-and-vinyl; (LeMans Safari) 211=Blue vinyl, 213=Saddle vinyl, 214=Green vinyl and 217=Burgundy vinyl; (LeMans two-door) 201=Blue cloth-and-vinyl, 204=Green cloth-and-vinyl, 205=Beige cloth-and-vinyl, 211=Blue vinyl, 212=White vinyl, 213=Saddle vinyl, 214=Green vinyl, 216=Black vinyl and 217=Burgundy vinyl; (LeMans Sport Coupe) 220=Burgundy vinyl, 231=Blue vinyl, 232=White vinyl, 233=Saddle vinyl, 234=Green vinyl, 235=Beige vinyl, and 236=Black vinyl; (Luxury LeMans) 241=Blue cloth-and-vinyl, 244=Green cloth-and-vinyl, 245=Beige cloth-and-vinyl, 251=Blue vinyl, 252=White vinyl, 253=Saddle vinyl, 254=Green vinyl, 255=Beige vinyl (coupe only), 256=Black vinyl (coupe only), 271=Beige cloth-and-vinyl and 276=Burgundy vinyl (coupe only); (Luxury LeMans Safari) 217=Burgundy vinyl, 280=Blue vinyl, 290=Saddle vinyl and 508=Green vinyl; (Grand Am) 263=Saddle cloth, 264=Green cloth, 265=Beige cloth, 267=Burgundy cloth, 273=Saddle vinyl, 274=Green vinyl, 275=Beige vinyl, 277=Burgundy vinyl and 551=White vinyl; (Ventura coupe/hatchback) 502=Black, Red and White plaid cloth, 503=Saddle vinyl, 523=Black, Whit and Green plaid cloth, 552=Black, White and Red plaid vinyl and 574=Green vinyl; (Ventura Custom coupe and hatchback) 522=Black

cloth, 542=White vinyl, 550=Red vinyl, 563=Saddle vinyl, 564=Green cloth, and 584=Green vinyl.

LEMANS — (SIX-CYL) — SERIES 2AD

Standard equipment in all A-body cars included wood-grained dashboard trim, a deluxe two-spoke steering wheel, a seat and shoulder belt warning system, a high-low level body ventilation system, nylon carpeting, an inside hood latch release, a trunk mat, concealed windshield wipers, an in-the-windshield radio antenna, energy-absorbing front and rear bumpers, hubcaps, manual front disc brakes, bright windshield moldings, bright roof drip moldings, bright body sill moldings, bright rear and rear quarter window moldings, F78-14 black sidewall tires, and a 250-cid six-cylinder engine with column-shifted three-speed manual transmission. Base LeMans models had cloth-and-Morrokide front bench seats. The LeMans Safari station wagon featured the same equipment as the base LeMans group, except it had no trunk mat, no wood-grained dash panel and no rear window moldings. It did include all-Morrokide vinyl interiors, a stowage compartment under the cargo load floor, a lift-type tailgate, a textured steel cargo floor, vertical tailgate rub strips and power front disc/rear drum brakes. The three-seat Safari also had a rear-facing third seat, an electric tailgate release and swing-out rear quarter vent windows.

Model Number	Body/Style Number	Body Type & Seating	Factory Price	Shipping Weight	Production Total
2AD	29	4d Hardtop-6P	$3,067	3,628 lbs.	17,266
2AD	37	2d Hardtop-6P	$3,047	3,552 lbs.	37,061
2AD	45	4d Sta Wagon-9P	$3,894	4,371 lbs.	4,743
2AD	35	4d Sta Wagon-6P	$3,761	4,333 lbs.	3,004

LEMANS SPORT COUPE — (SIX-CYL) — SERIES 2AF

In addition to the base LeMans features, the LeMans Sport Coupe featured a notchback front seat with center armrest, wood-grained glove box trim, and louvered rear quarter windows.

Model Number	Body/Style Number	Body Type & Seating	Factory Price	Shipping Weight	Production Total
2AF	37	2d Hardtop-6P	$3,131	3,580 lbs.	37,955

LUXURY LEMANS — (V-8) — SERIES 2AG

Luxury LeMans models had special vertically-segmented grille inserts, wide body sill moldings with front and rear extensions, distinctive curved vertical taillights accented with chrome moldings, a rear deck latch panel beauty strip, Luxury LeMans scripts behind the front wheel openings, and fender skirts. Standard equipment included: deluxe wheel covers, a Custom cushion steering wheel, and a V-8 engine. The Luxury LeMans hardtop provided buyers with a choice of front bucket seats or a notchback type with armrest. This model also incorporated ashtrays and glove box lamps, cloth-and-Morrokide or all-Morrokide trims, door-pull straps, pedal trim plates, dual horns, special taillight styling, bright windowsill moldings, a bright molding on the rear edge of the hood, rear fender skirts and wheel opening moldings. The Luxury LeMans Safari came with wood-grained dash trim, all-Morrokide seats, an under-the-floor storage compartment, a liftgate, a textured steel cargo floor, tailgate vertical rub strips, power front disc brakes, and all other base LeMans Safari station wagon features. The nine-passenger version had a rear-facing third seat, an electric tailgate release, and swing-out rear quarter windows.

Model Number	Body/Style Number	Body Type & Seating	Factory Price	Shipping Weight	Production Total
2AG	29	4d Hardtop-6P	$3,480	3,904 lbs.	4,513
2AG	37	2d Hardtop-6P	$3,410	3,808 lbs.	25,882
2AG	45	4d Sta Wagon-9P	$4,167	4,401 lbs.	1,178
2AG	35	4d Sta Wagon-6P	$4,034	4,363 lbs.	952

GRAND AM — (V-8) — SERIES 2AH

Other than having a new six-segment grille, vertical taillights, and different wood-grain dashboard trim, the '74 Grand Am was little changed from the original version. Standard equipment for all Grand Ams was based on the Luxury LeMans list, with the following variations: courtesy lamps, a Custom sport steering wheel, mahogany dashboard trim, an electric clock, a turn-signal-stalk headlight dimmer switch, an integrated console with mahogany trim, a floor-mounted gear shifter, lateral-restraint bucket seats with adjustable lumbar support; custom-finned wheel covers, Endura bumper protective strips, power brakes with front discs, a Rally gauge cluster with trip odometer, power steering, Turbo Hydra-Matic transmission, and a radial-tuned suspension with GR70-15 tires. Styling distinctions included a special vertically segmented polyurethane nose panel, an exclusive taillight design, and specific striping and badge ornamentation.

Model Number	Body/Style Number	Body Type & Seating	Factory Price	Shipping Weight	Production Total
2AH	29	4d Hardtop-5P	$4,623	4,073 lbs.	3,122
2AH	37	2d Hardtop-5P	$4,534	3,992 lbs.	13,961

VENTURA GTO — (V-8) — SERIES 2XY

The Firebird-style grille seen on 1973 Ventura Sprints was now used on all models in this line. There were minimal styling changes otherwise. Standard equipment included deluxe two-spoke steering wheel, bench front seat with cloth and Morrokide trim, wood-grained door inserts, front and rear armrests, high/low ventilation, rubber floor covering, hubcaps, vent windowless styling, and E78-14 tires. Cars with the Sprint option package (two-doors only) had black-textured grilles. The most interesting option was the GTO package, which was now available exclusively for Ventura coupes and hatchback coupes and Ventura Custom coupes and hatchback coupes. The Ventura GTO option package sold for $195 over the price of a comparable V-8 model. The option included the 350-cid four-barrel V-8, a front stabilizer bar, a rear stabilizer bars, a Radial Tuned Suspension, Pliacell shock absorbers, power steering, front and rear

drum brakes, E78-14 tires, a heavy-duty three-speed manual gearbox, dual exhausts with splitter extensions, a 3.08:1 ratio axle, Rally II wheel rims less trim rings, special grille driving lights, a rear-facing "shaker" air scoop, and computer selected high-rate rear springs. This was the 11th and last GTO.

Model Number	Body/Style Number	Body Type & Seating	Factory Price	Shipping Weight	Production Total
2XY	27	2d Coupe-5P	$3,035	3,147 lbs.	2,487
2XY	17	2d Hatchback-5P	$3,186	3,257 lbs.	687

VENTURA CUSTOM GTO — (V-8) — SERIES 2XZ

Ventura Customs had all features found on base models plus a choice of cloth or all-Morrokide trim, a Custom cushion steering wheel, bright metal front seat side panels, a glove box lamp, nylon carpeting, pedal trim plates, a right-hand door jamb switch, deluxe wheel covers, drip moldings, scalp moldings, and rocker panel moldings. Hatchback coupes also had load floor carpeting, fold-down seats, a Space-Saver spare tire, a cargo area dome light, and trimmed sidewalls. The GTO package was available teamed with either of these two-door Ventura Custom models. The GTO package contents were the same as described above. In both body styles, the Ventura Custom GTO was the more common version, but production of all cars with this option was quite low

Model Number	Body/Style Number	Body Type & Seating	Factory Price	Shipping Weight	Production Total
2XZ	27	2d Coupe-5P	$3,183	3,437 lbs.	2,848
2XZ	17	2d Hatchback-5P	$3,344	3,491 lbs.	1,036

ENGINES

LEMANS, LEMANS SPORT BASE 250-CID SIX-CYL: Inline. Overhead valve. Bore and stroke: 3.88 x 3.53. Displacement: 250 cid. Compression ratio: 8.50:1. Net hp: 100 at 3600 rpm. Net torque: 175 lbs.-ft. at 1600 rpm. Seven main bearings. Hydraulic valve lifters. Crankcase capacity: 4 qt (add 1 qt. for new filter). Cooling system capacity with heater: 13 qt. Carburetor: Rochester one-barrel carburetor. Engine code: D.

LUXURY LEMANS SAFARI BASE 350-CID V-8 (FEDERAL): Overhead valve. Cast-iron block. Bore and stroke: 3.88 x 3.53. Displacement: 350 cid. Compression ratio: 7.6:1. Net hp: 155 at 3600 rpm. Taxable hp: 48.00. Net torque: 275 lbs.-ft. at 2400 rpm. Five main bearings. Hydraulic valve lifters. Crankcase capacity: 5. Cooling system capacity with heater: 21.3 qt. Carburetor: Two-barrel. Not available in LeMans Safaris sold in California. Engine code M.

LEMANS, LEMANS SPORT COUPE, LUXURY LEMANS OPTIONAL 350-CID V-8: Overhead valve. Cast-iron block. Bore and stroke: 3.88 x 3.53. Displacement: 350 cid. Compression ratio: 7.6:1. Net hp: 170 at 4000 rpm. Taxable hp: 48.00. Net torque: 290 lbs.-ft. at 2400 rpm. Five main bearings. Hydraulic valve lifters. Crankcase capacity: 5 qt. Cooling system capacity with heater: 21.3 qt. Dual exhausts. Carburetor: Two-barrel. Engine code N.

GRAND AM BASE V-8; LEMANS, LEMANS SPORT COUPE, LUXURY LEMANS OPTIONAL 400-CID V-8: Overhead valve. Cast-iron block. Bore and stroke: 4.12 x 3.75. Displacement: 400 cid. Compression ratio: 8.0:1. Net hp: 175 at 3600 rpm. Taxable hp: 54.30. Net torque: 315 lbs.-ft. at 2000 rpm. Five main bearings. Hydraulic valve lifters. Crankcase capacity: 5 qt. Cooling system capacity with heater: 21.3 qt. Carburetor: Two-barrel. Engine code R.

LEMANS, LEMANS SPORT COUPE, LUXURY LEMANS OPTIONAL 350-CID V-8 (CALIFORNIA): Overhead valve. Cast-iron block. Bore and stroke: 3.88 x 3.53. Displacement: 350 cid. Compression ratio: 7.6:1.

Net hp: 185 at 4000 rpm. Taxable hp: 48. Net torque: 320 lbs.-ft. at 4400 rpm. Five main bearings. Hydraulic valve lifters. Crankcase capacity: 5 qt. Cooling system capacity with heater: 21.3 qt. Carburetor: Four-barrel. Engine code J.

LEMANS, LEMANS SPORT COUPE, LUXURY LEMANS, GRAND AM OPTIONAL 400-CID V-8: Overhead valve. Cast-iron block. Bore and stroke: 4.12 x 3.75. Displacement: 400 cid. Compression ratio: 8.00:1. Net hp: 190 at 4000 rpm. Taxable hp: 54.30. Net torque: 330 lbs.-ft. at 2400 rpm. Five main bearings. Hydraulic valve lifters. Crankcase capacity: 5 qt. Cooling system capacity with heater: 21.3 qt. Dual exhausts. Carburetor: Two-barrel. Engine code P.

John Gunnell photo

The 1974 Luxury LeMans came in two- and four-door models, and two different station wagon models.

GM Media Archives

**The LeMans two-door Colonnade hardtop was the most popular
midsized Pontiac in 1974 with more than 37,000 sold.**

**GTO BASE V-8; LEMANS, LEMANS SPORT COUPE,
LUXURY LEMANS, GRAND AM OPTIONAL 350-CID
V-8:** Overhead valve. Cast-iron block. Bore and stroke:
3.88 x 3.53. Displacement: 350 cid. Compression ratio:
7.6:1. Net hp: 200 at 4400 rpm. Taxable hp: 48. Net
torque: 295 lbs.-ft. at 2800 rpm. Five main bearings.
Hydraulic valve lifters. Crankcase capacity: 5 qt. Cooling
system capacity with heater: (GTO) 20 qt. (LeMans)
21.3 qt. Dual exhaust. Carburetor: Four-barrel. Engine
code K.

**LEMANS, LEMANS SPORT COUPE, LUXURY
LEMANS, GRAND AM OPTIONAL 350-CID V-8:**
Overhead valve. Cast-iron block. Bore and stroke: 4.12 x
3.75. Displacement: 400 cid. Compression ratio: 8.00:1.
Net hp: 200 at 4000 rpm. Taxable hp: 54.30. Net torque:
320 lbs.-ft. at 2400 rpm. Five main bearings. Hydraulic
valve lifters. Crankcase capacity: 5 qt. Cooling system
capacity with heater: 21.3 qt. Not available in LeMans
Safaris sold in California. Carburetor: Rochester two-

barrel. Engine code S.

**LEMANS, LEMANS SPORT COUPE, LUXURY
LEMANS, GRAND AM OPTIONAL 400-CID V-8:**
Overhead valve. Cast-iron block. Bore and stroke: 4.12 x
3.75. Displacement: 400 cid. Compression ratio: 8.00:1.
Net hp: 225 at 4000 rpm. Taxable hp: 54.30. Net torque:
330 lbs.-ft. at 2800 rpm. Five main bearings. Hydraulic
valve lifters. Crankcase capacity: 5 qt. Cooling system
capacity with heater: 21.3 qt. Not available in LeMans
Safaris sold in California. Carburetor: Rochester two-
barrel. Engine code T.

**LEMANS, LEMANS SPORT COUPE, LUXURY
LEMANS, GRAND AM OPTIONAL 455-CID V-8
(FEDERAL):** Overhead valve. Cast-iron block. Bore and
stroke: 4.15 x 4.21. Displacement: 455 cid. Compression
ratio: 8.00:1. Net hp: 250 at 4000 rpm. Taxable hp:
55.20. Net torque: 380 lbs.-ft. at 2800 rpm. Five main
bearings. Hydraulic valve lifters. Crankcase capacity: 5.

Cooling system capacity with heater: 21.1 qt. Dual exhaust. Carburetor: four-barrel. Engine code Y.

CHASSIS

Wheelbase: (LeMans, LeMans Sport Coupe, Luxury LeMans, and Grand Am two-door) 112 in., (LeMans, Luxury LeMans, Grand Am four-door and all LeMans Safari four-door station wagons) 116 in., (Ventura GTO) 111.1 in. Overall Length: (LeMans, LeMans Sport Coupe, Luxury LeMans and Grand Am two-door) 208 in., (LeMans, Luxury LeMans and Grand Am four-door) 215 in., (LeMans Safari) 215.4 in., (Ventura GTO) 199.6 in. Overall width: (Lemans, LeMans Sport Coupe, Luxury LeMans and Grand Am coupe) 77.4 in., (Lemans, LeMans Sport Coupe, Luxury LeMans and Grand Am sedan) 77 in., (Ventura GTO) 72.4 in. Overall height: (LeMans, LeMans Sport, Luxury LeMans and Grand Am two-door) 52.7 in., (LeMans, Luxury LeMans and Grand Am four-door) 53.4 in., (LeMans Safari) 55.3 in., (Ventura GTO) 52.2 in. Front headroom: (LeMans, LeMans Sport Coupe, Luxury LeMans and Grand Am two-door) 37.8 in., (LeMans, Luxury LeMans, Grand Am four-door) 38.5 in. Rear headroom: (LeMans, LeMans Sport Coupe, Luxury LeMans and Grand Am two-door) 36.9 in., (LeMans, Luxury LeMans, Grand Am four-door) 37.2 in. Front legroom: (LeMans, LeMans Sport Coupe, Luxury LeMans and Grand Am two-door) 42.4 in., (LeMans, Luxury LeMans and Grand Am four-door) 42.4 in. Rear legroom: (LeMans, LeMans Sport Coupe and Luxury LeMans two-door) 33.7 in., (Grand Am two-door) 33.5 in., (LeMans and Luxury LeMans four-door) 38.4 in., (Grand Am four-door) 38.6 in. Front shoulder room: (LeMans, LeMans Sport Coupe, Luxury LeMans and Grand Am two-door) 59.6 in., (LeMans, Luxury LeMans and Grand Am four-door) 59.6 in. Rear shoulder room: (LeMans, LeMans Sport Coupe, Luxury LeMans and Grand Am two-door) 57.5 in., (LeMans, Luxury Lemans and Grand Am four-door) 58.9 in. Trunk capacity: (All cars) 15.1 cu. ft. Top of front seat back to closed tailgate length: (Safari) 82.9 in. Rear opening width at floor: (Safari) 61.2 in. Maximum cargo height: (Safari) 30.1 in. Total cargo volume: (Safari) 85.1 cu. ft. Front tread: (All Lemans group except Grand Am) 61.5 in., (Grand Am) 61.9 in. Rear tread: (All LeMans group except Grand Am) 60.7 in., (Grand Am) 61.1 in.

LEMANS/GRAND AM OPTIONS

542 heavy-duty air cleaner ($9). 582 LeMans air conditioning, not available with 250-cid six-cylinder engine ($412). 581 Automatic Temperature Control air conditioning, Grand Am only ($488). 651 Automatic Level Control suspension, with trailering package ($36). 651 Automatic Level Control suspension, without trailering package ($77). 378 performance axle ratio ($10). 371 Safe-T-Track differential ($45). 574 Delco Maintenance-Free battery ($26). 592 heavy-duty battery, except with six-cylinder engine ($10). 691 Custom front and rear seat belts and front shoulder belts, all except three-seat safari ($13). 691 Custom front and rear seat belts and front shoulder belts in

three-seat safari ($16). 541 California assembly line emissions test, required in all cars registered in California ($20). 602 Safari cargo area carpeting ($19). 621 front floor mats ($7). 622 rear floor mats ($6). 621 carpeted front floor mats ($12). 711 electric clock, standard in Grand Am ($18). 712 Rally gauge cluster with clock, standard in Grand Am and not available with six-cylinder engine ($49). 714 Rally gauge cluster with clock and tachometer, not available in Grand Am or with M40 Turbo Hydra-Matic transmission ($100). 431 front seat center console with bucket seat interior, standard in Grand Am, not available with standard transmission with column shift ($61). 424 spare wheel and tire cover, all models except Safari ($13). 562 cruise control, except with six-cylinder engine ($63). 564 remote deck lid release, except Safaris ($14). 514 Safari rear window air deflector ($26). 592 electric rear window defroster, not available with six-cylinder engine or Safari ($64). 594 rear window defogger, except Grand Am, not available with LeMans GT option ($33). 682 dual exhausts, not available with six-cylinder engine ($30). 35D 250-cid six-cylinder engine (standard in base LeMans and LeMans Sport Coupe). 35M 350-cid two-barrel V-8 in base LeMans ($118). 35R 400-cid two-barrel V-8 in LeMans Safari ($51). 35R 400-cid two-barrel V-8 in LeMans coupe and sedan and LeMans Sport Coupe, standard in Grand Am ($169). 35S 400-cid four-barrel V-8, in Grand Am ($46). 35S 400-cid four-barrel V-8 in LeMans except base coupe and sedan and LeMans Sport Coupe ($97). 35S 400-cid four-barrel V-8, in base LeMans coupe and sedan and LeMans Sport Coupe ($215). 35J 350-cid four-barrel V-8 in base LeMans coupe and sedan and LeMans Sport Coupe ($164). 35J 350-cid four-barrel V-8 in Luxury LeMans ($46). 35W 455-cid four-barrel V-8 in Luxury LeMans and Safari ($154). 35W 455-cid four-barrel V-8 in Grand Am ($103). 601 engine block heater ($10). 571 all tinted glass ($43). 572 tinted windshield ($31). 492 door edge guards, two-door models ($6). 492 door edge guards, four-door models ($10). 731 front bumper guards ($15). 732 rear bumper guards ($5). 734 front and rear bumper impact strips ($24). 681 hood air scoop ($35). Hood decal LeMans coupe ($55). 664 ashtray lamp ($3). 664 glove box light in base LeMans and LeMans Sport Coupe ($3). 662 rear compartment courtesy lamp in Safari ($10). 661 dome reading lamp ($13). 662 luggage compartment lamp, except Safari ($3). 671 cornering lamps on Grand Am ($36). 674 instrument panel courtesy lamps ($4). 692 litter container ($5). 35J rear quarter window louvers ($35). 524 Safari roof top luggage carrier ($64). 444 remote-control left-hand outside rearview mirror ($12). 428 dual remote-control outside rearview mirrors ($38). 434 dual Sport-type outside rearview mirrors, left-hand remote controlled ($26). 424 dual remote-control Sport-type outside rearview mirrors, on Lemans without GT package ($47). 424 dual remote-control Sport-type outside rearview mirrors, on Lemans with GT package ($21). 441 left-hand visor-vanity mirror ($3). 442 right-hand visor-vanity mirror ($3). 482 side window reveal moldings on four-door sedan ($26). 491 wheel opening moldings on base LeMans ($15). SPS special solid paint, without vinyl top ($115). SPS special color solid paint with vinyl top ($97). RTT standard color two-tone paint LeMans Safari ($22). RTT standard color two-tone paint, except Safari ($39). STT special color two-tone paint, except Grand Am and Safaris ($152). STT special color two-tone paint on Safari ($134). 502 power front disc brakes ($46). 554 power door locks in coupe ($46). 554 power door locks, four-door models ($69). 561 6-way power left-hand front bucket seat, optional bucket seating required ($103). 561 Six-way power left-hand front bench seat ($103). 501 power steering, standard in Grand Am ($117). Power tailgate release in two-seat Safari ($14). 551 power side windows in coupes ($78). 551 power side windows in sedans and wagons ($117). 722 heavy-duty radiator, without air conditioning ($21). 411 AM radio ($65). 413 AM/FM radio ($135). 415 AM/FM stereo radio ($233). 417 AM radio and stereo tape player ($195). 419 AM/FM radio and stereo 8-track tape player ($363). 421 rear seat speaker, except Safari, requires AM radio or AM/FM radio ($18). 421 rear seat speaker in Safari, requires AM radio or AM/FM radio ($21). 804 speedometer marked in kilometers ($5). 652 Superlift rear shock absorbers, except with package 651 ($41). 721 Firm Ride springs and shocks ($9). 461 Custom Cushion steering wheel ($15). 462 Custom Sport steering wheel in base LeMans without Décor group ($56). 462 Custom Sport steering wheel in base LeMans with Décor group ($41). 504 tilt-adjustable steering column, requires Custom cushion ($41). 638 accent stripes for Grand Am and base LeMans coupe ($31). 452 electric sunroof, LeMans two-door ($325). 454 manual sunroof ($275). TFJ Radial Tuned Suspension, including G78-15 steel-belted radial white sidewall tires, special springs and shock absorbers, a rear stabilizer bar, and RTS identification badges ($86-$163 depending on other option combinations). TSJ Radial Tuned Suspension, including: G78-15 steel-belted radial white sidewall tires, special springs and shock absorbers, a rear stabilizer bar, and RTS identification badges for LeMans Safari ($165). 341 formal cordova or landau top on LeMans Sport Coupe, includes formal rear window ($97). SVT cordova vinyl top, except Safaris ($97). 451 cordova Landau top, LeMans coupes ($97). 701 light-duty trailer hitch ($25). 702 Five-wire trailer light cable ($14). 704 Seven-wire trailer light cable ($9). 36A three-speed manual transmission with column shift (standard). 36C heavy-duty three-speed manual transmission with floor shift in base LeMans or LeMans Sport Coupe with 350-cid two-barrel or 400-cid four-barrel V-8 ($82). 36E four-speed manual transmission in LeMans group except Safari and Grand Am with 350-cid two-barrel or 400-cid four-barrel V-8 ($197). 36E four-speed manual transmission in Grand Am ($45 credit). 36K M38 Turbo Hydra-Matic transmission in base LeMans or LeMans Sport Coupe ($221). 36K M38 Turbo Hydra-Matic transmission in Luxury LeMans ($211). 36L M40 Turbo Hydra-Matic transmission, standard in Grand Am, optional in LeMans except Safaris with 250-cid six-cylinder engine or 350-cid two-barrel V-8 ($242). 36L M40 Turbo Hydra-Matic transmission, in LeMans Safari ($21). 301 vinyl trim in base LeMans ($27). 472 Custom finned wheel covers, on base LeMans with Décor group ($24). 472 Custom finned wheel covers, on base LeMans without Décor group ($50). 476 deluxe wheel covers on base LeMans ($26). 478 honeycomb wheels on non-GT Lemans without Décor group ($123). 478 honeycomb wheels on Lemans with GT option or Décor group ($97). 478 honeycomb wheels on Lemans GT ($62). 478 honeycomb wheels on LeMans Safari without Décor group ($123). 478 honeycomb wheels on LeMans Safari with Décor group or Luxury LeMans ($97). 478 honeycomb wheels on Grand Am without 684 ($73). 478 honeycomb wheels on Grand Am with 684 ($53.60). 474 Rally II wheels on non-GT Lemans without Décor group ($87). 474 Rally II wheels on Lemans with GT option or Décor group ($61). 474 Rally II wheels on LeMans Safari without Décor group ($123). 474 Rally II wheels on LeMans Safari with Décor group or Luxury LeMans ($97). 474 Rally II wheels on Grand Am without 684 ($37). 474 Rally II wheels on Grand Am with 684 ($24). 471 wheel trim rings ($26). 521 swing-out rear quarter windows in two-seat Safari ($40). 512 wood-grain Safari paneling ($154). 324 Custom Trim Group for base LeMans sedan, includes notchback front bench seat with center armrest, body-color door handles and wood-grained vinyl glove box accents ($77). 724 Décor group, includes deluxe wheel covers, a Custom cushioned steering wheel, pedal trim, wheel opening moldings, window sill moldings and hood rear edge moldings, for Lemans without GT package ($77). 724 Décor group, includes deluxe wheel covers, a Custom cushioned steering wheel, pedal trim, wheel opening moldings, window sill moldings and hood rear edge moldings, for Lemans with GT package ($36). 342 LeMans GT option, includes Rally II wheels less trim rings, G70-14 white-letter tires, dual exhausts with chrome extensions, body accent stripes, a remote-control Sport-type left-hand rearview mirror, a Sport-type right-hand fixed rearview mirror, wheel opening moldings, and a three-speed manual transmission with floor-mounted gear shifter for base coupe or LeMans Sport Coupe with 582 or 35W combined with 682 ($232). 342 LeMans GT option, includes Rally II wheels less trim rings, G70-14 white letter tires, dual exhausts with chrome extensions, body accent stripes, a remote-control Sport-type left-hand rearview mirror, a Sport-type right-hand fixed rearview mirror, wheel opening moldings, and a three-speed manual transmission with floor-mounted gear shifter for base coupe or LeMans Sport Coupe with 582 or 35W without 682 ($202). 342 LeMans GT option, includes Rally II wheels less trim rings, G70-14 white-letter tires, dual exhausts with chrome extensions, body accent stripes, a remote-control Sport-type left-hand rearview mirror, a Sport-type right-hand fixed rearview mirror, wheel opening moldings and a three-speed manual transmission with floor-mounted gear shifter for base coupe or LeMans Sport Coupe without 582 or 35W, but with 682 ($246). 342 LeMans GT option, includes Rally II wheels less trim rings, G70-14 white-letter tires, dual exhausts with chrome extensions, body accent stripes, a remote-control sport-type left-hand rearview mirror, a sport-type right-hand fixed rearview mirror, wheel opening moldings and a three-speed manual transmission with floor-mounted gear shifter for base coupe or LeMans Sport Coupe without 582 or 35W or 682 ($216). 654 lamp group in base LeMans without dome reading lamp ($13). 654 lamp group in LeMans Safari without dome reading lamp ($20). 654 lamp group in Luxury LeMans without dome reading lamp, ashtray lamp and glove box lamp ($7). 642 medium trailer group ($60-$90 depending on other options). TDR H78-14 fiberglass-belted white sidewall tires ($35-$63 depending on body style and other options). TPL G70-14 fiberglass-belted raised-white-letter tires ($63-$77 depending on body style, model and other options). TRF G78-14 fiberglass-belted black sidewall tires for base LeMans, LeMans Sport Coupe and Luxury LeMans coupe ($14). TRR G78-14 fiberglass-belted white sidewall tires ($32-$46 depending on model and other options). TVJ GR70-15 steel-belted white sidewall tires for Grand Am without 684 ($32). TVJ GR70-15 steel-belted white sidewall tires for Grand Am with 684 ($25.60). TVK GR70-15 steel-belted raised-white-letter tires for Grand Am without 684 ($42). TVK GR70-15 steel-belted raised-white-letter tires for Grand Am with 684 ($33.60).

LEMANS OPTION INSTALLATION RATES

Of 149,637 Tempests built, 96.7 percent had automatic transmission, 0.6 percent had a four-speed synchromesh transmission, 27.2 percent had a standard V-8 engine, 67.6 percent had a standard V-8 engine, 5.2 percent had a six-cylinder engine, 58.9 percent had a AM radio, 16.4 percent had an AM/FM radio, 10.4 percent had an AM/FM stereo radio, 10.3 percent had a stereo tape player, 98.6 percent had power steering, 91.8 percent had power front disc/rear drum brakes, 8.2 percent had manual disc brakes, 5.2 percent had power door locks, 3.5 percent had a power seat, 10.5 percent had all power windows, 36 percent had bucket seats, 11.4 percent had reclining seats, 51.7 percent had a vinyl roof, 1.3 percent had a sun roof, 25.5 percent had steel-belted radial tires, 17.3 percent had a tinted windshield only, 71.3 percent had all tinted windows, 0.9 percent had automatic temperature control, 78.4 percent had an air conditioner, 16.2 percent had an adjustable steering column, 4.1 percent had a limited-slip differential, 12.9 percent had dual exhausts, 8.3 percent had standard wheel covers, 37.8 percent had optional wheel covers, 48 percent had optional styled wheels, 11.4 percent had a standard clock, 22.4 percent had an optional clock, 5.9 percent had a speed regulating device, 15.8 percent had a rear window defogger, and 77.2 percent had a remote-control outside rearview mirror.

VENTURA GTO OPTIONS

542 heavy-duty air cleaner ($9). 582 air conditioning ($396). 378 performance axle ratio ($10). 371 Safe-T-Track differential ($45). 592 heavy-duty battery ($15). 691 Custom front and rear seat belts and front shoulder belts without bucket seats ($15.25). 691 Custom front and rear seat belts and front shoulder belts with bucket seats ($12.75). 541 California assembly line emissions test, required in all cars registered in California ($20). 601 Custom carpets in standard Ventura ($21). 612 cargo area carpeting in hatchback ($19). 621 front floor mats ($6.50). 622 rear floor mats ($5.50). 614 fitted cargo area floor mat in hatchback ($8). 711 electric clock ($16). 601 engine block heater ($10). 571 all tinted glass ($40). 572 tinted windshield ($31). 492 door edge guards ($6). 731 front bumper guards ($15). 734 front and rear bumper impact strips ($24). 681 dual horns ($4). 694 unitized ignition ($77). 664 cigarette lighter ($4). 444 remote-control left-hand outside rearview mirror ($12). 434 dual sport-type outside rearview mirrors, left-hand remote controlled ($26). 442 non-glare day/night inside rearview mirror ($6). 484 rocker panel moldings on non-Custom Ventura ($10). 481 roof drip moldings on non-Custom Ventura without vinyl top ($13). 482 side window reveal moldings on coupes ($21). 491 wheel opening moldings ($15). SPS special color solid paint with vinyl top ($97). RTT standard color two-tone paint ($31). STT special color two-tone paint ($138). 512 power drum brakes ($46). 502 power front disc brakes ($68). 554 power door locks in coupe ($46). 501 power steering ($104). 722 heavy-duty radiator, without air conditioning ($14). 411 AM radio ($65). 413 AM/FM radio ($135). 415 AM/FM stereo radio ($233). 421 rear seat speaker ($15). 321 bucket seats in base Ventura coupe or hatchback ($132). 321 bucket seats in Custom Ventura coupe or hatchback ($67). 461 Custom Cushion steering wheel ($15). 462 Custom Sport steering wheel ($56). 504 tilt-adjustable steering column ($41). 638 vinyl accent stripes for Ventura ($41). TGJ Radial Tuned Suspension including FR78-14 steel-belted radial white sidewall tires, special springs, firm shock absorbers, a rear stabilizer bar and RTS identification badges on GTO coupe, not hatchback, with option 684 ($91.20). TGJ Radial Tuned Suspension including FR78-14 steel-belted radial white sidewall tires, special springs, firm shock absorbers, a rear stabilizer bar and RTS identification badges on GTO coupe, not hatchback, without option 684 ($113). TGK Radial Tuned Suspension including FR78-14 steel-belted radial white-letter tires, special springs, firm shock absorbers, a rear stabilizer bar and RTS identification badges on GTO coupe, not hatchback, with option 684 ($99.20). TGK Radial Tuned Suspension including FR78-14 steel-belted radial white-letter tires, special springs, firm shock absorbers, a rear stabilizer bar and RTS identification badges on GTO coupe without option 684 ($123). SVT cordova vinyl top ($82). 36A three-speed manual transmission with column shift (standard). 36B three-speed manual transmission with floor shift ($26). 36E four-speed manual transmission ($207). 36K M38 Turbo Hydra-Matic transmission ($206). 476 deluxe wheel covers on standard Ventura ($26). 474 Rally II wheels on Ventura GTO hatchback ($74.80). 474 Rally II wheels on Ventura Custom GTO hatchback ($74.80). 474 Rally II wheels on Ventura GTO coupe ($87). 474 Rally II wheels on Ventura Custom GTO coupe ($61). 341 Sprint option, includes specific front end styling, remote-control left-hand sport-type body-color outside rearview mirror, fixed right-hand sport-type body-color outside rearview mirror, a Custom cushioned steering wheel, Custom carpets, cargo area carpeting, vinyl accent stripes, Rally II wheels less trim rings and a rear

deck lid decal for Ventura hatchback ($168.80). 341 Sprint option, includes specific front-end styling, remote-control left-hand Sport-type body-color outside rearview mirror, fixed right-hand sport-type body-color outside rearview mirror, a Custom cushioned steering wheel, Custom carpets, cargo area carpeting, vinyl accent stripes, Rally II wheels (less trim rings) and a rear deck lid decal for Ventura Custom hatchback ($87.80). 341 Sprint option, includes specific front end styling, remote-control left-hand sport-type body-color outside rearview mirror, fixed right-hand sport-type body-color outside rearview mirror, a Custom cushioned steering wheel, Custom carpets, cargo area carpeting, vinyl accent stripes, Rally II wheels less trim rings, and a rear deck lid decal for Ventura coupe ($162). 341 Sprint option, includes specific front end styling, remote-control left-hand sport-type body-color outside rearview mirror, fixed right-hand sport-type body-color outside rearview mirror, a Custom cushioned steering wheel, Custom carpets, cargo area carpeting, vinyl accent stripes, Rally II wheels (less trim rings), and a rear deck lid decal for Ventura Custom coupe ($100). TCL E70-14 white letter tires GTO coupe with 684 or GTO hatchback ($30.40). TCL E70-14 white letter tires GTO coupe without 684 ($38).

NOTE: Ventura option installation rates would not be indicative of GTO option installation rates. Since we are only interested in GTOS in the catalog, the Ventura option installation rates are not being printed.

HISTORICAL FOOTNOTES

The 1974 Pontiacs were introduced on September 20, 1973. Martin J. Caserio was general manager of Pontiac Motor Division. Model-year production of LeMans and Grand Am models built in the United States or built in Canada for the U.S. market totaled 149,637

cars. This total included 62,074 base Lemans, 37,955 LeMans Sports, 32,525 Luxury Lemans and 17,083 Grand Ams. Model-year production of Venturas built for the U.S. market totaled 81,799 cars, but only 7,058 had the GTO option, which puts them within the scope of this catalog. U.S.-only model-year production of LeMans and Grand Am models included 6,367 made in Fremont, California, 40,209 make in the Lakewood, Georgia, assembly plant, 20,902 built in Framingham, Massachusetts, and 61,627 made in Pontiac, Michigan.

The total of 129,105 cars built in U.S. factories represented 1.59 percent of total U.S. industry production and included 6,540 cars with the six-cylinder engine and 122,565 with a V-8. U.S. model-year production of LeMans models only was 112,023 and included 5,691 base LeMans sixes, 47,926 base LeMans V-8s, 849 LeMans Sport sixes, 31,916 LeMans Sport V-8s and 25,641 Luxury LeMans V-8s. We can calculate that 20,532 cars were made in Oshawa, Canada for the model year. Ventura production included 34,247 units made in Van Nuys, California, and 47,552 cars made in Willow Run, Michigan. That represented 1.01 percent of industry output. Venturas were not built in Canada. Model-year sales of the LeMans toppled to 148,254, from 233,989 the previous year. The Ventura dropped from 80,406 in 1973 to 64,725 in 1974, but there is no way to compare GTO sales for the two years as the 1973 GTO was a LeMans and the 1974 GTO was a Ventura. Calendar-year sales of LeMans models by U.S. franchised dealers came to 128,689 cars for a 1.7 percent share of market. Sales of Venturas were 59,944 for a 0.8 percent market share.

All in all, it was a disappointing season for Pontiac production and sales. The catalytic converter was a new piece of government-mandated pollution hardware required this year.

GM photo

Little changed on the 1975 Grand Ams. The base engine remained the 400-cid/170-hp V-8. A 455-cid V-8 that produced 200 hp was optional.

The 1975 base LeMans and LeMans Sport series were basically unchanged from the previous year except for a new egg crate grille insert and some minor trim variations. An available styling option on two-door hardtop coupes was a louvered rear quarter window treatment, which was standard on LeMans Sport Coupes.

The Luxury LeMans became the Grand LeMans. The Grand Am continued to feature a unique vertically segmented polyurethane nose and louvered rear quarter windows on coupes. Little was changed except for some pin striping and grille insert details. General Motors' Efficiency System was added to all of the intermediate models. The GTO package was no longer available on either the LeMans or the Ventura platform.

I.D. NUMBERS

VIN on top of dash at left, viewable through windshield. First symbol tells GM division: 2=Pontiac. Second symbol tells series: Y=Ventura, Z=Ventura Custom, D=LeMans, F=LeMans Sport, G=Luxury LeMans, H=Grand Am. Third and fourth symbols indicate body style and appear as last two digits of body/style number in charts below. Fifth symbol indicates engine: D=250-cid one-barrel six-cylinder, J=350-cid four-barrel V-8 with single exhaust, K=350-cid four-barrel V-8 with dual exhausts, M=350-cid two-barrel V-8 with single exhaust, N=350-cid two-barrel V-8 with dual exhausts, P=400-cid two-barrel V-8 with single exhaust, R=400-cid two-barrel V-8 with dual exhausts, S=400-cid four-barrel V-8 with single exhaust, T=400-cid four-barrel V-8 with dual exhausts and Y=455-cid four-barrel V-8 with dual exhausts. Sixth symbol indicates model year: 5=1975. Seventh symbol indicates assembly plant: G=Framingham, Massachusetts, P=Pontiac, Michigan, Z=Fremont, California and 1=Oshawa, Canada. Remaining symbols are sequential unit production number at factory, starting with 100001. Fisher body plate on cowl tells style number (model year prefix 74, plus "2" for Pontiac and body/style number from charts below), plus body number, trim code, paint code and other data. Six-cylinder engine code stamped on distributor mounting on right-hand side of block. V-8 engine code on front of block below right-hand cylinder head. Engine production codes for 1975 were: (140-cid/78-nhp four-cylinder) BB-BC. (140-cid/87 hp four-cylinder) AM-AS-AR-AT-CAM-CAW-CBB-CBD-CAR-CAU. (140-cid/80-nhp four-cylinder) CAS-CAT. (250-cid/105-nhp six-cylinder) JU-JT-JL. (350-cid/155 hp V-8) YA-YB. (350-cid/175-nhp V-8) WN-YN-ZP-RN-RO. (400-cid/170-nhp V-8) YH. (400-cid/185-nhp V-8) YT-YM-YS-WT-ZT. (455-cid/200-nhp V-8) YW-YU-ZW-ZU-WX.

COLORS

Paint codes for 1975 were: 11=Cameo White, 13=Sterling Silver, 15=Graystone, 19=Starlight Black, 24=Arctic Blue, 26=Bimini Blue, 29=Stellar Blue, 31=Gray, 39=Burgundy, 44=Lakemist Green, 45=Agusta Green, 49=Alpine Green, 50=Carmel Beige, 51=Sunstorm Yellow, 55=Sandstone, 58=Ginger Brown, 59=Oxford Brown, 63=Copper Mist, 64=Persimmon, 66=Fire Coral Bronze, 72=Roman Red, 74=Honduras Maroon, 75=Buccaneer Red, and 80=Tampico Orange. Vinyl top colors for 1975 were: 1=White, 2=Black, 3=Sandstone, 4=Cordovan, 5=Green, 6=Burgundy, 7=Blue, 8=Red and 9=Silver. Interior trim combinations for 1975 were: (standard trim LeMans four-door sedan) 11V=White vinyl, 26C=Blue cloth-and-vinyl, 26V=Blue vinyl, 44V=Green vinyl, 63C=Saddle cloth-and-vinyl, 63V=Saddle vinyl, and 73S=Oxblood vinyl. (Custom trim LeMans four-door sedan) 11J=White vinyl, 26M=Blue cloth-and-vinyl, 26J=Blue vinyl, 44J=Green vinyl, 63M=Saddle cloth-and-vinyl, 63J=Saddle vinyl,

73M=Oxblood cloth-and-vinyl, and 73J=Oxblood vinyl (standard trim LeMans two-seat Safari). 11V=White vinyl, 26V=Blue vinyl, 44V=Green vinyl, 63V=Saddle vinyl, and 73V=Oxblood vinyl. (Custom trim LeMans two-seat Safari) 11Y=White vinyl, 26Y=Blue vinyl, 44Y=Green vinyl, 63Y=Saddle vinyl, and 73Y=Oxblood vinyl. (LeMans three-seat Safari) 11V=White vinyl, 26V=Blue vinyl, 44V=Green vinyl, 63V=Saddle vinyl, and 73V=Oxblood vinyl. (LeMans two-door coupe)11V=White vinyl, 19C=Black cloth-and-vinyl, 19V=Black vinyl, 26C=Blue cloth-and-vinyl, 26V=Blue vinyl, 44V=Green vinyl, 63C=Saddle cloth-and-vinyl, 63V=Saddle vinyl, and 73V=Oxblood vinyl. (LeMans Sport Coupe) 11W=White vinyl, 19W=Black vinyl, 26W=Blue vinyl, 44W=Green vinyl, 63W=Saddle vinyl and 73W=Oxblood vinyl. (Grand LeMans coupe or sedan) 11Y=White vinyl, 19Y (coupe only)=Black vinyl, 26E=Blue cloth-and-vinyl, 26Y=Blue vinyl, 44Y=Green vinyl, 63E=Saddle cloth-and-vinyl, 63Y=Saddle vinyl, 73E=Oxblood cloth-and-vinyl, 73Y=Oxblood vinyl. (Grand LeMans Safari) 11Y=White vinyl, 26Y=Blue vinyl, 44Y=Green vinyl, 63Y=Saddle vinyl, and 73Y=Oxblood vinyl. (Grand Am coupe or sedan) 11Z=White vinyl, 19G=Black cloth, 19Z (coupe only)=Black vinyl, 26G=Blue cloth, 26Z=Blue vinyl, 44G=Green cloth, 44Z=Green vinyl, 63G=Saddle cloth, 63Z=Saddle vinyl, 73G=Oxblood cloth, and 73Z=Oxblood vinyl.

LEMANS — (SIX-CYL) — SERIES 2AD

The 1975 base LeMans was basically unchanged from the previous year, except for a new egg crate grille insert and some minor trim variations. Standard equipment included wood-grained dashboard trim, a deluxe two-spoke steering wheel, a seat and shoulder belt warning system, a high-low level body ventilation system, Nylon carpeting, an inside hood latch release, a trunk mat, concealed windshield wipers, an in-the-windshield radio antenna, energy-absorbing front and rear bumpers, hubcaps, manual front disc brakes, bright windshield moldings, bright roof drip moldings, bright body sill moldings, bright rear and rear quarter window moldings, F78-14 black sidewall tires, and a 250-cid six-cylinder engine with column-shifted three-speed manual transmission. An available styling option on two-door hardtop coupes was the louvered rear quarter window treatment. Cloth-and-Morrokide front bench seats were standard. The LeMans Safari station wagon featured the same equipment as the base LeMans group, except that it had no trunk mat, no wood-grained dash panel, and no rear window moldings. It did include all-Morrokide vinyl interiors, a stowage compartment under the cargo load floor, a lift-type tailgate, a textured steel cargo floor, vertical tailgate rub strips, and power front disc/rear drum brakes. The three-seat Safari also had a rear-facing third seat, an electric tailgate release, and swing-out rear quarter vent windows.

Model Number	Body/Style Number	Body Type & Seating	Factory Price	Shipping Weight	Production Total
2AD	29	4d Hardtop-6P	$3,612	3,729 lbs.	15,065
2AD	37	2d Hardtop-6P	$3,590	3,656 lbs.	20,636

Model Number	Body/Style Number	Body Type & Seating	Factory Price	Shipping Weight	Production Total
2AD	45	4d Sta Wagon-9P	$4,688	4,500 lbs.	2,393
2AD	35	4d Sta Wagon-6P	$4,555	4,401 lbs.	3,898

LEMANS SPORT — (SIX-CYL) — SERIES 2AF

The louvered rear quarter window treatment was standard on LeMans Sport Coupes. These cars also featured a notchback front seat with center armrest and a wood-grained glove box trim panel. Vinyl upholstery, which was very much in vogue in the 1970s, was also included. Like the base LeMans, the Sport Coupe model came standard with an overhead-valve six-cylinder inline engine, and a three-speed manual transmission with column-mounted gear shifter.

Model Number	Body/Style Number	Body Type & Seating	Factory Price	Shipping Weight	Production Total
2AF	37	2d Hardtop-5P	$3,708	3,688 lbs.	23,817

GRAND LEMANS — (V-8) — SERIES 2AG

On the top-of-the-line Grand LeMans there was a distinctive grille design with six groupings of vertical blades arranged three on each side of the center divider. Stand-up hood ornaments appeared and fender skirts were used as standard equipment on all models except the Grand LeMans Safari station wagon. Additional standard equipment on the Grand LeMans included deluxe wheel covers, a Custom cushion steering wheel and a V-8 engine. The hardtop offered buyers the choice of front bucket seats or a notchback type with armrest. This model also incorporated ashtrays and glove box lamps, cloth-and-Morrokide or all-Morrokide trims, door-pull straps, pedal trim plates, dual horns, special taillight styling, bright windowsill moldings, a bright molding on the rear edge of the hood, rear fender skirts and wheel opening moldings. The Safari came with wood-grained dash trim, all-Morrokide seats, an under-the-floor storage compartment, a liftgate, a textured steel cargo floor, tailgate vertical rub strips, power front disc brakes, and all other base LeMans Safari station wagon features. The nine-passenger version had a rear-facing third seat, electric tailgate release and swing-out rear quarter windows.

Model Number	Body/Style Number	Body Type & Seating	Factory Price	Shipping Weight	Production Total
2AG	29	4d Hardtop-6P	$4,287	3,905 lbs.	4,906
2AG	37	2d Hardtop-6P	$4,231	3,942 lbs.	19,310
2AG	45	4d Sta Wagon-9P	$4,882	4,500 lbs.	1,501
2AG	35	4d Sta Wagon-6P	$4,749	4,462 lbs.	1,393

GRAND AM — (V-8) — SERIES 2AH

Standard equipment for all Grand Ams was based on the Luxury LeMans list, with the following substitutions or additions: courtesy lamps, a Custom sport steering wheel, mahogany dashboard trim, an electric clock, a turn-signal-stalk headlight dimmer switch, an integrated console with mahogany trim, a floor-mounted gear shifter, lateral-restraint bucket seats with adjustable lumbar support; custom-finned wheel covers, Endura

bumper protective strips, power brakes with front discs, a Rally gauge cluster with trip odometer, power steering, Turbo Hydra-Matic transmission, and radial tuned suspension with GR70-15 tires. Styling distinctions included a special vertically segmented polyurethane nose panel, an exclusive taillight design, and specific striping and badge ornamentation. The High Efficiency Ignition (HEI) system was also a new standard feature. At the end of the 1975 run the Grand Am nameplate was temporarily dropped.

Model Number	Body/Style Number	Body Type & Seating	Factory Price	Shipping Weight	Production Total
GRAND AM — (V-8) — SERIES 2AH					
2AH	29	4d Hardtop-5P	$4,976	4,055 lbs.	1,893
2AH	37	2d Hardtop-5P	$4,887	4,008 lbs.	8,786

ENGINES

LEMANS, LEMANS SPORT BASE 250-CID SIX-CYL: Inline. Overhead valve. Bore and stroke: 3.88 x 3.53. Displacement: 250 cid. Compression ratio: 8.50:1. Net hp: 100 at 3600 rpm. Net torque: 175 lbs.-ft. at 1600 rpm. Seven main bearings. Hydraulic valve lifters. Crankcase capacity: 4 qt (add 1 qt. for new filter). Cooling system capacity with heater: 13 qt. Carburetor: Rochester one-barrel carburetor. Engine code: D. Chevrolet built.

LEMANS BASE 350-CID V-8 (FEDERAL): Overhead valve. Cast-iron block. Bore and stroke: 3.88 x 3.53. Displacement: 350 cid. Compression ratio: 7.6:1. Net hp: 155 at 3600 rpm. Taxable hp: 48. Net torque: 280 lbs.-ft. at 2000 rpm. Five main bearings. Hydraulic valve lifters. Crankcase capacity: 5 qt. Cooling system capacity with heater: 21.3 qt. Carburetor: Two-barrel. Engine code M.

GRAND AM BASE 400-CID V-8: Overhead valve. Cast-iron block. Bore and stroke: 4.12 x 3.75. Displacement: 400 cid. Compression ratio: 7.6:1. Net hp: 170 at 4000 rpm. Taxable hp: 54.30. Net torque: 305 lbs.-ft. at 2000. Five main bearings. Hydraulic valve lifters. Crankcase capacity: 5 qt. Cooling system capacity with heater: 21.3 qt. Carburetor: Two-barrel. Engine code R.

LEMANS BASE 350-CID V-8 (CALIFORNIA): Overhead valve. Cast-iron block. Bore and stroke: 3.88 x 3.53. Displacement: 350 cid. Compression ratio: 7.6:1. Net hp: 175 at 4000 rpm. Taxable hp: 48. Net torque: 280 lbs.-ft. at 2000 rpm. Five main bearings. Hydraulic valve lifters. Crankcase capacity: 5 qt. Cooling system capacity with heater: 21.3 qt. Dual exhaust. Carburetor: Four-barrel. Engine code J.

LEMANS OPTIONAL 400-CID V-8: Overhead valve. Cast-iron block. Bore and stroke: 4.12 x 3.75. Displacement: 400 cid. Compression ratio: 7.6:1. Net hp: 185 at 3600 rpm. Taxable hp: 54.30. Net torque: 310 lbs.-ft. at 1600 rpm. Five main bearings. Hydraulic valve lifters. Crankcase capacity: 5 qt. Cooling system capacity with heater: 21.6 qt. Carburetor: Two-barrel. Engine code S.

The Grand Safari wagon came in two- and three-seat models.

GRAND AM OPTIONAL 455-CID V-8: Overhead valve. Cast-iron block. Bore and stroke: 4.15 x 4.21. Displacement: 455 cid. Compression ratio: 8.00:1. Net hp: 200 at 3500 rpm. Taxable hp: 55.20. Net torque: 330 lbs.-ft. at 2000 rpm. Five main bearings. Hydraulic valve lifters. Crankcase capacity: 5 qt. Cooling system capacity with heater: 19.9 qt. Dual exhaust. Carburetor: Four-barrel. Code Y engine.

CHASSIS

Wheelbase: (LeMans, LeMans Sport Coupe, Luxury LeMans and Grand Am two-door) 112 in., (LeMans, Luxury LeMans, Grand Am four-door and all LeMans Safari four-door station wagons) 116 in. Overall Length: (LeMans, LeMans Sport Coupe, Luxury LeMans and Grand Am two-door) 208 in., (LeMans, Luxury LcMans and Grand Am four-door) 215 in., (LeMans Safari) 215.4 in. Overall width: (Lemans, LeMans Sport Coupe, Luxury LeMans and Grand Am coupe) 77.4 in., (Lemans, LeMans Sport Coupe, Luxury LeMans and Grand Am sedan) 77 in. Overall height: (LeMans, LeMans Sport, Luxury LeMans and Grand Am two-door) 52.7 in., (LeMans, Luxury LeMans and Grand Am four-door) 53.4 in., (LeMans Safari) 55.3 in. Front headroom: (LeMans, LeMans Sport Coupe, Luxury LeMans and Grand Am two-door) 37.8 in., (LeMans, Luxury LeMans, Grand Am four-door) 38.5 in. Rear headroom: (LeMans, LeMans Sport Coupe, Luxury LeMans and Grand Am two-door) 36.9 in., (LeMans, Luxury LeMans, Grand Am four-door) 37.2 in. Front legroom: (LeMans, LeMans Sport Coupe, Luxury LeMans and Grand Am two-door) 42.4 in., (LeMans, Luxury LeMans and Grand Am four-door) 42.4 in. Rear legroom: (LeMans, LeMans Sport Coupe and Luxury LeMans two-door) 33.7 in., (Grand Am two-door) 33.5 in., (LeMans and Luxury LeMans four-door) 38.4 in., (Grand Am four-door) 38.6 in. Front shoulder room: (LeMans, LeMans Sport Coupe, Luxury LeMans and Grand Am two-door) 59.6 in., (LeMans, Luxury LeMans and Grand Am four-door) 59.6 in. Rear shoulder room: (LeMans, LeMans Sport Coupe, Luxury LeMans and Grand Am two-door) 57.5 in., (LeMans, Luxury Lemans and Grand Am four-door) 58.9 in. Trunk capacity: (all cars) 15.1 cu. ft. Top of front seat back to closed tailgate length: (Safari) 82.9 in. Rear opening width at floor: (Safari) 61.2 in. Maximum cargo height: (Safari) 30.1 in. Total cargo volume: (Safari) 85.1 cu. ft. Front tread: (All Lemans group except Grand Am) 61.5 in., (Grand Am) 61.9 in. Rear tread: (All LeMans group except Grand Am) 60.7 in., (Grand Am) 61.1 in.

OPTIONS

542 heavy-duty air cleaner. 582 LeMans air conditioning, not available with 250-cid six-cylinder engine. 581 Automatic Temperature Control air conditioning, Grand Am only. 651 Automatic Level Control suspension, with trailering package. 651 Automatic Level Control suspension, without trailering package. 378 performance axle ratio. 371 Safe-T-Track differential. 574 Delco Maintenance-Free battery. 592 heavy-duty battery, except with six-cylinder engine. 691 Custom front and rear seat belts and front shoulder belts, all except three-seat safari. 691 Custom front and rear seat belts and front shoulder belts in three-seat safari. 541 California assembly line emissions test, required in all cars registered in California. 602 Safari cargo area carpeting. 621 front floor mats. 622 rear floor mats. 621 carpeted front floor mats. 711 electric clock, standard in Grand Am. 712 Rally gauge cluster with clock, standard in Grand Am and not available with six-cylinder engine. 714 Rally gauge cluster with clock and tachometer, not available in Grand Am or with M40 Turbo Hydra-Matic transmission. 431 front seat center console with bucket seat interior, standard in Grand Am, not available with standard transmission with column shift. 424 spare wheel and tire cover, all models except Safari. 562 cruise control, except with six-cylinder

engine. 564 remote deck lid release, except Safaris. 514 Safari rear window air deflector. 592 electric rear window defroster, not available with six-cylinder engine or Safari. 594 rear window defogger, except Grand Am ($33). 682 dual exhausts, not available with six-cylinder engine. 35D 250-cid six-cylinder engine (standard in base LeMans and LeMans Sport Coupe). 35M 350-cid two-barrel V-8 in base LeMans. 35R 400-cid two-barrel V-8. 35S 400-cid four-barrel V-8. 35J 350-cid four-barrel V-8. 35W 455-cid four-barrel V-8. 601 engine block heater. 571 all tinted glass. 572 tinted windshield. 492 door edge guards, two-door models. 492 door edge guards, four-door models. 731 front bumper guards. 732 rear bumper guards. 734 front and rear bumper impact strips. Hood decal LeMans coupe. 664 ashtray lamp. 664 glove box light in base LeMans and LeMans Sport Coupe. 662 rear compartment courtesy lamp in Safari. 661 dome reading lamp. 662 luggage compartment lamp, except Safari. 671 cornering lamps on Grand Am. 674 instrument panel courtesy lamps. 692 litter container. 35J rear quarter window louvers. 524 Safari roof top luggage carrier. 444 remote-control left-hand outside rearview mirror. 428 dual remote-control outside rearview mirrors. 434 dual Sport-type outside rearview

mirrors, left-hand remote controlled. 424 dual remote-control Sport-type outside rearview mirrors. 441 left-hand visor-vanity mirror. 442 right-hand visor-vanity mirror. 482 side window reveal moldings on four-door sedan. 491 wheel opening moldings on base LeMans. SPS special solid paint. RTT standard color two-tone paint LeMans Safari. RTT standard color two-tone paint. STT special color two-tone paint on Safari. 502 power front disc brakes. 554 power door locks in coupe. 554 power door locks, four-door models. 561 Six-way power left-hand front bucket seat, optional bucket seating required. 561 Six-way power left-hand front bench seat. 501 power steering, standard in Grand Am. Power tailgate release in two-seat Safari. 551 power side windows. 722 heavy-duty radiator, without air conditioning. 411 AM radio. 413 AM/FM radio. 415 AM/FM stereo radio. 417 AM radio and stereo tape player. 419 AM/FM radio and stereo 8-track tape player. 421 rear seat speaker. 804 speedometer marked in kilometers. 652 Superlift rear shock absorbers. 721 Firm Ride springs and shocks. 461 Custom Cushion steering wheel. 462 Custom sport steering wheel in base LeMans without Décor group. 462 Custom sport steering wheel in base LeMans with Décor group. 504 tilt-adjustable steering column, requires

GM Media Archives photo

The louvered rear quarter windows were a calling card of the 1975 LeMans Sport.

Custom cushion. 638 accent stripes for Grand Am and base LeMans coupe. 452 electric sunroof, LeMans two-door. 454 manual sunroof. TFJ Radial Tuned Suspension including: G78-15 steel-belted radial white sidewall tires, special springs and shock absorbers, a rear stabilizer bar and RTS identification badges. TSJ Radial Tuned Suspension, including: G78-15 steel-belted radial white sidewall tires, special springs and shock absorbers, a rear stabilizer bar, and RTS identification badges for LeMans Safari. 341 formal cordova or landau top on LeMans Sport Coupe, includes formal rear window. SVT cordova vinyl top, except Safaris. 451 cordova Landau top, LeMans coupes. 701 light-duty trailer hitch. 702 five-wire trailer light cable. 704 seven-wire trailer light cable. 36A three-speed manual transmission with column shift (standard). 36C heavy-duty three-speed manual transmission with floor shift in base LeMans or LeMans Sport Coupe with 350-cid two-barrel or 400-cid four-barrel V-8. 36E four-speed manual transmission in LeMans group except Safari and Grand Am with 350-cid two-barrel or 400-cid four-barrel V-8. 36E four-speed manual transmission in Grand Am, delete option. 36K M38 Turbo Hydra-Matic transmission in base LeMans or LeMans Sport Coupe. 36K M38 Turbo Hydra-Matic transmission in Luxury LeMans. 36L M40 Turbo Hydra-Matic transmission. 301 vinyl trim in base LeMans. 472 Custom finned wheel covers. 476 deluxe wheel covers on base LeMans. 478 honeycomb wheels. 474 Rally II wheels. 471 wheel trim rings. 521 swing-out rear quarter windows in two-seat Safari. 512 wood-grain Safari paneling. 324 Custom Trim group for base LeMans sedan, includes notchback front bench seat with center armrest, body-color door handles and wood-grained vinyl glove box accents. 724 Décor Group, includes deluxe wheel covers, a Custom cushioned steering wheel, pedal trim, wheel opening moldings, window sill moldings and hood rear edge moldings. 342 LeMans GT option, includes Rally II wheels less trim rings, G70-14 white-letter tires, dual exhausts with chrome extensions, body accent stripes, a remote-control sport-type left-hand rearview mirror, a sport-type right-hand fixed rearview mirror, wheel opening moldings and a three-speed manual transmission with floor shifter for base coupe or LeMans Sport Coupe with 582 or 35W combined with 682. 654 lamp group. 642 medium trailer group. TDR H78-14 fiberglass-belted white sidewall tires. TPL G70-14 fiberglass-belted raised-white-letter tires. TRF G78-14 fiberglass-belted black sidewall tires. TRR G78-14 fiberglass-belted white sidewall tires ($32-$46 depending on model and other options). TVJ GR70-15 steel-belted white sidewall tires for Grand Am without 684 ($32). TVJ GR70-15 steel-belted white sidewall tires for Grand Am with 684. TVK GR70-15 steel-belted raised-white-letter tires for Grand Am without 684. TVK GR70-15 steel-belted raised-white-letter tires for Grand Am with 684.

OPTION INSTALLATION RATES

Of 103,688 LeMans built, 98 percent had automatic transmission, 2 percent had a synchromesh transmission, 14.3 percent had a standard V-8 engine, 77.3 percent had an optional V-8 engine, 8.5 percent had a six-cylinder engine, 53.8 percent had a AM radio, 18.6 percent had an AM/FM radio, 13.6 percent had an AM/FM stereo radio, 12.3 percent had a stereo tape player, 99.7 percent had power steering, 94 percent had power front disc/rear drum brakes, 6 percent had manual disc brakes, 8 percent had power door locks, 5.5 percent had a power seat, 14.6 percent had all power windows, 33.3 percent had bucket seats, 9 percent had reclining seats, 45 percent had a vinyl roof, 1.5 percent had a sun roof, 99.7 percent had steel-belted radial tires, 8.7 percent had a tinted windshield only, 79.6 percent had all tinted windows, 4.2 percent had Automatic Temperature Control, 77.1 percent had an air conditioner, 22.8 percent had an adjustable steering column, 4.2 percent had a limited-slip differential, 11.2 percent had standard wheel covers, 39.1 percent had optional wheel covers, 46.8 percent had optional styled wheels, 36.4 percent had a standard clock, 17.1 percent had an optional clock, 12 percent had a speed regulating device, 20.2 percent had a rear window defogger, and 79.2 percent had a remote-control outside rearview mirror.

HISTORICAL FOOTNOTES

The 1975 Pontiacs were introduced on September 27, 1974. Alex C. Mair was general manager of Pontiac Motor Division. Model-year production of LeMans and Grand Am models built in the United States or built in Canada for the U.S. market totaled 103,688 cars. This total included 42,082 base LeMans, 23,817 LeMans Sports, 27,110 Luxury LeMans and 10,679 Grand Ams. U.S.-only model-year production of LeMans and Grand Am models by factory included: 30,043 made in Lakewood, Georgia, 27,417 built in Framingham, Massachusetts, and 39,598 made in Pontiac, Michigan. The total of 97,058 cars built in U.S. factories represented 1.48 percent of total U.S. industry production and included 8,132 cars with the six-cylinder engine and 88,930 with a V-8. U.S. model-year production included 42,082 base LeMans and 23,817 LeMans Sport Coupes (of which 7,572 had six-cylinder engines), 27,110 Grand LeMans (of which 560 had six-cylinder engines), and 10,679 V-8-powered Grand Ams.

We can calculate that an additional 6,630 cars were made in Oshawa, Canada for the model year. Model-year sales of the LeMans dropped further to 92,542 units from 148,254 the previous year. Calendar-year sales of LeMans/Grand Am models by U.S. franchised dealers came to 93,382 cars for a 1.3 percent share of market.

GM Media Archives photo

**The LeMans series, this is a two-door Grand LeMans coupe, received
a new elegant front-end treatment for 1976.**

For the first time in 1976 the LeMans had a small 260-cid V-8. Quad rectangular headlights gave the LeMans a new front-end appearance. A horizontal rear taillight motif was another styling change. A five-speed manual transmission, which acted like an overdrive, was available on the LeMans Sport Coupe. LeMans and Grand LeMans cars included a Colonnade two-door hardtop and four-door sedan. The LeMans Safari and Grand LeMans Safari were two-seat station wagons. A rear-facing third seat was optional.

I.D. DATA

The 13-symbol vehicle identification number (VIN) was located on the upper left surface of the instrument panel, visible through the windshield. The first digit is 2, indicating Pontiac division. The second symbol is a letter indicating series: D=LeMans, F=LeMans Sport Coupe, G=Grand LeMans. Next come two digits that denote body type: 29=four-door hardtop, 35=four-door two-seat wagon, 37=two-door hardtop, 45=four-door three-seat wagon. The fifth symbol is a letter indicating engine code: D=250-cid I6 one-barrel, F=260-cid V-8 two-barrel, H or M=350-cid V-8 two-barrel, E or J=350-cid V-8 four-barrel, R=400-cid V-8 two-barrel, S=400-cid V-8 four-barrel W=455-cid V-8 four-barrel. The sixth symbol denotes model year (6=1976). Next is a plant code: A=Lakewood, Ga., P=Pontiac, Michigan, 1=Oshawa, Ontario, 2=Ste. Therese, Quebec. The final six digits are the sequential serial number, which began with 100,001.

COLORS

Paint codes for 1976 were: 11=Cameo White, 13=Sterling Silver, 16=Medium Gray, 19=Starlight Black, 28=Aethena Blue, 35=Polaris Blue, 36=Firethorn Red, 37=Cordovan Maroon, 40=Metalime Green, 49=Alpine Green, 50=Bavarian Cream, 51=Goldenrod Yellow, 55=Anniversary Gold, 57=Cream Gold, 65=Buckskin Tan. 67=Durango Bronze, 72=Roman Red and 78=Carousel Red. Interior trim codes were: 11M/11Y=White Cloth, 11W/11Y=White vinyl, 19B/19C Black leather, 19D/19E=Black vinyl, 91M/91N=Black cloth, 91V=Black cloth, 19V/19W=Black vinyl, 19Y=Black vinyl, 91Y=Black vinyl, 26B/26C=Blue leather, 26D=Blue leather, 26M/92M=Blue cloth, 26N=Blue cloth, 92N/26V=Blue vinyl, 92V=Blue vinyl, 26W/92W=Blue vinyl, 26Y=Blue vinyl, 92Y=Blue vinyl, 64M/64N=Buckskin cloth, 64V=Buckskin cloth, 64W/64Y=Buckskin vinyl, 64E/64J=Buckskin leather, 643=Buckskin leather, 71M/97M=Firethorn cloth, 71N=Firethorn cloth, 97N/71V=Firethorn vinyl, 97V=Firethorn vinyl, 71W/97W=Firethorn vinyl, 71Y=Firethorn vinyl, 97Y=Firethorn vinyl, 71C/71D=Firethorn leather, 71E=Firethorn leather, 98Y=Mahogany cloth, and 74J/743=Mahogany leather.

LEMANS — (V-6) / LEMANS SAFARI — (V-8) — SERIES 2AD

Quad rectangular headlights gave the LeMans a new front-end appearance. Two-door models had a formal-look rear quarter window. Park/signal lamps were at the outer ends of a single bumper slot, next to the bumper guards. The LeMans grille consisted of thin vertical bars, arranged in sections on each side of a peaked divider bar that displayed a Pontiac emblem. Two four-door (two-seat) station wagons were available with an optional rear-facing third seat. LeMans standard equipment included: the 250-cid six-cylinder engine with a three-speed manual transmission, rocker panel moldings, FR78 x 15 steel-belted-radial tires, RTS (radial-tuned suspension), and dual horns. Standard equipment for Safari station wagons included: a 400-cid two-barrel V-8, Turbo Hydra-Matic automatic transmission, power brakes, and HR78 x 15 tires.

Model Number	Body/Style Number	Body Type & Seating	Factory Price	Shipping Weight	Production Total
LEMANS — (SIX-CYL) — SERIES 2AD					
2AD	37	2d Hardtop-6P	$3,768	3,651 lbs.	21,130
2AD	29	4d Hardtop -6P	$3,813	3,760 lbs.	22,199
LEMANS SAFARI — (V-8) — SERIES 2AD					
2AD	35	4d Sta Wagon-6P	$4,687	4,336 lbs.	Note 1
2AD	45	4d Sta Wagon-9P	$4,820	4,374 lbs.	Note 1

LEMANS SPORT COUPE — (SIX-CYL) — SERIES 2AF

The LeMans Sport Coupe came only as a Colonnade coupe. Its standard equipment included louvered panels to cover the rear quarter windows. The LeMans Sport Coupe also had wheel opening moldings and either full-width seating or bucket seats. A new five-speed manual transmission was available on this model only.

Model Number	Body/Style Number	Body Type & Seating	Factory Price	Shipping Weight	Production Total
2AF	37	2d Hardtop -6P	$3,916	3,668 lbs.	15,582

GRAND LEMANS (V-6) — GRAND LEMANS SAFARI (V-8) — SERIES 2AG

Grand LeMans models had either a five-speed manual gearbox or Turbo Hydra-Matic transmission, deluxe wheel covers, an electric clock, wheel opening moldings, and either full-width seating or bucket seats.

Model Number	Body/Style Number	Body Type & Seating	Factory Price	Shipping Weight	Production Total
GRAND LEMANS (SIX-CYL)					
2AG	37	2d Hardtop -6P	$4,330	3,747 lbs.	14,757
2AG	29	4d Hardtop -6P	$4,433	3,860 lbs.	8,411
GRAND LEMANS SAFARI (V-8)					
2AG	35	4d Sta Wagon-6P	$4,928	4,389 lbs.	Note 1
2AG	45	4d Sta Wagon-9P	$5,061	4,427 lbs.	Note 1

NOTE 1: A total of 8,249 two-seat (six-passenger) and 5,901 three-seat (nine-passenger) LeMans Safari wagons were produced (base Safari and Grand Safari).

ENGINES

LEMANS BASE 350-CID SIX-CYL: Inline. Overhead valve. Six-cylinder. Cast-iron block and head. Displacement: 250 cid (4.1 liters). Bore and stroke: 3.87 x 3.53 in. Compression ratio: 8.3:1. Brake hp: 110 at 3600 rpm. Torque: 185 lbs.-ft. at 1200 rpm. Seven main bearings. Hydraulic valve lifters. Carburetor: Rochester one-barrel. VIN Code: D.

LEMANS OPTIONAL 260-CID V-8 ("BASE PASSENGER-CAR" V-8): Overhead valve. Cast-iron block and head. Bore and stroke: 3.50 x 3.39 in. Displacement: 260 cid (4.3 liters). Compression ratio: 7.5:1. Brake hp: 110 at 3400 rpm. Taxable hp: 39.20. Torque: 205 lbs.-ft. at 1600 rpm. Five main bearings. Hydraulic valve lifters. Crankcase capacity: 4 qt. Cooling system capacity: 23.5 qt. Carburetor: Rochester two-barrel. VIN Code: F.

LEMANS SAFARI BASE 350-CID V-8: Overhead valve. Cast-iron block and head. Bore and stroke: 3.80 x 3.85 in. Displacement: 350 cid (5.7 liters). Compression ratio: 8.0:1. Brake hp: 155 at 3400 rpm. Taxable hp: 48. Torque: 280 lbs.-ft. at 1800 rpm. Five main bearings. Hydraulic valve lifters. Crankcase capacity: 5 qt. Cooling system capacity: 21.4 qt. Carburetor: Rochester four-barrel.

LEMANS OPTIONAL 350-CID V-8: Overhead valve. Cast-iron block and head. Bore and stroke: 3.88 x 3.75 in. Displacement: 350 cid (5.7 liters). Compression ratio: 7.6:1. Brake hp: 160 at 4000 rpm. Taxable hp: 48. Torque: 280 lbs.-ft. at 2000 rpm. Five main bearings. Hydraulic valve lifters. 5 qt. VIN Cooling system capacity: 21.4 qt. Crankcase capacity: Carburetor: Rochester two-barrel. Code: H or M.

GM Media Archives photo

The 1976 Grand Safari wagon (left) and Grand LeMans Safari wagon were cousins.

LEMANS OPTIONAL 400-CID V-8: Overhead valve. Cast-iron block and head. Bore and stroke: 4.12 x 3.75 in. Displacement: 400 cid (6.6 liters). Compression ratio: 7.6:1. Brake hp: 170 at 4000 rpm. Taxable hp: 54.30. Torque: 310 lbs.-ft. at 1600 rpm. Five main bearings. Hydraulic valve lifters. Crankcase capacity: 5 qt. Cooling system capacity with heater: 21.4 qt. Carburetor: Rochester two-barrel. Engine code: J.

LEMANS OPTIONAL V-8 ("BASE PASSENGER-CAR" V-8 IN CARS REGISTERED IN CALIFORNIA): Overhead valve. Cast-iron block. Bore and stroke: 3.88 x 3.53. Displacement: 350 cid. Compression ratio: 7.6:1.

Net hp: 165 at 4000 rpm. Taxable hp: 48. Net torque: 260 lbs.-ft. at 2400 rpm. Five main bearings. Hydraulic valve lifters. Crankcase capacity: 5 qt. Cooling system capacity with heater: 21.3 qt. Dual exhaust. Carburetor: Four-barrel. Engine code J.

LEMANS OPTIONAL 400-CID V-8: Overhead valve. Cast-iron block and head. Bore and stroke: 4.12 x 3.75 in. Displacement: 400 cid (6.6 liters). Compression ratio: 7.6:1. Brake hp: 185 at 3600 rpm. Taxable hp: 54.30. Torque: 310 lbs.-ft. at 1600 rpm. Five main bearings. Hydraulic valve lifters. Crankcase capacity: 5 qt. Cooling system capacity with heater: 21.4 qt. Carburetor:

Rochester four-barrel. VIN Code: S.

LEMANS OPTIONAL 455-CID V-8: Overhead valve. Cast-iron block and head. Bore and stroke: 4.15 x 4.21 in. Displacement: 455 cid (7.5 liters). Compression ratio: 7.6:1. Brake hp: 200 at 3500 rpm. Taxable hp: 55.20. Torque: 330 lbs.-ft. at 2000 rpm. Five main bearings. Hydraulic valve lifters. Crankcase capacity: 5 qt. Cooling system capacity with heater: 21.6 qt. Carburetor: Rochester four-barrel. VIN Code: W.

CHASSIS

Wheelbase: (LeMans and Grand LeMans coupe) 112 in., (LeMans and Grand LeMans sedan) 116 in. Overall Length: (LeMans and Grand LeMans coupe) 208 in., (LeMans and Grand LeMans sedan) 212 in. Height: (LeMans and Grand LeMans coupe) 52.7 in., (LeMans and Grand LeMans sedan) 53.5 in., (LeMans station wagon) 55.3 in. Width: 77.4 in. Front tread: 61.6 in. Rear Tread: 61.1 in. Standard tires: (LeMans and Grand LeMans coupe and sedan) FR78 x 15, (LeMans Safari station wagon) HR78 x 15. Transmission: Three-speed manual transmission with column-mounted shifter. Standard final drive ratio: (with six-cylinder engine) 2.73:1 with three-speed transmission, 2.73:1 or 3.08:1 with automatic transmission; (with 260-cid V-8) 3.08:1 with three-speed transmission, 2.73:1 with automatic transmission, (with 350- or 400-cid V-8s) 2.41:1, except 2.56:1 with 400-cid V-8 in Safari station wagon) 2.56:1. Steering: re-circulating ball. Front suspension: coil springs with lower trailing links and anti-sway bar. Rear suspension: rigid axle with coil springs, lower trailing radius arms, upper torque arms and anti-sway bar. Brakes: front disc, rear drum. Ignition: electronic. Body construction: separate body and frame. Fuel tank: 21.8 gal.

OPTIONS

260-cid two-barrel V-8 ($90). 350-cid two-barrel V-8 ($140). 350-cid four-barrel V-8 ($195). 400-cid two-barrel V-8 ($203). 400-cid four-barrel in coupe or sedan V-8 ($258). 400-cid four-barrel in Safari ($55). 455-cid V-8 in coupe or sedan ($321). 455-cid four-barrel V-8 in Safari ($118). Three-speed manual transmission (standard). Five-speed manual transmission in LeMans sport coupe ($262). Turbo Hydra-Matic transmission in Grand LeMans (no charge). Turbo Hydra-Matic transmission in base LeMans ($262). M40 Turbo Hydra-Matic transmission in Grand LeMans or LeMans Safari ($24). M40 Turbo Hydra-Matic transmission in base LeMans ($286), Safe-T-Track differential ($55) Rally RTS handling package ($57-$101). Firm ride package ($10). Super lift shock absorbers ($46). Super-cooling radiator ($27-$49). Heavy-duty battery ($15-$17). Heavy-duty alternator ($42). Engine block heater ($11-$12). Medium trailer group LeMans ($97-$119). California emissions ($50). Air conditioning ($424-$512). Automatic air conditioning ($513). Cruise control ($73). Power seat ($124-$126). Power windows ($99-$159). Power sunroof ($370). Landau top ($109-

$119) Rear-facing third seat: Safari ($149). Wood-grain siding on Safari wagon ($154-$156). Custom trim group on sedan ($88).

OPTION INSTALLATION RATES

Of 96,229 LeMans built (including cars built in Canada for the U.S. market), 99.8 percent had automatic transmission, 0.2 percent had a five-speed manual transmission, 11.8 percent had a standard V-8 engine, 81.2 percent had an optional V-8 engine, 7.3 percent had a six-cylinder engine, 41.9 percent had a AM radio, 22.5 percent had an AM/FM radio, 10 percent had an AM/FM stereo radio, 3.9 percent had a stereo tape player, 99.8 percent had power steering, 98.6 percent had power front disc/rear drum brakes, 1.4 percent had manual disc brakes, 10.7 percent had power door locks, 5.9 percent had a power seat, 12.6 percent had all power windows, 17.8 percent had bucket seats, 0.4 percent had reclining seats, 40.1 percent had a vinyl roof, 0.9 percent had a sun roof, 100 percent had steel-belted radial tires, 1.5 percent had a tinted windshield only, 84.3 percent had all tinted windows, 6.1 percent had Automatic Temperature Control, 77.5 percent had an air conditioner, 28.1 percent had an adjustable steering column, 5.9 percent had a limited-slip differential, 8.4 percent had standard wheel covers, 44.1 percent had optional wheel covers, 36.2 percent had optional styled wheels, 24.1 percent had a standard clock, 28.3 percent had an optional clock, 15.4 percent had a speed regulating device, 25.3 percent had a rear window defogger, 78.5 percent had a remote-control left-hand outside rearview mirror, and 4.5 percent had a remote-control left-hand outside rearview mirror.

HISTORICAL FOOTNOTES

The 1976 Pontiacs were introduced on September 25, 1975. Alex C. Mair was general manager of Pontiac Motor Division. Model-year production of LeMans and Grand LeMans models built in the United States totaled 96,229 cars. That was 1.19 percent of the industry total. This total included 43,329 base Lemans coupes and sedans, 15,582 LeMans Sport Coupes, 23,168 Grand LeMans coupes and sedans, and 14,150 LeMans and Grand LeMans Safaris combined. Model-year production of LeMans and Grand LeMans models by factory included: 30,234 made in Lakewood, Georgia, 14,092 built in Framingham, Massachusetts, and 51,903 made in Pontiac, Michigan. Of the 96,229 cars built in U.S. factories, 7,053 had a six-cylinder engine, and 89,176 had a V-8. Model-year sales of LeMans through U.S. new-car dealers totaled 92,217 units compared to 92,542 the previous year. A total of 21,662 cars were reported built in Canada for model-year 1976. About 14,020 of these were 1976 models and approximately 8,271 cars of that model year were built late in calendar year 1975.

The first-generation Grand Am did not return in 1976. A concept vehicle called the Can Am was making the rounds of car shows in 1976 and would soon be made available at Pontiac dealerships.

The 1977 Grand LeMans was the last of the large LeMans cars. This Luxury model featured optional rear fender skirts.

The midsize LeMans had a new front-end appearance and revised engine selections. The base engine was the 231-cid (3.8-liter) V-6. Safari station wagons had a standard 350-cid (5.7-liter) V-8. A 6.6-liter V-8 was available in all models. New LeMans options included 15-in. cast-aluminum wheels, wire wheel covers, and newly styled deluxe wheel covers. Grand LeMans buyers could get a new AM/FM radio with a digital clock.

I.D. DATA

The 13-symbol vehicle identification number (VIN) was located on the upper left surface of the instrument panel, visible through the windshield. The first digit is 2, indicating Pontiac division. The second symbol is a letter indicating series: D=LeMans, F=LeMans Sport Coupe, G=Grand LeMans. Next come two digits that denote body type: 29=four-door Colonnade sedan, 35=four-door two-seat wagon and 37=two-door Colonnade sport coupe. The fifth symbol is a letter indicating engine code: C=231-cid two-barrel V-6, K=403-cid four-barrel V-8, L=350-cid four-barrel V-8, P=350-cid four-barrel V-8, R=350-cid four-barrel V-8, Y=301-cid two-barrel V-8 and Z=400-cid four-barrel V-8. The sixth symbol denotes model year (7=1977). Next is a plant code: A=Lakewood, Georgia, B=Baltimore, Maryland, P=Pontiac, Michigan, and 1=Oshawa, Ontario. The final six digits are the sequential serial number, which began with 100,001.

COLORS

Paint codes were: 11=Cameo White, 13=Sterling Silver, 15=Gray, 19=Starlight Black, 21=Lombard Blue, 22=Glacier Blue, 29=Nautilus Blue, 32=Royal Lime, 36=Firethorn Red, 37=Cordovan Maroon, 38=Aquamarine, 44=Bahia Green, 48=Berkshire Green, 50=Cream Gold, 51=Goldenrod Yellow, 61=Mojave Tan, 63=Buckskin, 64=Fiesta Orange, 72=Roman Red, 75=Buccaneer Red, and 78=Mandarin Orange. Interior trim codes were: (LeMans four-door) 19B/197=Black cloth and vinyl, 19C=Black cloth and vinyl notchback or 60/40 seat, 19R=Black vinyl bucket seats, 19N=Black vinyl notchback or 60/40 seat, 24B/247=Blue cloth and vinyl, 24C=Blue cloth and vinyl notchback or 60/40 seat, 24R=Blue vinyl bucket seats, 24N=Blue vinyl notchback or 60/40 seat, 64R/64R=Buckskin vinyl bucket seats, 64N=Buckskin vinyl notchback or 60/40 seat, 64C=Buckskin cloth and vinyl notchback or 60/40 seat, 71R/71R=Firethorn vinyl bucket seats, 71N=Firethorn vinyl notchback or 60/40 seat, 71C=Firethorn cloth and vinyl notchback or 60/40 seat; (LeMans Safari) 24R/24Y=Blue vinyl, 24N=Blue vinyl notchback or 60/40 seat, 24W=Blue Vinyl bucket seat or notchback or 60/40 seat, 64R/64Y=Buckskin vinyl, 64N=Bucksin vinyl notchback or 60/40 seat, 64W=Blue vinyl bucket seat or notchback or 60/40 seat, 71R/71Y=Firethorn vinyl seat, 71N=Firethorn vinyl notchback or 60/40 seat, 71W=Firethorn vinyl bucket seat or notchback or 60/40 seat; (LeMans Sport Coupe) 11R/11R=White vinyl bucket seats, 11N=White vinyl notchback or 60/40 seat, 19B/197=Black cloth and vinyl, 19C=Black cloth and vinyl notchback or 60/40 seat, 19R/19R=Black vinyl

bucket seats, 19N=Black vinyl notchback or 60/40 seat, 24B/247=Blue cloth and vinyl, 24C=Blue cloth and vinyl notchback or 60/40 seat, 92R/92R=Blue vinyl bucket seats, 24N=Blue vinyl notchback or 60/40 seat, 92N=Blue vinyl notchback or 60/40 seat, 64R/64R=Buckskin vinyl bucket seats, 64N=Buckskin vinyl notchback or 60/40 seat, 64C=Buckskin cloth and vinyl notchback or 60/40 seat, 71R/71R=Firethorn vinyl bucket seats, 97R/97R=Firethorn vinyl bucket seats, 71N=Firethorn vinyl notchback or 60/40 seat, 71C=Firethorn cloth and vinyl notchback or 60/40 seat; (Grand LeMans) 11W=White vinyl bucket seats or notchback or 60/40 seat, 19D=Black cloth and vinyl notchback or 60/40 seat, 19J=Black cloth and vinyl bucket seats or notchback or 60/40 seat, 19W=Black vinyl bucket seats or notchback or 60/40 seat, 24D=Blue cloth and vinyl notchback or 60/40 seat, 35J=Blue cloth and vinyl bucket seats or notchback or 60/40 seat, 24W=Blue vinyl bucket seats or notchback or 60/40 seat, 92W=Blue vinyl bucket seats or notchback or 60/40 seat, 64D=Buckskin cloth and notchback or 60/40 seat, 64J=Buckskin bucket seats or notchback or 60/40 seat, 64W=Buckskin bucket seats or notchback or 60/40 seat, 71D=Firethorn notchback or 60/40 seat, 71J=Firethorn bucket seats or notchback or 60/40 seat, 71W=Firethorn bucket seats or notchback or 60/40 seat, and 97W=Firethorn vinyl bucket seats or notchback or 60/40

The 1977 Can Am was short-lived, but it had plenty of personality.

seat. Vinyl roof colors were: 11T=White, 13T=Silver, 19T=Black, 22T=Light Blue, 36T=Firethorn, 44T=Medium Green and 61T=Light Buckskin. Glass sunroof color options were: CFT=Silver, CFL=Light Grey, CFZ=Gold, CFR=Rose, and CFG=Green.

LEMANS — (V-6) / LEMANS SAFARI — (V-8) — SERIES 2AD

Base LeMans models had quad rectangular headlights alongside a grille made up only of heavy vertical bars, forming six sections on each side of a protruding center divider. That divider formed a point that carried forward from the prominent hood creases and contained the Pontiac arrowhead emblem at its tip. Headlight frames continued outward to surround wraparound single-section marker lenses. Park/signal lights were at the outer ends of the twin bumper slots.

Model Number	Body/Style Number	Body Type & Seating	Factory Price	Shipping Weight	Production Total
LEMANS — (V-6) — SERIES 2AD					
2AD	37	2d Hardtop-6P	$4,045	3,550 lbs.	16,038
2AD	29	4d Hardtop-6P	$4,093	3,638 lbs.	23,060
LEMANS SAFARI — (V-8) — SERIES 2AD					
2AD	35	4d Sta Wagon-6P	$4,877	4,135 lbs.	10,081

LEMANS SPORT COUPE — (V-6) — SERIES 2AF

The LeMans Sport Coupe came only as a Colonnade coupe. Its standard equipment included louvered panels to cover the rear quarter windows. The LeMans Sport Coupe also had wheel opening moldings and either full-width seating or bucket seats. A LeMans GT option featured a distinctive two-tone paint treatment, bold body striping, a Rally RTS handling package, and body-color Rally II wheels.

The three varieties of LeMans for 1977: Grand LeMans (top), LeMans Sport Coupe, and LeMans.

Model Number	Body/Style Number	Body Type & Seating	Factory Price	Shipping Weight	Production Total
2AF	37	2d Hardtop-6P	$4,204	3,558 lbs.	12,277

CAN AM — (V-8) — SERIES 2AF

One of the more notable Pontiacs of the 1970s was the Can Am—a performance version of the LeMans Sport Coupe. The Can Am included the performance T/A 400-cid (6.6-liter) V-8 (or a 403-cid V-8 in California) along with body-colored Rally II wheels, a blacked-out grille assembly and GR70 x 15 SBR tires. The Can Am was promoted as a "fun car" along with the Trans Am. It was offered only in a Cameo White body color. Standard equipment included: Turbo Hydra-Matic transmission, power brakes, variable-ratio power steering, front and rear stabilizer bars, body-color Rally II wheels, front/rear protective rubber bumper strips and body-color dual sport mirrors (driver's side remote-controlled). A Grand Prix instrument panel assembly included a Rally gauge cluster and clock. A Rally RTS handling package was standard. Appearance features included tri-tone-colored accent tape striping on the hood, front fenders, doors and sport mirrors, black lower body sides (with accent striping), black rocker panel moldings, a full-width rear deck spoiler with tri-tone accent striping (front and rear), tri-tone "Can Am" identification on the front end, front fender and rear deck lid, black-out style windshield, backlight, door window and belt moldings, and unique "Can Am" interior identification. On the Can Am's hood was a Trans Am-style "shaker" scoop with tri-tone "T/A 6.6" identification and accent stripes. Early Can Am models also included a Safe-T-Track rear axle, GR70 x 15 white letter tires, a Custom sport steering wheel, Soft-Ray tinted glass, dual horns, front and rear floor mats and custom color-keyed seat belts. Other available options included: an air conditioning system, a radio, and a choice of White, Black, or Firethorn interior trim colors (or Firethorn-and-White) in notchback, full-

width, or bucket seats. The Can Am option was priced at $1,589.

Model Number	Body/Style Number	Body Type & Seating	Factory Price	Shipping Weight	Production Total
2AF	37	2d Hardtop-6P	$5,793	—	1,377

GRAND LEMANS (V-6) — GRAND LEMANS SAFARI (V-8) — SERIES 2AG

The Grand LeMans had a front-end look that was overall similar to that of the base LeMans, but its grille sections included a horizontal divider that created a 5 x 2 pattern of square holes on each side of center. Each of those 20 holes contained a smaller square. Grand LeMans buyers could add a new AM/FM radio with a digital clock.

Model Number	Body/Style Number	Body Type & Seating	Factory Price	Shipping Weight	Production Total
GRAND LEMANS — (V-6) — SERIES 2AG					
2AG	37	2d Hardtop-6P	$4,602	3,587 lbs.	7,581
2AG	29	4d HT Sedan-6P	$4,730	3,740 lbs.	5,584
GRAND LEMANS SAFARI — (V-8) — SERIES 2AG					
2AG	35	4d Sta Wagon-6P	$5,132	4,179 lbs.	5,393

ENGINES

LEMANS, GRAND LEMANS, BASE 231-CID V-6: Overhead-valve. Cast-iron block and head. Displacement: 231 cid. (3.8 liters). Bore and stroke: 3.80 x 3.40 in. Compression ratio: 8.0:1. Brake hp: 105 at 3200 rpm. Torque: 185 lbs.-ft. at 2000 rpm. Four main bearings. Hydraulic valve lifters. Carburetor: two-barrel Rochester 2GC. VIN Code: C.

LEMANS, GRAND LEMANS, SAFARI OPTIONAL 301-CID V-8: Overhead valve. Cast-iron block and head. Bore and stroke: 4.00 x 3.00 in. Displacement: 301 cid (4.9 liters). Compression ratio: 8.2:1. Brake hp: 135 at 4000 rpm. Taxable hp: 51.2. Torque: 235-245 lbs.-ft. at 2000 rpm. (fullsize: 250 at 1600). Five main bearings.

The 1977 Grand LeMans was a nice, if not tremendously popular, car. With Pontiac sales down significantly for the year, a restyling and down-sizing were on the way.

Hydraulic valve lifters. Carburetor: two-barrel. VIN Code: Y.

BASE SAFARI, LEMANS, GRAND LEMANS, SAFARI OPTIONAL 350-CID V-8: Overhead valve. Cast-iron block and head. Bore and stroke: 3.88 x 3.75 in. Displacement: 350 cid (5.7 liters). Compression ratio: 7.6:1. Brake hp: 170 at 4000 rpm. Taxable hp: 51.2. Torque: 280 lbs.-ft. at 1800 rpm. Five main bearings. Hydraulic valve lifters. Carburetor: Four-barrel Rochester M4MC. VIN Code: P.

LEMANS, GRAND LEMANS, SAFARI OPTIONAL 350-CID V-8: Overhead valve. Cast-iron block and head. Bore and stroke: 4.00 x 3.48 in. Displacement: 350 cid (5.7 liters). Compression ratio: 8.0:1. Brake hp: 170 at 3800 rpm. Taxable hp: 51.2. Torque: 275 lbs.-ft. at 2000 rpm. Five main bearings. Hydraulic valve lifters. Carburetor: Four-barrel Rochester M4MC. VIN Code: L. Chevrolet-built.

LEMANS, GRAND LEMANS, SAFARI OPTIONAL 350-CID V-8: Overhead valve. Cast-iron block and head. Bore and stroke: 4.06 x 3.38 in. Displacement: 350 cid (5.7 liters). Compression ratio: 8.0:1. Brake hp: 170 at 3800 rpm. Taxable hp: 51.2. Torque: 275 lbs.-ft. at 2000 rpm. Five main bearings. Hydraulic valve lifters. Carburetor: Four-barrel Rochester M4MC. VIN Code: R. Oldsmobile-built.

LEMANS, GRAND LEMANS, CAN AM OPTIONAL 400-CID V-8: Overhead valve. Cast-iron block and head. Bore and stroke: 4.12 x 3.75 in. Displacement: 400 cid (6.6 liters). Compression ratio: 7.6:1. Brake hp: 180 at 3600 rpm. Taxable hp: 54.30. Torque: 325 lbs.-ft. at 1600 rpm. Five main bearings. Hydraulic valve lifters. Carburetor: Four-barrel Rochester M4MC. VIN Code: Z.

LEMANS, GRAND LEMANS, SAFARI OPTIONAL 403-CID V-8: Overhead valve. Cast iron block and head. Bore and stroke: 4.35 x 3.38 in. Displacement: 403 cid (6.6 liters). Compression ratio: 8.0:1. Brake hp: 185 at 3600 rpm. Taxable hp: 60.6. Torque: 320 at 2200 rpm. Five main bearings. Hydraulic valve lifters. Carburetor: Four-barrel Rochester M4MC. VIN Code: K.

Paul Zazerine photo

The flashy 1977 Can Am came with a 400-cid (6.6-liter) V-8 and was offered only in Cameo White.

**Pontiac bragged about its 16 years of midsize car-building experience
when it promoted its 1977 LeMans Sport Coupe.**

CHASSIS

Wheelbase: (two-door) 112 in.; (four-door) 116 in. Overall length: (two-door) 208 in.; (four-door) 212 in. Height: (two-door) 52.7 in.; (four-door sedan) 53.5 in.; (Safari) 55.3 in. Width: 77.4 in. Front tread: 61.6 in. Rear tread: 61.1 in. Standard tires: FR78 x 15 except Safari HR78 x 15. Transmission: Three-speed manual transmission standard. Three-speed Turbo Hydra-Matic transmission optional. Standard final drive ratio: 3.08:1 with V-6, 2.56:1 with 301-cid V-8, 2.41:1 with 350- or 400-cid V-8, 2.56:1 with 403-cid V-8. Steering: re-circulating ball. Front suspension: coil springs with lower trailing links and anti-sway bar. Rear suspension: rigid axle with coil springs, lower trailing radius arms, upper torque arms and anti-sway bar. Brakes: Front disc, rear drum. Ignition: electronic. Body construction: separate body and frame. Fuel tank: 21.8 gal. (station wagon 22 gal.)

OPTIONS

C60 Custom air conditioning ($442-$540). C65 automatic temperature control ($539-$552). K97 heavy-duty alternator with 350- or 400-cid V-8. UA1 heavy-duty battery ($16-$18). AK1 Custom color-keyed seat belts. V31 front bumper guards, standard on Safari without VE5 rubber impact strips, optional with VE5. V32 rear bumper guards, optional with VE5 rubber impact strips only. VE5 protective rubber bumper strips. N92 California emissions for 231-cid V-6, 350-cid V-8, or 403-cid V-8 ($70). B39 Safari and Grand Safari load floor carpeting. U35 electric clock, standard in Grand LeMans. U14 instrument panel cluster with gauges and fuel economy indicator, optional in Grand LeMans with console only, includes fuel economy gauge. D55 front seat console, with Turbo Hydra-Matic transmission and bucket seats only. T58 rear wheel opening covers (fender skirts) with Grand LeMans only, not available with Safari or wire wheel covers. K30 cruise control, with V-8, Turbo Hydra-Matic transmission and power brakes only ($80-$84). A90 remote-control deck lid release with console or lamp group only on Grand LeMans. C31 Safari rear window air deflector. C49 electric rear window defroster. K05 engine block heater ($12-$13). Y96 Firm Ride package ($11). W63 Rally gauge cluster with clock with V-8 only. WW8 Rally gauge cluster with clock and instrument panel tachometer with V-8 and front seat console only. A01 Soft-Ray glass in all windows. WU2 LeMans GT package for Sport Coupe ($446-$463). B93 door edge guards. Y99 Rally RTS handling package, with V-8 and GR70-15 tires only ($36-$158). NA6 high-altitude performance and emission control package, optional with V-6, 350-and 400-cid V-8s with Turbo Hydra-Matic transmission only ($22). T44 interior hood latch. U05 dual horns. B51 additional acoustical insulation, standard in Grand LeMans. Y92 lamp group including rear doorjamb switch, rear compartment lamp, courtesy lamp, luggage lamp, glove box lamp, ash tray lamp and instrument panel courtesy lamp. C95 dome and reading lamp. VK3 front license plate bracket. D24 litter container. V55 luggage carrier. B48 luggage compartment trim, including luggage compartment lining and spare tire cover. B37 front and rear floor mats. D64 illuminated right-hand visor mirror. D35 right-hand manual and left-hand remote control Sport mirrors. D68 dual remote control sport mirrors. D33 left-hand remote control chrome mirror. DH9 dual visor-vanity mirrors. D34 right-hand visor-vanity mirror. B34 color-keyed body side moldings. B83 rocker panel molding. B96 wheel opening molding. B85 window sill molding, standard on LeMans Sport Coupe and Grand LeMans. JL2 front power disc brakes, required with V-8s or with V-6 and air conditioning ($61). AC3 power left-hand bucket seat ($137-$139). A42 power front bench seat ($137-$139). AU3 power door locks. A31 power windows ($108-$151). AG1 Six-way power 60/40 left-hand seat. N41 power steering, required with V-8s or with V-6 and air conditioning ($146). AU6 remote control power tailgate release for three-seat Safari. A87 louvered quarter window, optional only on LeMans Sport Coupe without vinyl top. V02 Super-Cooling radiator, standard with medium trailer group ($27-$55). U63 AM radio. U69 AM/FM radio. U58 AM/FM stereo radio. UM1 AM stereo with tape deck. UM2 AM/FM stereo radio and stereo 8-track tape player. UY8 AM/FM radio with digital clock for

Grand LeMans only, requires U14 instrument cluster. UN8 CB radio, not available with front seat console UP4 AM/FM stereo CB radio in Grand LeMans or GT only. UN9 radio accommodation package. WU7 third seat for Safari station wagon. G66 Superlift shock absorbers, rear only, standard with medium trailer group ($49). N65 stowaway spare tire, except Safaris. U80 rear seat speaker, optional with AM radio and U69 AM/FM radio. N30 luxury cushion steering wheel, standard in Grand LeMans. N31 Custom sport steering wheel. N33 tilt steering wheel, optional with Turbo Hydra-Matic transmission and optional steering wheels. CA1 electric sunroof, two-door models only ($394). V82 medium trailer group ($127-$151). U89 Five-wire trailer light cable, standard with medium trailer group. JL1 pedal trim package. P02 custom finned wheel covers. N93 wire wheel covers. YJ8 four cast-aluminum wheels, except Safaris. N98 four Rally II wheel rims. N67 four body-color Rally II wheel rims. A20 swing-out rear vent windows, standard with three-seat Safari. CD4 controlled-cycle windshield wipers. CF8 glass sunroof ($625). ZP2 color and trim override. V81 light-duty Class I trailer group ($109-$133). LD7 3.8-liter 231-cid two-barrel V-6 engine (standard equipment). L27 5.0-liter 301-cid two-barrel V-8 engine ($65). L34 5.7-liter 350-cid four-barrel V-8 engine ($155 in LeMans, $90 in LeMans Safari). L76 5.7-liter 350-cid four-barrel V-8 engine ($155 in LeMans, $90 in LeMans Safari). L78 6.6-liter 400-cid four-barrel V-8 ($220 in LeMans, $155 in LeMans Safari). L80 403-cid 6.6-liter four-barrel V-8 ($220 in Lemans, $155 in LeMans Safari. M15 three-speed manual transmission ($282). M40 three-speed Turbo Hydra-Matic transmission. Safe-T-Track differential ($54). Maintenance-free battery ($31). Heavy-duty alternator ($45). LeMans Custom trim group for four-door sedan and Safari ($92-$208). Padded landau top ($180). Cordova vinyl top ($111). Landau vinyl top ($111). Canopy vinyl top ($151). FR78-15 black sidewall tires (standard). FR78-18 white sidewall tires. GR78-18 black sidewall tires. GR78-15 white sidewall tires. Option package WV1 includes protective rubber bumper strips, a front seat console, Soft-Ray tinted glass in all windows, power front disc brakes, power steering, an AM radio, standard white sidewall tires, and deluxe wheel covers. Option package WV2 includes protective rubber bumper strips, a front seat console, Soft-Ray tinted glass in all windows, power front disc brakes, power steering, an AM radio, standard white sidewall tires, deluxe wheel covers, color-keyed Custom seat belts, color-keyed body side moldings, and wheel opening moldings.

OPTION INSTALLATION RATES

Of 80,014 LeMans built (including cars built in Canada for the U.S. market), 99.4 percent had automatic transmission, 12.6 percent had a standard V-8 engine, 74.6 percent had an optional V-8 engine, 12.8 percent had a V-6 engine, 38.6 percent had a AM radio, 20.8 percent had an AM/FM radio, 15.3 percent had an AM/FM stereo radio, 8 percent had a stereo tape player, 0.1 percent had a CB radio, 98.5 percent had power steering, 98.7 percent had power front disc/rear drum brakes, 1.3 percent had manual front brakes, 5.7 percent had a power seat, 10.5 percent had power side windows, 10.2 percent had power door locks, 14.8 percent had bucket seats, 29.5 percent had a vinyl roof, 1 percent had a sun roof, 87.7 percent had steel-belted radial tires, 12.3 percent had fiberglass-belted radial tires, 2.5 percent had a tinted windshield only, 85.2 percent had all tinted windows, 2 percent had Automatic Temperature Control, 83 percent had an air conditioner, 30.1 percent had an adjustable steering column, 6.5 percent had a limited-slip differential, 50.3 percent had optional wheel covers, 32.7 percent had optional styled wheels, 0.2 percent had a digital clock, 52.5 percent had a conventional clock, 16.8 percent had a speed regulating device, 28.9 percent had an electric rear window defogger, 80.9 percent had a remote-control left-hand outside rearview mirror, and 5.3 percent had a remote-control left-hand outside rearview mirror.

HISTORICAL FOOTNOTES

The 1977 Pontiacs were introduced on September 30, 1976. Alex C. Mair was general manager of Pontiac Motor Division. Model-year production included 49,179 base LeMans, 12,277 LeMans Sport Coupes, and 18,828 Grand LeMans. Model year production of LeMans and Grand LeMans models in the U.S., by factory, included: 16,536 made in Lakewood, Georgia, 13,178 made in Baltimore, Maryland, and 40,230 made in Pontiac, Michigan. Of the 80,014 cars built in all factories for the U.S. market, 10,206 had a V-6 and 69,808 had a V-8. The V-6-powered cars included 9,849 base LeMans models and only 357 Grand LeMans models. The V-8-powered cars included: 41,526 LeMans coupes and sedans, 12,808 Grand LeMans coupes and sedans, and 15,474 LeMans Safari and Grand LeMans Safari wagons combined. The 69,944 cars produced in factories in the U.S. represented 0.77 percent of total U.S. model-year production. Calendar-year sales of all LeMans models was 73,061 units for a 0.8 percent share of market.

Model-year sales of LeMans through U.S. new-car dealers totaled 68,941 units compared to 95,217 the previous year. A total of 10,340 cars were reported built in Canada for model-year 1977. Overall, Pontiac suffered a 27.6 percent fall off in LeMans sales, which explained why a major redesign and down-sizing was in the works for 1978. The 1977 LeMans police car option was one of the best Pontiac police cars. Many used ones were seen as stunt cars in various films.

The 1978 midsize Pontiacs were significantly shorter, but they were not lacking in comfort and styling. The Grand LeMans coupe came with plenty of amenities and a starting price of $4,777.

The downsized midsize Pontiacs were 8 to 17 inches shorter and 530 to 925 lbs. lighter than before, boosting fuel economy without loss of interior space. They were built on a 108.1-inch wheelbase, but were roomy enough to carry six passengers in comfort. They offered more headroom, legroom, and luggage room than the 1977 LeMans models. The LeMans models came in two-door coupe and four-door sedan body styles, along with a four-door Safari station wagon. The Grand LeMans line featured the same models with heavier exterior ornamentation and much richer interior trimmings.

Returning to the lineup this year was the Grand Am nameplate. The Grand Am was based on the LeMans, but featured a distinctive grille, sportier appointments inside and out and a standard 301-cid V-8. LeMans and Grand Am models were now built in factories in Baltimore, Maryland, Pontiac, Michigan, and Oshawa, Ontario, Canada.

I.D. DATA

The 13-symbol vehicle identification number (VIN) was located on the upper left surface of the instrument panel, visible through the windshield. The first digit is 2, indicating Pontiac division. The second symbol is a letter indicating car-line series: D=LeMans, F=Grand LeMans and G=Grand Am. Next come two digits that denote body type: 19=four-door notchback sedan, 27=two-door notchback coupe and 35=four-door Safari station wagon. The fifth symbol is a letter indicating engine code: A=Buick-built 231-cid two-barrel V-6, U=Chevrolet/GM of Canada-built 305-cid two-barrel V-8, W=Pontiac-built 301-cid four-barrel V-8, and Y=Pontiac-built 301-cid two-barrel V-8. The sixth symbol denotes model year (8=1978). Next is a plant code: B=Baltimore, Maryland, P=Pontiac, Michigan, and 1=Oshawa, Ontario. The final six digits are the sequential serial number, which began with 100,001.

COLORS

LeMans paint codes were: 11=Cameo White, 15=Platinum, 19=Starlight Black, 21=Dresden Blue, 22=Glacier Blue, 29=Nautilus Blue, 44=Seafoam Green, 45=Mayfair Green, 61=Desert Sand, 63=Laredo Brown, 67=Ember Mist, 69=Chesterfield Brown, 77=Carmine, and 79=Claret. Grand Am paint colors were: 11L/11U/22M=Cameo White body with Glacier Blue lower accent, 11L/11U/56M=Cameo White body color with Burnished Gold lower accent, 15L/15U/-77=Platinum body with Carmine lower accent, 19L/19U/56M=Starlight Black body with Burnished Gold lower accent, 29L/29U/15M=Nautilus Blue body with Platinum lower accent, 44L/44U/45M=Seafoam Green body with Mayfair Green lower accent, 61L/61U/56M=Desert Sand body with Burnished Gold lower accent, 69L/69U/56M=Chesterfield Brown body with Burnished Gold lower accent, and 72L/72U/-15M=Roman Red body with Platinum lower accent. Specific two-tone exterior paint colors for all models except Grand Ams and Safaris with vinyl tops were: 16L/15U=Cark Charcoal lower with Platinum hood and top, 29L/22U=Nautilus Blue lower with Glacier Blue hood and top, 45L/44U=Mayfair Green lower with Seafoam Green hood and top, 56L/61U=Burnished Gold lower with Desert Sand hood and top and 77L/79U=Carmine lower with Claret hood and top. (Note: for interior trim codes see accompanying charts.) Padded landau and full Cordova tops (not available on Safaris and Grand Am sedans) came in seven colors: 11T=White, 15T=Platinum, 19T=Black, 22T=Blue, 44T=Green, 61T=Sand, and 79T=Claret.

LEMANS — (V-6) — SERIES 2AD

The LeMans was the lowest-priced version of Pontiac's new midsize cars. Its styling was trim, clean, and contemporary. It had an eye-catching crosshatch grille, large single rectangular headlights of a new design and tasteful accents. Pontiac described its appearance as "a look you know will still be fresh years after the new car smell fades away." The body incorporated extensive corrosion-resisting treatments. In addition to using rust-inhibiting steel panels, Pontiac spayed them with zinc-rich primers, treated them with moisture-repelling sealants, and top-coated them with tough acrylic finishes. LeMans body features included soft, body-colored front/rear bumpers on coupes and sedans. A wide body-color divider with a Pontiac arrowhead emblem separated the split grille into two sections. Each section featured crosshatched chrome bars forming nine rectangular openings arranged in a 3 x 3 pattern. Inside each opening there were subdued vertical bars. The amber-colored wraparound side marker lenses were split into three sections. Two small air slots were seen below the bumper strip. Inside the car, the standard full-width seats were upholstered in a beautiful new fabric with

The Grand LeMans was downsized for 1978.

Bill Hylicke photo

The LeMans used a clean, non-cluttered exterior look for 1978. The body panels received improved rust-proofing treatments.

fully upholstered door panels and thick-pile carpeting. The headlight dimmer switch was now steering column mounted. A Deluxe cushion steering wheel was standard. An AM/FM stereo radio with cassette player was an available option. Another extra was a power vent rear window option for four-door sedans. The base engine was the 231-cid (3.8-liter) V-6. Also available were 301- and 305-cid V-8s, and a 350-cid V-8 could be ordered for the station wagon. The wraparound taillights had two horizontal dividers and stretched from each rear corner to the recessed license plate. Standard equipment included: a three-speed manual transmission with floor-mounted gear shifter, wheel opening moldings, a radial-tuned suspension, P185/75R14 black sidewall tires, hubcaps, and a heater/defroster. The LeMans Safari four-door station wagon boasted a 72.4 cu. ft. of load space and a new type of tailgate with a window that swung up independently of the drop-down gate. Its full-width seats were trimmed in supple vinyl and the dashboard carried a simulated walnut wood-grain appliqué.

Model Number	Body/Style Number	Body Type & Seating	Factory Price	Shipping Weight	Production Total
LEMANS — (V-6) — SERIES 2AD					
2AD	27	2d Coupe-6P	$4,405	3,038 lbs.	20,581
2AD	19	4d Sedan-6P	$4,480	3,047 lbs.	22,728
LEMANS SAFARI — (V-6) — SERIES 2AD					
2AD	35	4d Sta Wagon-6P	$4,937	3,225 lbs.	15,714

GRAND LEMANS — (V-6) — SERIES 2AF

On Grand LeMans models, the molding and impact strip that ran across the front bumper continued down the body sides and the taillights had five horizontal segments instead of just three. In addition, a stand-up hood ornaments and bright metal hood windsplit molding were standard, instead of optional as on base models. The same was true of rocker panel, windowsill, and side window reveal moldings. With the Grand LeMans, you also got dual horns and added acoustical insulation. Inside, the notchback seats had a new "loose pillow" look with soft velour upholstery and Custom color-keyed safety belts were standard. The Grand LeMans name appeared in chrome script on the front fenders. The three padded steering wheel spokes had wood-grained accents, and a slim horizontal wood-grained panel above the glove box door held a digital clock and a Grand LeMans nameplate. The Grand LeMans Safari four-door station wagon substituted full-width seats upholstered in supple vinyl, a luxury cushion steering wheel, plush nylon-blend carpeting on the floor and lower door panels, and new simulated-pine wood-grained body-side panels with a plank-style pattern.

Model Number	Body/Style Number	Body Type & Seating	Factory Price	Shipping Weight	Production Total
GRAND LEMANS — (V-6) — SERIES 2AF					
2A	F27	2d Coupe-6P	$4,777	3,070 lbs.	18,433
2A	F19	4d Sedan-6P	$4,881	3,098 lbs.	21,252

GRAND LEMANS SAFARI — (V-6) — SERIES 2AF

2A	F35	4d Sta Wagon-6P	$5,265	3,242 lbs.	11,125

GRAND AM — SERIES 2A — V-8

For a few glorious years in the early 1970s, the Pontiac Grand Am came blazing on the scene to establish itself as an impressive American grand touring car. Based on the '73-'75 LeMans, the GEN I Grand Am never really caught on with big numbers of buyers, but neither was it forgotten by enthusiasts who embraced the concept of a Euro-styled domestic coupe and sedan. With the downsizing of the '78 LeMans, some of those enthusiasts who worked at Pontiac decided it was time to bring the Grand Am name back. The new Grand Am was marketed in a single series with coupe and sedan models. Like the originals, they featured a soft front-end panel with a unique-looking vertically slotted split grille that slanted rearwards at the top. Recessed single rectangular headlights stood above clear park/signal lamps, with the same framework wrapping to clear/amber side marker lenses. Two-tone paint treatments were included. You could also order painted upper-body accent stripes with matching vinyl striping on the hood, rear-end panel, and available body-colored sport mirrors. Other standard Grand Am equipment included a 301-cid (4.9-liter) two-barrel V-8, an automatic transmission (a four-speed manual transmission was optional however), power brakes, power steering, 205/70R14 steel-belted radial tires, and a Rally RTS suspension. "Grand Am" nameplates went on the forward end of front fenders. At the rear were horizontally ribbed wraparound taillights.

The standard interior sported notchback seats in fine cloth or vinyl, carpeted lower door panels and added acoustical insulation. Bucket seats were optional, as was a new quick-readout dash with brushed aluminum dials and a regal walnut vinyl appliqué. The red, white, and blue Grand Am badge used in the early '70s was replicated on the front fender sides and the deck lid.

Model Number	Body/Style Number	Body Type & Seating	Factory Price	Shipping Weight	Production Total
2A	G27	2d Coupe-6P	$5,464	3,209 lbs.	7,767
2A	G19	4d Sedan-6P	$5,568	3,239 lbs.	2,841

ENGINES

LEMANS, GRAND LEMANS BASE 231-CID V-6: Overhead valve. Cast-iron block and head. Displacement: 231 cid (3.8 liters). Bore and stroke: 3.80 x 3.40 in. Compression ratio: 8.0:1. Brake hp: 105 at 3200 rpm. Torque: 185 lbs.-ft. at 2000 rpm. Four main bearings. Hydraulic valve lifters. Carburetor: two-barrel Rochester 2GC. VIN Code: A.

GRAND AM STANDARD 301-CID V-8: Overhead valve. Cast-iron block and head. Bore and stroke: 4.00 x 3.00 in. Displacement: 301 cid (4.9 liters). Compression ratio: 8.2:1. Brake hp: 140 at 3600 rpm. Taxable hp: 51.2. Torque: 235 lbs.-ft. at 2000 rpm. Five main bearings. Hydraulic valve lifters. Carburetor: Two-barrel Rochester M2MC. VIN Code: Y.

LEMANS, GRAND LEMANS, GRAND AM OPTIONAL 305-CID V-8: Overhead valve. Cast-iron block and

The Grand Ams returned in 1978 in either coupe of sedan versions.

GM photo

The LeMans was the least expensive of Pontiac's 1978 new midsize cars.

head. Bore and stroke: 3.74 x 3.48 in. Displacement: 305 cid (5.0 liters). Compression ratio: 8.4:1. Brake horsepower: 145 at 3800 rpm. Taxable hp: 44.7. Torque: 245 lbs.-ft. at 2400 rpm. Five main bearings. Hydraulic valve lifters. Carburetor: Two-barrel Rochester 2GC. VIN Code: U.

GRAND AM OPTIONAL V-8: Overhead valve. Cast-iron block and head. Bore and stroke: 4.00 x 3.00 in. Displacement: 301 cid (4.9 liters). Compression ratio: 8.2:1. Brake hp: 150 at 4000 rpm. Taxable hp: 51.2. Torque: 239 lbs.-ft. at 2000 rpm. Five main bearings. Hydraulic valve lifters. Carburetor: Two-barrel Rochester M2MC. VIN Code: W.

CHASSIS

Wheelbase: (LeMans/Grand LeMans/Safari/Grand Am) 108.1 in. Overall Length: (LeMans/Grand LeMans/Grand Am coupe) 199.2 in., (LeMans/Grand LeMans/Grand Am sedan) 198.5 in., (Safari) 197.8 in. Height: (LeMans/Grand LeMans/Grand Am coupe) 53.5 in., (LeMans/Grand LeMans/Grand Am sedan) 54.4 in., (Safari) 54.8 in. Width: (LeMans/Grand Lemans/Grand Am) 72.4 in., (Safari) 72.6 in. Front tread: (LeMans/Grand LeMans/Grand Am/Safari) 58.5 in. Rear tread: (LeMans/Grand LeMans/Grand Am/Safari) 57.8 in. Front headroom: (LeMans/Grand LeMans/Grand Am coupe) 37.9 in. Rear headroom: (LeMans/Grand LeMans/Grand Am coupe) 37.8 in. Front legroom: (LeMans/Grand LeMans/Grand Am coupe) 42.8 in. Rear legroom: (LeMans/Grand LeMans/Grand Am coupe) 35.1 in. Front hiproom: (LeMans/Grand LeMans/Grand Am coupe) 51.7 in. Rear hiproom: (LeMans/Grand LeMans/Grand Am coupe) 54.5 in. Front headroom: (LeMans/Grand LeMans/Grand Am sedan) 38.7 in. Rear headroom: (LeMans/Grand LeMans/Grand Am sedan) 37.7 in. Front legroom: (LeMans/Grand LeMans/Grand Am sedan) 42.8 in. Rear legroom: (LeMans/Grand LeMans/Grand Am sedan) 38 in. Front hiproom: (LeMans/Grand LeMans/Grand Am sedan) 52.2 in. Rear hiproom: (LeMans/Grand LeMans/Grand Am sedan) 55.6 in. Luggage capacity: (Lemans/Grand LeMans/Grand Am coupe) 16.4 cu. ft. (Lemans/Grand LeMans/Grand Am

sedan) 16.4 cu. ft. Cargo volume: (Safari) 72.4 cu. ft. Length of cargo space at floor: (Safari) 81.3 in. Length of cargo space at floor with tailgate lowered: (Safari) 103.9 in. Top of front seat back to closed tailgate: (Safari) 72.9 in. Minimum distance between rear wheelhousings at floor: (Safari) 43.6 in. Rear end opening width at belt; (Safari) 51.7 in. Maximum cargo height: (Safari) 30 in. Maximum height at rear opening with tailgate open: (Safari) 27.8 in. Standard tires: (LeMans/Grand LeMans) P185/75R14, (Grand Am) 205/70R14 steel-belted radials with Rally RTS suspension. Transmission: Three-speed manual transmission standard. Three-speed Turbo Hydra-Matic transmission optional on all. Steering: Re-circulating ball. Front suspension: coil springs with lower trailing links and anti-sway bar. Rear suspension: rigid axle with coil springs, lower trailing radius arms, upper torque arms and anti-sway bar. Brakes: front disc, rear drum. Ignition: electronic. Body construction: separate body and frame. Fuel tank: 17.5 gal. (except Safari 18.3 gal).

OPTIONS

C60 Custom air conditioning ($470-$581). C61 automatic temperature control ($584). UA1 heavy-duty battery ($17-$20). AK1 Custom color-keyed safety belts, standard in Grand Lemans models. V31 front bumper guards, not available with Grand Am. V32 rear bumper guards, not available with Grand Am. B39 Safari load floor carpeting. UE8 digital clock, requires lamp group and air conditioning. U35 electric clock. D55 front seat console, requires bucket seats, lamp group and automatic transmission. K30 cruise control, with automatic transmission only ($90-$95). A90 remote-control deck lid release. C51 Safari rear window air deflector. C49 electric rear window defroster. Y80 Custom exterior group including hood ornament, hood windsplit molding, rocker panel moldings, window sill moldings and reveal moldings, for base Lemans only. U14 instrument panel gauges without clock, requires V-8 engine. WW8 Rally gauges and instrument panel tachometer, without clock, requires V-8 engine. A01 Soft-Ray tinted glass in all windows. B93 door edge guards. U05 dual horns, optional on base LeMans only.

159

B51 added acoustical insulation, optional on base LeMans only. C95 dome reading lamp. Y92 lamp group including rear door jamb switch on sedans and Safaris, rear compartment courtesy lamp in Safaris, luggage lamp, glove box lamp, ashtray lamp and instrument panel courtesy lamp. V55 Safari luggage carrier. B48 luggage compartment trim, except Safaris. B32 front floor mats. B33 rear floor mats. D64 illuminated right-hand visor mirror. D34 right-hand visor mirror. D33 chrome left-hand remote-control rearview mirror. D68 dual remote-control Sport rearview mirrors. D35 dual sport mirrors, right-hand manual and left-hand remote controlled, requires specific two-tone paint treatments on Grand LeMans and Grand Am. B83 rocker panel moldings, standard on Grand LeMans and Grand Am. B90 side window reveal moldings, optional for LeMans sedan and Safari only. B85 windowsill moldings, standard on Grand LeMans and Grand Am. U75 power antenna, optional with air conditioning or automatic temperature control system only. U83 Tri-band power antenna for AM/FM and CB radio, requires proper radio and air conditioning. JL2 power front disc brakes, required with all V-8s and with V-6 teamed with air conditioning ($69). AU3 power door locks. AU6 power tailgate lock, Safari only. N41 power steering, required with V-8 or V-6 teamed with air conditioning ($152). A31 power front windows ($118-$190). U63 AM radio.

U69 AM/FM radio. U58 AM/FM stereo radio. UM1 AM radio and stereo 8-track player. UM2 AM/FM radio and stereo 8-track player. UY8 AM/FM stereo radio with digital clock. UP5 AM/FM radio with 40-channel CB includes tri-band power antenna. UP6 AM/FM stereo radio with 40-channel CB includes tri-band power antenna. UN3 AM/FM stereo radio and cassette player. UN9 radio accommodation package. U80 rear radio speaker with U63 or U69 radios only. AT6 reclining passenger seat, optional with bucket seat or notchback 60/40 seat only. N31 Custom Sport steering wheel. N30 Luxury Cushion steering wheel, standard in Grand LeMans. N33 tilt-adjustable steering wheel, with Custom Sport or Luxury Cushion steering wheels only. CF5 power glass sunroof, coupe only ($699). CA1 power steel sun roof, coupe only ($499). P02 Custom finned wheel covers. P01 deluxe wheel covers. N95 wire wheel covers. YJ8 four cast-aluminum wheels, available in 16P Gray or 55P Gold. N98 four Rally II wheel rims. N67 four body-color Rally II wheel rims. CD4 controlled-cycle windshield wipers. K76 heavy-duty 61-amp alternator. K81 heavy-duty 63-amp alternator. NB2 California emission requirements ($75-$100). Y91 cold weather group. W51 demo program. Y96 Firm Ride option ($12). NA6 high-altitude emission requirements ($33). VK3 front license plate bracket. VD2 Super-Cooling radiator ($31-$57). AW9 Safari security package ($35-$40). G67

Among the distinguishing characteristics of the 1978 Grand LeManses was the trim impact strip that started at the bumper and ran along the lower body sides.

GM Media Archives photo

auto level control shock absorbers ($63-$116). G66 Superlift shock absorbers ($52). V82 medium trailer group ($116-$141). U89 Five-wire trailer electrical harness. ZP2 color and trim incompatibility override. A40 power vent rear windows. W65 dual front and rear radio speakers. WY2 driver education. 305-cid, two-barrel V-8 ($150). 350-cid, four-barrel V-8 (in cars $265; in Safaris $265). Four-speed manual floor shift transmission ($125). Turbo Hydra-Matic transmission ($307). Safe-T-Track differential ($60). Rally RTS handling package ($42-$179). Engine block heater ($13-$14). LeMans exterior paint appearance ($159). WV1 Custom exterior package includes Soft-Ray tinted glass in all windows, front power disc brakes, power steering, AM radio, standard white sidewall tires and deluxe wheel covers ($40-$75). WV2 Custom trim group includes Soft-Ray tinted glass in all windows, front power disc brakes, power steering, AM radio, standard white sidewall tires, deluxe wheel covers, Custom color-keyed safety belts and remote-control left-hand outside rearview mirror ($134-$247). Full vinyl cordova top ($116). Padded landau top ($239). Rear-facing third seat: Safari ($175).

OPTION INSTALLATION RATES

Of 120,441 LeMans built (including cars built in Canada for the U.S. market) 99.7 percent had automatic transmission, 0.2 percent had a four-speed manual transmission, 4.7 percent had a standard V-8 engine, 61.2 percent had an optional V-8 engine, 34.1 percent had a V-6 engine, 34 percent had a AM radio, 21.3 percent had an AM/FM radio, 17.9 percent had an AM/FM stereo radio, 2.3 percent had an AM 8-track tape player, 3.9 percent had an AM/FM radio and 8-track stereo tape player, 1.6 percent had an AM/FM radio with cassette tape player, 0.7 percent had an AM/FM stereo CB radio, 0.1 percent had an AM/FM/CB radio, 99.8 percent had power steering, 98.8 percent had power front disc/rear drum brakes, 1.2 percent had manual front brakes, 7.8 percent had a power seat, 6.3 percent had power side windows, 14.1 percent had power door locks, 9.1 percent had bucket seats, 4.7 percent had reclining seats, 19.3 percent had a vinyl roof, 0.6 percent had a sunroof, 72.7 percent had steel-belted radial tires, 27.3 percent had fiberglass-belted radial tires, 1.5 percent had a tinted windshield only, 88.4 percent had all tinted windows, 2.1 percent had automatic temperature control, 84.8 percent had an air conditioner, 39.1 percent had an adjustable steering column, 4.2 percent had a limited-slip differential, 66.2 percent had optional wheel covers, 18.9 percent had styled steel wheels, 4.5 percent had styled aluminum wheels, 4.9 percent had a digital clock, 31.3 percent had a conventional clock, 27.6 percent had a speed regulating device, 0.1 percent had a blower-type rear window defogger, 35.4 percent had an electric rear window defogger, 84.1 percent had a remote-control left-hand outside rearview mirror, and 5.4 percent had a remote-control left-hand outside rearview mirror.

HISTORICAL FOOTNOTES

The 1978 Pontiacs were introduced on Oct. 6, 1977. Robert C. Stempel was named general manager of Pontiac Motor Division at the end of the year. It was the 70th year of Pontiac history marked from the sale of the first Oakland automobile in 1908. Oakland Motor Car Company became Pontiac in 1932.

Model-year production included 59,023 base LeMans, 50,810 Grand LeMans and 10,608 Grand Ams. Model-year production of LeMans, Grand LeMans and Grand Am models in the U.S., according to factory, included 40,576 made in Baltimore, Maryland, and 65,638 made in Pontiac, Michigan. Of the 120,441 cars built in all factories for the U.S. market, 41,061 had a V-6 and 79,380 had a V-8. The V-6-powered cars included 23,256 base LeMans models, 11,173 Grand LeMans models and 6,632 Safaris. The V-8-powered cars included 20,053 LeMans coupes and sedans, 39,120 Grand LeMans coupes and sedans and 20,207 LeMans Safari and Grand LeMans Safari wagons combined. The 106,214 cars produced in factories in the U.S. represented 1.19 percent of total U.S. model-year production. Calendar-year sales of all LeMans models was 125,020 units for a 1.3 percent share of market. Model-year sales of LeMans through U.S. new-car dealers totaled 114,577 units compared to 68,941 the previous year. A total of 14,227 cars were reported built in Canada for model-year 1978. The downsized LeMans's rise in popularity contributed to a record sales year for Pontiac in 1978, which registered a 7.5 percent increase in overall business.

The Grand LeMans added a new hood ornament and hood and body-side moldings for 1979. The grille was also changed slightly.

Styling of the midsize LeMans was similar to before, but the grille contained more openings. They were now arranged in a 6 x 4 pattern. Amber side-marker lenses now were split into four sections rather than three. The base engine was the 231-cid (3.8-liter) V-6 with three-speed manual transmission. The Pontiac-built 301-cid V-8 was available in two- and four-barrel versions. A new "Federal" engine option for Safari and Grand Safari station wagons was a 350-cid four-barrel V-8. Actually, three different 350-cid V-8s made by Buick, Chevrolet, and Oldsmobile were alternately used. In addition, only some station wagons sold in California got a 305-cid four-barrel V-8 supplied by Chevrolet or GM of Canada. As usual, the Grand LeMans and Grand LeMans Safari were a little brighter and a little more luxurious inside and out. Except for amber park/signal and marker lenses, the appearance of the LeMans-based Grand Am was changed little this year. It was, however, now available with a choice of a V-6 or a V-8 under the hood.

I.D. DATA

The 13-symbol vehicle identification number (VIN) was located on the upper left surface of the instrument panel, visible through the windshield. The first digit is 2, indicating Pontiac division. The second symbol is a letter indicating car-line series: D=LeMans, F=Grand LeMans and G=Grand Am. Next come two digits that denote body type: 19=four-door notchback sedan, 27=two-door notchback coupe and 35=four-door Safari station wagon. The fifth symbol is a letter indicating engine code: A=Buick-built 231-cid (3.8-liter) two-barrel V-6, H=Chevrolet or GM of Canada built 305-cid (5.0-liter) four-barrel V-8, L=Chevrolet or GM of Canada built 350-cid (5.7-liter) four-barrel V-8, R=Oldsmobile-built 350-

cid (5.7-liter) four-barrel V-8, W=Pontiac-built 301-cid (4.9-liter) four-barrel V-8, X=Buick-built 350-cid (5.7-liter) four-barrel V-8 and Y=Pontiac-built 301-cid two-barrel V-8. The sixth symbol denotes model year (9=1979). Next is a plant code: B=Baltimore, Maryland, P=Pontiac, Michigan, and 1=Oshawa, Ontario. The final six digits are the sequential serial number, which began with 100,001.

COLORS

LeMans paint codes for 1979 were: 11=Cameo White, 15=Platinum, 19=Starlight Black, 21=Skymist Blue, 22=Glacier Blue, 29=Nocturne Blue, 40=Willowmist Green, 44=Jadestone Green, 54=Montego Cream, 61=Mission Beige, 63=Sierra Copper, 69=Heritage Brown, 77=Carmine, and 79=Claret. Grand Am paint colors were: 11L/11U=Cameo White body with Carmine lower accent, 15L/15U=Platinum body with Nocturne Blue lower accent, 19L/19U=Starlight Black body with Burnished Gold lower accent, 29L/29U= Nocturne Blue body with Platinum lower accent, 44L/44U=Jadestone Green body with Burnished Gold lower accent, 54L/54U=Montego Cream body with Burnished Gold lower accent, 63L/63U=Sierra Copper body with Burnished Gold lower accent 77L/77U=Carmine body with Platinum lower accent, and 79L/79U=Claret body with Burnished Gold lower accent. Specific two-tone exterior paint colors for all models except Grand Ams and Safaris with vinyl tops were: 16L/15U=Cark Charcoal lower with Platinum hood and top, 85L/22U=Blue Metallic lower with Glacier Blue hood and top, 44L/40U=Jadestone Green lower with Willowmist Green hood and top, 63L/61U=Sierra Copper lower with Mission Beige hood and top, and 77L/79U=Carmine lower with Claret hood and top. Interior trim codes were: (LeMans coupe/sedan) 24B=Light Blue cloth and vinyl, 24R=Light Blue vinyl, 62B=Camel Tan cloth and vinyl, 62R=Camel Tan vinyl, 74B=Carmine cloth and vinyl and 74R=Carmine vinyl. (LeMans Safari) 24R=Light Blue vinyl, 24N=Light Blue vinyl bucket, notchback or 60/40 seat, 62C=Camel Tan cloth and vinyl vinyl bucket, notchback or 60/40 seat, 62R=Camel Tan vinyl, 62N=Camel Tan vinyl bucket, notchback or 60/40 seat, 74R=Carmine vinyl, 74N=Carmine vinyl bucket, notchback or 60/40 seat, 44C=Willow Green vinyl bucket, notchback or 60/40 seat. (Grand LeMans coupe/sedan)12N=Oyster vinyl bucket, notchback or 60/40 seat, 19G=Black cloth and vinyl bucket, notchback or 60/40 seat, 19N=Black vinyl bucket, notchback or 60/40 seat, 24G=Light Blue cloth and vinyl bucket, notchback or 60/40 seat, 24C=Light Blue cloth and vinyl bucket, notchback or 60/40 seat, 24N=Light Blue vinyl bucket, notchback or 60/40 seat, 62G=Camel Tan cloth and vinyl bucket, notchback or 60/40 seat, 62C=Camel Tan cloth and vinyl bucket, notchback or 60/40 seat, 62N=Camel Tan vinyl bucket, notchback or 60/40 seat, 74G=Carmine cloth and vinyl bucket, notchback or 60/40 seat, 74C=Carmine cloth and vinyl bucket, notchback or 60/40 seat, 74N=Carmine vinyl bucket, notchback or 60/40 seat, 44G=Willow Green cloth and vinyl bucket, notchback or 60/40 seat, 44C=Willow Green cloth and vinyl bucket, notchback or 60/40 seat, 44N=Willow Green vinyl bucket, notchback or 60/40 seat. (Grand Am coupe/sedan) 19G=Black cloth and vinyl bucket, notchback or 60/40 seat, 24G=Light Blue cloth and vinyl bucket, notchback or 60/40 seat, 62G=Camel Tan cloth and vinyl bucket, notchback or 60/40 seat, 74G=Carmine cloth and vinyl bucket, notchback or 60/40 seat, 44G=Willow Green cloth and vinyl bucket, notchback or 60/40 seat. Padded landau and full Cordova tops (not available on Safaris and Grand Am sedans) came in seven colors: 11T=White, 15T=Platinum, 19T=Black, 22T=Blue, 40T=Green, 61T=Beige, and 79T=Claret.

LEMANS — (V-6) — SERIES 2AD

Standard equipment included body-color bumpers with rub strips, P185/75R14 glass-belted radial tires, hubcaps, and wheel opening moldings.

Model Number	Body/Style Number	Body Type & Seating	Factory Price	Shipping Weight	Production Total
LEMANS — (V-6) — SERIES 2AD					
2AD	27	2d Coupe-6P	$5,031	3,036 lbs.	14,197
2AD	19	4d Sedan-6P	$5,134	3,042 lbs.	26,958
LEMANS SAFARI — (V-6) — SERIES 2AD					
2AD	35	4d Sta Wagon-6P	$5,587	3,200 lbs.	27,517

GRAND LEMANS — (V-6) — SERIES 2AF

The Grand LeMans added a hood ornament and hood windsplit molding, lower body-side moldings, brushed aluminum center pillars, Custom color-keyed safety belts, and door panel pull straps. Engine options included a 301-cid V-8 (with a two- or four-barrel carburetor), and a 305-cid four-barrel V-8. Safari wagons

had a 5.0-liter V-8 as standard and could also have a 5.7-liter (350-cid) V-8.

Model Number	Body/Style Number	Body Type & Seating	Factory Price	Shipping Weight	Production Total
GRAND LEMANS — (V-6) — SERIES 2AF					
2AF	27	2d Coupe-6P	$5,302	3,058 lbs.	13,020
2AF	19	4d Sedan-6P	$5,430	3,087 lbs.	28,577
GRAND LEMANS SAFARI — (V-6) — SERIES 2AF					
2AF	35	4d Sta Wagon-6P	$5,931	3,234 lbs.	20,783

GRAND AM — (V-6) — SERIES 2AG

Standard equipment was similar to that of the LeMans, but with power steering, two-tone body color, black-out taillights, P205/70R14 steel-belted radial tires, and a Rally RTS handling package.

Model Number	Body/Style Number	Body Type & Seating	Factory Price	Shipping Weight	Production Total
GRAND AM — (V-6) — SERIES 2AG					
2AG	27	2d Coupe-6P	$5,530	3,080 lbs.	4,021
2AG	19	4d Sedan-6P	$5,529	3,084 lbs.	1,865

ENGINES

LEMANS, GRAND LEMANS BASE 231-CID V-6: Overhead-valve. Cast-iron block and head. Displacement: 231 cid (3.8 liters). Bore and stroke: 3.80 x 3.40 in. Compression ratio: 8.0:1. Brake hp: 105 at 3200 rpm. Torque: 185 lbs.-ft. at 2000 rpm. Four main bearings. Hydraulic valve lifters. Carburetor: two-barrel Rochester 2GC. VIN Code: A.

LEMANS, GRAND LEMANS OPTIONAL 301-CID V-8: Overhead valve. Cast-iron block and head. Bore and stroke: 4.06 x 3.04 in. Displacement: 301 cid (4.9 liters). Compression ratio: 8.1:1. Brake hp: 140 at 3600 rpm. Taxable hp: 51.2. Torque: 235 lbs.-ft. at 2000 rpm. Five main bearings. Hydraulic valve lifters. Carburetor: Two-barrel Rochester M2MC. VIN Code: Y.

The interior of the 1979 Grand Am was decidedly sporty, in keeping with the car's image as the fun-to-drive member of the Pontiac midsize lineup.

LEMANS, GRAND LEMANS, GRAND AM OPTIONAL V-8: Overhead valve. Cast-iron block and head. Bore and stroke: 4.06 x 3.04 in. Displacement: 301 cid (4.9 liters). Compression ratio: 8.1:1. Brake hp: 150 at 4000 rpm. Taxable hp: 51.2. Torque: 240 lbs.-ft. at 2000 rpm. Five main bearings. Hydraulic valve lifters. Carburetor: Four-barrel Rochester M4MC. VIN Code: W.

LEMANS SAFARI, GRAND LEMANS SAFARI ALTERNATE OPTIONAL CALIFORNIA V-8: Overhead valve. Cast-iron block and head. Bore and stroke: 3.74 x 3.48 in. Displacement: 305 cid (5.0 liters). Compression ratio: 8.4:1. Brake hp: 150 at 3800 rpm. Taxable hp: 44.7. Torque: 230 lbs.-ft. at 2400 rpm. Five main bearings. Hydraulic valve lifters. Carburetor: Four-barrel. VIN Code: H.

LEMANS SAFARI, GRAND LEMANS SAFARI ALTERNATE OPTIONAL V-8: Overhead valve. Cast-iron block and head. Bore and stroke: 3.80 x 3.85 in. Displacement: 350 cid (5.7 liters). Compression ratio: 8.0:1. Brake hp: 155 at 3400 rpm. Taxable hp: 51.2. Torque: 280 lbs.-ft. at 1800 rpm. Five main bearings. Hydraulic valve lifters. Carburetor: Four-barrel Rochester M4MC. Chevrolet-built. VIN Code: X. Built by Buick.

LEMANS SAFARI, GRAND LEMANS SAFARI OPTIONAL V-8: Overhead valve. Cast-iron block and head. Bore and stroke: 4.00 x 3.48 in. Displacement: 350 cid (5.7 liters). Compression ratio: 8.2:1. Brake hp: 160 at 3800 rpm. Taxable hp: 51.2. Torque: 260 lbs.-ft. at 2400 rpm. Five main bearings. Hydraulic valve lifters. Carburetor: Four-barrel Rochester M4MC. VIN Code: L. Chevrolet-built.

LEMANS SAFARI, GRAND LEMANS SAFARI ALTERNATE OPTIONAL V-8: Overhead valve. Cast-iron block and head. Bore and stroke: 4.06 x 3.38 in. Displacement: 350 cid (5.7 liters). Compression ratio: 7.9:1. Brake hp: 160 at 3600 rpm. Taxable hp: 51.2. Torque: 270 lbs.-ft. at 2000 rpm. Five main bearings.

Hydraulic valve lifters. Carburetor: Four-barrel Rochester M4MC. Chevrolet-built. VIN Code: R. Built by Oldsmobile.

CHASSIS

Wheelbase: (LeMans/Grand LeMans/Safari/Grand Am) 108.1 in. Overall Length: (LeMans/Grand LeMans/Grand Am coupe) 199.2 in., (LeMans/Grand LeMans/Grand Am sedan) 198.5 in., (Safari) 197.8 in. Height: (LeMans/Grand LeMans/Grand Am coupe) 53.5 in., (LeMans/Grand LeMans/Grand Am sedan) 54.4 in., (Safari) 54.8 in. Width: (LeMans/Grand lemans/Grand Am) 72.4 in., (Safari) 72.6 in. Front tread: (LeMans/Grand LeMans/Grand Am/Safari) 58.5 in. Rear tread: (LeMans/Grand LeMans/Grand Am/Safari) 57.8 in. Front headroom: (LeMans/Grand LeMans/Grand Am coupe) 37.9 in. Rear headroom: (LeMans/Grand LeMans/Grand Am coupe) 37.8 in. Front legroom: (LeMans/Grand LeMans/Grand Am coupe) 42.8 in. Rear legroom: (LeMans/Grand LeMans/Grand Am coupe) 35.1 in. Front hiproom: (LeMans/Grand LeMans/Grand Am coupe) 51.7 in. Rear hiproom: (LeMans/Grand LeMans/Grand Am coupe) 54.5 in. Front headroom: (LeMans/Grand LeMans/Grand Am sedan) 38.7 in. Rear headroom: (LeMans/Grand LeMans/Grand Am sedan) 37.7 in. Front legroom: (LeMans/Grand LeMans/Grand Am sedan) 42.8 in. Rear legroom: (LeMans/Grand LeMans/Grand Am sedan) 38.0 in. Front hiproom: (LeMans/Grand LeMans/Grand Am sedan) 52.2 in. Rear hiproom: (LeMans/Grand LeMans/Grand Am sedan) 55.6 in. Luggage capacity: (Lemans/Grand LeMans/Grand Am coupe) 16.4 cu. ft. (Lemans/Grand LeMans/Grand Am sedan) 16.4 cu. ft. Cargo volume: (Safari) 72.4 cu. ft. Length of cargo space at floor: (Safari) 81.3 in. Length of cargo space at floor with tailgate lowered: (Safari) 103.9 in. Top of front seat back to closed tailgate: (Safari) 72.9 in. Minimum distance between rear wheelhousings at floor: (Safari) 43.6 in. Rear end opening width at belt; (Safari) 51.7 in. Maximum cargo height: (Safari) 30.0 in. Maximum height at rear opening with tailgate open: (Safari) 27.8 in. Standard tires: (LeMans/Grand LeMans)

The LeMans was marketed as a scaled-down luxury car. The starting price on a two-door coupe was just over $5,000.

P185/75R14, (Grand Am) 205/70R14 steel-belted radials with Rally RTS suspension. Transmission: Three-speed manual transmission standard. Three-speed Turbo Hydra-Matic transmission optional on all. Standard final drive ratio: (LeMans V-6) 2.73:1 with three-speed transmission; 2.93:1 with four-speed transmission, 2.41:1 or 3.23:1 with automatic transmission; (LeMans V-8) 2.14:1, 2.29:1 or 2.73:1. Steering: Re-circulating ball. Front suspension: coil springs with lower trailing links and anti-sway bar. Rear suspension: rigid axle with coil springs, lower trailing radius arms, upper torque arms and anti-sway bar. Brakes: front disc, rear drum. Ignition: electronic. Body construction: separate body and frame. Fuel tank: 17.5 gal., except Safari 18.3 gal.

OPTIONS

C60 Custom air conditioning ($496-$605). C61 automatic temperature control ($653). UA1 heavy-duty battery ($18-$21). AK1 Custom color-keyed safety belts standard with luxury trim on Grand LeMans and Grand Am. V31 front bumper guards, not available for Grand Am. V32 rear bumper guards, not available for Grand Am, B39 load floor carpeting for Safaris, included with Custom trim package. UE8 digital clock, optional with lamp group and air conditioning only. U35 electric clock. D55 front seat console, with bucket seats and lamp group only. K30 cruise control, with automatic transmission and power brakes only ($103-$108). A90 remote-control deck lid. C51 Safari rear window deflector. C49 electric rear window defroster. B57 Custom exterior group including hood ornament, hood windsplit molding, rocker panel moldings, window sill moldings and reveal moldings, for base Lemans only, not available with V-6 ($46-$98). U14 instrument panel gauges without clock, requires V-8 engine. U21 Rally gauges and instrument panel tachometer, without clock, requires V-8 engine. A01 Soft-Ray tinted glass in all windows. B93 door edge guards. U05 dual horns, standard in Grand LeMans and Grand Am. B51 added acoustical insulation, standard in Grand LeMans. C95 dome reading lamp. TR9 lamp group including rear doorjamb switch on sedans and Safaris, rear compartment courtesy lamp in Safaris, luggage lamp, glove box lamp, ash tray lamp and instrument panel courtesy lamp. V55 Safari luggage carrier. B48 luggage compartment trim, except Safaris. B32 front floor mats. B33 rear floor mats. D64 illuminated right-hand visor mirror. D34 right-hand visor mirror. D33 chrome left-hand remote-control rearview mirror, not available with specific two-tone colors. D68 dual remote-control Sport rearview mirrors, right-hand convex D35 dual Sport mirrors, right-hand manual and left-hand remote controlled, requires specific two-tone paint treatments. B83 rocker panel moldings, standard on Grand LeMans and Grand Am. B90 side window reveal moldings, optional for LeMans sedan and Safari only. B85 window sill moldings, standard on Grand Am. U75 power antenna, optional with air conditioning or automatic temperature control system only. U83 Tri-band power antenna for AM/FM and CB radio, requires proper radio and air conditioning. JL2 power front disc brakes, required with all V-8s and with V-6 teamed with

air conditioning ($76). AU3 power door locks. AU6 power tailgate lock, Safari only. A42 power driver's seat ($163-$166). N41 power steering, required with V-8 or V-6 teamed with air conditioning ($163). A31 power front windows ($126-$205). A40 power vent windows, for sedans and Safaris only. U63 AM radio. U69 AM/FM radio. U58 AM/FM stereo radio. UM1 AM radio and stereo 8-track player. UM2 AM/FM radio and stereo 8-track player. UY8 AM/FM stereo radio with digital clock. UP5 AM/FM radio with 40-channel CB includes tri-band power antenna. UP6 AM/FM stereo radio with 40-channel CB includes tri-band power antenna. UN3 AM/FM stereo radio and cassette player. UN9 radio accommodation package. UP8 rear radio speakers, dual front and rear, with U63, U69 or UP5 radios only. U80 rear radio speaker with U63 or U69 radios only. AT6 reclining passenger seat, optional with bucket seat or notchback 60/40 seat only. N31 Custom Sport steering wheel. N30 Luxury Cushion steering wheel, standard in Grand LeMans. N33 tilt-adjustable steering wheel, with Custom Sport or Luxury Cushion steering wheels only. CF5 power glass sunroof, coupe only ($729). CA1 power steel sunroof, coupe only ($529). P02 Custom finned wheel covers. P01 deluxe wheel covers. N95 wire wheel covers. N90 four cast-aluminum wheels, available in 16P Gray or 55P Gold. N66 four Rally II wheel rims. PH8 wire wheels, Grand Am only ($425-$499). CD4 controlled-cycle windshield wipers. D60 color and trim incompatibility override. K81 heavy-duty 63-amp alternator. NB2 California emission requirements ($83-$150). V10 cold weather group. F40 Firm Ride package ($13). NA6 High-altitude emissions requirements ($35). VK3 front license plate bracket. V02 Super-Cooling radiator ($32-$60). AW9 Safari security package ($37-$42). G67 Auto Level Control shock absorbers ($66-$121). G66 Superlift shock absorbers ($54). V82 medium trailer group ($121-$148). U89 5-wire trailer harness. W51 demo package. UX6 dual front speakers. 301-cid two-barrel V-8 ($195). 301-cid four-barrel V-8 ($255). 305-cid two-barrel V-8 ($195). 305-cid, four-barrel V-8 ($255). 350-cid, four-barrel V-8 LeMans Safari ($320). Four-speed manual floor shift transmission ($135). Turbo Hydra-Matic ($335). Limited-slip differential ($63). Rally RTS handling package ($44-$189). Heavy-duty radiator ($32-$59). Heavy-duty cooling ($26-$59). Heavy-duty alternator ($32). Engine block heater ($14-$15). LeMans luxury group ($148-$348). LeMans exterior paint appearance ($166). LeMans custom trim group ($145-$259). Full vinyl cordova top ($116). Padded landau top ($239). Rear-facing third seat: Safari ($183).

OPTION INSTALLATION RATES

Of 136,938 LeMans built (including cars built in Canada for the U.S. market) 99.5 percent had automatic transmission, 0.3 percent had a four-speed manual transmission, 51.9 percent had a V-8 engine, 48.1 percent had a V-6 engine, 40.7 percent had a AM radio, 20.2 percent had an AM/FM radio, 18.3 percent had an AM/FM stereo radio, 1.2 percent had an AM 8-track tape player, 3.1 percent had an AM/FM radio and 8-track

The four-door Grand LeMans was far more popular with buyers than the two-door.

GM Media Archives photo

stereo tape player, 1.2 percent had an AM/FM radio with cassette tape player, 0.4 percent had an AM/FM stereo CB radio, 0.1 percent had an AM/FM/CB radio, 95.5 percent had power steering, 99.4 percent had power front disc/rear drum brakes, 0.6 percent had manual front brakes, 6.5 percent had a power seat, 12.3 percent had power side windows, 12.4 percent had power door locks, 4.5 percent had non-reclining bucket seats, 4 percent had reclining seats (including reclining bucket seats), 13 percent had a vinyl roof, 0.3 percent had a sun roof, 62.4 percent had steel-belted radial tires, 37.6 percent had fiberglass-belted radial tires, 1.7 percent had a tinted windshield only, 85.6 percent had all tinted windows, 1.4 percent had automatic temperature control, 86.7 percent had an air conditioner, 35.6 percent had an adjustable steering column, 4.3 percent had a limited-slip differential, 79.6 percent had optional wheel covers, 10.9 percent had styled steel wheels, 1.8 percent had styled aluminum wheels, 2.6 percent had a digital clock, 31.9 percent had a conventional clock, 27 percent had a speed regulating device, 0.2 percent had a blower-type rear window defogger, 38.4 percent had an electric rear window defogger, 78 percent had a remote-control left-hand outside rearview mirror, and 5.4 percent had a remote-control left-hand outside rearview mirror.

HISTORICAL FOOTNOTES

The 1979 Pontiacs were introduced on September 28, 1979. Robert C. Stempel was general manager of Pontiac Motor Division. Model-year production included 68,673 base LeMans, 62,380 Grand LeMans, and 5,886 Grand Ams. Model-year production of LeMans, Grand LeMans, and Grand Am models in the U.S., according to factory, included 52,989 made in Baltimore, Maryland, and 59,714 made in Pontiac, Michigan. Of the 112,703 cars built in the U.S. market, 51,377 had a V-6 and 61,326 had a V-8. The V-6-powered cars included 18,853 base LeMans models, 12,787 Grand LeMans models, 367 Grand Ams and 19,370 LeMans Safari, and Grand LeMans Safari wagons combined. The V-8-powered cars included 10,179 LeMans coupes and sedans, 16,698 Grand LeMans coupes and sedans, 5,519 Grand Am coupes and sedans and 28,930 LeMans Safari and Grand LeMans Safari wagons combined.

The 112,703 cars produced in factories in the U.S. represented 1.22 percent of total U.S. model-year production. Calendar-year sales of all LeMans and Grand Am models was 114,993 units for a 1.4 percent share of market. Model-year sales of LeMans through U.S. new-car dealers totaled 119,709 units compared to 114,577 the previous year. The LeMans and the Sunbird were the only Pontiac models to gain sales in 1979. A total of 24,235 cars were reported built in Canada for model-year 1979.

The Grand LeMans and its stable mates received noticeably different front ends for 1980. The Grand LeMans was again the high-end Pontiac midsize car, with plenty of chrome and a stand-up hood ornament.

Pontiac's regular intermediate models—the LeMans, Grand LeMans, and Grand Am—all received a new front-end appearance and more stereo system options. Two new engine choices, the 4.9-liter E/C V-8 and lighter 4.3-liter V-8, were added. LeMans models came in three body styles: two-door notchback coupe, four-door notchback sedan, and four-door Safari station wagon. They had new chrome grilles, taillights, parking lights, signal lights, and front side-marker lights. The Grand Am came only as a performance-oriented coupe and was again a V-8-only series. Grand Ams featured a new soft-facia front end.

I.D. DATA

The 13-symbol vehicle identification number (VIN) was located on the upper left surface of the instrument panel, visible through the windshield. The first digit is 2, indicating Pontiac division. The second symbol is a letter indicating car-line series: D=LeMans, F=Grand LeMans, and G=Grand Am. Next come two digits that denote body type: 19=four-door notchback sedan, 27=two-door notchback coupe and 35=four-door Safari station wagon.

The fifth symbol is a letter indicating engine code: K=229-cid (3.8-liter) two-barrel V-6, H=Chevrolet or GM of Canada built 305-cid (5.0-liter) four-barrel V-8, S=265-cid (4.3-liter) two-barrel V-8, T=301-cid (4.9-liter) four-barrel V-8, and W and T=301-cid (4.9-liter) four-barrel V-8. The sixth symbol denotes model year (A=1980). Next is a plant code: B=Baltimore, Maryland, P=Pontiac, Michigan, and 1=Oshawa, Ontario. The final six digits are the sequential serial number, which began with 100,001.

COLORS

LeMans paint codes for 1980 were: 11=Cameo White, 15=Platinum, 19=Starlight Black, 21=Baniff Blue, 29=Nightwatch Blue (not available on Grand Am), 44=Piedmont Green (not available on Grand Am), 50=Mariposa Yellow (not available on Grand Am), 59=Stetson Beige (not available on Grand Am), 63=Fremont Gold, 69=Castilian Bronze (not available on Grand Am), 75=Bordeaux Red (not available on Grand Am), 76=Montreux Maroon (not available on Grand Am), 77=Agate Red and 85=Richmond Gray (not

The LeMans Safari wagon came with a base 3.8-liter V-6, but three different V-8s were also available.

available on Grand Am). Specific W53 double two-tone exterior paint colors for Grand LeMans Safari only were: 15L/19U=Platinum lower and Starlight Black hood, top, and lower accent, 16L/85U=Starlight Black lower and Richmond Gray hood, top and lower accent, 19L/63U=Starlight Black lower with Fremont Gold hood, top and lower accent, 29L/21U=Nightwatch Blue lower with Baniff Blue hood, top and lower accent, 29L/85U=Nightwatch Blue lower with Richmond Gray hood, top and lower accent, 59L/63U=Stetson Beige lower with Fremont Gold hood, top and lower accent, 75L/76U= Bordeaux Red lower with Montreux Maroon hood, top, and lower accent. Specific W50 two-tone exterior color combinations were the same as the W53 double two-tone combinations without the lower accent color. Interior trim codes were: (LeMans coupe/sedan) 26B2=Blue cloth full-width bench seat, 26R2=Blue vinyl full-width bench seat, 62B2=Camel Tan cloth full-width bench seat, 62R2=Camel Tan vinyl full-width bench seat, 79B2=Maroon cloth full-width bench seat, 79R2=Maroon vinyl full-width bench seat. (LeMans Safari) 26R2=Blue vinyl full-width bench seat, 62R2=Camel vinyl full-width bench seat, 79R2=Maroon vinyl full-width bench seat, 26N5=Blue vinyl custom notchback seat, 62C5=Camel cloth custom notchback seat, 62N5=Camel vinyl custom notchback seat, 79C5=Maroon cloth custom notchback seat, 79N5=Maroon vinyl custom notchback seat, 26N6=Blue vinyl Custom 60/40 seat, 62C6=Camel cloth Custom 60/40 seat, 82N6=Camel vinyl Custom 60/40 seat, 79C6=Maroon cloth Custom 60/40 seat, 79N6=Maroon vinyl Custom 60/40 seat, 26N1=Blue vinyl Custom bucket seats, 62C1=Camel cloth Custom bucket seats, 62N1=Camel vinyl Custom bucket seats, 79C1=Maroon cloth Custom bucket seats, 79N1=Maroon vinyl Custom bucket seats. (Grand LeMans Safari) 26Y2=Blue vinyl full-width bench seat, 82Y2=Camel vinyl full-width bench seat, 79Y2=Maroon vinyl full-width bench seat, 26N5=Blue vinyl custom notchback seat, 62C5=Camel

cloth custom notchback seat, 62N5=Camel vinyl custom notchback seat, 79C5=Maroon cloth custom notchback seat, 79N5=Maroon vinyl custom notchback seat, 26N6=Blue vinyl Custom 60/40 seat, 62C6=Camel cloth Custom 60/40 seat, 82N6=Camel vinyl Custom 60/40 seat, 79C6=Maroon cloth Custom 60/40 seat, 79N6=Maroon vinyl Custom 60/40 seat, 26N1=Blue vinyl Custom bucket seats, 62C1=Camel cloth Custom bucket seats, 62N1=Camel vinyl Custom bucket seats, 79C1=Maroon cloth Custom bucket seats, 79N1=Maroon vinyl Custom bucket seats. (Grand LeMans coupe) 12N5=Oyster vinyl notchback seat, 19C5=Black cloth notchback seat, 26C5=Blue cloth notchback seat, 26N5=Blue vinyl notchback seat, 82C5=Camel cloth notchback seat, 82N5=Camel vinyl notchback seat, 79C5=Maroon cloth notchback seat, 79N5=Maroon vinyl notchback seat, 12N6=Oyster vinyl Custom 60/40 seat, 19C6=Black cloth Custom 60/40 seat, 26C6=Blue cloth Custom 60/40 seat, 26N6=Blue vinyl Custom 60/40 seat, 62C6=Camel cloth Custom 60/40 seat, 62N6=Camel vinyl Custom 60/40 seat, 79C6=Maroon cloth Custom 60/40 seat, 79N6=Maroon vinyl Custom 60/40 seat, 12N1=Oyster vinyl Custom bucket seats, 19C1=Black cloth Custom bucket seats, 26C1=Blue cloth Custom bucket seats, 26N1=Blue vinyl Custom bucket seats, 62C1=Camel cloth Custom bucket seats, 62N1=Camel vinyl Custom bucket seats, 79C1=Maroon cloth Custom bucket seats, 79N1=Maroon vinyl Custom bucket seats, 26G5=Blue cloth Luxury notchback seat, 44G5=Green cloth Luxury notchback seat, 62G5=Camel cloth Luxury notchback seat, 79G5=Maroon cloth Luxury notchback seat, 26G5=Blue cloth Luxury 60/40 seat, 44G5=Green cloth Luxury 60/40 seat, 62G5=Camel cloth Luxury 60/40 seat, 79G5=Maroon cloth Luxury 60/40 seat, 26G1=Blue cloth Luxury bucket seats, 44G1=Green cloth Luxury bucket seats, 62G1=Camel cloth Luxury bucket seats, 79G1=Maroon cloth Luxury bucket seats. (Grand LeMans sedan) 19C5=Black cloth notchback seat, 26C5=Blue cloth notchback seat, 26N5=Blue vinyl notchback seat, 82C5=Camel cloth notchback seat, 82N5=Camel vinyl notchback seat, 79C5=Maroon cloth notchback seat, 79N5=Maroon vinyl notchback seat, 19C6=Black cloth Custom 60/40 seat, 26C6=Blue cloth Custom 60/40 seat, 26N6=Blue vinyl Custom 60/40 seat, 62C6=Camel cloth Custom 60/40 seat, 62N6=Camel vinyl Custom 60/40 seat, 79C6=Maroon cloth Custom 60/40 seat, 79N6=Maroon vinyl Custom 60/40 seat, 19C1=Black cloth Custom bucket seats, 26C1=Blue cloth Custom bucket seats, 26N1=Blue vinyl Custom bucket seats, 62C1=Camel cloth Custom bucket seats, 62N1=Camel vinyl Custom bucket seats, 79C1=Maroon cloth Custom bucket seats, 79N1=Maroon vinyl Custom bucket seats, 26G5=Blue cloth Luxury notchback seat, 44G5=Green cloth Luxury notchback seat, 62G5=Camel cloth Luxury notchback seat, 79G5=Maroon cloth Luxury notchback seat, 26G5=Blue cloth Luxury 60/40 seat, 44G5=Green cloth Luxury 60/40 seat, 62G5=Camel cloth Luxury 60/40 seat, 79G5=Maroon cloth Luxury 60/40 seat, 26G1=Blue cloth Luxury bucket seats, 44G1=Green cloth Luxury bucket seats, 62G1=Camel cloth Luxury bucket seats, 79G1=Maroon cloth Luxury bucket seats. (Grand Am) 12N1=Oyster vinyl bucket seats, 19C1=Black cloth bucket seats, 26C1=Blue cloth bucket seats, 26N1=Blue vinyl bucket seats, 62C1=Camel cloth bucket seats, 62N1=Camel vinyl bucket seats, 79C1=Maroon cloth bucket seats, 79N1=Maroon vinyl bucket seats, 12N6=Oyster vinyl bucket seats, 19C6=Black cloth bucket seats, 26C6=Blue cloth bucket seats, 26N6=Blue vinyl bucket seats, 62C6=Camel cloth bucket seats, 62N6=Camel vinyl bucket seats, 79C6=Maroon cloth bucket seats, 79N6=Maroon vinyl bucket seats. Padded landau and full Cordova tops (not available on Safaris and Grand Am sedans) came in: 11T=White, 19T=Black, 21T=Blue, 44T=Green, 63T=Gold, 76T=Maroon, and 85T=Gray.

LEMANS — (V-6) — SERIES 2AD

Design changes for the LeMans included new grilles, park/signal lamps, front side-marker lamps, and taillights (for coupes and sedans). Two new interior colors, Blue and Maroon, were available. LeMans door panels had new simulated welt-and-stitch lines centered between bright mylar moldings. Safari wagons could have a double two-tone paint treatment at no extra cost, instead of the standard simulated wood-graining. The exterior wood-grain trim came in a new red elm pattern this year. New options included electronic-tuned-radio (ETR) stereos and extended-range speakers. The new grille continued Pontiac's trademark "split grille" styling. Each grille section consisted of horizontal bars with clear park/signal lamps behind the outer ends. The wide center panel held a Pontiac arrowhead emblem above "Pontiac" block lettering. Wraparound clear/amber marker lenses had four horizontal trim ribs. Single rectangular headlamps were used. The base engine for coupes and sedans was Chevrolet's 229-cid (3.8-liter) V-6 with a three-speed manual gearbox. Options included a new 265-cid (4.3-liter) V-8 and Turbo Hydra-Matic transmission, as well as a 301-cid (4.9-liter) four-barrel V-8. Cars sold in California could have a 305-cid V-8.

Model Number	Body/Style Number	Body Type & Seating	Factory Price	Shipping Weight	Production Total
LEMANS — (V-6) — SERIES 2AD					
2AD	27	2d Coupe-6P	$5,652	3,024 lbs.	9,110
2AD	19	4d Sedan-6P	$5,758	3,040 lbs.	20,485
LEMANS SAFARI — (V-6) — SERIES 2AD					
2AD	35	4d Sta Wagon-6P	$6,257	3,232 lbs.	12,912

GRAND LEMANS — (V-6) — SERIES 2AF

The Grand LeMans again included such upscale trim items as a stand-up hood ornament, a hood windsplit molding, rocker panel moldings, windowsill moldings, side window reveal moldings, Custom color-keyed safety belts, dual horns, added acoustical insulation, a luxury cushion steering wheel, and door panels with wide mylar moldings. The Grand LeMans Safari also had load floor carpeting.

Model Number	Body/Style Number	Body Type & Seating	Factory Price	Shipping Weight	Production Total
GRAND LEMANS — (V-6) — SERIES 2AF					
2AF	27	2d Coupe-6P	$5,947	3,050 lbs.	—
2AF	19	4d Sedan-6P	$6,120	3,089 lbs.	—
GRAND LEMANS SAFARI — (V-6) — SERIES 2AF					
2AF	35	4d Sta Wagon-6P	$6,682	3,265 lbs.	12,912

GRAND AM — (V-8) — SERIES 2AG

The Grand Am now came in coupe form only and only with a V-8. It carried the same 301-cid E/C engine (as in Trans Am) with automatic transmission. California Grand Ams had a 305-cid V-8 instead. In addition to a new soft-fascia front end, the Grand Am added ample standard equipment in an attempt to attain a performance image. The list included: bucket seats (with console), sport mirrors, Rally IV wheels, and a custom sport steering wheel. A new silver upper body accent stripe was standard. The Rally RTS suspension had larger front and rear stabilizer bars. All Grand Am bodies had a new Ontario Gray lower accent color. Each of the twin grille sections was divided into three sections, with thin body-color separators between. Each section held horizontal strips. A wide, peaked center divider held a V-shaped Pontiac emblem that extended from the hood crease. The front bumper had two air slots. Single rectangular headlamps stood directly above clear park/signal lamps.

Model Number	Body/Style Number	Body Type & Seating	Factory Price	Shipping Weight	Production Total
GRAND AM — (V-8) — SERIES 2AG					
2AG	27	2d Coupe-6P	$7,504	3,299 lbs.	1,647

ENGINES

LEMANS, GRAND LEMANS BASE 229-CID V-6: Overhead-valve. Cast-iron block and head. Displacement: 229 cid (3.8 liters). Bore and stroke: 3.38 x 3.48 in. Compression ratio: 8.6:1. Brake hp: 115 at 3800 rpm. Torque: 175 lbs.-ft. at 2000 rpm. Four main bearings. Hydraulic valve lifters. Carburetor: two-barrel Rochester M2ME. VIN Code: K.

169

LEMANS, GRAND LEMANS OPTIONAL 265-CID V-8: Overhead valve. Cast-iron block and head. Bore and stroke: 3.75 x 3.00 in. Displacement: 265 cid (4.3 liters). Compression ratio: 8.3:1. Brake hp: 120 at 3600 rpm. Taxable hp: 45. Torque: 210 lbs.-ft. at 1600 rpm. Five main bearings. Hydraulic valve lifters. Carburetor: Two-barrel. VIN Code: S.

GRAND AM BASE V-8; LEMANS, GRAND LEMANS OPTIONAL 301-CID V-8: Overhead valve. Cast-iron block and head. Bore and stroke: 4.06 x 3.04 in. Displacement: 301 cid (4.9 liters). Compression ratio: 8.1:1. Brake hp: 140 at 4000 rpm. Taxable hp: 51.2. Torque: 240 lbs.-ft. at 1800 rpm. Five main bearings. Hydraulic valve lifters. Carburetor: Four-barrel Rochester. VIN Code: W.

GRAND AM, LEMANS, GRAND LEMANS OPTIONAL 305-CID V-8: Overhead valve. Cast-iron block and head. Bore and stroke: 3.74 x 3.48 in. Displacement: 305 cid (5.0 liters). Compression ratio: 8.4:1. Brake hp: 150 at 3800 rpm. Taxable hp: 44.7. Torque: 230 lbs.-ft. at 2400 rpm. Five main bearings. Hydraulic valve lifters. VIN Code: H.

GRAND AM OPTIONAL 301-CID V-8: Overhead valve. Cast-iron block and head. Bore and stroke: 4.06 x 3.04 in. Displacement: 301 cid (4.9 liters). Compression ratio: 8.1:1. Brake hp: 155 at 4400 rpm. Taxable hp: 51.2. Torque: 240 lbs.-ft. at 2200 rpm. Five main bearings. Hydraulic valve lifters. Carburetor: Four-barrel Rochester. VIN Code: T.

CHASSIS

Wheelbase: (LeMans/Grand LeMans/Safari/Grand Am) 108.1 in. Overall length: (LeMans/Grand LeMans/Grand Am coupe) 199.2 in., (LeMans/Grand LeMans sedan) 198.6 in., (Safari) 197.8 in. Height: (LeMans/Grand LeMans/Grand Am coupe) 53.5 in., (LeMans/Grand LeMans sedan) 54.4 in., (Safari) 54.8 in. Width: (LeMans/Grand lemans/Grand Am) 72.4 in., (Safari) 72.6 in. Front tread: (LeMans/Grand LeMans/Grand Am/Safari) 58.5 in. Rear tread: (LeMans/Grand LeMans/Grand Am/Safari) 57.8 in. Front headroom: (LeMans/Grand LeMans/Grand Am coupe) 37.9 in. Rear headroom: (LeMans/Grand LeMans/Grand Am coupe) 37.8 in. Front legroom: (LeMans/Grand LeMans/Grand Am coupe) 42.8 in. Rear legroom: (LeMans/Grand LeMans/Grand Am coupe) 35.1 in. Front hiproom: (LeMans/Grand LeMans/Grand Am coupe) 51.7 in. Rear hiproom: (LeMans/Grand LeMans/Grand Am coupe) 54.5 in. Front headroom: (LeMans/Grand LeMans sedan) 38.7 in. Rear headroom: (LeMans/Grand LeMans sedan) 37.7 in. Front legroom: (LeMans/Grand LeMans sedan) 42.8 in. Rear legroom: (LeMans/Grand LeMans sedan) 38 in. Front hip room: (LeMans/Grand LeMans sedan) 52.2 in. Rear hip room: (LeMans/Grand LeMans/Grand Am sedan) 55.6 in. Luggage capacity: (Lemans/Grand LeMans/Grand Am coupe) 16.4 cu. ft. (Lemans/Grand LeMans sedan) 16.4 cu. ft. Cargo volume: (Safari) 72.4 cu. ft. Length of cargo space at floor: (Safari) 81.3 in.

Length of cargo space at floor with tailgate lowered: (Safari) 103.9 in. Top of front seat back to closed tailgate: (Safari) 72.9 in. Minimum distance between rear wheelhousings at floor: (Safari) 43.6 in. Rear end opening width at belt; (Safari) 51.7 in. Maximum cargo height: (Safari) 30 in. Maximum height at rear opening with tailgate open: (Safari) 27.8 in. Standard tires: (LeMans/Grand LeMans) P185/75R14, (LeMans Safari/Grand LeMans Safari) P195/75R14, (Grand Am) 205/70R14 steel-belted radials with Rally RTS suspension. Transmission: Three-speed manual transmission standard. Three-speed Turbo Hydra-Matic transmission optional on all. Standard final drive ratio: (LeMans V-8) 2.29:1 or 2.14:1, (LeMans Safari) 2.73:1 with V-6, 2.41:1 with 265-cid V-8, 2.29:1 with 301-cid V-8, (Grand Am) 2.93:1. Steering: Re-circulating ball. Front suspension: coil springs with lower trailing links and anti-sway bar. Rear suspension: rigid axle with coil springs, lower trailing radius arms, upper torque arms and anti-sway bar. Brakes: front disc, rear drum. Ignition: electronic. Body construction: separate body and frame. Fuel tank: 18.1 gal., except Safari 18.2 gal.

OPTIONS

C60 Custom air conditioning, requires power steering and required with 305-cid four-barrel V-8 ($531-$647). C61 Automatic Temperature Control, requires power steering and required with 305-cid four-barrel V-8 ($700). UA1 heavy-duty battery. AK1 Custom color-keyed safety belts standard with luxury trim on Grand LeMans and Grand Am and with Custom trim on Safaris. V31 front bumper guards, not available for Grand Am. V32 rear bumper guards, not available for Grand Am. NB2 California emission requirements ($250). B39 load floor carpeting for Safaris, standard on Grand LeMans Safaris and included with Custom trim package. UE8 digital quartz clock, optional with lamp group and air conditioning only. U35 electric quartz clock, standard in Grand Am and not available with Rally gauges or ETR radio. D55 front seat console, with bucket seats and lamp group only. K30 cruise control, with automatic transmission only ($105-$118). A90 remote-control deck lid. C51 Safari rear window deflector. C49 electric rear window defroster. B57 Custom exterior group including hood ornament, hood windsplit molding, rocker panel moldings, windowsill moldings and reveal moldings, for base Lemans only, not available with V-6 ($51-$107). U14 instrument panel gauges without clock, standard with Grand Am. U21 Rally gauges and instrument panel tachometer, without clock, on Grand Am optional with digital clock or ETR stereo only; not available with electric quartz clock U35. A01 Soft-Ray tinted glass in all windows. B93 door edge guards. U05 dual horns, standard in Grand LeMans and Grand Am. B51 added acoustical insulation, standard in Grand LeMans. TR9 lamp group including rear doorjamb switch on sedans and Safaris, rear compartment courtesy lamp in Safaris, luggage lamp, glove box lamp, ashtray lamp and instrument panel courtesy lamp. C95 dome reading lamp. V55 Safari luggage carrier. B32 front floor mats. B33 rear floor mats. D64 illuminated right-hand visor mirror. D34 right-hand visor mirror. D35 dual sport mirrors, right-hand manual and left-hand remote controlled, requires specific two-tone paint treatments; standard on Grand Ams and required with specific two-tone color combinations. D68 dual remote-control Sport rearview mirrors, right-hand convex. D33 chrome left-hand remote-control rearview mirror, not available with Grand Am. B83 rocker panel moldings, standard on Grand LeMans and Grand Am, included with Custom interior group. B90 side window reveal moldings, optional for LeMans sedan and Safari only, included with Custom interior group. B85 window sill moldings, standard on Grand Am, included with Custom interior group. U75 automatic power antenna. U83 Tri-band power antenna for AM/FM and CB radio, included with CB radio. AU3 power door locks. AU6 power tailgate lock, Safari only. A42 power driver's seat ($165-$179). N41 power steering, standard on Grand Am and required with air conditioning and V-8 engine ($174). A31 power windows, front door only on coupes, front door and rear vents on sedan and Safari ($132-$221). A32 power windows, front door only on sedans and Safaris ($132). U63 AM radio. U69 AM/FM radio. U58 AM/FM stereo radio. UN3 AM/FM stereo radio and cassette player. UM7 ETR AM/FM stereo radio with seek/scan. UM1 AM radio and stereo tape player. UM2 AM/FM radio and stereo tape player. UP6 AM/FM stereo radio with 40-channel CB includes tri-band power antenna. U80 rear radio speaker with U63 or U69 radios only. UP8 rear radio speakers, dual front and rear, with U63, U69 or UP5 radios only. UX6 dual front radio speakers. UQ1 dual rear extended-range radio speakers. UN9 radio accommodation package. AT6 reclining passenger seat, optional with bucket seat or notchback 60/40 seat only. N31 Custom sport steering wheel, standard in Grand Am. N30 Luxury Cushion steering wheel, standard in Grand LeMans, not available in Grand Am. N33 tilt-adjustable steering wheel, with Custom Sport or Luxury Cushion steering wheels and automatic transmission only. CF5 power glass sunroof, coupe only ($773). CA1 power steel sunroof, coupe only ($561). P02 Custom finned wheel covers, not available on Grand Am. P01 deluxe wheel covers. N95 wire wheel covers. N90 four cast-aluminum wheels, available in 15P Silver or 55P Gold. N66 four Rally II wheel rims, standard on Grand Am. CD4 controlled-cycle windshield wipers. D60 color and trim incompatibility override. K73 heavy-duty 70-amp alternator ($15-$51). V10 cold weather group. F40 Firm Ride package ($14). VK3 front license plate bracket. AW9 Safari security package ($40-$45). N18 wire wheel locking package. V82 medium trailer group ($132-$161). W52 demo package. 265-cid two-barrel V-8 ($180). 301-cid four-barrel V-8 ($295). 305-cid four-barrel V-8 ($295). Turbo Hydra-Matic transmission ($358). Limited-slip differential ($68). Power steering: ($174). Rally RTS handling package ($142-$228). Engine block heater ($16). LeMans luxury trim group ($161-$271). W50 LeMans two-paint appearance ($180). LeMans custom trim group ($131-$305). Full vinyl cordova top ($124). Padded landau top ($239). Rear-facing third seat: Safari ($199).

OPTION INSTALLATION RATES

Of 84,024 LeMans built (including cars built in Canada for the U.S. market), 99.8 percent had automatic transmission, 27.6 percent had a V-8 engine, 72.4 percent had a V-6 engine, 38.3 percent had an AM radio, 17.9 percent had an AM/FM radio, 23.7 percent had an AM/FM stereo radio, 0.9 percent had an AM 8-track tape player, 1.7 percent had an AM/FM radio and 8-track stereo tape player, 2.8 percent had an AM/FM radio with cassette tape player, 0.3 percent had an AM/FM/CB radio, 99.9 percent had power steering, 100 percent had power front disc/rear drum brakes, 5.6 percent had a power seat, 12.9 percent had power side windows, 13.6 percent had power door locks, 3.3 percent had non-reclining bucket seats, 3.2 percent had reclining seats (including reclining bucket seats), 10.6 percent had a vinyl roof, 0.2 percent had a sun roof, 58.4 percent had steel-belted radial tires, 41.6 percent had fiberglass-belted radial tires, 1.2 percent had a tinted windshield only, 85.2 percent had all tinted windows, 1 percent had automatic temperature control, 86.8 percent had an air conditioner, 33.6 percent had an adjustable steering column, 3.4 percent had a limited-slip differential, 76.8 percent had optional wheel covers, 14.4 percent had styled steel wheels, 1.4 percent had styled aluminum wheels, 2.9 percent had a digital clock, 28.4 percent had a conventional clock, 33.8 percent had a speed regulating device, 0.3 percent had a blower-type rear window defogger, 42.1 percent had an electric rear window defogger, 85.6 percent had a remote-control left-hand outside rearview mirror and 3.8 percent had a remote-control left-hand outside rearview mirror.

HISTORICAL FOOTNOTES

The 1980 Pontiacs were introduced on October 11, 1979. William E. Hoglund became general manager and Robert Stempel was promoted. Model-year production included 42,507 base LeMans, 39,870 Grand LeMans, and 1,647 Grand Ams. Model-year production of LeMans, Grand LeMans, and Grand Am models in the U.S., according to factory, included 25,774 made in Baltimore, Maryland, and 35,449 made in Pontiac, Michigan. Of the 84.024 LeMans and Grand Am models built in the U.S. and Canada for the U.S. market, 60,835 had a V-6 and 23,189 had a V-8. The V-6-powered cars included 23,614 base LeMans models, 18,378 Grand LeMans models, and 18,843 LeMans Safari and Grand LeMans Safari wagons combined. The V-8-powered cars included 5,981 LeMans coupes and sedans, 6,660 Grand LeMans coupes and sedans, 1,647 Grand Am coupes and 8,901 LeMans Safari and Grand LeMans Safari wagons combined. The 61,223 cars produced in factories in the U.S. represented 0.9 percent of total U.S. model-year production. Calendar-year sales of all LeMans and Grand Am models was 77,911 units for a 1.2 percent share of market. Model-year sales of LeMans through U.S. new-car dealers totaled 84.975 units compared to 119,709 the previous year. Not only Pontiac was suffering, as the 1980 model year turned out to be one of the most disastrous ever for U.S. automakers.

The Grand LeMans took one final bow in 1981 before the entire Pontiac LeMans line was discontinued.

The LeMans had a lower, more horizontal front-end look that included a revised front fascia panel and grille. The twin egg crate-style grilles had a 4 x 3 pattern on each side of a tapered center panel with the Pontiac emblem and contained new park/signal lamps at their outer ends. Rectangular quad headlights were new and the wraparound marker lenses had two horizontal trim ribs. Wide wraparound taillights had one horizontal trim strip and a series of vertical strips. These formed squares and the back-up light lenses were at the center, adjoining the license plate. Sedans added a new formal roof. A fully padded vinyl top was optional. A new luxury LJ package was available for the LeMans four-door sedan. The fancier Grand LeMans was back for 1981, but the Grand Am was discontinued again. This was to be the last season for the midsize LeMans.

I.D. DATA

The 17-symbol vehicle identification number (VIN) was located on the upper left surface of the instrument panel, visible through the windshield. The first digit is 1 indicating U.S. built, The second symbol is a G indicating a General Motors Product. The third symbol is a 2 indicating Pontiac. The fourth symbol is a letter indicating the type of restraint system: A=non-passive manual belts, B=passive automatic belts, C=passive inflatable airbag. The fifth symbol is a letter indicating car-line series: D=LeMans and F=Grand LeMans. The sixth and seventh symbols indicate body type: 19=four-door notchback sedan, 27=two-door notchback coupe and 35=four-door Safari station wagon. The eighth symbol is a letter indicating engine code: A=Buick-built 231-cid (3.8-liter) two-barrel V-6, S=Pontiac-built 265-

cid (4.3-liter) two-barrel V-8, W=Pontiac-built 301-cid (4.9-liter) four-barrel V-8. The ninth symbol is a check digit. The 10th symbol is a letter denoting model year (B=1981). Next is a plant code: B=Baltimore, Maryland, P=Pontiac, Michigan, and 1=Oshawa, Ontario. The final six digits are the sequential serial number, which began with 100,001.

COLORS

LeMans paint codes were: 11=White, 16=Silver Metallic, 19=Black, 21=Light Blue Metallic, 29=Dark Blue Metallic, 35=Pastel Champagne, 36=Champagne Metallic, 45=Light Jadestone (Blue-Green) Metallic, 47=Jadestone (Blue-Green) Metallic, 63=Medium Beige, 68=Light Brown Metallic, 69=Medium Brown Metallic, 72=Medium Maroon Metallic, and 77=Dark Maroon Metallic. Specific W53 double two-tone exterior paint colors for Grand LeMans Safari only were: 16/29 Silver Metallic lower with Dark Blue Metallic hood, top and lower accent, 16/77=Silver Metallic lower with Dark Maroon Metallic hood, top and lower accent, 21/29=Light Blue Metallic lower with Dark Blue Metallic hood, top and lower accent, 35/36=Pastel Campagne lower with Champagne Metallic hood, top and lower accent, 37/36=Medium Campagne Metallic lower with Champagne Metallic hood, top and lower accent, 47/45=Jadestone (Blue-Green) Metallic lower with Light Jadestone (Blue-Green) Metallic hood, top, and lower accent, 63/11=Medium Beige lower with White hood, top, and lower accent, 69/63=Medium Brown Metallic lower with Medium Beige hood, top, and lower accent, 69/68=Medium Brown Metallic lower with Light Brown Metallic hood, top, and lower accent, 72/77= Medium

Maroon Metallic lower with Dark Maroon Metallic hood, top, and lower accent, 77/63=Dark Maroon Metallic lower with Medium Beige hood, top, and lower accent. Specific W50 two-tone exterior color combinations for coupes and sedan only were the same as the W53 double two-tone combinations without the lower accent color. (Note: For interior trim codes see accompanying charts.) Padded landau and full cordova tops (not available on Safaris) came in: 11=White, 19=Black, 29=Dark Blue, 36=Champagne, 45=Light Jadestone (Blue-Green), 63=Medium Beige, and 77=Dark Maroon.

LEMANS — (V-6) — SERIES 2AD

The base LeMans came with a 231-cid (3.8-liter) V-6 as standard equipment. A three-speed manual transmission was also standard, except in station wagons and cars sold in California, which came with Turbo Hydra-Matic. The automatic transmissions had a torque converter clutch. New standard equipment included power steering, a compact spare tire, and a side-lift frame jack. Custom finned wheel covers were a new option. Regular standard equipment included P185/75R14 fiberglass-belted black sidewall tires, power brakes and steering, wheel opening moldings, body-color bumpers with bright rub strips, and hubcaps with the Pontiac crest. Coupes had black/bright pillar moldings.

Model Number	Body/Style Number	Body Type & Seating	Factory Price	Shipping Weight	Production Total
LEMANS — (V-6) — SERIES 2AD					
2AD	27	2d Coupe-6P	$6,689	3,035 lbs.	2,578
2AD	69	4d Sedan-6P	$6,797	3,052 lbs.	22,186
LEMANS LJ — (V-6) — SERIES 2AD + Y83					
2AD	69/Y83	4d Sedan-6P	$7,100	—	Note 1
LEMANS SAFARI — (V-6) — SERIES 2AD					
2AD	35	4d Sta Wagon-6P	$7,316	3,240 lbs.	13,358

NOTE 1: A specific production total for 2AD sedans with the LJ package is not available.

GRAND LEMANS — (V-6) — SERIES 2AF

The Grand LeMans added a stand-up hood ornament, a hood windsplit molding, window reveal moldings, lower body-side moldings, black rocker panel moldings, Custom color-keyed seat belts, dual horns, extra acoustical insulation, and a front seat with a folding center armrest.

Model Number	Body/Style Number	Body Type & Seating	Factory Price	Shipping Weight	Production Total
GRAND LEMANS — (V-6) — SERIES 2AF					
2AF	27	2d Coupe-6P	$6,976	3,063 lbs.	1,819
2AF	69	4d Sedan-6P	$7,153	3,108 lbs.	25,241
GRAND LEMANS — (V-6) — SERIES 2AF					
2AF	35	4d Sta Wagon-6P	$7,726	3,279 lbs.	16,683

ENGINES

LEMANS, GRAND LEMANS BASE V-6: Overhead-valve V-6. Cast-iron block and head. Displacement: 231 cid (3.8 liters). Bore and stroke: 3.80 x 3.40 in. Compression ratio: 8.0:1. Brake hp: 110 at 3800 rpm. Torque: 190 lbs.-ft. at 1600 rpm. Four main bearings. Hydraulic valve lifters. Carburetor: two-barrel Rochester M2ME. Buick-built. VIN Code: A.

LEMANS, GRAND LEMANS OPTIONAL V-8: Overhead valve. Cast iron block and head. Bore and stroke: 3.75 x 3.00 in. Displacement: 265 cid (4.3 liters). Compression ratio: 8.3:1. Brake hp: 120 at 4000 rpm. Taxable hp: 45.00. Torque: 205 lbs.-ft. at 2000 rpm. Five main bearings. Hydraulic valve lifters. Carburetor: Two-barrel Rochester E2ME. VIN Code: S.

LEMANS SAFARI, GRAND LEMANS SAFARI OPTIONAL V-8: Overhead valve. Cast iron block and head. Bore and stroke: 4.00 x 3.00 in. Displacement: 301 cid (4.9 liters). Compression ratio: 8.1:1. Brake hp: 135 at 3600 rpm. Taxable hp: 51.2. Torque: 235 lbs.-ft. at 1600 rpm. Five main bearings. Hydraulic valve lifters. Carburetor: Four-barrel Rochester E4ME. VIN Code: W.

CHASSIS

Wheelbase: (LeMans/Grand LeMans/Safari) 108.1 in. Overall length: (LeMans/Grand LeMans coupe) 199.2 in., (LeMans/Grand LeMans sedan) 198.6 in., (Safari) 197.8 in. Height: (LeMans/Grand LeMans coue) 53.5 in., (LeMans/Grand LeMans sedan) 54.4 in., (Safari) 54.8 in. Width: (LeMans/Grand Lemans/Grand Am) 72.4 in., (Safari) 72.6 in. Front tread: (LeMans/Grand LeMans/Safari) 58.5 in. Rear tread: (LeMans/Grand LeMans/Safari) 57.8 in. Front headroom: (LeMans/Grand LeMans coupe) 37.9 in. Rear headroom: (LeMans/Grand LeMans coupe) 37.8 in. Front legroom: (LeMans/Grand LeMans coupe) 42.8 in. Rear legroom: (LeMans/Grand LeMans coupe) 35.1 in. Front hip room: (LeMans/Grand LeMans coupe) 51.7 in. Rear hip room: (LeMans/Grand LeMans coupe) 54.5 in. Front headroom: (LeMans/Grand LeMans sedan) 38.7 in. Rear headroom: (LeMans/Grand LeMans sedan) 37.7 in. Front legroom: (LeMans/Grand LeMans sedan) 42.8 in. Rear legroom: (LeMans/Grand LeMans sedan) 38 in. Front hiproom: (LeMans/Grand LeMans sedan) 52.2 in. Rear hiproom: (LeMans/Grand LeMans sedan) 55.6 in. Luggage capacity: (Lemans/Grand LeMans coupe) 16.4 cu. ft. (LeMans/Grand LeMans sedan) 16.4 cu. ft. Cargo volume: (Safari) 72.4 cu. ft. Length of cargo space at floor: (Safari) 81.3 in. Length of cargo space at floor with tailgate lowered: (Safari) 103.9 in. Top of front seat back to closed tailgate: (Safari) 72.9 in. Minimum distance between rear wheelhousings at floor: (Safari) 43.6 in. Rear end opening width at belt; (Safari) 51.7 in. Maximum cargo height: (Safari) 30 in. Maximum height at rear opening with tailgate open: (Safari) 27.8 in. Standard tires: (LeMans/Grand LeMans) P185/75R14, (LeMans Safari/Grand LeMans Safari) P195/75R14. Transmission: three-speed manual transmission standard. Three-speed Turbo Hydra-Matic transmission optional on all. Standard final drive ratio: (LeMans V-8) 2.29:1 or 2.14:1, (LeMans Safari) 2.73:1 with V-6, 2.41:1 with 265-cid V-8, 2.29:1 with 301-cid V-8. Steering: recirculating ball. Front suspension: coil springs with lower trailing links and anti-sway bar. Rear suspension: rigid axle with coil springs, lower trailing radius arms, upper torque arms and anti-sway bar. Brakes: front disc, rear drum. Ignition: electronic. Body construction: separate body and frame. Fuel tank: 18.1 gal., except Safari 18.2 gal.

OPTIONS

C60 Custom air conditioning, requires power steering and 305-cid four-barrel V-8 ($560-$625). C61 automatic temperature control ($677). K73 heavy-duty 70-amp alternator, required with air conditioning or with electric rear window defroster ($15-$51). G80 limited-slip differential ($67). OPT optional axles. UA1 heavy-duty battery. V31 front bumper guards. V32 rear bumper guards. NB2 California emissions requirements ($46). UE8 digital quartz clock, optional with Lamp Group and air conditioning only. V10 cold weather group. D55 front seat console, with bucket seats and Lamp Group only. A90 remote-control deck lid. C49 electric rear window defroster. WS2 demo package. U14 instrument panel gauges without clock, includes trip odometer. U21 Rally gauges and instrument panel tachometer, without clock, includes trip odometer; not available with electric quartz clock U35. B93 door edge guards. TT5 tungsten quartz halogen headlights. BS1 added acoustical insulation, standard in Grand LeMans. C95 dome reading lamp. VK3 front license plate bracket. D33 chrome left-hand remote-control rearview mirror, not available with specific two-tone paint combinations. D68 dual remote-control sport rearview mirrors, right-hand convex. D64 illuminated right-hand visor mirror. D34 right-hand visor mirror. B83 rocker panel moldings, standard on Grand LeMans, included with Custom interior group. B90 side window reveal moldings, optional for LeMans sedan and Safari only, included with Custom interior group. B85 windowsill moldings, included with Custom interior group. U75 automatic power antenna. U83 Tri-band power antenna for AM/FM and CB radio, included with CB radio. AU3 power door locks. A42 power driver's seat ($173). U69 AM/FM radio. U58 AM/FM stereo radio. UN3 AM/FM stereo radio and cassette player. UM7 ETR AM/FM stereo radio with seek/scan. UM1 AM radio and stereo tape player. UM2 AM/FM radio and stereo tape player. UP6 AM/FM stereo radio with 40-channel CB includes tri-band power antenna. U80 rear radio speaker with U63 or U69 radios only. UP8 rear radio speakers, dual front and rear, with U63, U69 or UP5 radios only. UX6 dual front radio speakers. UQ1 dual rear extended-range radio speakers. UN9 radio accommodation package. AT6 reclining passenger seat, optional with bucket seat or notchback 60/40 seat only. F40 load carrying springs. N31 Custom sport steering wheel. CF5 power glass sunroof, coupe only ($773). CA1 power steel sunroof, coupe only ($561). V81 light trailer group ($129-$158). U89 Five-wire trailer wiring harness. MM3 three-speed manual transmission, with V-6 coupes and sedans only. P02 Custom finned wheel covers. N95 wire wheel covers. N18 wire wheel locking package, with optional wire wheel package only. N90 four cast-aluminum wheels, available in 15P Silver or 55P Gold. N66 four Rally II wheel rims. CD4 controlled-cycle windshield wipers.

(ORDER PROCESSING OPTIONS): D60 color and trim incompatibility override. ZV1 manufacturer's statement of origin. VC8 substitution or deletion authorization. (New Options) D08 heavy-duty radiator. P42 puncture-sealant tires, optional with QXW tires only. WS1 option program. WS8 priced order acknowledgement. Y83 LJ option.

(SAFARI OPTIONS): B39 load floor carpeting. C51 rear window deflector. V55 luggage carrier. AU6 power tailgate lock. AW9 Safari security package ($40). 301-cid four-barrel V-8 in Safari ($50). Turbo-Hydra-Matic ($349). Rally handling suspension ($202-$241). Heavy-duty springs ($14-$15). Heavy-duty cooling ($34). Engine block heater ($16). LeMans Luxury trim group ($160-$270). LeMans appearance package ($180). LeMans Custom exterior ($44-$100). LeMans Custom rim group ($130-$303). Cruise control ($132-$135). Power windows ($140-$211). Full vinyl cordova top ($115). Padded landau cordova top ($192). Rear-facing third seat: Safari ($194).

OPTION INSTALLATION RATES

Of 81,865 LeMans built (including cars built in Canada for the U.S. market), 99.1 percent had automatic transmission, 11.9 percent had a V-8 engine, 88.1 percent had a V-6 engine, 27.9 percent had a AM radio, 11.3 percent had an AM/FM radio, 42.3 percent had an AM/FM stereo radio, 0.2 percent had an AM 8-track tape player, 1.4 percent had an AM/FM radio and 8-track stereo tape player, 4 percent had an AM/FM radio with cassette tape player, 0.3 percent had an AM/FM/CB radio, 100 percent had power steering, 100 percent had power front disc/rear drum brakes, 8.7 percent had a power seat, 18 percent had power side windows, 26.3 percent had power door locks, 0.9 percent had non-reclining bucket seats, 4.8 percent had reclining seats (including reclining bucket seats), 19.8 percent had a vinyl roof, 0.1 percent had a sunroof, 63.9 percent had steel-belted radial tires, 36.1 percent had fiberglass-belted radial tires, 1.8 percent had a tinted windshield only, 88 percent had all tinted windows, 1.2 percent had automatic temperature control, 90.3 percent had an air conditioner, 50.3 percent had an adjustable steering column, 3.3 percent had a limited-slip differential, 84.7 percent had optional wheel covers, 9.9 percent had styled steel wheels, 0.3 percent had styled aluminum wheels, 2.9 percent had a digital clock, 39.1 percent had a conventional clock, 43.7 percent had a speed regulating device, 43.8 percent had an electric rear window defogger, 87.2 percent had a remote-control left-hand outside rearview mirror, and 4 percent had a remote-control left-hand outside rearview mirror.

HISTORICAL FOOTNOTES

The 1981 Pontiacs were introduced on September 24, 1980. William E. Hoglund was general manager of Pontiac Motor Division. Model-year production included 38,122 base LeMans and 43,743 Grand LeMans.

2004 GTO

Produced by General Motors Australian subsidiary Holden, the 2004 GTO will be based on the Holden Monaro, a modern car that shares many traits with the legendary GTOs of the '60s and '70s. The Monaro was the first all-Australian performance coupe when it was introduced in 1968. The current version debuted in 2001 and quickly became one of the most sought-after vehicles in Australia.

Actually, the Monaro, and consequently the 2004 GTO, can be traced further back to the four-door Holden SS Commodore. After creating this high-performance four-door sedan, Holden designed the Monaro coupe on the same platform. The SS Commodore fitted with an optional HSV (for "Holden Special Vehicles") kit has taken victories in all major touring car events held in

Australia. The SS Commodore sells for approximately 50,000 Australian dollars, which equates to $30,000 in U.S. money.

Bob Lutz, the ex-Chrysler exec and car collector who is now chairman of GM's North American Operations (and perhaps the only enthusiast left in the corporate hierarchy), played the key role in turning the Monaro into the 2004 GTO. It has been reported that Lutz drove a Holden Monaro while in Australia. He liked the car and felt that it was a machine that could live up to the original GTO's genuine high-performance image.

To give America's car-buying public its first look at the rebirth of the legend, Pontiac introduced show-car versions of the 2004 GTO to audiences at the Los

Angeles Auto Show, the North American International Auto Show in Detroit, and the Chicago Auto Show early in 2003. Pontiac said that production versions of the GTO would be available in Pontiac showrooms later in the year.

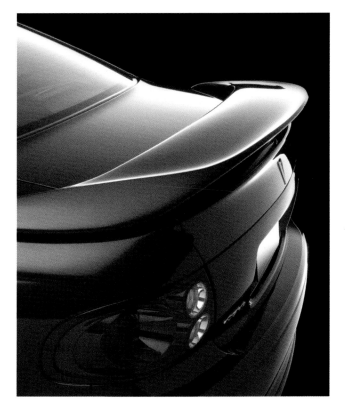

"The public's interest in the GTO has been everything we hoped it would be and more," Lutz said at the show. "This car is a strong statement from both Pontiac and GM that we are determined to re-energize the car market with vehicles that command attention and excite the customer's senses." The introduction of the show-car versions comes only seven months after GM announced it was bringing back the GTO. "This latest GTO will carry on the proud tradition of a legendary line," Lutz said.

Later, when GTO enthusiasts criticized the Los Angeles show car for not being "retro" styled, Lutz posted answers to the critics on the Internet. He told them that the idea behind the car was not to go down the retro road like Ford's T-Bird, but to develop a modern counterpart to the '60s American muscle car. Lutz did add that the lack of a hood scoop—which the car really does need to reinforce its GTO identity—would be corrected by the time the 2005 model arrives. Buyers will have to decide if they want first-year status or a scooped hood, or maybe both.

Hot looks and hotter engine

Sporting special red or yellow high-gloss paint, the GTO show cars exhibited a strong Pontiac brand character with their signature dual-port grille and a wide and aggressive stance. For the record, the yellow show car was reported to have Aussie-type right-hand drive. The red car that your editor saw at the Chicago Automobile Show was a left-hand drive unit. Both show cars rode on 18-in. alloy wheels and sported a high-performance power train worthy of the name "GTO."

Under the hood was a specially tuned LS1 5.7-liter V-8 aluminum-block engine that produced an estimated 340 hp at 5200 rpm and 360 lbs.-ft. of torque at 4000 rpm. The throaty V-8 was said to have had "an appropriately tuned Pontiac exhaust note." While sharing its basic configuration with the first-level Corvette, the GTO V-8 has been modified with a high-lift camshaft and increased air induction. These changes create greater horsepower and low-end torque than the standard Monaro offers. The changes are designed to meet the needs of American drivers.

Geared up for handling and performance

Although performance testing of the GTO had not been completed at the time this catalog went to press, the production model was expected have a 0-to-60 acceleration time of less than 6 seconds. Pontiac estimated that it should be able to run the standing-start quarter-mile in approximately 14 seconds with a terminal speed of 105 mph. The top speed of the vehicle is expected to be about 160 mph.

Buyers will be able to mate the 2004 GTO's substantial power to either an electronically controlled Hydra-Matic 4L60-E four-speed automatic transmission or a six-speed, close-ratio manual transmission like that currently available in Corvette ZO6 models. Both transmissions will drive to the same low-geared 3.46:1 rear axle. Maximum off-the-line performance will be assured with a limited-slip differential and a three-channel traction control system that will enhance the driver's control of the car.

The GTO will feature power-assisted four-wheel ventilated disc brakes and a standard four-channel anti-lock braking system. Additional standard safety features will include dual front airbags, side airbags, a three-point safety belt system at all seating positions and an "emergency mode" that will automatically shut down the engine, turn off the fuel pump, unlock the doors, and illuminate the dome light any time the airbags are deployed.

Performance-oriented interior

The 2004 GTO will seat four adults in a 2+2 configuration on front and rear bucket seats. Customers will have a choice of standard black leather seats or color-coordinated leather seats. The door panels and instrument panel will also be color-coordinated. A six-disc CD changer with a premium 10-speaker sound system will be standard along with cruise control, a multi-function driver information center, a remote keyless entry system and a host of other features designed to make driving easier and more fun.

Production of the 2004 Pontiac GTO will begin in September 2003 at Holden's Elizabeth plant. Pontiac said that up to 18,000 GTOs will be produced annually.

1964-74 GTO Production Breakout by Engine and Transmission

B x S	CID	Compr.	Carb.	HP	Torque	Prod.

1964

LeMans GTO (Base)

B x S	CID	Compr.	Carb.	HP	Torque	Prod.
4.06 x 3.75	389	10.75:1	1 x 4 Bbl.	325 @ 4800	428 @ 3200	24,205

LeMans GTO (Tri-Power)

B x S	CID	Compr.	Carb.	HP	Torque	Prod.
4.06 x 3.75	389	10.75:1	3 x 2 Bbl.	348 @ 4900	428 @ 3600	8,245

NOTE 1: Model-year production of GTOs by transmission type not available.

1965

LeMans GTO (Base)

B x S	CID	Compr.	Carb.	HP	Torque	Prod.
4.06 x 3.75	389	10.75:1	1 x 4 Bbl.	335 @ 5000	431 @ 3200	54,805

LeMans GTO (Tri-Power)

B x S	CID	Compr.	Carb.	HP	Torque	Prod.
4.06 x 3.75	389	10.75:1	3 x 2 Bbl.	360 @ 5200	424 @ 3600	20,547

NOTE 2: Model-year production of GTOs included 18,974 cars with automatic transmission and 56,378 cars with manual transmission.

1966

GTO (Base)

B x S	CID	Compr.	Carb.	HP	Torque	Prod.
4.06 x 3.75	389	10.75:1	1 x 4 Bbl.	335 @ 5000	431 @ 3200	77,901

GTO (Tri-Power)

B x S	CID	Compr.	Carb.	HP	Torque	Prod.
4.06 x 3.75	389	10.75:1	3 x 2 Bbl.	360 @ 5200	424 @ 3600	19,045

NOTE 3: Model-year production of GTOs included 35,667 cars with automatic transmission and 61,279 cars with manual transmission.

1967

GTO (Econmy option)

B x S	CID	Compr.	Carb.	HP	Torque	Prod.
4.12 x 3.75	400	8.6:1	1 x 2 Bbl.	255 @ 4400	397 @ 2400	2,967

GTO (Base)

B x S	CID	Compr.	Carb.	HP	Torque	Prod.
4.12 x 3.75	400	10.75:1	1 x 4 Bbl.	335 @ 5000	441 @ 3400	64,177

GTO (H.O.)

B x S	CID	Compr.	Carb.	HP	Torque	Prod.
4.12 x 3.75	400	10.75:1	1 x 4 Bbl.	360 @ 5100	438 @ 3600	13,827

Ram Air GTO

B x S	CID	Compr.	Carb.	HP	Torque	Prod.
4.12 x 3.75	400	10.75:1	1 x 4 Bbl.	360 @ 5400	438 @ 3800	751

NOTE 4: Model-year production of GTOs included 42,594 cars with automatic transmission and 39,128 cars with manual transmission.

1968

GTO (Economy option)
Hardtop (Automatic transmission)

B x S	CID	Compr.	Carb.	HP	Torque	Prod.
4.12 x 3.75	400	8.6:1	1 x 2 Bbl.	265 @ 4600	397 @ 2400	2,841

Convertible (Automatic transmission)

B x S	CID	Compr.	Carb.	HP	Torque	Prod.
4.12 x 3.75	400	8.6:1	1 x 2 Bbl.	265 @ 4600	397 @ 2400	432

GTO (Base)
Hardtop (Automatic transmission)

B x S	CID	Compr.	Carb.	HP	Torque	Prod.
4.12 x 3.75	400	10.75:1	1 x 4 Bbl.	350 @ 5000	445 @ 3000	39,215

Hardtop (Manual transmission)

B x S	CID	Compr.	Carb.	HP	Torque	Prod.
4.12 x 3.75	400	10.75:1	1 x 4 Bbl.	350 @ 5000	445 @ 3000	25,371

Convertible (Automatic transmission)

B x S	CID	Compr.	Carb.	HP	Torque	Prod.
4.12 x 3.75	400	10.75:1	1 x 4 Bbl.	350 @ 5000	445 @ 3000	5,091

Convertible (Manual transmission)

B x S	CID	Compr.	Carb.	HP	Torque	Prod.
4.12 x 3.75	400	10.75:1	1 x 4 Bbl.	350 @ 5000	445 @ 3000	3,116

GTO (H.O.)
Hardtop (Automatic transmission)

B x S	CID	Compr.	Carb.	HP	Torque	Prod.
4.12 X 3.75	400	10.75:1	1 x 4 Bbl.	360 @ 5100	445 @ 3600	3,140

Hardtop (Manual transmission)

B x S	CID	Compr.	Carb.	HP	Torque	Prod.
4.12 X 3.75	400	10.75:1	1 x 4 Bbl.	360 @ 5100	445 @ 3600	6,197

Convertible (Automatic transmission)

B x S	CID	Compr.	Carb.	HP	Torque	Prod.
4.12 X 3.75	400	10.75:1	1 x 4 Bbl.	360 @ 5100	445 @ 3600	461

Convertible (Manual transmission)

B x S	CID	Compr.	Carb.	HP	Torque	Prod.
4.12 X 3.75	400	10.75:1	1 x 4 Bbl.	360 @ 5100	445 @ 3600	766

Ram Air GTO (Early)

B x S	CID	Compr.	Carb.	HP	Torque	Prod.
4.12 X 3.75	400	10.75:1	1 x 4 Bbl.	360 @ 5400	445 @ 3600	751

Ram Air GTO (Late)

B x S	CID	Compr.	Carb.	HP	Torque	Prod.
4.12 X 3.75	400	10.75:1	1 x 4 Bbl.	370 @ 5500	445 @ 3900	751

NOTE 5: Combined production of 1968 GTOs with early and late Ram Air V-8s included 183 hardtops with automatic transmission, 757 hardtops with automatic transmission, 22 convertibles with automatic transmission, and 92 convertibles with manual transmission.

1969

GTO (Economy option)
Hardtop (Automatic transmission)

B x S	CID	Compr.	Carb.	HP	Torque	Prod.
4.12 x 3.75	400	8.6:1	1 x 2 Bbl.	265 @ 4600	397 @ 2400	1,246

Convertible (Automatic transmission)

B x S	CID	Compr.	Carb.	HP	Torque	Prod.
4.12 x 3.75	400	8.6:1	1 x 2 Bbl.	265 @ 4600	397 @ 2400	215

GTO (Base)
Hardtop (Automatic transmission)

B x S	CID	Compr.	Carb.	HP	Torque	Prod.
4.12 x 3.75	400	10.75:1	1 x 4 Bbl.	350 @ 5000	445 @ 3000	32,744

Hardtop (Manual transmission)

B x S	CID	Compr.	Carb.	HP	Torque	Prod.
4.12 x 3.75	400	10.75:1	1 x 4 Bbl.	350 @ 5000	445 @ 3000	22,032

Convertible (Automatic transmission)

B x S	CID	Compr.	Carb.	HP	Torque	Prod.
4.12 x 3.75	400	10.75:1	1 x 4 Bbl.	350 @ 5000	445 @ 3000	4,385

Convertible (Manual transmission)

B x S	CID	Compr.	Carb.	HP	Torque	Prod.
4.12 x 3.75	400	10.75:1	1 x 4 Bbl.	350 @ 5000	445 @ 3000	2,415

GTO (Ram Air III)
Hardtop (Automatic transmission)

B x S	CID	Compr.	Carb.	HP	Torque	Prod.
4.12 X 3.75	400	10.75:1	1 x 4 Bbl.	366 @ 5100	445 @ 3600	1,986

Hardtop (Manual transmission)

B x S	CID	Compr.	Carb.	HP	Torque	Prod.
4.12 X 3.75	400	10.75:1	1 x 4 Bbl.	366 @ 5100	445 @ 3600	6,143

Convertible (Automatic transmission)

B x S	CID	Compr.	Carb.	HP	Torque	Prod.
4.12 X 3.75	400	10.75:1	1 x 4 Bbl.	366 @ 5100	445 @ 3600	113

Convertible (Manual transmission)

B x S	CID	Compr.	Carb.	HP	Torque	Prod.
4.12 X 3.75	400	10.75:1	1 x 4 Bbl.	366 @ 5100	445 @ 3600	249

GTO (Ram Air IV)

Type	B x S	CID	Compr.	Carb.	HP	Torque	Prod.
Hardtop (Automatic transmission)	4.12 X 3.75	400	10.75:1	1 x 4 Bbl.	370 @ 5500	445 @ 3900	151
Hardtop (Manual transmission)	4.12 X 3.75	400	10.75:1	1 x 4 Bbl.	370 @ 5500	445 @ 3900	549
Convertible (Automatic transmission)	4.12 X 3.75	400	10.75:1	1 x 4 Bbl.	370 @ 5500	445 @ 3900	14
Convertible (Manual transmission)	4.12 X 3.75	400	10.75:1	1 x 4 Bbl.	370 @ 5500	445 @ 3900	45

1970

GTO (Base)

Type	B x S	CID	Compr.	Carb.	HP	Torque	Prod.
Hardtop (Automatic transmission)	4.12 x 3.75	400	10.25:1	1 x 4 Bbl.	350 @ 5000	445 @ 3000	18,148
Hardtop (Manual transmission)	4.12 x 3.75	400	10.25:1	1 x 4 Bbl.	350 @ 5000	445 @ 3000	9,348
Convertible (Automatic transmission)	4.12 x 3.75	400	10.25:1	1 x 4 Bbl.	350 @ 5000	445 @ 3000	2,173
Convertible (Manual transmission)	4.12 x 3.75	400	10.25:1	1 x 4 Bbl.	350 @ 5000	445 @ 3000	887

GTO (Ram Air III)

Type	B x S	CID	Compr.	Carb.	HP	Torque	Prod.
Hardtop (Automatic transmission)	4.12 X 3.75	400	10.50:1	1 x 4 Bbl.	366 @ 5100	445 @ 3600	1,302
Hardtop (Manual transmission)	4.12 X 3.75	400	10.50:1	1 x 4 Bbl.	366 @ 5100	445 @ 3600	3,054
Convertible (Automatic transmission)	4.12 X 3.75	400	10.50:1	1 x 4 Bbl.	366 @ 5100	445 @ 3600	114
Convertible (Manual transmission)	4.12 X 3.75	400	10.50:1	1 x 4 Bbl.	366 @ 5100	445 @ 3600	174

GTO (Ram Air IV)

Type	B x S	CID	Compr.	Carb.	HP	Torque	Prod.
Hardtop (Automatic transmission)	4.12 X 3.75	400	10.50:1	1 x 4 Bbl.	370 @ 5500	445 @ 3900	140
Hardtop (Manual transmission)	4.12 X 3.75	400	10.50:1	1 x 4 Bbl.	370 @ 5500	445 @ 3900	627
Convertible (Automatic transmission)	4.12 X 3.75	400	10.50:1	1 x 4 Bbl.	370 @ 5500	445 @ 3900	13
Convertible (Manual transmission)	4.12 X 3.75	400	10.50:1	1 x 4 Bbl.	370 @ 5500	445 @ 3900	24

GTO (455 Four-Barrel)

Type	B x S	CID	Compr.	Carb.	HP	Torque	Prod.
Hardtop (Automatic transmission)	4.15 X 4.21	455	10.00:1	1 x 4 Bbl.	360 @ 4300	500 @ 2700	1,986
Hardtop (Manual transmission)	4.15 X 4.21	455	10.00:1	1 x 4 Bbl.	360 @ 4300	500 @ 2700	1,761
Convertible (Automatic transmission)	4.15 X 4.21	455	10.00:1	1 x 4 Bbl.	360 @ 4300	500 @ 2700	241
Convertible (Manual transmission)	4.15 X 4.21	455	10.00:1	1 x 4 Bbl.	360 @ 4300	500 @ 2700	158

1971

GTO (Base)

Type	B x S	CID	Compr.	Carb.	HP	Torque	Prod.
Hardtop (Automatic transmission)	4.12 x 3.75	400	8.2:1	1 x 4 Bbl.	300 @ 4800	400 @ 3600	6,421
Hardtop (Manual transmission)	4.12 x 3.75	400	8.2:1	1 x 4 Bbl.	300 @ 4800	400 @ 3600	2,011
Convertible (Automatic transmission)	4.12 x 3.75	400	8.2:1	1 x 4 Bbl.	300 @ 4800	400 @ 3600	508
Convertible (Manual transmission)	4.12 x 3.75	400	8.2:1	1 x 4 Bbl.	300 @ 4800	400 @ 3600	79

GTO (455)

Type	B x S	CID	Compr.	Carb.	HP	Torque	Prod.
Hardtop (Automatic transmission)	4.15 X 4.21	455	8.2:1	1 x 4 Bbl.	325 @ 4400	455 @ 3200	534
Convertible (Automatic transmission)	4.15 X 4.21	455	8.2:1	1 x 4 Bbl.	325 @ 4400	455 @ 3200	43

GTO (455 H.O.)

Type	B x S	CID	Compr.	Carb.	HP	Torque	Prod.
Hardtop (Automatic transmission)	4.15 X 4.21	455	8.4:1	1 x 4 Bbl.QJ	335 @ 4800	480 @ 3600	412
Hardtop (Manual transmission)	4.15 X 4.21	455	8.4:1	1 x 4 Bbl.QJ	335 @ 4800	480 @ 3600	476
Convertible (Automatic transmission)	4.15 X 4.21	455	8.4:1	1 x 4 Bbl.QJ	335 @ 4800	480 @ 3600	27
Convertible (Manual transmission)	4.15 X 4.21	455	8.4:1	1 x 4 Bbl.QJ	335 @ 4800	480 @ 3600	21

1972

GTO (Base)

Type	B x S	CID	Compr.	Carb.	HP	Torque	Prod.
Hardtop (Automatic transmission)	4.12 x 3.75	400	8.2:1	1 x 4 Bbl.	250 @ 4400	325 @ 3200	3,284
Hardtop (Manual transmission)	4.12 x 3.75	400	8.2:1	1 x 4 Bbl.	250 @ 4400	325 @ 3200	1,519
Coupe (Automatic transmission)	4.12 x 3.75	400	8.2:1	1 x 4 Bbl.	250 @ 4400	325 @ 3200	60
Coupe (Manual transmission)	4.12 x 3.75	400	8.2:1	1 x 4 Bbl.	250 @ 4400	325 @ 3200	59

GTO (455)

Type	B x S	CID	Compr.	Carb.	HP	Torque	Prod.
Hardtop (Automatic transmission)	4.15 X 4.21	455	8.2:1	1 x 4 Bbl.	250 @ 3600	370 @ 2400	235
Coupe (Automatic transmission)	4.15 X 4.21	455	8.2:1	1 x 4 Bbl.	250 @ 3600	370 @ 2400	5

GTO (455 H.O.)

Type	B x S	CID	Compr.	Carb.	HP	Torque	Prod.
Hardtop (Automatic transmission)	4.15 X 4.21	455	8.4:1	1 x 4 Bbl.QJ	300 @ 4000	415 @ 3200	325
Hardtop (Manual transmission)	4.15 X 4.21	455	8.4:1	1 x 4 Bbl.QJ	300 @ 4000	415 @ 3200	310
Coupe (Automatic transmission)	4.15 X 4.21	455	8.4:1	1 x 4 Bbl.QJ	300 @ 4000	415 @ 3200	7
Coupe (Manual transmission)	4.15 X 4.21	455	8.4:1	1 x 4 Bbl.QJ	300 @ 4000	415 @ 3200	3

1973

GTO (Base)

Type	B x S	CID	Compr.	Carb.	HP	Torque	Prod.
Sport Coupe (Automatic transmission)	4.12 x 3.75	400	8.0:1	1 x 4 Bbl.	230 @ 4400	325 @ 3200	2,867
Sport Coupe (Manual transmission)	4.12 x 3.75	400	8.0:1	1 x 4 Bbl.	230 @ 4400	325 @ 3200	926
Coupe (Automatic transmission)	4.12 x 3.75	400	8.0:1	1 x 4 Bbl.	230 @ 4400	325 @ 3200	282
Coupe (Manual transmission)	4.12 x 3.75	400	8.0:1	1 x 4 Bbl.	230 @ 4400	325 @ 3200	187

GTO (455)

Type	B x S	CID	Compr.	Carb.	HP	Torque	Prod.
Sport Coupe (Automatic transmission)	4.15 X 4.21	455	8.0:1	1 x 4 Bbl.	250 @ 4000	370 @ 2800	519
Coupe (Automatic transmission)	4.15 X 4.21	455	8.0:1	1 x 4 Bbl.	250 @ 4000	370 @ 2800	25

1974

GTO (Base)

Type	B x S	CID	Compr.	Carb.	HP	Torque	Prod.
Coupe (Automatic transmission)	3.88 x 3.53	350	7.6:1	1 x 4 Bbl.	200 @ 4400	295 @ 2800	2,848
Coupe (Manual transmission)	3.88 x 3.53	350	7.6:1	1 x 4 Bbl.	200 @ 4400	295 @ 2800	2,487
Hatchback (Automatic transmission)	3.88 x 3.53	350	7.6:1	1 x 4 Bbl.	200 @ 4400	295 @ 2800	1,036
Hatchback (Manual transmission)	3.88 x 3.53	350	7.6:1	1 x 4 Bbl.	200 @ 4400	295 @ 2800	687

Table abbreviations:

Compr.=Compression

Carb.=Carburetion

QJ=Quadra-Jet

BxS=Bore & Stroke

CID=Cubic-inch Displacement

1961-81
Tempest—Le Mans—GTO —Grand Am—Can Am

Model-Year Production

1961

Tempest
2 dr sdn	7,432
4 dr sdn	22,557
wgn, 6-pass	7,404
SUB-TOTAL:	37,393

Tempest Custom
2 dr sdn	7,455
4 dr sdn	40,082
wgn, 6-pass	15,853
SUB-TOTAL:	63,390

1961 TOTAL:	100,783

1962

Tempest
2 dr sdn	15,473
4 dr sdn	16,057
wgn, 6-pass	6,504
SUB-TOTAL:	38,034

Tempest Custom
2 dr sdn	12,319
4 dr sdn	21,373
2 dr conv	5,076
wgn, 6-pass	11,170
SUB-TOTAL:	49,938

Tempest LeMans
2 dr sdn	39,662
3 dr conv	15,559
SUB-TOTAL:	55,221

1962 TOTAL:	143,193

1963

Tempest
2 dr sdn	13,307
4 dr sdn	12,808
wgn, 6-pass	4,203
SUB-TOTAL:	30,318

Tempest Custom
2 dr sdn	13,157
4 dr sdn	15,413
2 dr conv	5,012
wgn, 6-pass	5,932
SUB-TOTAL:	39,514

Tempest LeMans
2 dr sdn	45,701
2 dr conv	15,957
SUB-TOTAL:	61,658

1963 TOTAL:	131,490

1964

Tempest
2 dr sdn	21,765
4 dr sdn	19,427
wgn, 6-pass	6,834
SUB-TOTAL:	48,026

Tempest Custom
2 dr sdn	25,833
4 dr sdn	29,948
2 dr conv	7,987
wgn, 6-pass	10,696
SUB-TOTAL:	74,464

LeMans
2 dr sdn	31,317
2 dr hdtp	31,310
2 dr conv	17,559
SUB-TOTAL:	80,186

LeMans GTO
2 dr sdn	7,384
2 dr hdtp	18,422
2 dr conv	6,644
SUB-TOTAL:	32,450

1964 TOTAL:	235,126

1965

Tempest
2 dr sdn	18,198
4 dr sdn	15,705
wgn, 6-pass	5,622
SUB-TOTAL:	39,525

Tempest Custom
2 dr sdn	18,367
2 dr hdtp	25,242
4 dr sdn	21,906
3 dr conv	8,346
wgn, 6-pass	10,792
SUB-TOTAL:	84653

LeMans
2 dr sdn	18,881
4 dr sdn	14,227
2 dr hdtp	60,548
2 dr conv	13,897
SUB-TOTAL:	107,553

LeMans GTO
2 dr sdn	8,319
2 dr hdtp	55,722
2 dr conv	11,311
SUB-TOTAL:	75,352

1965 TOTAL:	307,083

1966

Tempest
2 dr sdn	22,266
4 dr sdn	17,392
wgn, 6-pass	4,095
SUB-TOTAL:	43,753

Tempest Custom
2 dr sdn	17,182
4 dr sdn	23,988
2 dr hdtp	31,322
4 dr hdtp	10,996
2 dr conv	5,557
wgn, 6-pass	7,614
SUB-TOTAL:	96,659

LeMans
2 dr sdn	16,654
2 dr hdtp	78,109
4 dr hdtp	13,897
2 dr conv	13,080
SUB-TOTAL:	121,740

GTO
2 dr sdn	10,363
2 dr hdtp	73,785
2 dr conv	12,798
SUB-TOTAL:	96,946

1966 TOTAL:	359,098

1967

Tempest
2 dr sdn	17,978
4 dr sdn	13,136
wgn, 6-pass	3,495
SUB-TOTAL:	34,609

Tempest Custom
2 d sdn	12,469
4 dr sdn	17,445
2 dr hdtp	30,512
4 dr hdtp	5,493
2 dr conv	4,082
wgn, 6-pass	5,324
SUB-TOTAL:	75,325

LeMans
2 dr sdn	10,693
2 dr hdtp	75,965
4 dr hdtp	8,424
2 dr conv	9,820
SUB TOTAL:	104,902

GTO
2 dr sdn	7,029
2 dr hdtp	65,176
2 dr conv	9,517
SUB-TOTAL:	81,722

Tempest Safari
wgn, 6-pass	4,511
SUB-TOTAL:	4,511

1967 TOTAL:	301,069

1968

Tempest
2d sdn	19,991
4 dr sdn	11,590
SUB-TOTAL:	31,581

Tempest Custom
2 dr sdn	10,634
4 dr sdn	17,304
2 dr hdtp	40,574
4 dr hdtp	6,147
2 dr conv	3,518
wgn. 6-pass	8,253
SUB-TOTAL:	86,430

LeMans
2 dr sdn	8,439
2 dr hdtp	110,036
4 dr hdtp	9,002
2 dr conv	8,820
SUB-TOTAL:	136,297

GTO
2 dr hdtp	77,704
2 dr conv	9,980
SUB-TOTAL:	87,684

Tempest Safari
wgn, 6-pass	4,414
1968 TOTAL:	346,406

1969

Tempest
2 dr sdn	17,181

4 dr sdn 9,741
SUB-TOTAL: 26,922

Tempest Custom
2 dr sdn 7,912
4 dr sdn 16,532
2 dr hdtp 46,886
4 dr hdtp 3,918
2 dr conv 2,379
wgn, 6-pass 6,963
SUB-TOTAL: 84,590

LeMans
2 dr sdn 5,033
2 dr hdtp 82,817
4 dr hdtp 6,475
2 dr conv 5,676
wgn, 6-pass 4,115
SUB-TOTAL: 104,116

GTO
2 dr hdtp 58,126
2 dr conv 7,328
Judge hdtp 6,725
Judge conv 108
SUB-TOTAL: 72,287

1969 TOTAL: 287,915

1970

Tempest
2 dr sdn 11,977
T-37 2 dr hdtp 9,187
4 dr sdn 20,883
SUB-TOTAL: 42,047

LeMans
2 dr sdn 5,656
2 dr hdtp 15,255
4 dr hdtp 52,304
2 dr conv 3,872
wgn, 6-pass 7,165
SUB-TOTAL: 84,252

LeMans Sport
2 dr sdn 1,673
2 dr hdtp 58,356
4 dr hdtp 3,657
2 dr conv 4,670
wgn, 6-pass 3,823
SUB-TOTAL: 72,179

GTO
2 dr hdtp 32,737
2 dr conv 3,615
Judge hdtp 3,629
Judge conv 168
SUB-TOTAL: 40,149

1970 TOTAL: 238,627

1971

T-37
2 dr sdn 7,184
2 dr hdtp 8,336
4 dr sdn 29,466
SUB-TOTAL: 44,986

LeMans
2 dr sdn 2,374
4 dr sdn 11,979
2 dr hdtp 40,966
4 dr hdtp 3,186
2 dr conv 6,311
wgn, 6-pass 4,363
SUB-TOTAL: 69,179

LeMans Sport
2 dr hdtp 34,625
4 dr hdtp 2,451
2 dr conv 3,865
SUB-TOTAL: 40,941

GTO
2 dr hdtp 9,497
2 dr conv 661
Judge hdtp 357
Judge conv 17
SUB-TOTAL: 10,532

1971 TOTAL: 165,638

1972

LeMans
2 dr sdn 6,855
4 dr sdn 19,463
2 dr hdtp 80,383
4 dr hdtp 3,438
2 dr conv 8,332
wgn, 6-pass 5,266
SUB-TOTAL: 123,737

LeMans Sport
2 dr hdtp 37,615
4 dr hdtp 8,641
SUB-TOTAL: 46,256

1972 TOTAL: 169,993
Includes 5,807 LeMans GTO.

1973

LeMans
2 dr sdn 68,230
4 dr sdn 26,554
wgn, 6-pass 10,446
wgn, 9-pass 6,127
SUB-TOTAL: 111,357

LeMans Sport
2 dr sdn 50,999
SUB-TOTAL: 50,999

Luxury LeMans
2 dr sdn 33,916
4 dr sdn 9,377
SUB-TOTAL: 43,293

Grand Am
2 dr sdn 34,445
4 dr sdn 8,691
SUB-TOTAL: 43,136

1973 TOTAL: 248,785
Includes 4,806 LeMans GTO.

1974

Ventura
2 dr sdn 47,782
2 dr htbk 16,694
SUB-TOTAL: 81,799

Includes 7,058 Venturas with the GTO option package.

LeMans
2 dr sdn 37,061
4 dr sdn 17,266
wgn, 6-pass 4,743
wgn, 9-pass 3,004
SUB-TOTAL: 62,074

LeMans Sport
2 dr sdn 37,955
SUB-TOTAL: 37,955

Luxury LeMans
2 dr sdn 25,882
4 dr sdn 4,513
wgn, 6-pass 952
wgn, 9-pass 1,178
SUB-TOTAL: 32,525

Grand Am
2 dr sdn 13,961
4 dr sdn 3,122
SUB-TOTAL: 17,083

1974 TOTAL: 231,436

1975

LeMans
2 dr sdn 20,636
4 dr sdn 15,065
wgn, 6-pass 3,988
wgn, 9-pass 2,393
SUB-TOTAL: 42,082

LeMans Sport
2 dr sdn 23,817
SUB-TOTAL: 23,817

Grand LeMans
2 dr sdn 19,310
4 dr sdn 4,906
wgn, 6-pass 1,393
wgn, 9-pass 1,501
SUB-TOTAL: 27,110

Grand Am
2 dr sdn 8,786
4 dr sdn 1,893
SUB-TOTAL: 10,679

1975 TOTAL: 103,688

1976

LeMans
2 dr sdn 21,130
4 dr sdn 22,199
wgn, 6-pass 8,249
wgn, 9-pass 5,901
SUB-TOTAL: 57,479

LeMans Sport
2 dr sdn 15,582
SUB-TOTAL: 15,582

Grand LeMans
2 dr sdn 14,757
4 dr sdn 8,411
SUB-TOTAL: 23,168

1976 TOTAL: 96,229

1977

LeMans
2 dr sdn 16,038
4 dr sdn 23,060
wgn, 6-pass 10,081
SUB-TOTAL: 49,179

LeMans Sport
LeMans Sport 12,277
SUB-TOTAL: 12,277

Grand LeMans
2 dr sdn 7,851
4 dr sdn 5,584
wgn, 6-pass 5,393
SUB-TOTAL: 18,828

Can Am 1,377

1977 TOTAL: 81,661

1978

LeMans
2 dr sdn 20,581
4 dr sdn 22,728
wgn, 6-pass 15,714
SUB-TOTAL: 59,023

Grand LeMans
2 dr sdn 18,433
4 dr sdn 21,252
wgn, 6-pass 11,125
SUB-TOTAL: 50,810

Grand Am
2 dr sdn 7,767
4 dr sdn 2,841
SUB-TOTAL: 10,608

1978 TOTAL: 120,441

1979

LeMans
2 dr sdn 14,197
4 dr sdn 26,958
wgn, 6-pass 27,518
SUB-TOTAL: 68,673

Grand leMans
2 dr sdn 13,020
4 dr sdn 28,577
wgn, 6-pass 20,783
SUB-TOTAL: 62,380

Grand Am
2 dr sdn 4,021
4 dr sdn 1,865
SUB-TOTAL: 5,886

1979 TOTAL: 136,939

1980

LeMans
2 dr sdn 9,110
4 dr sdn 20,485
wgn, 6-pass 12,912
SUB-TOTAL: 42,507

Grand LeMans
2 dr sdn 6,477
4 dr sdn 18,561
wgn, 6-pass 14,832
SUB-TOTAL: 39,870

Grand Am
Grand Am 1,647
SUB-TOTAL: 1,647

1980 TOTAL: 84,024

1981

LeMans
2 dr sdn 2,578
4 dr sdn 22,186
wgn, 6-pass 13,358
SUB-TOTAL: 38,122

Grand LeMans
2 dr sdn 1,819
4 dr sdn 25,241
wgn, 6-pass 16,683
SUB-TOTAL: 43,743

1981 TOTAL: 81,865

1964-81

GTO/Tempest/LeMans

Vehicle Condition Scale

1: **Excellent:** Restored to current maximum professional standards of quality in every area, or perfect original with components operating and apearing as new. A 95-plus point show car that is not driven.

2: **Fine:** Well-restored or a combination of superior restoration and excellent original parts. Also, extremely well-maintained original vehicle showing minimal wear.

3. **Very Good:** Complete operable original or older restoration. Also, a very good amateur restoration, all presentable and serviceable inside and out. Plus, a combination of well-done restoration and good operable components or a partially restored car with all parts necessary to compete and/or valuable NOS parts.

4: **Good:** A driveable vehicle needing no or only minor work to be functional. Also, a deteriorated restoration or a very poor amateur restoration. All components may need restoration to be "excellent," but the car is mostly useable "as is."

5. **Restorable:** Needs complete restoration of body, chassis and interior. May or may not be running, but isn't weathered, wrecked or stripped to the point of being useful only for parts.

6. **Parts car:** May or may not be running, but is weathered, wrecked and/or stripped to the point of being useful primarily for parts.

	6	5	4	3	2	1

1961

Tempest Compact, 4-cyl.

	6	5	4	3	2	1
4d Sed	350	1,050	1,750	3,500	6,100	8,700
2d Cpe	350	1,050	1,750	3,500	6,150	8,800
2d Cus Cpe	400	1,200	2,000	4,000	7,000	10,000
4d Safari Wag	400	1,200	2,000	4,000	7,000	10,000

NOTE: Add 20 percent for Tempest V-8.

1962

Tempest, 4-cyl., 122" wb

	6	5	4	3	2	1
4d Sed	300	900	1,550	3,100	5,400	7,700
2d Cpe	300	950	1,550	3,100	5,450	7,800
2d HT	550	1,700	2,800	5,600	9,800	14,000
2d Conv	700	2,050	3,400	6,800	11,900	17,000
4d Safari	400	1,200	2,000	4,000	7,000	10,000

NOTE: Add 20 percent for Tempest V-8.

1963

Tempest (Compact), 4-cyl., 112" wb

	6	5	4	3	2	1
4d Sed	300	900	1,500	3,000	5,250	7,500
2d Cpe	400	1,200	2,000	4,000	7,000	10,000
2d HT	450	1,400	2,300	4,600	8,050	11,500
2d Conv	700	2,050	3,400	6,800	11,900	17,000
4d Sta Wag	400	1,200	2,000	4,000	7,000	10,000

NOTE: Add 20 percent for Tempest V-8.

LeMans, V-8, 112" wb

	6	5	4	3	2	1
2d HT	600	1,800	3,000	6,000	10,500	15,000
2d Conv	700	2,150	3,600	7,200	12,600	18,000

1964

Tempest Custom 21, V-8, 115" wb

	6	5	4	3	2	1
4d Sed	300	900	1,550	3,100	5,400	7,700
2d HT	450	1,400	2,300	4,600	8,050	11,500
2d Conv	700	2,050	3,400	6,800	11,900	17,000
4d Sta Wag	400	1,200	2,000	4,000	7,000	10,000

NOTE: Deduct 10 percent for 6-cyl. where available.

LeMans, V-8, 115" wb

	6	5	4	3	2	1
2d HT	700	2,050	3,400	6,800	11,900	17,000
2d Cpe	600	1,850	3,100	6,200	10,900	15,500
2d Conv	700	2,150	3,600	7,200	12,600	18,000
2d GTO Cpe	850	2,500	4,200	8,400	14,700	21,000
2d GTO Conv	1,100	3,250	5,400	10,800	18,900	27,000
2d GTO HT	900	2,750	4,600	9,200	16,100	23,000

NOTE: Deduct 20 percent for Tempest 6-cyl.

1965

Tempest, V-8, 115" wb

	6	5	4	3	2	1
4d Sed	350	1,050	1,700	3,450	6,000	8,600
2d Spt Cpe	400	1,200	2,000	4,050	7,050	10,100
2d HT	450	1,400	2,300	4,600	8,050	11,500
2d Conv	600	1,800	3,000	6,000	10,500	15,000
4d Sta Wag	400	1,200	2,000	4,000	7,000	10,000

NOTE: Add 20 percent for V-8.

LeMans, V-8, 115" wb

	6	5	4	3	2	1
4d Sed	400	1,200	2,000	4,000	7,000	10,000
2d Cpe	450	1,400	2,300	4,600	8,050	11,500
2d HT	600	1,850	3,100	6,200	10,900	15,500
2d Conv	800	2,400	4,000	8,000	14,000	20,000
2d GTO Conv	1,150	3,500	5,800	11,600	20,300	29,000
2d GTO HT	1,000	3,000	5,000	10,000	17,500	25,000
2d GTO Cpe	900	2,750	4,600	9,200	16,100	23,000

NOTE: Deduct 20 percent for 6-cyl. where available. Add 5 percent for 4-speed.

1966

Tempest Custom, OHC-6, 115" wb

	6	5	4	3	2	1
4d Sed	350	1,050	1,700	3,450	6,000	8,600
4d HT	400	1,150	1,950	3,900	6,800	9,700
2d HT	550	1,700	2,850	5,700	10,000	14,300
2d Cpe	450	1,300	2,200	4,400	7,700	11,000
2d Conv	600	1,800	3,000	6,000	10,500	15,000
4d Sta Wag	350	1,000	1,700	3,400	5,950	8,500

NOTE: Add 20 percent for V-8.

Lemans, OHC-6, 115" wb

	6	5	4	3	2	1
4d HT	400	1,200	2,000	4,000	7,000	10,000
2d Cpe	450	1,300	2,150	4,300	7,550	10,800
2d HT	600	1,800	3,000	6,000	10,500	15,000
2d Conv	650	2,000	3,300	6,600	11,600	16,500

NOTE: Add 20 percent for V-8.

GTO, V-8, 115" wb

	6	5	4	3	2	1
2d HT	900	2,650	4,400	8,800	15,400	22,000
2d Cpe	800	2,400	4,000	8,000	14,000	20,000
2d Conv	1,100	3,250	5,400	10,800	18,900	27,000

NOTE: Add 5 percent for 4-speed. Add 20 percent for tri power option.

1967

Tempest, 6-cyl., 115" wb

	6	5	4	3	2	1
4d Sed	350	1,000	1,700	3,400	5,950	8,500
2d Cpe	400	1,200	2,000	4,000	7,000	10,000
4d Sta Wag	400	1,250	2,100	4,250	7,400	10,600

NOTE: Add 20 percent for V-8.

Tempest Custom, 6-cyl., 115" wb

	6	5	4	3	2	1
2d Cpe	400	1,200	2,000	4,050	7,050	10,100
2d HT	450	1,400	2,300	4,650	8,100	11,600
2d Conv	600	1,800	3,000	6,000	10,500	15,000
4d HT	400	1,200	2,050	4,100	7,150	10,200
4d Sed	350	1,050	1,700	3,450	6,000	8,600
4d Sta Wag	400	1,200	2,000	4,000	7,000	10,000

NOTE: Add 20 percent for V-8.

Lemans, 6-cyl., 115" wb

	6	5	4	3	2	1
4d HT	400	1,200	2,000	4,000	7,000	10,000
2d Cpe	400	1,200	2,050	4,100	7,150	10,200
2d HT	550	1,700	2,800	5,600	9,800	14,000
2d Conv	650	2,000	3,300	6,600	11,600	16,500

NOTE: Add 20 percent for V-8.

Tempest Safari, 6-cyl., 115" wb

	6	5	4	3	2	1
4d Sta Wag	400	1,200	2,000	4,000	7,000	10,000

NOTE: Add 20 percent for V-8.

GTO, V-8, 115" wb

	6	5	4	3	2	1
2d Cpe	700	2,150	3,600	7,200	12,600	18,000
2d HT	850	2,500	4,200	8,400	14,700	21,000
2d Conv	950	2,900	4,800	9,600	16,800	24,000

NOTE: Add 10 percent for Ram Air 400 GTO.

1968

Tempest, 6-cyl., 112" wb

	6	5	4	3	2	1
2d Spt Cpe	400	1,200	2,000	4,000	7,000	10,000
2d Cus "S" Cpe	400	1,250	2,100	4,200	7,350	10,500
2d Cus "S" HT	550	1,700	2,800	5,600	9,800	14,000
2d Cus "S" Conv	600	1,800	3,000	6,000	10,500	15,000
2d LeMans	400	1,200	2,000	4,000	7,000	10,000
2d LeMans Spt Cpe	450	1,300	2,200	4,400	7,700	11,000
2d LeMans Conv	750	2,300	3,800	7,600	13,300	19,000

NOTE: Add 20 percent for V-8.

GTO, V-8, 112" wb

	6	5	4	3	2	1
2d HT	800	2,400	4,000	8,000	14,000	20,000
2d Conv	950	2,900	4,800	9,600	16,800	24,000

NOTE: Add 25 percent for Ram Air I, 40 percent for Ram Air II.

1969

Tempest, 6-cyl., 116" wb, 2d 112" wb

	6	5	4	3	2	1
4d Sed	300	950	1,600	3,250	5,650	8,100
2d Cpe	350	1,000	1,650	3,300	5,750	8,200

NOTE: Add 20 percent for V-8.

Tempest "S" Custom, 6-cyl., 116" wb, 2d 112" wb

	6	5	4	3	2	1
4d Sed	350	1,000	1,650	3,300	5,750	8,200
4d HT	350	1,000	1,700	3,350	5,900	8,400
2d Cpe	350	1,000	1,650	3,300	5,800	8,300
2d HT	450	1,300	2,200	4,400	7,700	11,000
2d Conv	550	1,700	2,800	5,600	9,800	14,000
4d Sta Wag	350	1,000	1,700	3,400	5,950	8,500

NOTE: Add 20 percent for V-8.

Jerry Heasley photo

1970 GTO

	6	5	4	3	2	1

Tempest Lemans, 6-cyl., 116" wb, 2d 112" wb

	6	5	4	3	2	1
4d HT	350	1,000	1,700	3,400	5,950	8,500
2d Cpe	350	1,000	1,700	3,350	5,900	8,400
2d HT	450	1,400	2,300	4,600	8,050	11,500
2d Conv	600	1,850	3,100	6,200	10,900	15,500

NOTE: Add 20 percent for V-8.

Tempest Safari, 6-cyl., 116" wb

	6	5	4	3	2	1
4d Sta Wag	350	1,050	1,750	3,500	6,100	8,700

NOTE: Add 20 percent for V-8.

GTO, V-8, 112" wb

	6	5	4	3	2	1
2d HT	900	2,650	4,400	8,800	15,400	22,000
2d Conv	1,050	3,100	5,200	10,400	18,200	26,000

NOTE: Add 40 percent for GTO Judge option.

1970

Tempest, 6-cyl., 116" wb, 2d 112" wb

	6	5	4	3	2	1
4d Sed	350	1,000	1,650	3,300	5,800	8,300
2d HT	450	1,300	2,200	4,400	7,700	11,000
2d Cpe	350	1,000	1,700	3,400	5,950	8,500

NOTE: Add 20 percent for V-8.

LeMans, 6 cyl., 116" wb, 2d 112" wb

	6	5	4	3	2	1
4d Sed	350	1,000	1,700	3,350	5,900	8,400
4d HT	400	1,200	2,000	4,000	7,000	10,000
2d Cpe	350	1,050	1,700	3,450	6,000	8,600
2d HT	450	1,400	2,300	4,600	8,050	11,500
4d Sta Wag	350	1,050	1,750	3,500	6,150	8,800

NOTE: Add 20 percent for V-8.

LeMans Sport, 6-cyl., 116" wb, 2d 112" wb

	6	5	4	3	2	1
4d HT	400	1,200	2,050	4,100	7,150	10,200
2d Cpe	400	1,250	2,100	4,200	7,350	10,500
2d HT	550	1,700	2,800	5,600	9,800	14,000
2d Conv	600	1,750	2,900	5,800	10,200	14,500
4d Sta Wag	400	1,200	2,000	4,000	7,000	10,000

NOTE: Add 20 percent for V-8.

LeMans GT 37, V-8, 112" wb

	6	5	4	3	2	1
2d Cpe	550	1,700	2,800	5,600	9,800	14,000
2d HT	600	1,850	3,100	6,200	10,900	15,500

GTO, V-8, 112" wb

	6	5	4	3	2	1
2d HT	900	2,750	4,600	9,200	16,100	23,000
2d Conv	1,100	3,250	5,400	10,800	18,900	27,000

NOTE: Add 40 percent for GTO Judge option.

1971

LeMans T37, 6-cyl., 116" wb, 2d 112" wb

	6	5	4	3	2	1
2d Sed	350	1,000	1,700	3,400	5,950	8,500
4d Sed	300	950	1,600	3,200	5,600	8,000
2d HT	450	1,300	2,200	4,400	7,700	11,000

LeMans, 6-cyl., 116" wb, 2d 112" wb

	6	5	4	3	2	1
2d Sed	300	950	1,600	3,250	5,650	8,100
4d Sed	300	950	1,600	3,200	5,600	8,000
4d HT	400	1,150	1,900	3,750	6,600	9,400
2d HT	550	1,700	2,800	5,600	9,800	14,000
4d 3S Sta Wag	400	1,150	1,900	3,800	6,650	9,500

LeMans Sport, 6-cyl., 116" wb, 2d 112" wb

	6	5	4	3	2	1
4d HT	400	1,150	1,900	3,800	6,650	9,500
2d HT	600	1,750	2,900	5,800	10,200	14,500
2d Conv	650	1,900	3,200	6,400	11,200	16,000

NOTE: Add 20 percent for V-8.

LeMans GT 37, V-8, 112" wb

	6	5	4	3	2	1
2d HT	650	1,900	3,200	6,400	11,200	16,000

GTO

	6	5	4	3	2	1
2d HT	850	2,500	4,200	8,400	14,700	21,000
2d Conv	1,150	3,500	5,800	11,600	20,300	29,000

NOTE: Add 40 percent for GTO Judge option.

1964 GTO

1965 GTO

	6	5	4	3	2	1

1972

LeMans, 6-cyl., 116" wb, 2d 112" wb

	6	5	4	3	2	1
2d Cpe	300	900	1,500	3,000	5,250	7,500
4d Sed	300	900	1,450	2,900	5,100	7,300
2d HT	550	1,700	2,800	5,600	9,800	14,000
2d Conv	600	1,850	3,100	6,200	10,900	15,500
4d 3S Sta Wag	300	900	1,500	3,000	5,250	7,500

GTO

	6	5	4	3	2	1
2d HT	700	2,100	3,500	7,000	12,300	17,500
2d Sed	600	1,750	2,900	5,800	10,200	14,500

Luxury LeMans, V-8

	6	5	4	3	2	1
4d HT	300	900	1,550	3,100	5,400	7,700
2d HT	600	1,750	2,900	5,800	10,200	14,500

NOTE: Add 10 percent for Endura option on LeMans models. Add 20 percent for V-8.

1973

LeMans

	6	5	4	3	2	1
4d Sed	300	850	1,400	2,800	4,900	7,000
2d HT	350	1,000	1,650	3,300	5,750	8,200

LeMans Spt

	6	5	4	3	2	1
2d Cpe	300	900	1,500	3,000	5,250	7,500

Luxury LeMans

	6	5	4	3	2	1
2d Cpe	300	900	1,550	3,100	5,400	7,700
4d HT	300	900	1,500	3,000	5,250	7,500

LeMans Safari, V-8, 116" wb

	6	5	4	3	2	1
4d 2S Sta Wag	300	850	1,400	2,800	4,900	7,000
4d 3S Sta Wag	300	850	1,400	2,850	4,950	7,100

1974

LeMans

	6	5	4	3	2	1
4d HT	200	550	950	1,900	3,300	4,700
2d HT	250	750	1,250	2,500	4,350	6,200
4d Sta Wag	200	600	1,000	2,000	3,500	5,000

LeMans Sport

	6	5	4	3	2	1
2d Cpe	200	650	1,100	2,200	3,850	5,500

Luxury LeMans

	6	5	4	3	2	1
4d HT	200	650	1,050	2,100	3,700	5,300
2d HT	250	800	1,350	2,700	4,700	6,700
4d Safari	200	650	1,100	2,200	3,850	5,500

NOTE: Add 10 percent for GT option.

1975

LeMans

	6	5	4	3	2	1
4d HT	180	540	900	1,800	3,150	4,500
2d HT	220	660	1,100	2,200	3,850	5,500
4d Safari	184	552	920	1,840	3,220	4,600

NOTE: Add 10 percent for Grand LeMans.

LeMans Sport

	6	5	4	3	2	1
2d HT Cpe	228	684	1,140	2,280	3,990	5,700

1976

LeMans, V-8

	6	5	4	3	2	1
4d Sed	192	576	960	1,920	3,360	4,800
2d Cpe	196	588	980	1,960	3,430	4,900
4d 2S Safari Wag	184	552	920	1,840	3,220	4,600
4d 3S Safari Wag	188	564	940	1,880	3,290	4,700

LeMans Sport Cpe, V-8

	6	5	4	3	2	1
2d Cpe	208	624	1,040	2,080	3,640	5,200

Grand LeMans, V-8

	6	5	4	3	2	1
4d Sed	196	588	980	1,960	3,430	4,900
2d Sed	200	600	1,000	2,000	3,500	5,000
4d 2S Safari Wag	192	576	960	1,920	3,360	4,800
4d 3S Safari Wag	196	588	980	1,960	3,430	4,900

1977

LeMans, V-8

	6	5	4	3	2	1
4d Sed	160	480	800	1,600	2,800	4,000
2d Cpe	164	492	820	1,640	2,870	4,100
4d 2S Sta Wag	156	468	780	1,560	2,730	3,900
4d 3S Sta Wag	160	480	800	1,600	2,800	4,000

LeMans Sport Cpe, V-8

	6	5	4	3	2	1
2d Cpe	208	624	1,040	2,080	3,640	5,200
	6	5	4	3	2	1

NOTE: Add 20 percent for Can Am option.

Grand LeMans, V-8

	6	5	4	3	2	1
4d Sed	164	492	820	1,640	2,870	4,100
2d Cpe	168	504	840	1,680	2,940	4,200
4d 2S Sta Wag	160	480	800	1,600	2,800	4,000
4d 3S Sta Wag	164	492	820	1,640	2,870	4,100

1978

LeMans

	6	5	4	3	2	1
4d Sed	160	480	800	1,600	2,800	4,000
2d Cpe	168	504	840	1,680	2,940	4,200
4d 2S Sta Wag	160	480	800	1,600	2,800	4,000

1969 Judge

1964 Tempest Custom

Tom Sparano photo

	6	5	4	3	2	1

Grand LeMans

	6	5	4	3	2	1
4d Sed	164	492	820	1,640	2,870	4,100
2d Cpe	172	516	860	1,720	3,010	4,300
4d 2S Sta Wag	164	492	820	1,640	2,870	4,100

1979

LeMans

	6	5	4	3	2	1
4d Sed	164	492	820	1,640	2,870	4,100
2d Cpe	172	516	860	1,720	3,010	4,300
4d Sta Wag	164	492	820	1,640	2,870	4,100

Grand LeMans

	6	5	4	3	2	1
4d Sed	168	504	840	1,680	2,940	4,200
2d Cpe	180	540	900	1,800	3,150	4,500
4d Sta Wag	168	504	840	1,680	2,940	4,200
	6	5	4	3	2	1

1980

LeMans, V-8

	6	5	4	3	2	1
4d Sed	148	444	740	1,480	2,590	3,700
2d Cpe	156	468	780	1,560	2,730	3,900
4d Sta Wag	152	456	760	1,520	2,660	3,800

NOTE: Deduct 10 percent for V-6.

Grand LeMans, V-8

	6	5	4	3	2	1
4d Sed	152	456	760	1,520	2,660	3,800
2d Cpe	160	480	800	1,600	2,800	4,000
4d Sta Wag	156	468	780	1,560	2,730	3,900

NOTE: Deduct 10 percent for V-6.

1981

LeMans, V-8

	6	5	4	3	2	1
4d Sed	156	468	780	1,560	2,730	3,900
4d Sed LJ	160	480	800	1,600	2,800	4,000
2d Cpe	160	480	800	1,600	2,800	4,000
4d Sta Wag	160	480	800	1,600	2,800	4,000

NOTE: Deduct 10 percent for V-6.

Grand LeMans, V-8

	6	5	4	3	2	1
4d Sed	184	552	920	1,840	3,220	4,600
2d Cpe	168	504	840	1,680	2,940	4,200
4d Sta Wag	168	504	840	1,680	2,940	4,200

NOTE: Deduct 10 percent for V-6.

Standard Catalogs...
your best source for history, technical specifications, pricing and more!

Created by Krause Publications 25 years ago, Standard Catalogs have become the ultimate automotive reference books. They combine history, photos, buyer's guide information, technical specifications and pricing into one handy, easy-to-use publication that tells you all there is to know about cars and trucks. You get original equipment, serial numbers, factory prices, production totals, engine data, technical specifications and current collector prices. Standard Catalogs are available by era (prewar, postwar, etc.); by type of vehicle (domestic, import, truck, etc.); by brand (Chevrolet, Ford, Chrysler, etc.) or by model (Camaro, Chevelle, Corvette, Firebird, GTO and Mustang).

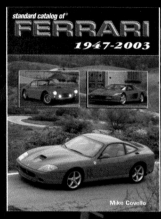

Standard Catalog of® Ferrari 1947-2002
by Mike Covello
Softcover
8-1/4 x 10-7/8
224 pages
250+ color photos
Item# FERI1
$24.99

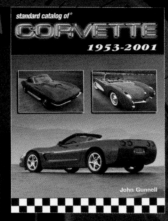

Standard Catalog of® Corvette 1953-2001
by John Gunnell
Softcover
8-1/4x10-7/8
224 pages
225 color photos
Item# VET01
$24.95

Standard Catalog of® Mustang 1964-2001
by Brad Bowling
Softcover
8-1/2x11
256 pages
300 color photos
Item# MUS01
$24.95

Standard Catalog of® Pontiac 1926-2002, 2nd Edition
by John Gunnell
Softcover • 8-1/2x11
368 pages
700+ b&w photos
16-page color section
Item# APO02
$21.95

Standard Catalog of® Camaro 1967-2002
by John Gunnell
Softcover
8-1/4x10-7/8
224 pages
200+ color photos
Item# CMRO1
$24.95

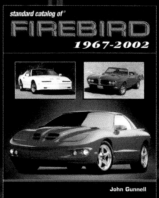

Standard Catalog of® Firebird 1967-2002
by John Gunnell
Softcover
8-1/4x10-7/8
224 pages
200+ color photos
Item# BIRD1
$24.95

Available from Krause Publications by calling 800-258-0929 or online at www.krausebooks.com. Books are also available from your local bookseller.

kp krause publications
Offer AUB3

Standard Catalog of® 4x4s 1945-2000, 2nd Edition
by Robert C. Ackerson
Softcover • 8-1/2x11 • 736 pages
300+ b&w photos • 8-page color section
Item# FX02 • $34.95

Standard Catalog of® American Light-Duty Trucks, 3rd Edition
edited by James T. Lenzke
Softcover • 8-1/2x11 • 944 pages
3,600+ b&w photos
Item# PT03 • $34.95

Standard Catalog of® Buick 1903-2000, 2nd Edition
edited by Ron Kowalke
Softcover • 8-1/2x11 • 304 pages
500 b&w photos • 8-page color section
Item# AK02 • $21.95

Standard Catalog of® Cadillac 1903-2000, 2nd Edition
edited by James T. Lenzke
Softcover • 8-1/2x11 • 304 pages
600+ b&w photos • 16-page color section
Item# AL02 • $21.95

Standard Catalog of® Chevelle 1964-1987
by John Gunnell
Softcover • 8-1/4x10-7/8 • 256 pages
150+ color photos
Item# CHVL1 • $24.99

Standard Catalog of® Chevrolet 1912-2003, 3rd Edition
by John Gunnell
Softcover • 8-1/2x11 • 520 pages
1,000+ b&w photos • 8-page color section
Item# AV03 • $24.99

Standard Catalog of® Chrysler 1914-2000, 2nd Edition
edited by James T. Lenzke
Softcover • 8-1/2x11 • 552 pages
500 b&w photos • 8-page color section
Item# AY02 • $22.95

Standard Catalog of® Ford 1903-2003, 3rd Edition
by John Gunnell
Softcover • 8-1/2x11 • 640 pages
1,800 b&w photos • 16-page color section
Item# AF03 • $24.95

Standard Catalog of® Imported Cars 1946-2002, 2nd Edition
Updated by Mike Covello
Softcover • 8-1/2x11 • 912 pages
1,500+ b&w photos
Item# AI02 • $32.95

Standard Catalog of® Jeep 1945-2002
by Patrick R. Foster
Softcover • 8-1/4x10-7/8 • 224 pages
300+ b&w photos • 300+ color photos
Item# JPSC1 • $24.99

Standard Catalog of® Light-Duty Dodge Trucks 1917-2002
by John Gunnell
Softcover • 8-1/2x11 • 264 pages
500+ b&w photos • 16-page color section
Item# LDDG1 • $24.95

Standard Catalog of® Light-Duty Ford Trucks 1905-2002
by John Gunnell
Softcover • 8-1/2x11 • 360 pages
500+ b&w photos
Item# LDFT1 • $24.95

Standard Catalog of® Oldsmobile, 1897-1997
by John Chevedden & Ron Kowalke
Softcover • 8-1/2x11 • 304 pages
800 b&w photos
Item# OLDS • $21.95

Standard Catalog of® V-8 Engines 1906-2002
by John Gunnell
Softcover • 8-1/2x11 • 264 pages
100 b&w photos
Item# VEE1 • $24.95

Muscle Mania

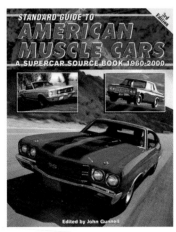

Standard Guide to American Muscle Cars
A Supercar Source Book 1960-2000, 3rd Edition

Edited by John Gunnell

This ultimate guide for muscle car collectors and enthusiasts features more than 300 American high-performance machines. Four decades of Detroit's most muscular models from Chevrolet, Chrysler, Ford, General Motors and Studebaker receive individual listings that include model history, factory specifications, and options information plus current values in six condition grades.

**Softcover • 8¼ x 10-⅞
304 pages
200+ color photos
Item# AM03 • $24.95**

75 Years of Pontiac
The Official History

by John Gunnell

From the Chief of the Sixes and Silver Streaks to the famed GTO, Firebird and Trans Am, this all-new full-color reference chronicles the rich 75-year history of Pontiac from its introduction in 1926 through today. Produced in full cooperation with Pontiac Motor Division, trace the development of the legend in this official hardcover anniversary edition featuring production figures for all models and 250 full-color photos.

**Hardcover • 11½ x 9
224 pages
250 color photos
Item# SPONT • $29.95**

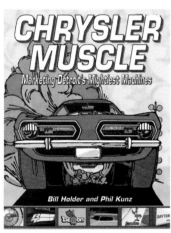

Chrysler Muscle
Marketing Detroit's Mightiest Machines

by Bill Holder and Phil Kunz

With youthful, hip, and bold marketing techniques, MOPAR left an incredible legacy! Ad campaigns with eye-popping colors and cartoon mascots-never before has the automotive business seen engines used as marketing tools similar to the pavement-pounding Plymouth and Dodge machines of the late 1960s and early 1970s. This richly illustrated presentation, with more than 200 full-color images, chronicles the mystique surrounding Chrysler's muscle cars and takes a look at how the marketing behind these cars made them desirable.

**Softcover • 8¼ x 10-⅞ • 160 pages
200+ color photos
Item# MOPAR • $24.99**

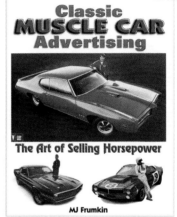

Classic Muscle Car Advertising

by MJ Frumkin

Strap yourself in for a powerful, historic ride through muscle car advertisements of the '50s, '60s, and '70s. You'll uncover hard-to-find factory facts and muscle car images from more than 160 near full size, restored-to-original-color advertisements. Includes popular models from American Motors, Buick, Chevrolet, Chrysler, Dodge, Ford, General Motors, Mercury, Oldsmobile, Plymouth, and Pontiac. Humorous text accompanies each advertisement for maximum enjoyment.

**Softcover • 8¼ x 10-⅞
160 pages
160+ color photos
Item# CMCLC • $21.95**

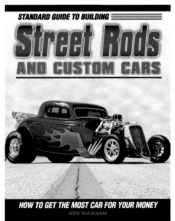

Standard Guide to Building Street Rods and Custom Cars

by Ken Wickham

Learn how to build the street rod of your dreams without going broke using these step-by-step instructions that detail the costs, plans, and safety precautions. You'll save time, money, and avoid costly mistakes. All major restoration steps are generously illustrated and include chassis, engine, and bodywork, paint, and upholstery. Author Ken Wickham has been rebuilding cars for more than a decade.

**Softcover • 8½ x 11 • 184 pages
200 b&w photos
8-page color section
Item# SRCB • $21.95**

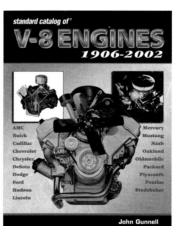

Standard Catalog of® V-8 Engines 1906-2002

by John Gunnell

Comprehensive coverage is provided for thousands of domestic V-8s, from the early 20th century to today's compact powerhouses. Engine listings consist of serial number codes, bore and stroke, cubic-inch displacement, and horsepower ratings. Various sidebars throughout the book identify correct engine colors and list decals available for specific engines.

**Softcover • 8½ x 11 • 288 pages
100 b&w photos
Item# VEE1 • $24.95**

krause publications
P.O. Box 5009, Iola WI 54945-5009
www.krausebooks.com

To order call 800-258-0929 **Offer AUB3**

Please add $4.00 for the first book and $2.25 each additional for shipping & handling to U.S. addresses. Non-U.S. addresses please add $20.95 for the first book and $5.95 each additional.

Residents of CA, IA, IL, KS, NJ, PA, SD, TN, WI please add appropriate sales tax.